ADVANCEMENT IN ORGANIZATIONAL BEHAVIOUR

© Keith Hill

Derek S. Pugh

b.1930. M.A., M.Sc. (Edinburgh), D.Sc. (Aston). F.S.S., F.B.Ps.S.
Research Assistant, Assistant Lecturer, University of Edinburgh (1953–1957)
Lecturer, Senior Research Fellow, Reader, University of Aston (1957–1968)
Reader, Professor of Organizational Behaviour, London Business School (1968–1982)
Professor of Systems, Open University (1983–1988)
Professor of International Management, Open University Business School (OUBS) (1988–1995)
Visiting Research Professor of International Management, OUBS (1995–)

ADVANCEMENT IN ORGANIZATIONAL BEHAVIOUR

ESSAYS IN HONOUR OF DEREK S. PUGH

Edited by
TIMOTHY CLARK

Ashgate

Aldershot • Brookfield USA • Singapore • Sydney

Published by
Ashgate Publishing Company Limited
Gower House
Croft Road
Aldershot
Hants GU11 3HR
England

Ashgate Publishing Company
Old Post Road
Brookfield
Vermont 05036
USA

British Library Cataloguing in Publication Data
Advancement in organizational behaviour : essays in honour
    of Derek S. Pugh
    1. Organizational behaviour
    I. Clark, Timothy
    302.3'5

Library of Congress Cataloging-in-Publication Data
Clark, Timothy, 1964–
    Advancement in organizational behaviour : essays in honour of
    Derek S. Pugh / edited by Timothy Clark.
        p.   cm.
    Includes bibliographical references.
    ISBN 1–85521–796–1 (hardcover). — ISBN 1–85521–801–1 (pbk.)
    1. Organizational behaviour.   2. Pugh, Derek Salman.   I. Pugh,
    Derek Salman.   II. Title.
    HD58.7.C519   1997
    302.3'5—dc20
                                                                96–35392
                                                                    CIP

ISBN 1 85521 796 1 (HB)
ISBN 1 85521 801 1 (PB)

Typeset by Manton Typesetters, 5–7 Eastfield Road, Louth, Lincolnshire LN11 7AJ, UK
Printed and bound in Great Britain by Biddles Limited, Guildford and King's Lynn

Contents

List of Figures

List of Tables

List of Contributors

Chris Argyris is James B. Conant Professor of Education and Organizational Behaviour, Emeritus, Harvard Business School, Harvard University.

Moshe Banai has a BA from the Ben Gurion University, Israel, an MSc from Recanati Graduate School of Management at Tel Aviv University and a PhD from The London Business School, gained under the supervision of Derek Pugh. He has held teaching appointments at the InterAmericana University in Puerto Rico, Kazan State University Tatarstan, Russia, and in Sydney Graduate School of Management, Australia. Currently he is an Associate Professor at Baruch College, The City University of New York. He has published book chapters and articles in learned journals in the area of international human resource management, comparative management and Russian management. He has also consulted to major MNCs, government agencies and private businesses in Eastern and Western Europe, The USA, and Israel.

John Child has an MA in Economics and a PhD in Management from the University of Cambridge, which in 1984 also awarded him a ScD for outstanding scholarly work. In 1996 he was awarded the Honorary Doctorate by the Helsinki School of Economics, one of the first business schools to be founded in Europe. His career started with posts in marketing and personnel at Rolls-Royce Ltd. He worked with Derek Pugh as a Research Fellow at Aston University from 1966 to 1968 and subsequently at the London Business School until 1973. In that year he was appointed Professor of Organizational Behaviour at Aston University. From 1986–1989 he was Dean of the Aston Business School. During 1989–90 he was seconded to the position of Dean and Director of the China-European Community Management Centre in Beijing with which he had been connected since 1985. He became Guinness Professor of Management Studies at Cambridge in 1991. He was Editor-in-Chief of the international journal *Organization Studies* from 1992–6. He is the author or co-author of ninety articles in learned journals and fourteen books, most recently *Management in China During the Age of Reform* (1996, with Yuau Lu).

Timothy Clark has two principal areas of research. First, since completing his PhD into the development of the executive recruitment industry in the UK he has continued to examine different aspects of the management constancy industry, focusing most recently on the nature of client-consultant interaction, factors underpinning managers' use of management consultants and the factors accounting for the success of management guru ideas. Second, he has conducted a number of cross-national research projects, particularly in the area of human resource management. Between 1991 and 1996 he worked with Derek Pugh at the Open University Business School as a member of the International Organization Observatory. Since January 1997 he has been Reader in Management at King's College, University of London. He is author or co-author of numerous articles and six books, the most recent of which are *Managing Consultants* (1995), *European Human Resource Management* (1996), *HRM – The Inside Story* (1997).

Dale Cunningham is currently studying law at the University of Alberta. Prior to this he was a research student in the departments of Sociology and Sport Studies.

Lex Donaldson is Professor of Organization Design at the Australian Graduate School of Management in the University of New South Wales. His PhD was supervised by Derek Pugh, who also led the Organisational Behaviour Research Group of the London Graduate School of Business Studies, in which Lex served (1971–6). His interest is in theories of organization, especially of structure. Books include *In Defence of Organization Theory: A Reply to the Critics* (1985) and *American Anti-Management Theories of Organization: A Critique of Paradigm Proliferation* (1995). He has also edited a collection of key articles by classic contributors in *Contingency Theory* (1995). He has recently published a detailed argument for the Aston approach to the study of organizations, *For Positivist Organization Theory: Proving the Hard Core* (1996). He has published articles in *Administrative Science Quarterly, Academy of Management Journal, Academy of Management Review, Human Relations, Journal of Management Studies* and *Organization Science and Organization Studies*.

Dagmar Ebster-Grosz has a BSc in Sociology, a degree in International Trade and a PhD in Sociology and Philosophy from Comenius University, Bratislava. Prior to her academic career she worked in a Czechoslovakian import-export firm and was a business advisor to British companies operating on the Continent and in Eastern Europe. In 1990 she joined the Open University Business School to work under the direction of Derek Pugh on an Anglo-German comparative study supported by the Anglo-German Foundation. She is the co-author with Derek Pugh of *Anglo-German Business Collaboration: Pitfalls and Potentials.*

Charles Handy is a self-employed writer and broadcaster. He is a Fellow of the London Business School, where he taught for 20 years. Before that he was an oil executive and an economist. His books on the workings of organizations and the future of work and society have sold more than one million copies around the world.

Frank Heller is a director of the Centre for Decision Making Studies at the Tavistock Institute, Visiting Professor in the Department of Economics and Administration at the University of Chile at Santiago, Visiting Professor at Hangzhou University, China and Visiting Fellow, the Management College, Henley. He took an engineering diploma and worked in the motor car industry for six years before taking an economics degree at the London School of Economics, followed by a PhD in psychology. After a stint as Head of a department of management, he took a six-year consulting assignment in South America, first with the ILO and later with the UN Special Fund. His special interest is in comparative research, with particular emphasis on leadership and decision making theory and practice and, more recently, in the application of an open-system sociotechnical model to organizational change. Since 1970, when he joined the Tavistock Institute, he has been involved in a number of cross-national studies in Europe, the USA, Japan, China, Chile and, most recently, in Central Europe. He is the executive editor of the *International Handbook of Organizational Democracy* and the *International Handbook of Participation in Organizations* and has published numerous books, chapters in books and papers in refereed journals.

David Hickson is Research Professor of International Management and Organization at the University of Bradford Management Centre, England. His principal research interests are how societal cultures affect managerial decision making in different nations and what influences the success of major decisions. His previous research has included processes of managerial decision making, power in organizations and bureaucratization as co-leader with Derek Pugh of the Aston Programme. He was founding editor-in-chief of the international research journal, *Organization Studies*, a founder of the European Group for Organizational Studies (EGOS) and a founding member of the British Academy of Management. He has held appointments in university business schools and research institutes in Canada, the USA, and the Netherlands, has an honorary PhD from the University of Umeå in Sweden and has lectured widely around the world. He has published numerous research journal papers and book chapters and is author or editor of eight books, most recently *Management in Western Europe* (1993) and *Management Worldwide: The Impact of Societal Culture on Organizations Around the Globe* (with Derek S. Pugh, 1995). Prior to becoming an academic, David Hickson worked in financial administration and qualified professionally in personnel management and as a chartered secretary.

C.R. (Bob) Hinings is Thornton A. Graham Professor of Business at the University of Alberta, Canada. He is also Director of the Centre for Professional Service Firm Management. Before going to Canada he was a founder member, with Derek Pugh, of the Aston Programme. His current research interests are in changes in the management of professional service firms and Canadian national sport organizations.

Geert Hofstede is Emeritus Professor of Organizational Anthropology and International Management at the University of Limburg at Maastricht, the Netherlands. He was founder and first director of the Institute for Research on Intercultural Co-operation (IRIC), an independent foundation now cooperating with Tilburg University and the University of Limburg. He is at present chairman of the board of IRIC, a fellow of the Centre for Economic Research at Tilburg, and an Honorary Professor at the University of Hong Kong.

Kerr Inkson is Professor of Management Studies at the Department of Management and Employment Relations, University of Auckland, New Zealand. He was educated at the University of Aberdeen and Birkbeck College, University of London, and was on the staff of the University of Aston from 1965 to 1970 (for the first three years working with Derek Pugh on the Aston Programme). He moved to Auckland in 1980, was appointed to a chair in 1988, and is currently Associate Dean of Commerce. His current research interests include career theory and management of sport and recreation.

Tom Lupton was born in County Durham in 1918. After leaving elementary school he became an apprentice marine engineer. During the Second World War he was a design draughtsman of the Corvette programme and also saw active service with the Royal Engineers. After the war he went to Ruskin College Oxford and later to Oriel College. In 1951, he joined Joan Woodward's team at Liverpool, leaving in 1954 to supervise a research project in the Department of Social Anthropology at Manchester. In 1959, he became head of the Department of Industrial Administration at the Birmingham C.A.T. (later Aston University) where he initiated the Aston Programme. After a short spell at Leeds University, he joined the founding team at Manchester Business School, eventually becoming deputy director and then director. He has published many books and articles. He retired from MBS in 1988 and now lives and works in Spain. He is currently coordinating projects in Central Europe.

Geoff Mallory is currently a Lecturer in Strategic Management and leads the Strategic Management Research Group within the Open University Business School. Following industrial experience in both marketing and management services he graduated from the Universities of Bradford and Leeds with a specialization in Organization Studies. Between 1982 and 1985 he was a Research Fellow and then a Temporary Lecturer at Bradford Management Centre where he worked the Power and Decision Making project directed by David Hickson. He then completed his PhD in 1987 whilst an Assistant Professor in the School of Business, Carleton University, Ottawa. He retains his link with Carleton through an Adjunct Research Professorship associated with a project into decision making and International Business with Professors Haines and Cray. He has published articles in the *British Journal of Management*, the *Journal of Management Studies, Omega*, and the *European Journal of Operations Research.*

Roy L. Payne graduated in Psychology at Liverpool University and spent two years postgraduate study in the MRC Unit for Occupational Aspects of Ageing. From there he joined the Aston Group, then followed Derek Pugh to the London Business School. Seventeen years after leaving there he went as Professor of Organizational Behaviour to Manchester Business School, having spent the intervening years at the MRC/ESRC Social and Applied Psychology Unit at Sheffield University. He returned to Sheffield University in 1992 to a chair in the Management School, and from January 1997 has been Professor of Organizational Psychology at School of Psychology, Curtin University of Technology, Perth, W. Australia. His work at Aston led to publications on organizational climate in particular, and he has also published in the occupational stress area. These remain active interests as well as more recent work on trust in organizations.

Vincenzo Perrone received his PhD from Bocconi University, Milan. He is currently Professor of Organization Management and Theory and holder of the Chair in Business Organization in the Department of Business Administration at the University of Cassino. He also serves as Chairman of the *Area Organizzazione e Personale* (OB, OMT and HRM Department) at SDA-Boconi School of Management. From 1986 to 1992 he was a member, with Derek Pugh and other colleagues coming from leading European Business School, of the International Organizational Observatory. The aim of this cross-cultural research project was to collect quantitative data on the organization of a large sample of European manufacturing firms, longitudinally. His current research interests include the development of networks within and between organizations, the role of trust in intra and inter-organizational relations and the evolutionary processes of populations of organizations.

Andrew M. Pettigrew is Professor of Organisational Behaviour at Warwick Business School. Between 1985 and 1995 he founded and directed the Centre for Corporate Strategy and Change at the University of Warwick. He has written, co-authored or edited 10 books. He has published many articles in international scholarly journals such as the *Administrative Science Quarterly, Organization Science, Organization Studies, Journal of Management Studies, Human Relations, International Journal of Human Resource Management, Strategic Management Journal* and *Public Administration*. He was the first chairman of the British Academy of Management (1987–90) and was president of the British Academy of Management (1990–3). In 1995, he was the recipient of the Distinguished Scholar Award by the Organization and Management Theory Division of the US Academy of Management.

Gordon Redding has been at the University of Hong Kong School of Business since 1973, researching Asian aspects of comparative management and also developing a regional business school. His main research is on Chinese capitalization. Currently he is at INSEAD Euro-Asia Centre, where he continues to research varieties of Asian capitalism.

Violina P. Rindova is a doctoral candidate at the Stern School of Business, New York University. She has an LLB and an MBA, and extensive experience in transition work for business, government and educational institutions. She has published book chapters on the role of academic institutional evaluations. Her current research focus is on the use of language and communications in firms' competitive positioning.

Trevor Slack is Director of the School of Physical Education at De Montfort University, England. Previously he was a professor in sport studies at the University of Alberta. His research interests are in socio-cultural studies of sport and leisure.

Arndt Sorge has conducted research on the organization and management of industrial enterprises, vocational education and training personnel policy and industrial relations. In particular, he has taken part in a number of international comparitive studies, and he has studied the development and utilization of new technology. Since 1972, he has had university or research positions in Germany, England, France and the Netherlands. He is presently the editor in chief of *Organization Studies* and he was the sub-editor for the Organization Behaviour articles in the *International Encyclopedia of Business and Management* (1996). Between 1992 and 97, he was Professor of Industrial and Organizational Sociology at Humboldt University, Berlin. He is now research professor and the Director of WORC (the Work and Organization Research Centre) at Tilburg University in the Netherlands.

William H. Starbuck is ITT Professor of Creative Management at New York University. He formerly worked at Purdue, Johns Hopkins, Cornell, University of Wisconsin-Milwaukee and International Institute of Management (Berlin), and he has visited London Business School, Norwegian School of Economics, University of Gothenburg and Stockholm School of Economics. He has edited *Administrative Science Quarterly*, chaired the screening committee for senior Fulbright awards in business management and directed the doctoral programme in business at New York University. He is president elect of the American Academy of Management. He has published articles on accounting, bargaining, business strategy, computer programming, computer simulation, forecasting, decision making, human–computer interaction, learning, organizational design, organizational growth and development, perception, scientific methods and social revolutions. He has also edited four books, including the *Handbook of Organization Design*, which won an award as the best book on management published in 1981.

1 Derek Pugh: his Contribution to the Advancement of Organizational Behaviour

TIMOTHY CLARK, *King's College, University of London*

Organization behaviour (OB) is a relatively recent and still growing area of academic inquiry, having only emerged since the 1950s. This book is a collection of essays to mark the retirement of one of the most influential scholars in the field. Derek Pugh's career has spanned 40 years and during that time he has made a significant and lasting impression on the development of OB as a field of study and the advancement of management research in general. Through his research, his writings and his professional values which have underpinned these, he has sought to nurture and establish OB as a distinctive field of study and one in which knowledge is advanced through innovative research conducted to the highest academic standards.

The chapters which comprise this volume are organized around the central theme of 'advancement in organizational behaviour'. This theme is particularly appropriate to a celebration of Derek's career, for two reasons: (1) his career has been intimately connected with the emergence of OB as a field of study; and (2) the contributions consider and reflect how the field has developed since Derek's seminal work, as well as indicating his continuing influence.

Derek's contribution to the advancement of OB has been considerable and has been made in a number of different ways. As the first British Professor of Organizational Behaviour (at London Business School) one of Derek's most important contributions was to distinguish OB as a new and distinctive discipline area at a time when it was struggling to gain a presence in many universities partly because it lacked a clear identity. In the most cited paper he has written, Derek defined OB as:

> the study of the structure and functioning of organizations and behaviour of groups and individuals within them. It is an emerging interdisciplinary quasi-independent science, drawing primarily on the disciplines of sociology and psychology, but also on economics and, to a lesser extent, production engineering. (Pugh, 1966, p. 235)

The critical feature of this definition is its stress on the interdisciplinary character of OB. As a consequence of his experiences while working in the interdisciplinary environment of the Social Sciences Research Unit at Edinburgh University in the late 1950s, Derek developed a considerable scepticism towards the utility of academic discipline areas: in particular, the arbitrariness of the boundaries (see Pugh, 1996). For Derek what mattered, and continues to matter, is that the phenomenon being investigated should be illuminated in as many different ways as possible. While OB is concerned with structure, functioning, organization, behaviour, groups and individuals, these elements should not be separated out so that they become the province of individual discipline areas. So the structure and functioning of organizations should not become the exclusive territory of sociologists. Similarly, the study of the behaviour of individuals within organizations should not be restricted to psychologists. For Derek the emergence of this new field of study was an opportunity to break away from the compartmentalization of knowledge associated with the traditional boundaries between discipline areas. In recognizing this, Derek sought to create a 'unified science of people in organizations' by utilizing whatever concepts, theories and methods were useful and relevant to the study of organizational phenomena from a number of base discipline areas, such as psychology, sociology and economics. Hence the priorities, concerns and foci of any one discipline area should not preclude OB from advancing knowledge with regard to organizational phenomena. Rather, in Derek's view, OB would grow and flourish precisely because it would become a melting pot within which elements from different discipline areas would be uniquely combined to create new insights into the functioning of organizations and the behaviour of their members.

Several consequences follow from emphasizing the interdisciplinary nature of OB. One relates to the character and make-up of the academics working in this area. To be successful, real interdisciplinary research should take place in the researcher's head. OB researchers therefore need to straddle several discipline areas if they are to use and combine the theories, concepts and methods of different disciplines to develop new insights into organizational phenomena. Derek has personified this interdisciplinary approach to research and so in a sense represents the prototypical OB researcher since, during his career, he has eschewed affiliation to any one discipline. Over four decades he has held posts in social sciences, social medicine, human relations, industrial administration, organizational behaviour, systems and international management.

A second implication is the need for interdisciplinary research teams in order to maximize the collaboration between discipline areas. Again much of Derek's best known work has been conducted in teams of this kind. For example, the Aston Studies began with the establishment of the Industrial Administration (IA) Research Unit in January 1961, with a senior research fellow (Derek), a research fellow (David Hickson) and two research assistants (Bob Hinings, a sociologist, and Graham Harding, a psychologist). At London Business School, Derek's research team included John Child, Lex Donaldson and Roger Mansfield (who had each straddled the disciplines in their previous degrees), Roy Payne (a psychologist) and Malcolm Warner (an economist). In the entry on the Aston Group in the *International Encyclopaedia of Business and Management*, Jerald Hage (1996, p. 291) has written that 'the single most important lesson to be learned from the Aston Group is how to manage research'.

In this interdisciplinary environment successful team management becomes critical if high-quality research is to be produced and long-term integrated programmes of the sort envisaged by the Aston Group are to be sustained. This is an area in which Derek has excelled. He has proved that interdisciplinary groups can produce work which is both original and of high quality. When one examines the way in which he has managed teams of researchers at Aston University, London Business School and the Open University, a number of common elements emerge. The first element is the way in which he has sought to appoint one or two core researchers for whom the research project is their primary academic task. These individuals form the nucleus around which the project is built. Given their importance to the success of a project, Derek has sought to protect researchers from the intrusion of other responsibilities (that is, teaching and administration) so that they focus wholly on the task at hand, and supported researchers on fixed-term contracts by seeking long-term funding. This has entailed actively managing the research group's relations with the wider university. In doing this, Derek has established a number of different research groups with whom he has worked over long periods. This has given his various research projects a longevity that few others have enjoyed.

The second element is the extent and level of participation within his research teams. While Derek's research teams have invariably been comprised of people at different levels in academic hierarchy (for example, a professor, research fellows and research assistants) he has always encouraged members to participate in the different stages of the research process. Derek has long realized that the feeling of 'working on someone else's research' has a limiting effect on an individual's level of participation and long-term commitment to a project. One example of this is the second generation of Aston researchers. It has been argued that they failed to sustain their interest in the Aston research because they had not participated in the design and conceptual development of the project, but arrived to work on other people's research. To overcome this in Derek's teams all members, regardless of level, are encouraged to participate in the development of the conceptual framework, the formulation of the research strategy, the operationalizion of the concepts, collecting the data, the analysis and the writing up of the results for publication. Although individual members of the research team may have specific responsibilities, and so part of the work 'belongs' to them, they also have contact with all of it so that the final product is owned by the group as a whole. This is manifested most clearly in Derek's approach to publication. In believing that a research project is a collective effort, he has been guided by the principle that each member is named on the publications, without having to claim it, irrespective of what part of the work they did. The research then becomes known as W, X, Y and Z's, or invariably by the group name, rather than just as Y and Z's. While the sequence of names remains an issue, this approach nevertheless drastically reduces intra-group rivalry and supports a more harmonious and egalitarian atmosphere.

The third and final element is the quality of the intellectual environment within the research team. Derek has the ability to create an environment in which groundbreaking ideas are generated, operationalized and then tested. This is partly attributable to the quality of people that Derek has recruited, many of whom now occupy senior positions in universities throughout the world. As William Starbuck (1981, p. 167) wrote in a major review of the Aston Studies, 'The participants amount to a Who's Who of British organization theory.' However, it also relates to Derek's personal style. Derek is someone who is always open to ideas. He therefore permits people space in which they can develop and test their own ideas. Indeed, Derek has always actively encouraged members of his research teams to try out *their* ideas on the data. Apart from supporting their intellectual development, such an approach also builds people's commitment to the project since they have a personal stake and therefore come to identify with and 'own' the work. It is worth noting that (1) his teams collaborate for long periods, (2) they are incredibly productive and (3) the intra-group ties are so strong that members continue to collaborate even when they move to other academic institutions.

Derek's primary contribution to the development of OB was inaugurating, with Tom Lupton and then David Hickson, one of the most influential and long-running research programmes in the field – the Aston Studies. It is not my intention to outline the theoretical foundations, empirical results and subsequent critiques of this body of work here since these are discussed in detail in many of the contributions to this book; indeed, the first section of this book focuses on the legacy of the Aston Studies. Rather, I wish to emphasize that, although the original study was conducted over 30 years ago, the results of the programme have had an enormous and continuing impact on the field. No fewer than three papers have been designated 'citation classics' by the Institute of Scientific Information on the basis of citation counts. The work is regularly referred to in most leading textbooks on the subject. John Freeman's 'editorial essay' (1986) on assuming the editorship of *Administrative Science Quarterly* cited the Hawthorne Studies, the American Soldier studies during the Second World War and the Aston Studies as examples of research projects that had major impacts beyond their original intentions. Thus the intellectual legacy of these studies has been considerable and has done much to shape the subsequent research agenda and research efforts of scholars in the field. It is therefore appropriate that, at a time when both the organizational and academic worlds are facing increasing turbulence, the theme of the 1996 British Academy of Management Conference should be 'Back to Aston and thirty years on … what have we really learned in management theory?' This recognizes the continuing influence of the Aston Studies in contemporary OB research. After 30 years, this programme of research remains a key benchmark against which more recent contributions to the field are still compared. There are perhaps three reasons for the continuing interest in this programme of research.

The first reason is that the concepts used are central to the study of the organization and researchers in this field continually have to struggle with them. Since the Aston Studies represent perhaps the first attempt to systematically define and operationalize key features of the organization, constant reference to this work is necessary. Furthermore, some of the scales upon which they based their measurements of organization structure–context relations have not been bettered.

The second reason is that through their many publications the group have made the methodology completely explicit and the methods openly available. The items used, the questions asked and the analyses carried out have all been published, so that it is comparatively easy for others to utilize the methods developed. Thus studies have been conducted throughout the world which have been based entirely on the published methods. Currently, the ESRC Data Archive at Essex University holds data from 24 studies which have used the Aston methods and/or instruments in such countries as the UK, Canada, Germany, Japan, Sweden and USA. As a consequence, the Aston Studies have perhaps had more worldwide impact than any other programme of research in the field.

The third reason is the group basis of the original research. Many of the members of the research team continued to conduct research using the Aston instruments with new collaborators – the 'fourth generation of Aston' researchers – even after moving to different academic institutions. Thus, in addition to the original work at Aston, work was also conducted in collaboration with earlier Aston generations at London Business School, the universities of Birmingham, Bradford and Sheffield, and the Open University in the UK, and universities in Canada, Poland, Egypt, Germany, Japan, the USA and Sweden. The continuing commitment of the original members of the research group to the programme, even after leaving Aston, has given it a stability and continuity that few other projects have been able to duplicate. This has resulted in a continuous stream of publications for almost 30 years emanating from a single research programme. As a consequence, the Aston Studies have rarely been far from the academic agenda in OB. Rather, they have been a core feature of the intellectual environment for three generations of organizational researchers.

The contributors to this book are leading researchers in OB and most have been fortunate enough to work with Derek at some point in their careers, although in very different capacities. Their commitment and enthusiasm towards the idea of producing this book demonstrates the affection and respect with which Derek is held. For many of the contributors, the time they worked with Derek was a critical, if not the most important, formative period of their working lives. The lineage of empirical, conceptual and theoretical work for which they are now known can, in many cases, be traced back to working with Derek.

The subsequent chapters cover a wide variety of subjects including the Aston Studies, organization climate, organization structure, the role of taxonomies in organization studies, the impact of national culture on organizational functioning, the nature of bureaucracy, management in Russia and pre-modern management theory (before the year zero). The diversity of organizational issues examined in this book reflects and celebrates the nature of the field Derek sought to create. Like the 'philosopher's stone' of medieval alchemy, OB has become a medium through which the theoretical, conceptual and empirical 'base metal' from other disciplines has become continually reconstituted and transformed in order to provide new and revealing insights into the nature of organizations and the behaviour of their members. With this in mind, the book is divided into four parts which reflect key aspects of Derek's professional life. Part I focuses on the Aston Studies and their legacy. The chapters in Part II are all concerned with a major empirical and theoretical preoccupation of Derek's throughout his career – organization structure. The third part is devoted to issues relating to his current concern with cross-cultural management. The final cluster of chapters examines the future of management research which Derek has done so much to develop.

References

Freeman, J. (1986), 'Data quality and the development of organizational social science: an editorial essay', *Administrative Science Quarterly*, **31**, 298–303.

Hage, J. (1996), 'Aston Group', in M. Warner (ed.), *International Encyclopaedia of Business and Management*, London: International Thomson Business, pp. 286–92.

Pugh, D.S. (1966), 'Modern organization theory: a psychological and sociological study', *Psychological Bulletin*, **66**, 235–51.

Pugh, D.S. (1996), 'A taste for innovation', in A.G. Bedeian (ed.), *Management Laureates*, Vol. 4, Greenwich, Conn.: JAI Press, pp. 235–76.

Starbuck, W.H. (1981) 'A trip to view the elephants and rattlesnakes in the garden of Aston', in A.H. Van de Ven and W.F. Joyce (eds), *Perspectives on Organization Design and Behavior*, New York: Wiley, pp. 167–98.

PART I
THE ASTON LEGACY

2 The Ivory Tower in a Basement: Reminiscences of Aston

DAVID HICKSON, *University of Bradford Management Centre*

How does a research team happen? The team that happened at Aston was the greatest single influence in bringing Derek Pugh to prominence. Yet he was not the first of its researchers. No indeed. That was me! I was the first researcher appointment. But Derek was first on the ground, so to speak. When I arrived he was already there. No one told me about him, though. And perhaps no one told him about me. It happened like this. Well, it happened like this in memory. Others' memories would hold the same picture but see it differently with differing details and emphases.

Getting a Job

The municipal College of Technology in Birmingham had just grandly become the Birmingham College of Advanced Technology. In 1960, in Manchester, I had for some months been failing to get a job in industry (I never meant to become an academic) when a friend told me of this research fellow position advertised in a Birmingham college. I went. I got it. I was amazed. I had not dreamed of such academic eminence or of so much money. Long afterwards, I found that my success was partly due to my cheek in tossing the interview question about what research I should do back to the interview panel itself, cruelly exposing that they did not know either. Sadly, I also found that, far from crushing my towering competitors, I was the only serious applicant for the only research post the college had ever had, which until then they had been unable to fill. So was I humbled.

Where then was Pugh? Be patient, he will enter very soon. My post was in the industrial administration department. This was headed

11

by Tom Lupton, then and ever since a distinguished figure in British management education. His is a much better story, but it is not for me to tell, except briefly. He took pride in being an anthropologist of full pedigree. Remarkably, before that he had been in the engineering industry. So how could this university-trained anthropological researcher have become head of a local industrial administration department? Somewhere along the way was the influence of Joan Woodward, that outstanding early researcher in this field, who knew Tom because they both originated in the source of much British industrial sociology, the sociology department of Liverpool University. She had been consulted by the college, and had been persuasive. Tom it was who appreciated my perky discomfiting of the interview panel. Previously, he had once met me for lunch in Manchester where I was doing two years' masters research on worker group behaviour and knew of his record in that area.

Enter Derek

Tom brought with him to Birmingham research grants which were substantial for those days. This is where Derek comes in. For Tom found that his department head responsibilities did not allow him time for research himself, a formative warning to me which always shaped my career. However, on the department staff was one Pugh, with whom Tom had a special relationship since only Pugh could talk research talk with him. This was because Derek had been four years in the multidisciplinary Social Sciences Research Centre at Edinburgh. He was now 'taking a sabbatical', as he once put it, teaching human relations to classes of supervisors and union shop stewards, often in the evenings (he sometimes said that teaching was easier than research). Tom asked him to make something of Tom's idle money.

I had not yet decided what to do. Advised by Tom to think carefully rather than rush into anything, I was taking an initial one-term pause for breath and, incidentally, teaching a class of shop stewards in public speaking (maybe teaching a *skill* is *harder* than research?).

Consternation

Derek still says he recalls the consternation on my face when he met me in the corridor and asked me if I would like to join in the research he was about to launch. Yes, I was aghast. It was a complete surprise. I had thought that here I alone led the way in research. Why had no one told me what was afoot? Why was this concealed from me? Who was going behind my back and undermining my position? Which way now, flight or fight?

I chose fight, taking it that lack of communication was inadvertent rather than Machiavellian. I decided to come forward and be positive. I decided that, as you are only as good as those you can learn from, better risk working with and being bossed about by this experienced Pugh than stand aloof on my own. Was I right! I had almost everything to learn. I had had no research training, just one do-it-yourself factory project, solo. And while this experienced Pugh certainly led intellectually, he never domineered. He was ever patient, ever willing to listen, ever ready to explain, as I floundered mentally among academics much of whose conversation left me behind. He was the same to all of us.

Next was Bob Hinings, recruited by us as a research assistant, a sociologist with one of the best grade degrees ever awarded by Leeds sociology department. He was some years younger than Derek and me, who were both 30 (Derek being the elder, just). Bob had done his compulsory military service as a typist in the Air Force, paid sixpence per day extra for learning to shoot! He could give hilarious (and disturbing) demonstrations of how to stick a bayonet into an enemy with a bloodthirsty yell. He himself would never have got beyond practising on a sandbag.

And then Graham Harding, a psychologist. His was a relatively short sojourn. Derek soon saw that he was technically minded. He did, after all, give as much attention to the model locomotives in his desk drawer as to the research objectives. So he proved more in touch with the EEG machines in the head-reading labs to which he transferred.

Ivory Tower

By now we were ensconced in our academic ivory tower in a basement. Always astute, Derek willingly accepted on our behalf that we be pushed out into the below ground level of an office block opposite the college (negotiating a free electric kettle in compensation) and that most of our limited teaching be in the evenings. Marginalized we might be in a wholly teaching institution, but he saw that this way we could concentrate wholeheartedly on the research, free of interruptions. Few of us have been able to concentrate so single-mindedly again.

The decrepit office block awaited demolition. No one else was in it. Our feet echoed on its wooden stairs. We worked by flickering fluorescent strips, hearing the buses rumble by above us. The office block and the college, were in Aston, a city neighbourhood of factories and tenements on the edge of central Birmingham. Aston had been there before Birmingham was. Industrial Revolution Birmingham had swallowed it, and all but obliterated its ancient origins. Aston lives now in the names of a football team (once supported by my father who was raised in nearby back streets) and of the university which the college turned into.

Share and Share Alike

The name lives too in the so-called Aston Group and Aston Programme. It could have been Pugh Group, Pugh Programme, but Derek early on put forward the principle that, at its simplest, is 'everyone goes on everything, unless they don't want to'. That is, each will get a full share of naming on publications, without having to claim it, irrespective of what part of the work they have done. This principle still leaves the question of sequence of names, but it virtually removes intra-group competition. There is common ownership. Everyone becomes willing to work on anything, with anyone. So the group was extremely egalitarian. It, including Derek, wanted to be known, if it were known at all, by an impersonal name above that of any one of us. In this, as in many things, Derek gave us all an example of how to lead such a group, and how to try and understand its members and the relationships between them.

How, then, was it that our first four publications, in the new *Administrative Science Quarterly* (*ASQ* – 40 years old in 1996) began with Pugh and Pugh and Pugh and Pugh? This was well merited by intellectual input but, just as much, we all discussed what to do and agreed that unknowns like we were needed to put across a brand name that would stick. Each would benefit, whoever's name it was, more than having different names fronting the list every time. Once a publication has more than two authors it becomes known as '*X et al.*', so better for us that ours were all known as '*X et al.*', than confusingly as '*X et al.*', '*Y et al.*', '*Z et al.*', and so on. We all were there in '*et al.*', in lists of names unusually long at the time, over which *ASQ* editorially swallowed hard. Among ourselves the papers were just numbers: *ASQ*1, *ASQ*2, *ASQ*3 and *ASQ*4.

Research on a Blackboard

Tom Lupton's money had been awarded for the study of shopfloor working practices. On the blackboard on our basement wall we had scrawled on the right 'worker behaviour', or some such, and to the left we began to list factors which might influence that. Woodward had not long before made 'technology' a popular explanation, so we wrote that on the board. We wrote 'corporate ownership' (maybe people worked harder if nationalized?). We talked to economists and wrote 'market'. Crucially, the day came when Derek clattered down the stairs and said, 'Where's management?'

We were never the same again. It led to *ASQ*. It led far away from what Tom Lupton intended, but fortunately he was benignly far-sighted and when he became aware we were heading off somewhere else he said, 'If that's what you buggers want to do,' (well, he had been in engineering) 'you'd better do it.' The penetrating mind of Albert Cherns (later a professor at Loughborough, now deceased) said the same, more elegantly, when he discovered what was up during one of his occasional visits from the research agency (the Department of Scientific and Industrial Research, an ancestor of the present Economic and Social Research Council) where he was in charge of funding. That, they both showed, is true wisdom in re-search administration. To let enthusiasts have their head and hope for the best, which may well come. Better than tying thinking down to detailed contracts and specific practical applications, for that hin-ders ideas from going further than the point where the research began. Without Tom and Albert's perspicacity, there would never have been 'Aston', just another study of shopfloor life.

So we added 'management' to the list of factors supposed to affect workers. But what was management? You could define technology per Woodward, look up who owned shares, even think about 'mar-ket' (though the economists never did tell us how to measure it), but what was 'management'? Bob knew Weber. I read Fayol. Derek knew Urwick and Brech. We interrogated some managers. The question remained. What was it, and how could you get at it empirically? We looked around. No one seemed to have done anything compara-tively, across different sorts of organizations. We became absorbed by the difficulty, cocky and excited by the challenge. We would excel the great single case merchants, Gouldner, Selznick, Dalton and the like! We would show just what was possible on a broader scale.

From this I learned, looking back in later years, that the chief spur to each generation of researchers is to outdo the last one; that the variables with the most explanatory power for what happens are life cycle and age spectrum; that the methodological pendulum swings slowly decade by decade: from hard to soft, soft to hard; small 'n' to large 'n', large 'n' to small 'n'; subjectivist to objectivist, objectivist to subjectivist; artistic to scientistic, scientistic to artistic.

Variables and Levels and Typing

Little by little, 'management' for us became disassembled into features usually thought of as structural. So many of these were chalked up that they had to have a column of their own on the board, in the space to the right of 'technology' and so on to which size and other possibilities were added. 'Worker behaviour' was pushed off the far edge, to be dealt with one day – we never had time. The management-cum-structure variables became what had to be explained, dependent variables, with 'contextual' variables being some possible explanations. Further to the left was 'society', the ultimate explanation – for which we never had time either. So the great almighty plan was 'soggy', SOGI. It was to straddle all four levels of analysis: Societal, Organizational, Group and Individual. Eventually we did reach G and I.

There were sceptics everywhere. Reg Revans, Britain's first professor of management, said no one could do everything. Anthropologists said it would not mean anything. College teachers asked with humorous cynicism, 'What have you discovered today?' On we went. The Organization-level work reached a stage where we needed a typist. We interviewed applicants, purported to test their typing proficiency (here Bob's military experience was useful) and chose one. Pretty soon we, and she, had to admit that she could not type – well, not well enough. For the rest of my life I have been pointedly asked at home how it was that this female, selected by a bunch of males, just happened to be the most visually dazzling of the candidates.

Impending demolition moved us from our basement to rooms high in the college building, though still remote from the Industrial Administration Department. Much later on again, we repeated the basement strategy by voluntarily moving out once more into another rickety building down a side street. To the bafflement of everyone but ourselves, we also clung to another principle of common commitment promulgated by Derek: no individual rooms; no pretentious names on blank closed doors; all desks together in one room. Casual conversations prompted by proximity were the stimulus to ideas, Derek argued. Individual thought occurred in the bath, in bed, on the train, wherever. Real work was done at home. That was not what our college room was for. It was for interaction – though we did now have a side room for quiet retreat.

There was more money and, for a while, our sociological streak became pre-eminent with the recruitment of Chris Turner, Keith McDonald and Theo Nichols, all of whose careers have been pursued subsequently in sociology departments, whereas everyone else has continued in management schools. Keith and Theo pitched in loyally but were uneasy outside the sociological mainstream, and

moved on. Theo preferred workers anyway. I wonder if he was influenced by the misapprehension, which I have frequently encountered,
that making things managerial your subject of study makes you
managerial, even a 'tool of capitalism' when that accusation was
fashionable. Just as if to study rabbits makes your nose twitch.

Derek was, and underneath may still be, a social psychologist
and, awesomely, a Fellow of the Statistical Society. He saw how
large numbers of cases could be compared and, when even he
lagged behind the latest developments in methods, he drew in as
adviser Phil Levy from the University of Birmingham whose expertise this was. So we came, in effect, to apply what were then seen as
psychological methods to sociological data, as the nature of the
data was even though it was outside the purview of the sociologists
of the day.

Foolish Questions

Being least trained (I had no undergraduate degree) my part was to
ask the foolish questions during mystifying discussions. Sometimes I
did this half knowingly, mostly it was innocence: 'What does
unidimensional mean?'. Or 'orthogonal', or 'Brogden-Clemans coefficient', and so on. Sometimes I still don't know. Which is not Derek's
fault. He never treated foolish questions as fool questions. Moreover,
he had a vital knack of seeing that such a question could expose
something that was being taken for granted but should be questioned. It might open up fresh possibilities, and quite often did. And
I learned that, when dealing with lots and lots, words are too bulky
and that numbers, like words, are just a way of labelling data.

Derek's team-view of holding things in common ensured that everyone did everything. We did not specialize. Everyone went out
interviewing managers (I envied Derek who somehow got Cadburys,
which held the promise of free chocolates – all I ever got from data
collection, years later, was cartons of beer from breweries in Canada,
which I gave to Bob Hinings as I don't drink the stuff). Everyone
entered up their data into the collective files. Everyone laboured on
data analysis and on inventing scales.

That was the big labour. It took years. Which showed that basic
research, substantial research, needs a long time horizon. It contrasts
pointedly with contemporary practice that funds almost all research
for a mere year or two. Luckily for us, overlapping grants gave us
the years. There were frustrations. Why were we not moving faster?
Why was Derek dawdling? Why was his mind more on editing the
Association of Teachers of Management Newsletter than the rest of us
thought it should be? But we stuck to it laboriously, to month after

month of categorizing from interview notes, of careful definition and redefinition of what we meant by this or that.

Purists at Work

Concepts had to be defined and operationalized in terms of the aims and thinking behind the research, whatever casual lay terms might be. For 'specialization', for instance, departmental titles would not do. They covered different work in different organizations, and meant different things to different people. We would not cheat by counting departments on organization charts. What we had to do was extract, from what we knew of the organizations, definitions of activities that could potentially be specialized (and by any sort of organization), whittle the number of possible activities down to those which scaled in a unidimensional way (it became 16), find out which were done by specialists, irrespective of job title or department title, and count the score for each organization. Not realizing all this, others have subsequently published research which for one reason or another leaves out a few of the specializable activities, adds back in a few titles of departments, and counts with that assemblage, never attending to whether or not it is countable. Such a compilation might not represent a single countable-along dimension. Whereas Derek's intellectual discipline held us to the establishing of ordinality in nonordinal data ('please, what is ordinality?').

We did the same with all other scales that needed it. We then correlated and yes, factor analysed, which was the latest wheeze. Even the zero-order correlation coefficient was a novelty here. Joan Woodward, in whose shadow we worked, along with that of Max Weber, had not got that far. We were further on, so far on that we did not have to work out a coefficient with pencil and paper. If all went well, we could get one from the computer in a mere week or two!

By now the arrival of Kerr Inkson and Roy Payne, both psychologists, had tilted the balance of the team in that direction. Bob Hinings had begun a series of shifts between posts at the University of Birmingham and back at Aston which went so fast that they are a blur in my memory, though presumably not in his. So we were ripe for G level and a little I level, group and individual characteristics.

Wide and Deep

We did now have to specialize so that we could play it both ways, 'wide' and 'deep'. Diana Pheysey, too, had joined us. She was the hardest working of us all. It was frightening. Mention a possibility one afternoon and she was excitedly there next morning with it fully worked out, having toiled into the night hours. The rest of us never kept pace, though somehow I hung on while she and I produced, with Derek, *ASQ5*, on technology and structure, in retrospect our memorial to Joan Woodward.

We specialized in two pairs. Kerr and myself took the 'wide', which we came to call shallow-G, Roy and Diana the deep-G. Shallow-G meant a questionnaire study of managers' roles in another large number of organizations, including collecting further structural data with an interview schedule of items selected from the compendious, carefully formulated interview schedule that covered the whole of such data. That one was known as Full-O, the smaller version as, well, 'er, yes, Skimpy-O(!). Whereas Deep-G meant in-depth case studies of two contrasting firms, including some I-level individual attitudinal data.

Derek kept a guiding hand in both, and at the same time moved on towards a replication-type O-level study, which because of its extending beyond the Birmingham region we call the National project. John Child was recruited to work with Derek on this.

National and deep-G were both published, Shallow-G very little. Peculiarities in the questionnaire results led me, and Kerr too, to doubt their meaningfulness. I shrank from publication. Times have changed. As the full force of 'publish or perish' has been imported over the Atlantic, so now I would probably have to be more reckless.

Varying Weber

In the exhilaration of O level we had hoped that, as the first researchers sallying forth to capture this kind of information in the academically untrodden wild West Midlands, we would stumble across some previously undreamed of form of organization. More even than Burns' organismic and mechanistic. We did not find it. Almost certainly it was not there: that is, not there as our eyes saw it. In effect, 'Aston' came up with instrumental variations on the Weberian theme (apologies to musical classicists). So it seems to have become known more for its methods than for its concepts or for its typology of bureaucracies.

Often it is misunderstood as being 'deterministic', whatever that might mean in a complex world that changes moment to moment. Perhaps it means a belief that X causes Y and there is no more to be said. 'Aston' never was so. The outstanding feature of its results, the product of Derek's thinking more than anyone's, is that they are multivariate; there is not one 'cause' but many. 'Astonians' were never size theorists, as they are sometimes erroneously said to be.

Size, dependence, technology, the second and the third especially being themselves composites representing many multiple factors, play different proportionate parts in the explanation of different facets of structure.

It was left to John Child to put into print subsequently what had been implicit, that all are subjects of meaningful choice and can work both ways 'causally'. Moreover, no correlation coefficient was 1.0. Some were amazingly high and amazingly robust, linking a core 'paradigm' of organization (though we did not say 'paradigm' in those times), but even then they could never be more than a part of explanation. There was and is much more to it.

So there were and are disappointments in what was not achieved and what is misunderstood, as well as gratification. Perhaps these would have been fewer had there been a book. The four books of collected and edited journal papers are not a book in that sense. None of us, Derek included, was able then to write a book that thought through what was done, grasped the purport for theory that lay within it, and expounded 'Aston' fully. Perhaps we were not capable of doing so. Certainly, we were too drained by the effort and too close to it. Yet later on was too late, unfortunately.

Of course, we were not used to writing big tomes. None of us who were in at the beginning have PhDs: Derek does not, Bob does not, I do not. I am perversely proud of that, and I suspect the others are too. In those days there was no one to supervise and award such niceties. Ever since, we have been saying to succeeding generations of sweating candidates, 'Do as I say, not as I did not.' Times have changed.

The Diaspora

One day in 1967, I opened a letter on my desk in the collective room. It had a Canadian stamp, but I knew no one there for I had hardly ever left England, let alone flown to North America. The letter offered me a professorship at the University of Alberta, a place I had never heard of. I was astonished. I realized they must read *ASQ*.

Now Derek and I shared a sneaky feeling that research groups had a seven-year life, more or less. That seemed so for the Woodward group and for groups at the Tavistock Institute. We did not want to break up, not the Aston Group nor our relationship, but maybe if we engineered a controlled dispersion we could then regroup after the break. Alberta was the chance to do this. So I went, and enticed Bob to come along too. We had two invigorating years, enjoying working together and with new colleagues. Each of us owes Alberta a great deal. Neither of us returned to Aston.

For everyone else, too, was moving on. Aston University itself made the supreme error in prevaricating over a Chair for Derek, so he was not surprisingly drawn away to London Business School in his 'home town', and was soon sitting in its OB Chair, then the premier one in Britain. John went with him to finish the National study and ponder strategic choice.

From Alberta, I came back to Bradford, not Aston. Bob, many years afterwards, settled at Alberta, via a wide loop back through Birmingham. Kerr ended in Auckland (New Zealand), Roy in Sheffield, Chris in Stirling (Scotland), Keith and Theo in Surrey and Bath, respectively, John in Cambridge. Diana alone among the researchers continued at Aston right up to her retirement. Derek himself went on from LBS to the Open University, a vehicle for educating widely and well in a way that is close to his heart.

So many took part in 'Aston' that not everyone has been mentioned in these recollections. Derek would want them all in. There are Rita Austin, Cindy Fazey, Will McQuillan, our last and longest serving secretarial member Ruth Goodkin and, the ultimate survivor, Pat Clark (who still works at Aston in research administration).

Nothwithstanding all else he did and does, 'Aston' is Derek's foremost academic landmark, a tribute to his scholarly vision and team-building skills. Nowadays he describes himself as an unreconstructed positivist. I suppose he was so all those years ago. I suppose, too, that I remain still under construction.

Bibliography

Organization-level *ASQ* Papers

Hickson, D.J., Pugh, D.S. and Pheysey, D.C. (1969), 'Operations technology and organization structure: an empirical reappraisal', *Administrative Science Quarterly*, **14**, 378–97.

Inkson, J.H.K., Hickson, D.J. and Pugh, D.S. (1970), 'Organization context and structure: an abbreviated replication', *Administrative Science Quarterly*, **15**, 318–29.

Pugh, D.S., Hickson, D.J., Hinings, C.R., Macdonald, K.M., Turner, C. and Lupton, T. (1963), 'A conceptual scheme for organizational analysis', *Administrative Science Quarterly*, **8**, 289–315.

Pugh, D.S., Hickson, D.J., Hinings, C.R. and Turner, C. (1968), 'Dimensions of organization structure', *Administrative Science Quarterly*, **13**, 65–105.

Pugh, D.S., Hickson, D.J., Hinings, C.R. and Turner, C. (1969), 'The context of organization structures', *Administrative Science Quarterly*, **14**, 91–114.

Pugh, D.S., Hickson, D.J. and Hinings, C.R. (1969), 'An empirical taxonomy of structures of work organizations', *Administrative Science Quarterly*, **14**, 115–26.

Books of Edited Collected Papers

Hickson, D.J. and McMillan, C.J. (1981), *Organization and Nation: The Aston Programme*, IV, Aldershot: Gower.

Pugh, D.S. and Hickson, D.J. (1976), *Organizational Structure and its Context: The Aston Programme*, I, Aldershot: Gower.

Pugh, D.S. and Hinings, C.R. (1976), *Organization Structure – Extensions and Replications: The Aston Programme*, II, Aldershot: Gower.

Pugh, D.S. and Payne, R.L. (1977), *Organizational Behaviour in its Context: The Aston Programme*, III, Aldershot: Gower.

3 Derek Pugh: Scientific Revolutionary in Organization Studies

LEX DONALDSON, *Australian Graduate School of Management, University of New South Wales*

Derek Pugh is one of the great scientific revolutionaries in organization studies. He helped inaugurate the modernist approach to the study of organizations. And he provides in our field a role model of a person living professional values. In particular, he exemplifies commitment to value-neutrality and a readiness to challenge the validity of fondly held but erroneous theories and beliefs. His life and work provide an enduring lesson for present and future researchers.

Derek has enjoyed a long and fruitful professional life, which continues today. This *festschrift* marks his retirement from a full-time position, but not, happily, from making professional contributions. I knew Derek personally, principally in the early 1970s, when I served under his leadership in the Organizational Behaviour Research Group of the London Graduate School of Business Studies. My perceptions of Derek are therefore skewed somewhat towards this period, though I shall not limit myself to just that phase in his life. I want to emphasize what I see as his great contribution to our field. Thus I will focus on his philosophical position and seek to explain why it was such an important contribution, and why it remains important. I shall dwell on his philosophical position as well as on his research projects since I believe that both have been significant. Moreover, there is perhaps more danger of overlooking his underlying philosophical position as his research is more tangible and has been discussed in the literature, whereas the philosophical position is more abstract.

One must acknowledge at the outset that Derek chose to work in teams for some of his best known projects and so those achievements are shared with those colleagues. However, it is possible to discern a distinctive position that is apparent in his solo work as much as in the team projects. Moreover, some of his team colleagues have said to me that one of his particular contributions to their work was his firm sense of the philosophy of scientific inquiry. Thus, while recognizing the collaborative nature of much of his research, it is appropriate in discussing his particular achievements to highlight his philosophical position. This is welcome because it raises some central issues in organization studies.

His Philosophical Position

Derek Pugh epitomizes commitment to science in organization studies. The mission is to build a body of objective knowledge that transcends personal subjectivity. This involves the forging of abstract concepts that powerfully summarize aspects of the world. Such concepts, when linked together, form theories from which are derived hypotheses that are tested against the data. Only theories whose hypotheses survive empirical testing are considered to be true. Theories that fail empirical testing are discarded as false and misleading, however appealing or popular they may be. The stuff of science is concepts, but they must be tested in the crucible of empirical inquiry. This is a very Popperian view and Popper (1945) was held up as a major authority on the philosophy of science. It is also a very sceptical and empirical view of knowledge, and Derek was fond of saying that, while an undergraduate at the University of Edinburgh, he had sat on the same benches as Hume. Today this philosophical position would be classified as that of a modernist.

   Later critics of his research criticized it as empiricist. By this they meant that it was underlain by an inductive view of knowledge as emerging from the accumulation of facts. They criticize empiricism as wrong and naive, because it overlooks the crucial role of concepts and theories in shaping what is observed and how data are interpreted. This criticism of Derek's work is a mistaken caricature, however. Derek always understood that data do not speak for themselves and that concepts and theories provide the interpretation. This idea was clear to any follower of Popper (1945) who lampooned empiricism as the bucket theory of the mind and asserted instead the searchlight theory, with concepts and theories providing the searchlight that illuminates the object under study.

   Concepts were central to Derek's work. He strove to find and articulate concepts. He also produced several conceptual frameworks which were architectural arrangements of concepts. An example is the idea that organizational behaviour could be studied at four different but interacting levels: the environment, the organization, the groups of organizational members and the individual organizational

member (Pugh and Hickson, 1976). Such conceptual schemas provide ways of ordering lower-level concepts (such as concepts about
the environment as distinct from concepts about the organization).
Theories were relations between concepts that ran within or between
any one level in the schema. There could be many theories, and some
would compete. There was no a priori commitment to one theory as
against another. The task of social scientists was to define the schemas
that made possible identification of different theories and then to test
them. Whereas Derek and others defined the conceptual schemas
that gave intellectual structure to the field, the task of theory construction and testing was a larger one to which many different
colleagues and students could contribute.

Another important conceptual schema and programme put forward by Derek was to define organizational behaviour as an
interdisciplinary field of study (Pugh, 1966). The understanding of
organizations and the behaviour of their members involves compre-
hending a range of phenomena and he argued that this would be
best attained by combining insights from several disciplines, such as
psychology, sociology and economics, into the interdisciplinary field
of organizational behaviour. OB focuses on organizational phenomena and uses whatever theories, concepts and methods are most
helpful from whatever base discipline. Thus OB is defined pragmati-
cally rather than by traditional academic disciplines whose own
concerns should not dominate and preclude OB from obtaining the
best insights possible. By implication, OB should launch itself on a
programme of interdisciplinary research across many topics. The
article defining OB was published at a time when OB was seeking to
establish itself at the start of its growth in universities across the
world. The article has been much cited and has been helpful in
defining and legitimating OB. It advocates a change that diminishes
the influence of older academic departments while asserting the need
for a newer field that more adequately captures the nature of life in
organizations. This was a progressive rather than conservative act by
Derek.

Thus part of Derek's contribution consisted of programmatic writings that sought to set a course for long-term research endeavours.
These endeavours required work not just by Derek but by a team, as in
the original Aston Study, and indeed by a host of individuals and
teams stretching out over generations. The results of pioneering studies were not to be trusted until replicated by others to ensure their
validity and objectivity. Once replicated, further research was needed
to ensure that the results generalized; that is, that they held true across
different settings, such as nations, or across organizations of different
types. Again the underlying philosophy was one of scepticism about
any proposition being true until actually shown to hold by empirical

tests. To aid replication and generalization there was an emphasis on explicit operational definitions, full reporting of procedures and making procedures and data available to other scholars (as with the Aston databank (Richards, 1980)). Thus Derek saw his role as that of defining conceptual frameworks and operationalizations that would allow a scientific programme to unfold over the long term.

While concepts were the building blocks of theory, Derek often expressed some scepticism about theories, seeing any theory as just one possible conjunction between concepts. Indeed, he surprised many people by his lack of commitment to particular theories. He was willing to entertain a variety of causal interpretations of his data: for example, if X and Y were correlated then it could mean that X caused Y or that Y caused X or that both were caused by W or that there was no causal connection between X and Y (Pugh and Hickson, 1972). He was often willing to admit that some variable other than those included in his data might be a cause. The commitment was not to a theory, but rather to scientific method. All disputes between theory would 'come out in the wash', as he would say, as successive studies empirically tested between them.

Latter-day critics of Derek's work in the Aston project on organizational structure sometimes depict it as a dogmatic assertion that size drives structure. This is because of the prominence given to size in the Aston publications (Pugh *et al.*, 1969; Pugh and Hinings, 1976), but this reflects the prominence of size in the Aston findings. Organizational size was the major correlate of many aspects of organizational structure (Pugh *et al.*, 1969) and subsequent studies also found that size was a major correlate of structure (Pugh and Hinings, 1976). Thus the role accorded to size follows directly from the empirical findings. It is not produced by dogmatic conviction, nor is it even produced by commitment to a prior theory.

There is relatively little in the way of a systematic theory of the effects of size on structure in the writings of Derek. This is better appreciated when contrasted with the formal theory of Blau (1970) which asserts strong, general and pervasive size effects. The main theory of the effects of size on structure within the Aston programme is by Child (1973a) and this comes after his replication study (Child, 1972a) had been conducted and hence after the Aston Study (Pugh *et al.*, 1968). There is no Astonian published theory of size prior to the Aston study collection of their data, nor does the Aston study claim that it expected to find strong size effects because of a prior theory (Pugh *et al.*, 1969). Thus there was no commitment to some theory that was held by Derek and his colleagues prior to their data collection, so it could not have shaped their results.

In fact, the dominance of size seems to have surprised them and was almost something of an embarrassment. The Aston Study went to considerable lengths to include many different aspects of context additional to size, based on a comprehensive reading of prior work, so that a long list of context variables was studied – charter, technology, dependence and so on (Pugh *et al.*, 1963). A rationale for the Aston project was that, with so many putative causes of structure a comprehensive inquiry was needed to identify the true causes. A desirable finding that would have justified the study would have been that structure was caused by many different aspects of context, that different structural variables were each caused by distinct combinations of context variables and that the context variables interacted in complex ways to cause structure. Instead, size dominated for many structural variables (Pugh *et al.*, 1969). This led critics to sneer at the Aston findings as banal (for example, Starbuck, 1981). This is too harsh a judgement, but the immediate point is that the dominance of size was not the result of prior theoretical commitment or professional self-interest. It is a genuinely emergent empirical finding. As such it is in keeping with the philosophy of research of Derek that research should be open to empirical discoveries.

Critics of the Aston Study also criticize it as being functionalist and for offering managerial prescriptions. However, the functionalism is very muted. It only comes to the fore in later writings such as in Child (1975), where increasing bureaucratization as size grows is held to increase performance, or where bureaucratization and centralization are discussed as alternative modes of control (Child, 1972a). Moreover, Child (1972b) also made a major contribution to the critical discussion of functionalist interpretations of organizational structure. There cannot be much functionalist theory in the Aston Study, because there is not much theory, with rather sparing use of cause and effect interpretations. This is part of Derek's scepticism about theories, as discussed above, that leads to a rather agnostic discussion of data. He is particularly cautious about trying to make causal inferences from cross-sectional data (such as the Aston Study), seeing the need for longitudinal data to establish causality (Pugh and Hickson, 1972). Given the sparing approach to theory, it necessarily follows that Derek offers little prescriptive advice, which necessarily would involve commitment to a theory. Hence Derek's writing is mainly free of prescriptions, managerial or otherwise.

His lack of commitment to a theory contrasted with the other style which was often found among organizational behaviour researchers, and is still found today. This other style is commitment to a particular theory. A certain view about organizations or the behaviour of people in them is strongly held. The mission is to show the truth of this theory and to persuade others of its truth. Research and writing takes on the character of advocacy. There is no entertaining the possibility that the theory may be false. The theory is true and the task is to get data to show this, or find compelling examples, or show how contradictory findings really mask the deeper truth of the theory. There is no real discovery in the advocacy approach, because the truth is known at the outset. In contrast, for sceptics like Derek, since theories are fallible there is the very real possibility that research may uncover something not previously known, or at least that surprising empirical findings may force alternate explanations to be entertained and novel theory development to occur.

His Value-neutrality

Commitment to a theory is widespread and one theory in particular has long enjoyed a following among some organizational behaviour faculty members. This is human relations theory, which holds that organizations are structured in ways that stifle human beings and so cause dissatisfaction and ineffectiveness (Roethlisberger and Dickson, 1939; Likert, 1961). This theory enjoyed increasing popularity among industrial psychologists and sociologists from the 1930s onwards. Human relations was the basic theory underlying the work of Burns and Stalker (1961) and Woodward (1958, 1965). Both projects held that traditional organizational structures of the bureaucratic and mechanistic kinds were ineffectual once new technology was adopted, and these structures needed to be replaced by more participatory or organic structures that gave more scope to initiative and power sharing. Both these projects advanced sophisticated human relations theories, conceding that traditional technologies required fewer human relations style structures, but, for both, the future need was for human relations. The purpose of their books was to alert managers to the necessity to adopt human relations practices as technologies changed. Subsequent writings by Burns (1963) and Woodward (Flanders *et al.*, 1968) show their commitment to human relations as the right approach for almost all organizations; that is, the theory becomes universal rather then contingent. The work of Burns and Woodward carried strong theoretical interpretations, had definite claims about organizational effectiveness and strong prescriptions for management. These were pioneering contributions in establishing what came to be known as contingency theory, or structural contingency theory (Donaldson, 1995a, 1996a).

The works of Burns and Stalker and of Woodward were already established when the Aston project was commencing (Pugh *et al.*, 1963). The Aston project broke radically from their tradition by not following their human relations theoretical base. The Aston project did not conclude that organizations had increasingly to adopt human relations practices, such as participation. It made little in the way of statements about effectiveness and almost no prescriptions about what managers should do. This lack of prescriptive conclusions irritated many of its readers. But for Derek and his colleagues this was because they were taking a scientific approach. They were conducting basic research to find how organizations actually were structured. These concepts would allow future assessments about consequences for satisfaction and effectiveness. These assessments, in turn, were part of the long-run programme, which eventually would reveal which theory was correct. This would provide a valid base from which prescriptions might be made, again at some time in the future.

The human relations movement is more than a theory; it is a value position which asserts that organizations should be run humanistically, that is so as to respect their human members. Thus followers of the theory are committed to a set of values. They have a world-view that sees many organizations and managers as trampling on human feelings and have a mission to change organizations and their managers to bring about liberation. There is much that is appealing about this value position. However, the human relations and other value positions run counter to the principle that social science should be a value-neutral inquiry. This holds that scientific inquiry about people and organizations should aim to find the truth without being deflected through reverence for some value presupposition. Social science concerns revealing the world as it is, because focus on what ought to be impairs objectivity. Thus the task of social science is to build a body of objective knowledge rather than to advocate solutions. Committing oneself to solutions before knowing how the organizational world actually works is potentially foolish. Again we arrive at the idea that the aim for organizational researchers must be to build a science through a programme of researches over a long term, rather than cling to values and beliefs fashioned when the real world is only dimly understood. Thus the social scientist is committed neither to a theory nor to social values. To put it another way, the commitment is to scientific method and to the values of scientific inquiry. Derek embodied this position, a position very different from that of leading authorities of the time, such as Burns and Woodward.

Thus Derek championed value-neutral inquiry into organizations, which conflicted with the approach of existing authority figures. He was a scientific revolutionary. He sought to bring to organization studies an approach that was scientific, and this upset the status quo.

The Scientific Revolution in Organization Studies

In addition to value-neutrality, there were other elements that distinguished the scientific approach. There were differences also in methods. The pre-existing mode of studying organizations relied on qualitative methods and case histories (Crozier, 1964). Burns and Stalker (1961) broadened this with a comparison across organizations, but without quantitative measurement. Woodward (1958, 1965) used quantitative measures, but simple ones of limited reliability and without use of statistical procedures. The Aston project on organizational structure gave emphasis to developing reliable, multi-item scales and it used multivariate statistical procedures (Pugh *et al.*, 1968). The results challenged the status quo, by questioning the validity of established theories.

Burns and Stalker (1961) and Woodward (1958, 1965) argued that organizations were becoming less bureaucratic because of new technology. The Aston Study showed weak technology effects (Hickson *et al.*, 1969). The major replication showed weaker technology effects (Child and Mansfield, 1972). A review showed that Woodward's technology effects failed to replicate (Donaldson, 1976). Thus Derek and his colleagues laid down a challenge to human relations theory by questioning the idea that technology was bringing about human relations practices. Considerable controversy ensued with many subsequent studies being conducted, with a variety of outcomes (for example, Blau *et al.*, 1976; Reimann, 1980; Lincoln *et al.*, 1986). The challenge to human relations-based theories of organization that Derek and his colleagues made continues in current debate. Recurrently it forces a close examination of fresh empirical data rather than letting the discussion slide back to cozy beliefs. Thus Derek acted as a revolutionary by challenging human relations and value-led beliefs and so generating a scientific discourse with attention to empirical data and methodology.

The scientific revolutionary nature of his work is seen also in another cardinal aspect of the Aston project on organizational structure. The pre-existing mode of inquiry in organization studies relied much on typologies and ideal-types. This in turn was linked to the reverence held for Max Weber (1968) and his use of ideal-types. The Aston project empirically examined the Weberian ideal-type of bureaucracy and concluded that it was flawed (Pugh *et al.*, 1968). Through statistical analysis of data from real organizations they showed that the unitary concept of bureaucracy was misleading because organizational structure was multidimensional (Pugh *et al.*, 1968). Subsequent empirical studies were conducted that produced a variety of findings, some confirming multidimensionality and some confirming Weber (for example, Child, 1972a; Reimann, 1973). The Aston Study

by Derek and his colleagues was revolutionary to the point of iconoclasm. Weber was a giant not only in organization theory but in the
whole of sociology. His writings were seen as seminal and authori-
tative. Derek and his colleagues had the temerity to challenge Weber.
Moreover, they did so by empirically studying real organizations
rather than by a scholarly reinterpretation of classical texts. This is
the Baconian empirical tradition. It moved the whole issue of the
dimensions of organizational structure away from armchair
conceptualization towards empirical study and refutation.

The issue of the number of dimensions underlying organizational
structure was pursued by making a factor analysis of the structural
variables. Inquiries into dimensionality by factor analysis, such as
research into the dimensionality of personality, had already been
conducted in psychology. In pursuing this issue, and in other ways,
such as computing reliability coefficients, the Aston project drew
upon approaches used in psychology that were more novel in sociology. As a trained psychologist, Derek would be familiar with such
psychometric approaches.

Again the Astonian emphasis on empirical field testing is important because many organization studies, especially under the influence
of sociological theory, took the form of essays. These were exegeses
and commentaries upon classical writers, such as Weber, Marx,
Durkheim and so on. The new social science approach of Derek and
others radically challenged this, by asserting an important role for
empirical studies of real organizations. The ethos was hostile to ver-
bose theorizing, however learned, if empirical evidence was lacking.
As Derek was wont to say in seminars: 'Show me the colour of your
data.' Organizational sociology in the 1970s and later witnessed a
large increase in the number of studies of actual organization. Much
of this was following the example set by Derek and his Aston colleagues (together with other exemplars, such as Blau).

The Legacy

What has been the impact of Derek's professional contribution to
date? He helped inaugurate a scientific revolution in organization
studies and that revolution has caused large and continuing changes.
Part of Derek's legacy is seen in the continuing prosecution and
success of the Aston programme of studies of organizational structure. The insistence on scientific procedures in developing reliable
scales and then making the procedures available to subsequent researchers has paid off handsomely. Through the 1970s, 1980s and
1990s, researchers have followed in the steps of Derek and his colleagues, empirically studying organizations by using the Aston scales

Table 3.1   Generality of size and functional specialization relationship

Study	Country	r	n
Manufacturing organizations			
Hinings & Lee (1971)	UK	0.92	9
McMillan*	UK	0.90	12
Pheysey*	UK	0.86	10
Grinyer & Yasai-Ardekani (1981)	UK	0.86	45
Child & Kieser (1979)	Germany	0.83	51
Hickson *et al.* (1974)	USA	0.82	21
Routamaa (1985)	Finland	0.81	122
Hickson *et al.* (1974)	UK	0.79	25
Ayoubi (1981)	Jordan	0.78	34
Zeffane (1989)	France	0.77	61
Zeffane (1989)	UK	0.73	70
Shenoy (1981)	India	0.73	35
Reimann (1977)	USA	0.70	20
Clark (1990)	Canada	0.70	47
Kuc *et al.* (1981)	Poland	0.67	11
Tai (1987)	Singapore	0.67	30
Tayeb (1987)	India	0.66	7
Tayeb (1987)	England	0.56	7
Zeffane (1989)	Algeria	0.50	50
Hickson *et al.* (1974)	Canada	0.49	24
Azumi & MacMillan (1981)	Japan	0.42	51
Payne & Mansfield (1973)	UK	0.34	14
Marsh & Mannari (1981)	Japan	0.29	50
Horvath *et al.* (1981)	Sweden	0.28	14
Blau *et al.* (1976)	USA	0.25	110
Mixed manufacturing and service organizations			
Bryman *et al.* (1983)	UK	0.77	71
Aston (Pugh & Hickson, 1976)	UK	0.67	46
National (Child & Mansfield, 1972)	UK	0.61	82
Mansfield *et al.* (1980)†	UK	0.55	78
Badran and Hinings (1981)	Egypt	0.53	31
Conaty *et al.* (1983)	Iran	0.47	64
Conaty *et al.* (1983)	USA	0.36	65
Service organizations			
Churches			
(Hinings *et al.*, 1976)	UK	0.79	7

Table 3.1 continued

Study	Country	r	n
Community colleges (Heron*)	Canada	0.84	77
Labour unions (Donaldson & Warner, 1974)	UK	0.73	7
Commercial banks (Wong & Birnbaum-More, 1994)	Hong Kong	0.62	39
Local government (Greenwood & Hinings, 1975)	UK	0.59	84
Colleges (Holdaway *et al.*, 1976)	Canada	0.56	23
Hospitals (Glueck*)	UK	0.46	11
General and mental hospitals (Tauber, 1968)	UK	0.41	6

Notes:
Size is transformed logarithmically for all studies except the three by Zeffane and the one by Tai (unknown for Shenoy); all logarithmic transformations are to base 10 except for studies by Routamaa, Marsh & Mannari and Wong & Birnbaum, More that use natural logarithms.
* Source is Aston Databank.
† Revised scale fewer items, probably less reliable.

Source: Donaldson (1996b).

(Hickson and McMillan, 1981; Lammers and Hickson, 1979). These have now been applied across many different countries and across many different sorts of organizations. For the variables that formed the structuring of activities factor in the Aston Study – functional specialization, formalization and standardization – there is an impressive degree of replication and generalization (Donaldson, 1986). The positive relationship found in the Aston Study between size and each of functional specialization, formalization and standardization holds consistently across the studies (Donaldson, 1996b).

Functional specialization has been the most often studied of these structuring variables. There have been 40 studies and every one finds a positive correlation between size and functional specialization (see Table 3.1). The studies range over 16 different countries: Algeria, Canada, Egypt, Finland, France, Germany, Hong Kong, India, Iran, Japan, Jordan, Poland, Singapore, Sweden, UK and USA. Thus the size–specialization relationship holds over nations differing in culture and social system. The organizations studied range over labour unions, electrical engineering manufacturers, textile firms, churches, community colleges, colleges, local government, hospitals and commercial banks. Thus the size–specialization relationship holds over organizations of very differing types and technologies. The programme of conducting studies of replication and generalization over a long term has produced impressive evidence that the size–structuring relationship holds robustly. The programme of carefully ascertaining the validity of each proposition in each different setting has produced a body of evidence that meets the stringent requirements of the sceptic for systematic proof.

Establishing the general validity of the size–structuring relationship finding in the Aston project is important. Blau and his colleagues (Blau and Schoenherr, 1971; Blau, 1972) showed that size was a major factor of structural differentiation, and the Aston programme showed that it was a major factor for other aspects of structure such as functional specialization and standardization. Blau and Schoenherr (1971) had produced some evidence of a positive connection between formalization and size but their correlations were only modest because of shorter scales and lower reliabilities. The Aston researches used more reliable scales and so were able to reveal stronger relationships, similar in magnitude to the relationships of Blau, between size and structural differentiation. Thus one could combine Blau and Aston and say that increasing size led both to increasing structural differentiation and structuring of activities. Thus increasing size leads to increasing bureaucratization (Donaldson, 1976). This is a parsimonious and elegant finding.

Further, the effects of size on structure found by the Aston Program increased at a decreasing rate with size (that is structure increases as size increases, but the slope becomes shallower) (Child, 1973a). This was similar to the relationship of size and structural differentiation found by Blau and his colleagues (Blau and Schoenherr, 1971; Blau, 1972). The fact that the slope becomes shallower as size increases contradicts the belief that bureaucracy grows cancerously as size increases, which is the basis for many misguided prescriptions about needing to rid organizations of bureaucracy.

As mentioned above, the fact that size correlated with the structural variables in the first major replication study, as it had in the original Aston Study, led Child (1973a) to construct a theory of how size affects structure. This filled the lacuna left by the lack of theory in the original Aston Study. Moreover, it argued a role for human actors (that is managers and administrators). This was useful in that systems–level analyses such as Aston had been criticized for neglecting human actors and thus not fully enough explaining how the structural adaptations to increasing size came about.

Thus the period since the original Aston study has seen many dozens of studies which use the Aston measures and examine replication and generalization or dimensionality of structure or the effects of size and technology and so on. The Aston Programme has had a wider influence than its individual studies in that it helped to establish an approach to organization studies that features quantitative variables, reliability of measures, multivariate statistics and others (Price and Mueller, 1986). These methods are now commonplace across many organization studies and also allied fields such as strategy. The Aston project helped to inaugurate such an approach by being one of the first large-scale studies to emphasize these features. They show how the introduction of psychometrics into the study of organizational structure has spread more pervasively throughout organization studies and beyond.

The Counter-revolution Against Science in Organization Studies

While Derek and his colleagues left a clear legacy, it is not uncontested. The revolution that they started has been challenged by a counter-revolution. The theory and method of studies such as Aston has been challenged, but so too has the aim of building a value-neutral science. This value-neutral stance was explicitly rejected by many working in organization studies. In particular, from the late 1960s onwards many OB faculty members have taken a partisan stance. Commitments are displayed to a variety of values, including those for democracy, for the working class, for women, against capitalism, for 'greening' the environment and so on. Such value commitments often in turn lead to commitments to particular theories and prescriptions, as exemplified by human relations, which value individuals and sees them as being degraded by organizations in ways that could be reversed through more participation and so on. A problem is that, since partisans already believe in a theory, they have little incentive to consider seriously alternative theories or to cleave to rigorous methods of inquiry. There is little point in learning rival theories which are seen a priori as wrong and offensive, or in committing oneself to scientific methods which may lead to scepticism about a deeply cherished belief.

There have been attempts to reassert an approach to organization studies that is similar to the old tradition that Aston sought to overthrow. Qualitative methods and case studies have come back into fashion, especially in the UK (for example, Pettigrew, 1985; Johnson, 1987; Smith *et al.*, 1990; Whittington, 1989). A number of those graduating with PhDs in the UK in the past couple of decades have received little training in scientific methods and are generally hostile to such methods, because they have limited understanding of their role and purpose.

A broad attack has been mounted against analyses of the organization as a system, especially where made through functionalist theory. Critics have argued for the superiority of alternative theories such as interpretism or social action theory (Silverman, 1970), or conflict or Marxian theories (Clegg and Dunkerley, 1980). These are asserted to be paradigms which are incommensurable with functionalism (Burrell and Morgan, 1979). The doctrine of paradigm incommensurability is used to reject Aston-type work and to ignore work done within a paradigm different from that favoured by the scholar in question. Aston and the like are labelled as positivist, not only in method, but in theory, by giving emphasis to material causes such as size and to deterministic causal laws. Much of the critique is mounted in philosophical and sociological theory terms. Many of the critical writings take the form of essays with reliance on arguments of an a priori kind, at the expense of considering in depth the results of empirical studies. There is a penchant for arguing for whole new programmes of research rather than studying what research to date has found; moreover, the programmatic statements seem to yield little in the way of subsequent studies. For example, the much publicized programme of social action theory advanced by Silverman has led to little subsequent research (Donaldson, 1994). But, in the circles of the avant-garde organization theorist or organization sociologist, lack of empirical study seems not to matter. Such is the new scholasticism.

Dissension occurred within the ranks of the Aston researchers. Having conducted the major replication of the original Aston Study, Child (1972b) expressed strong reservations about the positivist, functionalist type of explanations used in the Aston Study. He argued that material factors and functionalist imperatives had only some influence on the organizational structure, with a considerable strategic choice being left for the dominant coalition who control the organization. He called for more study of the decision-making process and politics, and more recognition of the role of managerial values, interests and ideologies (ibid.). Other members of the original Aston group, such as Hickson, went on to study intra-organizational power (Hickson *et al.*, 1971) and then organizational decision making in quantitative, comparative researches in the Aston mould (Hickson *et al.*, 1986). Pettigrew (1973) championed a more qualitative and intensive case history approach to the study of political processes. This became increasingly the dominant mode of organizational research in the UK in the 1980s (for example, Johnson, 1987; Whittington, 1989), even being followed by Child (Smith *et al.*, 1990).

Aston saw as one of its great achievements the laying of the ghost of Weber (1968), in the sense of proving that ideal-types were unfruitful for studying organizations. Instead of having a few ideal-types, such as bureaucracy, and then discussing whether an organization was more like that idea-type or some other ideal-type, Aston offered what can be called a Cartesian framework (Donaldson, 1996b). There were several distinct structural dimensions which were independent of each other, such as structuring of activities and concentration of authority. Each organization was scored as lying at one of the large number of different points along the continuum of structuring and of the continuum of concentration of authority. The score on one dimension was independent of the score on the other dimension. Thus there are a very large number of points, or coordinates, in the two-dimensional space at which an organization can lie. This is a very finely-grained way of modelling the organization which is more accurate and useful than analysis in terms of ideal-types. Thus one of the major achievements of research in the 1960s was to move from ideal-types to multivariate, multidimensional Cartesian frameworks for the study of organizations.

Notwithstanding this progress, a retrogressive movement has developed to go back to using ideal-types, often today called configurations or gestalts. Mintzberg (1979) identified five structural types and Miller (1986) reduced this to four strategy–structure gestalts. Lately, a spate of researchers has sought to study organizations using such configurations (see Meyer *et al.*, 1993). Unsurprisingly, these researchers often conclude that their data fail to fall into the few configurations and so they must have recourse to hybrid configurations. Former Aston researcher Hinings has participated in the configurations movement.

Thus the scientific revolution inaugurated by Derek and others has faced a counter-revolution. In the UK, the counter-revolution has gone a long way and has had a large impact on research, though some continue the scientific style of research (for example, Ezzamel and Watson, 1993) and some who were involved in qualitative case history have latterly conducted more scientific types of research (Bailey and Johnson, 1995). However, many of the basic issues remain contested and so there remains a need for professionals to adopt Derek's position. We cannot take for granted the past commitments of Derek and his like: each new generation of doctoral students needs to internalize his value commitment to a science of organizations.

Continuing the Scientific Revolution

The tribulations in the UK have not ended the scientific programme that Derek led. Some among us continue to fight for the revolution that he helped initiate and to continue building the science of organizations. I have long agreed with Derek's vision and have sought to continue his scientific revolution in organization studies.

I have considered elsewhere at length the philosophical and socio-logical critiques of systems-level analyses of organizations and have shown these critiques to be flawed and systems-level analyses to be sound (Donaldson, 1985). Functionalism has also been shown to be cogent and empirically supportable. The claim that organizational sociology is composed of incommensurable paradigms has been dem-onstrated to be false (ibid.). Thus there are considerable prospects for accommodation between functionalism on the one hand and conflict and culturalist theories on the other. Reed (1985) rightly character-izes my position as that of an integrationist. Many of the claims about how alternate theories such as social action theory or Marxian organization theory can and should be developed as separate, rival theories to functionalism are shown to be false (Donaldson, 1985). I have sought to demonstrate the unfolding evidence for replication and generalization by tracking the studies that continue to appear using the Aston variables of organizational structure (for example, Routamaa, 1985) and showing how they replicate the original Aston findings (Donaldson, 1996b).

Child (1972b) and others have made their case for strategic choice, by arguing that the contingency factors such as size only weakly determine organizational structure. I have shown that the connection between size and structure is strong, despite qualifying factors such as slack organizational resources (Donaldson, 1996b). Moreover, whereas Child claims that organizations can escape from misfit by altering their contingencies to fit their structure and thereby avoid adapting structure to contingency, in fact organizations overwhelm-ingly have to adapt their structure to their contingency to attain fit. A review of these and other arguments against determinism shows that they are mostly invalid and that organizational structure is to a con-siderable degree determined by contingencies with little role for choice (Donaldson, 1996b).

The central claim of the configuration or gestalt approach is that organizations can be reduced to a few types that are internally coher-ent (Mintzberg, 1979; Miller, 1986). An analysis reveals that the idea of internal coherence is theoretically flawed and that there are many more types than these few gestalts (Donaldson, 1996b). In order to account for empirically observed structures and organizational change it is necessary to revert to the Cartesian approach such as in the Aston programme.

As part of the counter-revolution, the call has been made to aban-don the search for simple positivist explanations, such as size, and replace them with complex political process models in which self-interested actors struggle with each other. One arena in which this argument has been advanced is the growth of managers and administrative staff (for example, Child, 1973b). Since managerial self-interest favours such growth, researchers have examined it and argued that positivistic, functionalist size-based explanations fail and need to be replaced by political explanations. However, a closer analysis reveals that the political explanations are flawed, whereas the size explanations work well, yielding simple, general relationships (Donaldson, 1996b). Thus positivist, functionalist explanations of this topic of growth of managers and administrative staff are valid, and more valid than the political explanations.

In the USA there has been no successful counter-revolution against positivism or systematic empirical study, as there has been in the UK. There has been no return to the essay nor even to case histories as a general mode of research. However, neither has there been a smooth build-up in organizational science. There has been some continuing work therein on the Aston programme (for example, Lincoln *et al.*, 1986); and there has been work in research traditions that are closely allied to Aston, in that they examine other aspects of the contingency–structure relationships (for example, Gresov, 1989). But parallel to such structural contingency theory research has been other work that takes a different view and tends to argue against structural contingency theory.

From about the mid-1970s onwards several new theories have arisen in the USA, of which the main ones are population–ecology, institutional theory, resource dependence theory, agency theory and transaction cost economics (Hannan and Freeman, 1989; Powell and DiMaggio, 1991; Pfeffer and Salancik, 1978; Jensen and Meckling, 1976; Williamson, 1985, respectively). Each of these explicitly or implicitly rejects structural contingency theory. They each lead to their own programmes of research, which leads away from the completion of the earlier programme, as envisaged by Derek. Moreover, these newer theories tend to work separately from each other. Thus organization studies is fragmented and cumulation of research into a solid science is frustrated. I have offered a critique of each of these theories and sought to show the continuing cogency of structural contingency theory (Donaldson, 1995b). Moreover, I have sought to show how the valid parts of each of these theories may be synthesized with contingency theory into a model of organizational structure that reintegrates this topic (ibid.). In essence, the problem in the USA is the rapid proliferation of fads and fashions. Less emphasis on chasing fads would leave more room for completing long-term programmes such as that envisioned by Derek. A contemporary agenda for future research on organizational structure that builds on the scientific achievements to date is outlined in Donaldson (1995b).

While the emphasis upon novelty seems to be a cultural facet of the USA, faddism is not confined to that country. Novel management fads come and go, but they command the attention of researchers to the detriment of scientific development. Moreover, the popularity of many of the fads seems to depend in part upon their attractiveness in value terms. Much of the contemporary scene reflects the evergreen appeal of human relations theory. For example, flatter structures are depicted as a present trend with beneficial consequences for organizational productivity. Again, modern organizations are seen as evolving towards the N-Form: a network form in which the organization interacts with other organizations to which it out-sources many of its erstwhile core functions such as manufacturing or product design (this is discussed in more detail in Chapter 9). Much of the thinking on both topics is motivated by dislike of hierarchy and the wish to see hierarchy flattened or replaced by contracting between firms, and this reflects the human relations theory distaste for authority hierarchies. There is much simplistic thinking. For example, if some organizations had too tall a hierarchy and benefited from flattening it, this does not mean that all organizations have too tall a hierarchy and would benefit, so case examples are a hazardous basis for a general prescription.

On many topic areas today one sees the way ideas about organizations have become widely accepted despite the absence of empirical evidence that they are valid. For example, regarding boards of directors, some organization theories assert that a board that is composed of outsiders who are independent of management will better control management and so will produce superior corporate profits and shareholder returns (Jensen and Meckling, 1976; Williamson, 1985). However, empirical studies are mixed in their findings: some find that non-executive directors and a non-executive board chairman raise organizational performance and shareholder wealth, while others find that non-executives *reduce* organizational performance and shareholder wealth (Donaldson, 1995b; for a review, see Donaldson and Davis, 1994). Thus the general proposition that corporations would benefit from introducing more non-executives onto their boards is false. Theories that assert such a view, such as agency theory and transaction cost economics, need to be examined critically. Prescriptive advice that corporations should adopt more independent boards is unwarranted at present and may be counter-productive. Thus in topics other than those Derek has researched there is need for the scientific approach and the scepticism that he personifies.

Yet people, including OB faculty members, are enduringly victims in believing in simplistic theories because they find them appealing on value grounds. This is a problem when these theories are empirically invalid. Worse yet, such people broadcast these theories to their students and to managers and policy makers. We need now, as much as ever in the history of organization studies, to follow a scientific approach. Theories should be considered just speculations until they have been empirically tested and shown to be true. This a long, hard road, but it is the only one which produces dependable knowledge. Derek pointed us down that road and we should continue in that direction. The struggle to build a science goes on. The forces of counter-revolution are considerable but we are making progress towards the goal of building a science of organizations. Therefore we should salute Derek and push forward with the scientific revolution.

References

Bailey, A. and Johnson, G. (1995), 'Strategy development processes: a configurational approach', paper to Business policy and Strategy Division, Academy of Management, Best Paper Proceedings, Vancouver, British Columbia, Canada, pp. 2–6.

Blau, P.M. (1970), 'A formal theory of differentiation in organizations', *American Sociological Review*, **35**, 201–18.

Blau, P.M. (1972), 'Interdependence and hierarchy in organizations', *Social Science Research*, **1**, 1–24.

Blau, P.M. and Schoenherr, P.A. (1971), *The Structure of Organizations*, New York: Basic Books.

Blau, P.M., Falbe, M., McHugh, C., McKinley, W. and Phelps, T.K. (1976), 'Technology and organization in manufacturing', *Administrative Science Quarterly*, 21–40.

Burns, T. (1963), 'Industry in a New Age', *New Society*, **18**, 17–20.

Burns, T. and Stalker, G.M. (1961), *The Management of Innovation*, London: Tavistock.

Burrell, G. and Morgan, G. (1979), *Sociological Paradigms and Organizational Analysis: Elements of the Sociology of Corporate Life*, London: Heinemann.

Child, J. (1972a), 'Organization structure and strategies of control: a replication of the Aston Study', *Administrative Science Quarterly*, **17**, 163–77.

Child, J. (1972b), 'Organizational structure, environment and performance: the role of strategic choice', *Sociology*, **6**, 1–22.

Child, J. (1973a), 'Predicting and understanding organization structure', *Administrative Science Quarterly*, **18**, 168–85.

Child, J. (1973b), 'Parkinson's progress: accounting for the number of specialists in organizations', *Administrative Science Quarterly*, **18**, 328–48.

Child, J. (1975), 'Managerial and organizational factors associated with company performance, Part 2: A contingency analysis', *Journal of Management Studies*, **12**, 12–27.

Child, J. and Mansfield, R. (1972), 'Technology, size and organization structure', *Sociology*, **6**, 369–93.

Clegg, S. and Dunkerley, D. (1980), *Organization, Class and Control*, London: Routledge & Kegan Paul.

Crozier, M. (1964), *The Bureaucratic Phenomenon*, London, Tavistock.

Donaldson, L. (1976), 'Woodward, Technology, Organizational Structure and Performance – a Critique of the Universal Generalization', *Journal of Management Studies*, **13**, 255–73.

Donaldson, L. (1985), *In Defence of Organization Theory: A Reply to the Critics*, Cambridge: Cambridge University Press.

Donaldson, L. (1986), 'Size and Bureaucracy in East and West: a preliminary meta analysis', in S.R. Clegg, D. Dunphy and S.G. Redding (eds), *The Enterprise and Management in East Asia*, Hong Kong: University of Hong Kong Press, pp. 67–91.

Donaldson, L. (1994), 'The liberal revolution and organization theory', in J. Hassard and M. Parker (eds), *Towards a New Theory of Organizations*, London: Routledge, pp. 190–208.

Donaldson, L. (1995a), *Contingency Theory*, volume 9 in *History of Management Thought Series*, Aldershot: Dartmouth.

Donaldson, L. (1995b), *American Anti-Management Theories of Organization: A Critique of Paradigm Proliferation*, Cambridge: Cambridge University Press.

Donaldson, L. (1996a), 'The normal science of structural contingency theory', in S.R. Clegg, C. Hardy and W. Nord (eds), *The Handbook of Organization Studies*.

Donaldson, L. (1996b), *For Positivist Organization Theory: Proving the Hard Core*, London: Sage.

Donaldson, L. and Davis, J.H. (1994), 'Boards and company performance – research challenges the conventional wisdom', *Corporate Governance: An International Review*, **2**, 151–60.

Ezzamel, M.A. and Watson, R. (1993), 'Organizational form, ownership structure and corporate performance: a contextual empirical analysis of UK companies', *British Journal of Management*, **4**, 161–76.

Flanders, A.D., Pomeranz, R. and Woodward, J. (1968), *Experiments in Industrial Democracy: A Study of the John Lewis Partnership*, London: Faber.

Gresov, C. (1989), 'Exploring fit and misfit with multiple contingencies', *Administrative Science Quarterly*, **34**, 431–53.

Hannan, M.T. and Freeman, J. (1989), *Organizational Ecology*, Cambridge, Mass.: Harvard University Press.

Hickson, D.J. and McMillan, C.J. (eds) (1981), *Organization and Nation: The Aston Programme IV*, Farnborough: Gower.

Hickson, D.J., Pugh, D.S. and Pheysey, D.G. (1969), 'Operations technology and organization structure: an empirical reappraisal', *Administrative Science Quarterly*, **14**, 378–97.

Hickson, D.J., Butler, R.J., Cray, D., Mallory, G.R. and Wilson, D.C. (1986), *Top Decisions: Strategic Decision-Making in Organizations*, Oxford: Blackwell.

Hickson, D.J., Hinings, C.R., Lee, C.A., Schneck, R.E. and Pennings, J.M. (1971), 'A strategic contingencies theory of intraorganizational power', *Administrative Science Quarterly*, **16**, 216–29.

Jensen, M.C. and Meckling, W.H. (1976), 'Theory of the firm: managerial behavior, agency costs and ownership structure', *Journal of Financial Economics*, **3**, 305–60.

Johnson, G. (1987), *Strategic Change and the Management Process*, Oxford: Blackwell.

Lammers, C.J. and Hickson, D.J. (1979), *Organizations Alike and Unlike: International and Inter-Institutional Studies in the Sociology of Organization*. London: Routledge & Kegan Paul.

Lincoln, J.R., Hanada, M. and McBride, K. (1986), 'Organizational structures in Japanese and U.S. manufacturing', *Administrative Science Quarterly*, **31**, 338–64.

Likert, Rensis (1961), *New Patterns of Management*, New York: McGraw-Hill.

Meyer, A.D., Tsui, A.S. and Hinings, C.R. (1993), 'Configurational approaches to organizational analysis', *Academy of Management Journal*, **36**, 1175–95.

Miller, D. (1986), 'Configurations of strategy and structure: towards a synthesis', *Strategic Management Journal*, **7**, 233–49.

Mintzberg, H. (1979), *The Structuring of Organizations: A Synthesis of the Research*, Englewood Cliffs, NJ: Prentice-Hall.

Pettigrew, A.M. (1973), *The Politics of Organizational Decision-Making*, London: Tavistock.

Pettigrew, A.M. (1985), *The Awakening Giant: Continuity and Change in ICI*, Oxford: Blackwell.

Pfeffer, J. and Salancik, G.R. (1978), *The External Control of Organizations: A Resource Dependence Perspective*, New York: Harper & Row.

Popper, K.R. (1945), *The Open Society and Its Enemies, Volume 2, The High Tide of Prophecy: Hegel, Marx and the Aftermath*, London: Routledge & Kegan Paul.

Powell, W.W. and DiMaggio, P.J. (1991), *The New Institutionalism in Organizational Analysis*, Chicago: University of Chicago Press.

Price, J.L. and Mueller, C.W. (1986), *Handbook of Organizational Measurement*, Marshfield, Mass.: Pitman.

Pugh, D.S. (1966), 'Modern organization theory: a psychological and sociological study', *Psychological Bulletin*, **66**, 235–51.

Pugh, D.S. and Hickson, D.J. (1972), 'Causal inference and the Aston Studies', *Administrative Science Quarterly*, **17**, 273–6.

Pugh, D.S. and Hickson, D.J. (1976), *Organizational Structure in its Context: The Aston Programme I*, Farnborough: Saxon House.

Pugh, D.S. and Hinings, C.R. (1976), *Organizational Structure: Extensions and Replications: The Aston Programme II*, Farnborough: Saxon House.

Pugh, D.S., Hickson, D.J., Hinings, C.R. and Turner, C. (1968), 'Dimensions of organization structure', *Administrative Science Quarterly*, **13**, 65–105.

Pugh, D.S., Hickson, D.J., Hinings, C.R. and Turner, C. (1969), 'The context of organization structures', *Administrative Science Quarterly*, **14**, 91–114.

Pugh, D.S., Hickson, D.J., Hinings, C.R., Macdonald, K.M., Turner, C. and Lupton, T. (1963), 'A conceptual scheme for organizational analysis', *Administrative Science Quarterly*, **8**, 289–315.

Reed, M. (1985), *Redirections in Organizational Analysis*, London: Tavistock.

Reimann, B.C. (1973), 'On the dimensions of bureaucratic structure: an empirical reappraisal', *Administrative Science Quarterly*, **18**, 462–76.

Reimann, B.C. (1980), 'Organization structure and technology in manufacturing: system versus work flow level perspectives', *Academy of Management Journal*, **23**, 61–77.

Richards, V.G. (1980), 'Research note: the Aston Databank', *Organization Studies*, **1**, 271–8.

Roethlisberger, F.J. and Dickson, W.J. (1939), *Management and the Worker*, Cambridge, Mass.: Harvard University Press.

Routamaa, V. (1985), 'Organizational structuring: an empirical analysis of the relationships and dimensions of structures in certain Finnish companies', *Journal of Management Studies*, **22**, 498–522.

Silverman, D. (1970), *The Theory of Organizations*, London: Heinemann.

Smith, C., Child, J. and Rowlinson, M. (1990), *Reshaping Work: The Cadbury Experience*, Cambridge: Cambridge University Press.

Starbuck, W.H. (1981), 'A trip to view the elephants and rattlesnakes in the garden of Aston', in A.H. Van de Ven and W.F. Joyce (eds), *Perspectives on Organization Design and Behavior*, New York: Wiley, pp. 167–98.

Weber, M. (1968), *Economy and Society: An Outline of Interpretive Sociology*, eds G. Roth and C. Wittich, New York: Bedminster Press.

Whittington, R. (1989), *Corporate Strategies in Recession and Recovery: Social Structure and Strategic Choice*, London: Allen & Unwin.

Williamson, Oliver E. (1985), *The Economic Institutions of Capitalism: Firms, Markets, Relational Contracting*, New York: Free Press.

Woodward, J. (1958), *Management and Technology*, London: HMSO.

Woodward, J. (1965), *Industrial Organization: Theory and Practice*, London: Oxford University Press.

4 From the Aston Programme to Strategic Choice: a Journey from Concepts to Theory

JOHN CHILD, *Judge Institute of Management Studies, University of Cambridge*

Personal Background

I joined the Aston Programme 30 years ago, in November 1966, and in so doing entered the most important formative period of my whole career. The Aston team, and Derek Pugh in particular, imbued in me a deep and lasting sense of the economic and social significance of the way our collective activities are organized in modern society, and a firm belief that we should not take this for granted. The forms that organizations take, I learned, can be examined comparatively, in order to find out whether there are other, perhaps better, ways of achieving their stated goals. For this, we need a tool kit of concepts and measures, and the Aston Programme under Derek Pugh's leadership was the world's pioneer in providing a comprehensive set of such tools. Derek also set the highest standards of professionalism for his colleagues to follow when applying the Programme's measures for comparative organizational analysis. He insisted on a thorough on-site training for new researchers like me, and emphasized the meticulous recording of information, the value of learning from the unexpected, and the transparency of analyses and procedures used for the reporting of findings.

My brief was to organize and conduct a new study to replicate the original Aston research into 46 Birmingham organizations, and to extend the sampling onto a national basis. It was also to be an opportunity to explore how the structure of organizations might relate to their performance. The project appeared to present an exciting chance to make both a theoretical and a practical contribution, and I was greatly encouraged in this view by one of Derek's favourite academic aphorisms, taken from Kurt Lewin, that 'there is nothing so practical as a good theory'. My previous experience suggested, however, that the relation of organizational structure and performance might not be a straightforward one. My PhD had researched the historical process through which the body of knowledge on organization had developed in response to both technical and legitimatory needs (Child, 1969). This suggested that organizations might be structured in ways that were intended not only to contribute to securing good performance but also to justify the role of those managers who were designing and approving the structural arrangements. For some two years prior to joining the Aston Programme, I had worked in industry and, as I describe below, this brought me into close contact with the processes through which organizational structuring was actually realized within a major British company. These pointed to the presence of contrasting rationalities held by different groups in the company, and the significance of selection and negotiation between them for the structural outcomes that ensued.

I therefore had to find a way of making sense of the study on which I was now engaged. This study was located within a research programme whose founding members consciously preferred to keep theory implicit in favour of an inductive approach which relied on the application of conceptually driven operational measurement. I could not avoid the conclusion that the concepts which Derek and his colleagues had isolated were looking for a theory, and that the theory which was implicit in the Aston Programme was underdeveloped.

The present chapter explains how this conclusion led to the development of the 'strategic choice' perspective, which was therefore a direct consequence of the opportunity I had to work with Derek and his colleagues. The chapter then goes on to clarify the nature and purpose of this perspective when it was formulated, and to comment on the ensuing debate over agency and environment as influences on organizational structuring. This debate still continues in the form of the post-Aston structural contingencies theory and its critics (for example, Donaldson, 1985, 1995; see also Chapter 3). The chapter concludes by examining the potential contribution of the strategic choice perspective to the development of an evolutionary learning-based approach to organizational analysis which is of current interest but very far removed from the original, essentially static perspective of the Aston Programme. In this respect, at least, strategic choice analysis can be seen to have provided a bridge over the past 30 years from 'the ancient to the modern'. But first, we should go back to the beginning.

The Aston Programme: Concepts Looking for a Theory

The original Aston team set out the specifications for their programme of research in an article published in the December 1963 issue of the *Administrative Science Quarterly*. It presented 'a *conceptual* scheme for organizational analysis' (Pugh *et al.*, 1963). Its purpose was

> to develop an empirically based multidimensional analysis of the struc-
> tural variables of organization. In order to do this we must first of all
> isolate the conceptually distinct elements that go into Weber's formu-
> lation of bureaucracy. Then the relationships between these elements
> become a subject for empirical investigation and not for a priori pos-
> tulation. (p. 298)

As is clear from this extract, the emphasis was on identifying and operationalizing the dimensions of organization, rather than on the-orizing their possible interconnections and understanding how such connections might arise. While the Aston researchers recognized that an organization's structure relates to its activities, they used this insight to inform their conceptualization of structural dimensions, rather than as a resource for a theory of structural formation.

Although it eschewed 'a priori postulation', the Aston Programme did contain an implicit theory. A number of 'independent variables for the study of organizational structure' (Pugh *et al.*, 1963, p. 308) were identified: origin and history, ownership and control, size, char-ter, technology, location, resources and interdependence. The Aston team labelled the variables in this category 'contextual variables'. The variables of organizational 'context' were seen to present contin-gencies which organizational structuring had to satisfy. Of these, size, technology and charter received most prominence in the Pro-gramme's research. The way organizations are structured was expected to impinge on, and therefore predict, group composition and interaction. Group characteristics would in turn have an impact upon individual features through, for example, the process of role definition. In other words, the main theoretical postulate implicit in the Aston Programme was that the configuration of variables at each level would be determined to a significant degree by their immediate context.

The Aston writers also referred to individual personality, but with-out further elaboration. It is not clear whether individual personality was expected to exert an independent influence on organizations through the personalities of their leaders or whether the prediction was that managers who structured organizations in certain ways would seek to attract and select personality types which would fit – such as the so-called 'bureaucratic personality' (Merton, 1940). Internal discussions within the team indicated that its guiding assumption was one of contextual determinism all the way through the levels of analysis from context to structure, to group and to individual. There was, however, really no consideration of how these relationships might come about – how, for instance, structure would adjust to context.

The implicit theory of the Aston Programme can be summarized in the following way:

Environment → Context → Organization Structure → Group → Individual

The distinction between environment and context drawn here was not made explicit in Aston thinking. I recall asking Derek Pugh once whether environment and context were the same and, after some thought, he replied 'Yes, they are.' Some of the younger Aston researchers were concerned that the task and institutional environments of organizations should be taken into account. Colin Fletcher and I drafted half a book on the subject, which unfortunately never saw the light of day.[1] We were influenced by the contributions of writers like Burns and Stalker (1961) and Lawrence and Lorsch (1967) on the significance of the 'task environment' and of institutionalists like Selznick (1949) on the significance of the sociopolitical environment. We believed that organizational form would be shaped, not only by contingencies arising from the market and technological conditions which characterize task environments, but also by pressures emanating from different political and cultural regimes. So we moved towards the view that environment had to be distinguished from context, and that within the Aston theoretical perspective so-called 'contextual' variables like organizational size and technology would be constrained by environmental features. Organizational size would be constrained by the size of markets and producer concentration within them, and organizational technology both by the level of demand and by the technical knowledge available to a given sector of operations.

The rather mechanical perspective through which Derek and his team appeared to view the contextual determination of organization structure particularly concerned me, for what I had seen in industrial practice before joining the Aston Programme suggested that the relationship was far from mechanical and deterministic either in its process or in its effect. If it were accepted as such, even implicitly, I believed that this would close off the exploration of options for organizational design in a way that was both theoretically pathological and socially dangerous. This generated a strong personal imperative to reconcile the conceptual breakthrough which the Aston Programme had made with a theory that resounded with my practical experience.

I came to the Aston Programme from employment with the then Oil Engine Division of Rolls-Royce. Rolls-Royce had gone into the commercial production of diesel engines in partnership with Vickers, building on wartime experience with the Vickers tank. In anticipation of a large post-war demand for agricultural mechanization, the companies produced a tractor which, however, was not a commercial success. This left Rolls-Royce still looking for a market that would permit the mass, or at least large-batch, production of its diesels, such as the automotive market. In the meantime it had to rely on a great deal of small and 'one-off' orders requiring ad hoc specifications. Anyone working in that organization could not fail to be aware of how important the market strategies pursued by its senior management were for the production profile and associated use of technology that the division could sustain.

At the time, there was considerable discussion about the competitive domain in which the division should seek to place itself. The outcome would have consequences for the division's development programmes, on which considerable sums of money could be spent. Should it, for example, concentrate investment on developing a new automotive diesel in order to strengthen its position in that market? What was the appropriate balance between price and quality as competitive strategies, and how significant was the Rolls-Royce image as a factor in this decision? These strategic choices were debated and different departments argued for their own preferred options. The context was not simply a given factor; it was to an important degree being selected over the course of time.

A project that colleagues and I were asked to undertake involved an examination of the division's internal organization and proposals for its improvement. It is instructive to consider how the goals of this exercise emerged. It began as a rather localized part of a company-wide 'Management Systems Survey', initiated by the Rolls-Royce head office in Derby and stimulated by the company's intention to upgrade its computing facilities. However, we soon realized that, while an upgrading of computing opened up new possibilities, this did not by itself specify the improvements which such possibilities might realize. We therefore had to engage with senior divisional managers to arrive at the goals of the organizational examination we were supposed to undertake, and we found that they were not entirely agreed on its priorities. We had to accommodate these divergencies and also translate them into what appeared to be the relevant specifics which we could adopt as meaningful guidelines. So the definition of the 'context' for the proposed reorganization was by no means a clear and straightforward matter. It emerged from a process of debate and interpretation.

When we got into the details of the project, we found that there was usually more than one possible organizational and sociotechnical way of meeting a given requirement. In the event, the proposals we put forward were ones which we felt were workable. 'Workable' meant not just technically feasible, but also solutions which different departmental stakeholders within the division could accept and felt able to work with.

The theoretical perspective which emerged from subsequent reflection on this experience could not be one of simple contextual determination. It had to take account of how the actors involved in discussions and decisions interpreted the significance of the context and accepted or rejected the legitimacy of proposed organizational adaptations to it, from the vantage point of their own, often differing, criteria and roles. It was these people who were deciding on organizational structure. In so doing, they certainly referred to contextual 'requirements', or what Mary Parker Follett called 'the law of the situation' (Graham, 1995), but they mapped their own constructions onto such needs. These constructions had quite significant consequences.

So, on joining the Aston Programme, I faced a disjuncture between the conclusions to be drawn from personal organizational experience and the implicit theoretical assumptions guiding the work of my new academic colleagues. They were studiously avoiding what they called 'a priori postulation', so as to keep an open mind and let the data recently collected with their new concepts and measures 'speak for themselves'. Derek Pugh was very insistent on this. I had tremendous respect for the craft and professionalism of the way the Aston team went about the process of their research, but I could not help feeling that their avoidance of the 'how' and 'why' questions relating to their findings was intellectually unsatisfying and at variance with what appeared to be significant in practice. Most important of all, their stance seemed to reject the questions which for me legitimized the whole comparative research endeavour, namely, 'Was there a genuine choice in how we organized collective effort' and 'Could there be a better way of doing this?' (cf. Child, 1973).

The Emergence of a Strategic Choice View of Organizational Structure

The Aston model of contextual determination assumed a linear progression from higher- to lower-order variables. It did not allow for recursive patterns of influence which would imply a cyclical dynamic. It was basically an equilibrium model which assumed that organizational stability was most likely when each dimension was consistent with its relevant higher-order contingencies. Structure was also thought to contribute maximally to performance when its design was consistent with an organization's context and environment. The general argument of the Aston Programme and other contemporary research of a similar theoretical orientation (for example, Blau and Schoenherr, 1971; Woodward, 1965) was that, 'if organizational structure is not adapted to its context, then opportunities are lost, costs rise, and the maintenance of the organization is threatened' (Child, 1972, p. 8).

The Aston researchers always intended to include an assessment of organizational performance within the scope of their programme (Pugh *et al.*, 1963, pp. 312–13). This would permit a test of the underlying 'structural contingency' perspective: namely, that the goodness of fit between contextual and structural variables would contribute to better performance (Donaldson, 1985). This test was, in fact, conducted. It appeared to support the argument while at the same time leaving much of the variance in performance unexplained (Child, 1975). One consequence of bringing performance variations into the picture, however, was to draw attention to the fact that choices are being made about organizational design. Some choices can be expected to lead to better performance, some to worse.

This led to the question of how a goodness of fit between environment and context, on the one hand, and organizational structure, on the other hand, comes about. In what terms do those organizational actors who exert influence over structural and other organizational choices understand what they are doing, and how do they reconcile possibly differing views on the matter? Are they likely to view these choices as a purely technical matter, or is it possible that considerations of organizational politics will intrude? Do managers see the requirement simply in terms of adjusting organizational structure to suit context and environment, or do they also consider what adjustments they could make to the latter and to their positioning within the environment? Might they indeed regard structures as difficult and costly to change if they are strongly embedded in what Johnson (1990) has more recently called their 'cultural webs'?

My experience in industry indicated that these were not irrelevant questions. I believed at the time (and still do) that they called for a substantial revision of theories, implicit or explicit, of contextual determinism so as to incorporate the logic and consequence of social action. I also believed (and still do) that it is an oversimplification to argue, as Donaldson (1985, 1995) has done, that, whatever the perspectives and preferences of organizational decision makers, there is an overriding logic of structural contingency which will force their hand, given that they face the imperative of organizational survival. This makes a very strong assumption about the relative importance of organizational design for performance and it also assumes that there is only one strategy–structure combination which is viable for a particular organization. And, of course, in the end, it makes managers irrelevant, which is the very assumption against which Donaldson inveighs in his recent book (1995).

The view that context–structure matching should be regarded as the product of actions taken by those individuals or groups with the power both to choose structures and (over time) to select or position themselves in contexts led to the development of the so-called 'strategic choice' perspective (Child, 1972). This began as an attempt to offer a more developed theory within which the conceptual scheme of the Aston Programme could be lodged, which would recognize the dual role in organizational structuring played by social action and situational contingencies. The recursive processes which emerged from a conjunction of action and contingency, however, led naturally towards a dynamic perspective which enabled possibilities to be explored that lay beyond the theoretical reach of the original Aston equilibrium model. I believe that this dynamic perspective has contemporary relevance in contributing to an understanding of organizational learning and transformation, and comment further on this towards the end of this chapter.

Burrell and Morgan (1979) placed the theoretical orientation of the Aston Programme squarely within the 'functionalist' paradigm and there are continuities with it in several contemporary approaches, namely the *strategic contingencies* perspective (Donaldson, 1985, 1995), the *ecological* approach (Hannan and Freeman, 1989) and the *institutional* perspective (Powell and DiMaggio, 1991). The first stresses the functional importance for organizational performance of matching internal organizational capabilities to external conditions, and regards this as a key strategic issue. The second considers that units which do not have organizational forms characteristic of their sector or 'niche' have a poorer chance of survival; its focus is primarily on organizational populations and it gives little attention to the way decision makers might endeavour to adapt to the environment. The institutional perspective is a rather 'broader church', but most of its adherents find common ground in the assumption that the structural forms (as well as the identities and values sustaining these) of relevant external institutions map themselves onto organizations which depend on them for legitimacy, resourcing or staffing. All of these contemporary approaches therefore regard environmental conditions as ultimate determinants of organizational characteristics. Put simply, they stress the environmental selection of organizational structures.

Consideration of strategic choice led to the conclusion that this deterministic view was inadequate because of its failure 'to give due attention to the agency of choice by whoever have the power to direct the organization' (Child, 1972, p. 2). 'Strategic choice' was defined as the process whereby power holders within organizations decide upon courses of strategic action. Such action could be directed towards different targets, though the 1972 paper focused on the design of an organization's structure. 'Strategic choice' extends to the environment within which the organization is operating, to the standards of performance against which the pressure of economic constraints has to be evaluated, and to the design of the organization's structure itself' (ibid.). Strategic choices were seen to be made through initiatives within the network of internal and external organizational relationships – through *proaction* as well as *reaction*. It was assumed that effective strategic choice required the exercise of power and was therefore an essentially *political* phenomenon:

> Incorporation of the process whereby strategic decisions are made directs attention onto the degree of choice which can be exercised... whereas many available models direct attention exclusively onto the constraints involved. They imply in this way that organizational behaviour can only be understood by reference to functional imperatives rather than to political action. (Child, 1972, p. 2)

Such statements identified the need for a corrective to, and not an outright rejection of, the prevailing paradigm, exemplified by the Aston Programme. Indeed, they implied a *potential synthesis* between the political process and functionalist perspectives, between the role of actors and that of structural contingencies. For the power available to decision makers was seen to be accountable in terms of the consequences for organizational performance that flowed from its exercise. Those accorded the authority to make decisions were in effect exercising organizational property rights which were conditional rather than absolute. It was therefore assumed that such actors would take the consequences of their actions quite seriously. They would make some assessment of those consequences, conditioned by factors such as their knowledge, understanding and prior preferences, which would then enter as informational inputs into their subsequent thinking and decision making. The model towards which strategic choice analysis led would therefore

> direct our attention towards those who possess the power to decide upon an organization's structural rationale, towards the limits upon that power imposed by the operational context, and towards the process of assessing constraints and opportunities against values in deciding organizational strategies. (Child, 1972, p. 13)

The 1972 paper offered the outline of a processual model under the title of 'the role of strategic choice in a theory of organization'. This model is reproduced as Figure 4.1. It locates strategic choice within the organizational context and, through the feedback of information to decision makers, depicts the conditions for what today some would call an *organizational learning process*. Since the discussion in the last section of this chapter will refer to the model, a brief explanation now follows.

In the model, the exercise of strategic choice by organizational decision makers refers to a process in which the first stage is their evaluation of the organization's position – the expectations placed on it by external resource providers, the trend of relevant external events, the organization's recent performance, how comfortable the decision makers are with its internal configuration, and so on. Their prior values, experience and training are assumed to colour this evaluation in some degree. A choice of objectives for the organization is assumed to follow on from this evaluation, and to be reflected in the strategic actions on which they decide. This process is, in practice, often formalized into an annual planning round and/or procedure for making capital expenditure, which appears usually to be accompanied by considerable informal lobbying and negotiation (cf. Lu and Heard, 1995).

Externally oriented actions may include a move into or out of given markets or areas of activity in order to try and secure a favourable demand or response that will be expressed by a high consumer valuation of the organization's products or services. They could also include attempts to negotiate the terms of acceptable organizational performance with external resource providers or institutions holding sanction over the organization, though this possibility was not considered in the 1972 paper. Rather common examples occur when companies go to banks for a substantial loan and when they seek permission to erect a new processing facility that has an environmental impact. Internally oriented actions may involve an attempt, within the limits of resource availability and indivisibility, to establish a configuration of personnel, technologies and work organization which is both internally consistent and compatible with the scale and nature of the operations planned. The 'goodness of fit' that is in the event achieved is seen to determine the level of efficiency expressed by output in relation to costs. The conjunction of efficiency with external demand will determine the organization's overall level of performance. Performance realized becomes in turn a significant informational input to the organization's decision makers when they next make an evaluation of the organization's position and decide whether this warrants any changes. Thus a circular and potentially evolutionary process is established.

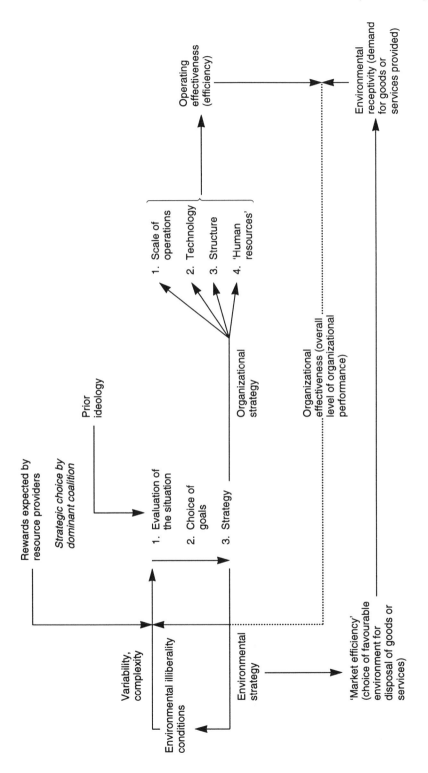

Figure 4.1   The role of strategic choice in a theory of organization

Agency and Environment

The earlier exposition of strategic choice gave some attention to the choice of internal organization with reference to the 'contextual' parameters of size and technology: how, for example, formalization could be a response to increasing scale. It was more fundamentally concerned, however, with the relationship between agency and environment. The ability of decision makers ('agents') to make a 'choice' between policies was seen to depend ultimately upon how far they could preserve autonomy within the environment, through achieving the levels of performance expected of them. The term 'strategic' was used to signify matters of importance to an organization as a whole, particularly those bearing upon its ability to prosper within an environment where it faces competition or the need to maintain its credibility. It is closely related to the idea of 'stratagem', which is a way of attempting to accomplish an objective in interaction with, or against, others.

It is not possible to abstract from the environment when considering the strategic choices available to organizational actors. This is partly because the environment presents threats and opportunities for the organization which establish the parameters of choice. It is also because the ways in which organizational actors understand the environment affect the extent to which they believe they enjoy an autonomy of choice between alternatives.

Strategic choice analysis recognizes both a proactive and a reactive aspect in organizational decision making vis-à-vis the environment. Organizational agents are seen to enjoy a kind of 'bounded' autonomy. They can take external initiatives, including the choice to enter and leave environments, and also make adaptive internal arrangements. At the same time, the environment within which they are operating is seen to limit their scope for action because it imposes certain conditions for their organizations to perform well. It is assumed that organizational actors will themselves have a similar understanding of the environment, because this is what experience teaches them.

Weick (1969) maintains that people in organizations 'enact' their environments. This can be interpreted in two ways. The first is that people can only be aware of a literally all-embracing concept like 'the environment' in terms of how they enact it in their minds. Organizational actors therefore necessarily respond to their own subjective definitions of the environment. This interpretation is fundamental to strategic choice analysis and indeed to any view of organizations that admits of human agency. The second interpretation is that people in organizations can enact the environment in the sense of 'making it happen as they wish'. A very qualified form of this second interpretation informed the original description of strategic choice that could be exercised by organizational decision makers:

> to an important extent, their decisions as to where the organization's operations shall be located, the clientele it shall serve, or the types of employees it shall recruit determine the limits to its environment – that is, to the environment significant for the functions which the organization performs. (Child, 1972, p. 10)

The possibility of environmental enactment is here limited to the selection of environments in which to operate, and even this decision cannot necessarily be entered into lightly or frequently since it may incur large entry and exit costs. Enactment in strategic choice analysis thus refers mainly to actions which bring certain environments into relevance – which introduce them onto the organizational stage. Once entered, the conditions of an environment assume an objective reality which is consequential for an organization, however much they are filtered by a subjective interpretation. That interpretation will shape the actions taken within the environment, which will amount to further enactment insofar as the actors are able to effect intended changes in it. The level of change which the managers of an organization can effect within its environment is always liable to be limited by the countervailing powers of institutions, as telecommunication companies found under previously regulatory regimes, and/ or by the possibility of new competition, as former market leaders like IBM have experienced.

When the original article was written at the beginning of the 1970s, a 'task environment' view predominated which focused on economic and technological variables. These were generally treated as impersonal factors such as market demand or the rate of technological change, and as quite distinct from the organizations for which they were relevant. Today, we are much more conscious of the social network properties of organizations and their contexts. The growth of organizational networks and collaborative arrangements between organizations means that it is not necessarily productive to look for clear and fixed boundaries to organizations. Rather, what used to be called boundary relationships are now often conducted through sets of arrangements which are themselves organized. An appropriate contemporary extension of strategic choice analysis would take this into account. It would continue, on the one hand, to maintain that environments have properties which cannot simply be enacted by organizational actors. This poses to those actors the question of whether they can select the most attractive environment in which to operate. It would, however, recognize, on the other hand, that the implications of some environmental properties may be negotiable through social interaction between organizational actors and their external contacts. Attention to the ways in which actors seek to realize their goals through selection between environments needs to be complemented by attention to the ways they may seek to attain their objectives through mutual accommodation and collaboration with the parties within an existing environment.

Strategic choice analysis thus incorporates both subjectivist and objectivist perspectives on organizational environment. This dualism does not result only from identifying organizational decision makers' subjective evaluations of the environment as a critical link between its objective features and organizational action, though that is an important element in it. It also reflects a recognition that organizational actors do not necessarily, or even typically, deal with an 'environment' at arm's length through the impersonal transactions of classical market analysis. On the contrary, they often engage in relationships with external parties that are sufficiently close and long-standing as to lend a mutually pervasive character to organization and environment. This indicates that the environment of organizations has an institutional character and, indeed, that people inside and outside the formal limits of an organization may share institutionalized norms and relationships. The 'environment' contains cultural and relational dimensions in addition to the 'task' and market variables identified respectively by strategic contingencies and economic theories. This is particularly true of organizations in personal service sectors such as health care, but it has, in other forms, been noted as a characteristic of East Asian business systems (Whitley, 1992). Mary Douglas (1987) expressed the dualism of the personally subjective and the institutionally objective in the following incisive way: 'For better or worse, individuals really do share their thoughts and they do to some extent harmonize their preferences, and they have no other way to make the big decisions except within the scope of institutions they build' (p. 128).

Porter (1990) has argued that the way economies are organized is more important for their success than the quality of the specific production factors within them. This is consistent with a view that corporate environments are themselves social organizations, which exhibit a degree of cohesion around a shared identity. The concept of 'firm-in-sector' emphasizes the interaction between environments and their constituent organizations (Child and Smith, 1987). They both shape and are, to some extent, shaped by each of these organizations, a process which has proceeded historically in the field of business as firms became embedded within increasingly institutionalized and internationalized sectors. Each sector has an economic dimension signified primarily by markets and the players in them; a cultural dimension signified primarily by a set of shared prescriptions and a common identity; and a relational dimension signified by networks between members of the organizations within the sector, including governmental agencies with responsibilities bearing on the sector. This conception of the organizational environment as a social entity has provided useful additional insights into the way companies have developed over time (for example, Smith *et al.*, 1990). It also helps to clarify two long-standing issues in the relationship between organizational agents and the environment which arise from strategic choice analysis: (1) *whether or not the environment is constraining or enabling*, and (2) *how externalized the environment actually is.*

Whittington (1988) criticizes environmental determinism in which exogenous structural constraints are assumed necessarily to limit and regulate the actions that can be taken by organizational decision makers. This point is consistent with the strategic choice argument, which drew attention to various possibilities allowing for choice on the part of organizational actors without their incurring intolerable penalties. Whittington conceives of environment in terms of the way it is socially structured and argues that this structuring can be enabling as well as constraining for strategic choice. Thus, organizational actors who are members of a professional occupation, and bound by norms of appropriate conduct, may thereby be externally constrained in their actions, whereas owner-managers supported by entrepreneurial ideologies and the rights of capitalist ownership may thereby be externally enabled to consider a wider range of action alternatives.

A more extended consideration of the enabling and constraining features of the environment is similarly encouraged by the sectorial concept of environment just described. This indicates how, for instance, long-standing relationships between members of the same sector, structured within industry associations, can furnish a basis for concerted action on matters of common interest such as political lobbying. Or it may show how the sharing of sector-specific strategic recipes (Spender, 1989) can facilitate the interpretation of the environment by a firm's managers. At the same time, the cultural and relational norms shared by members of a sector are likely to constrain organizational actors who seek to diverge from them. For example, divergence from normal strategic recipes may be perceived as risky by members of the capital market familiar with the sector, with the result that they impose a premium on its cost of raising external funds. Thus, while the social nature of an organization's environment will under some circumstances act as a constraint upon action, even to the point of determining it, it can also enable action and widen the range of available strategic alternatives. It is a misleading oversimplification to treat the environment simply as an external determinant of organizational action.

The concept of an organizational environment as a social network also raises doubts about how externalized it really is from its constituent organizations. The distinction between organization and environment contained in the original strategic choice article (Child, 1972) has to be softened by the recognition that organizational actors often create choice possibilities through their relationships with people who are formally outside the organization. They may, for example, be able to secure from officials with whom a good relationship has been developed a rather more liberal interpretation of environmental controls, especially in countries where the application of regulations is open to a flexible interpretation. Organization and environment are becoming interpenetrated through collaboration between actors in such a way as to diffuse the distinction between the two entities and, incidentally, to blur the distinction between 'firm' and 'market'. With the rapid growth of collaborative relationships between organizations, in the form of joint ventures and other strategic alliances (Lorange and Roos, 1992), this interpenetration assumes a fully operational form. It is, of course, qualified by the terms on which the parties can agree to cooperate and by how far they can identify mutual complementarities. Such alliances can indeed be unstable, and many survive for only a limited period. Nevertheless, they constitute an increasingly important arrangement through which part of the relevant environment is internalized, often with the motive of affording greater control over, or access to, other areas of the environment (such as markets) in a bid to extend strategic choice. Airbus Industrie furnishes a prominent example (Dussauge and Garrette, 1993).

Strategic choice analysis therefore allows for the objective presence of environments while at the same time it recognizes that organizations and environments are mutually pervasive. This pervasiveness occurs in two main ways. The first is through the interpretation of environments as being consequential for organizational action. The second is through the relationships that extend across an organization's 'boundaries'. It takes the very definition of those boundaries to be in large part the consequence of 'the kinds of relationships which its decision-makers choose to enter upon with their equivalents in other organizations, or ... the constraints which more dominant counterparts impose upon them' (Child, 1972, p. 10). Organization and environment therefore permeate one another both cognitively and relationally – that is, both in the minds of actors and in the process of conducting relationships between the two.

The concept of strategic choice was for some time misleadingly interpreted as justifying a sharp distinction between organizational agency and organizational environment, with the former being emphasized by voluntaristic perspectives and the latter by deterministic approaches (see the comprehensive review by Astley and Van de Ven, 1983). Strategic choice was associated with an absence of external determination, an assumption maintained even in later analyses which explored the possibility of different combinations of choice and determinism (for example, Hrebiniak and Joyce, 1985). This is understandable, given the intention of the Child (1972) article to criticize the then prevailing dominance of determinism, but it overlooked that article's statement that organizational decision makers are in a position of responding to feedback from the environment. This feedback may in turn provide them with a learning opportunity which brings to light new action choices, but the process overall was seen as an *interactive* one between organizational agents and the environment, and in effect between choice and constraint.

This interactive view is one which writers on strategic management have generally adopted, exemplified by the influential study of US firms and hospitals conducted in the 1970s by Miles and Snow (1978). They recognized how strategic choice analysis identified the continuing relationship between organizational agents and the environment, giving rise to what they termed 'the adaptive cycle': 'The strategic-choice approach essentially argues that the effectiveness of organizational adaptation hinges on the dominant coalition's perceptions of environmental conditions and the decisions it makes concerning how the organization will cope with these conditions' (ibid., p. 21). From their investigation, Miles and Snow concluded that the policies which organizational agents adopted towards the environment could be placed into the four generic categories of 'defender', 'prospector', 'analyser' and 'reactor'. This categorization was an important refinement of the strategic choice concept.

Bourgeois (1984), in similar vein, argued for a view of strategic management as a creative activity which is intrinsic to a dialectic between choice and constraint: 'so, though environmental and internal forces act as constraints, strategy making often selects and later modifies the sets of constraints' (p. 593). Hambrick and Finkelstein (1987) developed and explored the concept of chief executive discretion, defined as 'latitude of action'. They argued that this concept reconciled polar views of organizations as either inertial or highly adaptive. Their premise was that chief executives vary in how much discretion they possess and that this variation is due to a combination of (1) factors in the environment, (2) organizational characteristics which promote inertia (such as size, age and culture) and (3) the chief executive's own attributes. While Hambrick and Finkelstein in this way focus on discrete factors rather than the processes and relationships through which choice and constraint work themselves out, they identify the influences which might enter interactively into the process.

More recently, Neergaard (1992) has developed a 'partial contingency model'. This recognizes that the nature of the environment, such as its levels of dynamism and complexity, can impact upon the internal control systems which it is functional for an organization to adopt. At the same time, the model also recognizes that environmental management is possible through two main strategies which (borrowing from previous writers) Neergaard calls 'buffering' and 'bridging'. Through buffering, managers aim to protect their core activities from external influences – examples include stockpiling, attempts to reduce input and output fluctuations such as marketing campaigns, and public relations activities. With bridging, managers endeavour to manage their environments through various forms of negotiation, cooperation, exchange of information and other forms of reciprocity. Neergaard illustrates through case studies from Denmark how environmental management has a direct bearing on the type and degree of organizational control that it is necessary to adopt. His conclusion in effect reiterates the basic strategic choice argument: 'Only by studying the interplay between environment and environmental management is it possible to gain a more full understanding of different controls [that is, internal organization]' (p. 29).

Strategic choice is recognized and realized through a process whereby those with the power to make decisions for the organization interact among themselves (so constituting a shifting 'dominant coalition') with other organizational members and with external parties. Analytical centrality is given to organizational agents' interpretations (their goals and views of the possibilities for realizing them) as they engage in these relationships. This is to say that organization, as a social order, is the subject of adjustment through negotiation on a continuing, though not necessarily continual, basis (cf. Strauss, 1978). The possibilities for this negotiation are at any one point in time framed by existing structures, both within and without the organization. The reference to 'framing' here is intended to convey a sense that the issues and options open to negotiation by actors have some structured limits, though it may be possible to change the limits themselves over time through the negotiation process. Structures within the organization include the channels through which relevant information is obtained and processed, and formalized policies which define action priorities for the organization. External structures include the configuration of competitor organizations within the organization's operating domain, that of its suppliers and customers, and the regulations and other institutional obligations relevant to its activities.

Strategic choice in organizational analysis thus furnishes an example of 'structuration' (Giddens, 1984). That is, action is bounded by existing structures but at the same time impacts upon those structures.

Through their actions, agents endeavour to modify and redefine structures in ways that will admit of different possibilities for future action. The process is a continuing one. Strategic choice thus presents a dynamic rather than a static perspective on organizations and their environments. In keeping with structuration theory, it also addresses the so-called problem of levels of analysis. For while the actions taken in the name of organizations are driven by individuals and therefore draw for some of their explanation on individual motivations, they are organizational both in how they are represented and in the resources and relationships which are activated. When these actions become a constituent element in the relations between an organization and external bodies, they move onto an even higher level of social process. The consequences of this process for the organization, which strategic choice analysis depicts as being transmitted to it through a feedback of information on its performance and external standing, are social in origin but may be interpreted in some circumstances by individual actors primarily in terms of their own personal values or priorities.

Strategic choice analysis admits of a role for the individual organizational actor (qua entrepreneur), assumes that actors will more often constitute a collective (qua dominant coalition) and treats the cycle of action and response as one that is environmentally and therefore socially contextualized. It does not regard the wider social arena simply as a constraining or defining context for lower-order units of analysis like groups and individuals, as did, for instance, the Aston Programme founders in their original 'conceptual framework' (Pugh *et al.*, 1963). Nor does it do the opposite and treat action as explicable only by reference to individuals and their understanding of the situation. Rather, its conception of agency entering into a cycle of organizational development within an environment cuts across these levels of analysis and in this respect helps to bridge what has sometimes been a source of division among theorists of organization.

Strategic Choice and Evolutionary Organizational Learning

These characteristics of strategic choice analysis – its recognition of the interaction between agency and structure, and the cyclical nature of organizational development – contribute to the refinement of an evolutionary view of organizational development over time. There is a parallel between the adaptive structuration cycle posited by strategic choice and analyses of knowledge formation and organizational learning of the kind advanced by Boisot (1986). Both approaches regard new circumstances as posing a potential challenge to knowledge which has been previously codified into formalized/structured organizational practices. If adaptation is to take place, this challenge will initiate a process of enquiry and search, mostly outside the organization, which initially brings ill-defined information specific to the new situation within the purview of organizational actors (uncodified/undiffused knowledge, in Boisot's terminology). From the process of evaluating this new knowledge, proposals emerge for the definition and formalization of new actions and structures, which if acceptable and successful become standardized and hence widely applied ('diffused'). The contribution that this adaptive cycle model can offer stems largely from the fact that it bridges the subjective/objective and change/continuity dichotomies in the study of organizations (cf. Burrell and Morgan, 1979). Interpretation becomes objectified into structures and individual learning becomes translated into organizational practice. The challenge is to develop an adequate theoretical account of the process. Recognition that the interplay between organization and environment is mediated by the interpretation and evaluation of actors, operating within the arenas of organizational subcultures and micropolitics, also reconciles the paradox of simultaneous radical change and continuity within this conception of organizational dynamics.

Strategic choice analysis therefore has some affinity with an evolutionary view of organizations which focuses on their capacity to 'learn' and to adapt within their environments. Organizational learning has become a prominent topic within the study of organizations, attracting much attention over the past 20 years. Nevertheless, it displays considerable theoretical disarray (for a wide-ranging review, see Pawlowsky, 1992). The term 'organizational learning' appears to be quite beguiling, even contradictory, in the light of the Burrell and Morgan scheme. Does it reflect a subjective or objective view of organizations? Individuals can learn through a process of internalization, but what about organizations? Organizational learning implies the acquisition of new understanding and competence but is this learning used to bring about change, or to devise new ways of maintaining the status quo in the light of different circumstances?

A great deal of the work on organizational learning has modelled itself on studies of individual learning, borrowing terms such as 'organizational memory' (for example, Levitt and March, 1988). Both cognitive and behaviourist theories of individual learning have been imported into discussions of organizational learning. A cognitive orientation is reflected in terms such as 'organizational intelligence' and a behavioural orientation in concepts such as 'organizational routines', which are regarded as codifications of understanding and competence acquired by the organization. A subjective–objective distinction is also present here, in that cognition is by definition subjective whereas behaviour can, in principle, be externally observed. Although frequently attempted, the application of individual learning models to organizations is deeply problematic. It reifies the organization into a mechanism or organism and wholly avoids the politics of agency which are integral to strategic choice analysis. It does this because it lacks a conception of learning as a social process in which ideas and understanding are not free-standing and neutral but are subject to approval or disapproval, development or modification, through interaction with others. This is particularly evident among the writers on organizational learning who prefer to confine the term to the acquisition of potentially useful knowledge and to leave aside consideration of the processes through which such knowledge would come to be used (for example, Huber, 1991). In this interpretation, 'organizational learning' does not extend to the ability of those in an organization to take action consequent upon their understanding.

This lacuna arises because much of the organizational learning literature fails to locate the prime movers of the process, the relevant actors, within the political systems of organizations and their relevant external groups. In recognizing that there are barriers to learning, this literature explores defensiveness as a personal attribute, but usually fails to enquire into its non-psychological sources such as the organizational micropolitics which lead to learning and innovation being contested between groups (Child and Loveridge, 1990). For the actors involved in organizational learning and adaptation often belong to several groups which have different views about the desirable future path for their organization to follow. They may, for instance, be a mix of top managers, technical experts, functional managers and external consultants. Strategic choice analysis, by focusing upon a leading or initiating group operating within a political context that is both internal and external to the organization, draws attention not just to the capacity of individuals or groups to learn but equally to those people who are controlling and managing the learning process 'on behalf of' the organization. It admits the possibility that existing structures may limit learning because of the way they close off certain options, through, for example, the absence of procedures or staff that can gain access to certain areas of information, or because the options are too politically sensitive to consider. At the same time, it also allows for the possibility that such structures may offer some resources for the achievement of change.

Strategic choice analysis thus recognizes that it may be necessary to sustain certain paradoxes for learning to take place as a collective phenomenon in organizations, such as the need to achieve consensus from a diversity of views and the preservation of some continuities within the process of introducing change. In particular, it can bring an appreciation of the politics of change to bear upon the understanding of organizational learning and, in this way, locate the process within the organization and its environment as social contexts. Failure to do this not only betrays a theoretical inadequacy, but also severely limits insight into the way learning may be promoted in practice.

The relevance of these considerations may be illustrated by quoting just three of the conclusions drawn from a detailed study of successful organizational transformation in the Cadbury chocolate company:

1   'a lengthy process of re-cognition preceded transformation. This involved a combination of symbolic and power-relevant activities, namely (a) re-framing the definition of relevant contextual conditions and appropriate internal arrangements with (b) the ascension into powerful positions of those advocating new interpretations and solutions';

2   'competing frames of meaning and recipes for improvement were advanced by actors whose views were conditioned by their training, speciality, and previous experience in the company';

3   'the traditional and hitherto dominant corporate ideology was not simply a barrier to transformation. Its wide acceptance and cohesion provided a clear position against which the case for change had to be developed. This was easier because the ideology was itself malleable, stressing receptivity to new techniques and intellectual enquiry, and management had been encouraged to proceed in that mode' (Child and Smith, 1987, p. 590).

Students of organizational learning are directly concerned with the issue of individual (and sometimes group) competence and its development through knowledge creation. They do not reify the firm or the organization; rather the opposite. In the main, they have yet to address the question of how individuals and groups form part of, and relate to, the wider organizational social system. They face the challenge of explaining how individual learning is translated into enhanced organizational capabilities, and how these are translated into innovative policies and procedures. The strategic choice perspective would maintain that political forces are likely to play an important role here. For instance, are HRM managers who have knowledge on the design of work organization permitted to join project teams which have the task of recommending how people shall have access to new information technology systems in the course of their work (cf. Child and Loveridge, 1990)? The question of how competences enter into organizational adaptation or evolution requires further analysis of a kind to which strategic choice theory can contribute.

The same applies to the intentionality of learning in organizations. Few discussions of organizational learning address the issue of the goals for learning in organizations and how they are established. They tend simply to treat the establishment of such goals as part of the learning process itself (the 'double loop learning' of Argyris and Schön, 1978). Organizational learning makes at least implicit reference to success criteria insofar as they regard adaptation as a necessary condition for the survival of organizations. The questions which then arise are: who lays down the success criteria articulated, who evaluates the degree of success achieved, and who decides on subsequent action? With the exception of the lone entrepreneur, these are necessarily collective actions. It is for the same reason problematic to ascribe intentions to 'the organization'. This equally obscures the issues of who are defining these intentions and enacting related decisions. Only a theory of social action within organizations can make sense of the way intentionality gives rise to outcomes, and how definitions of success are articulated and applied in the process.

Institutional analysis (Powell and DiMaggio, 1991; Scott, 1995) points to ways in which those bodies in society which accord social legitimacy to organizations are thereby contributing to the definition of organizational success criteria. For example, an equal opportunities commission will examine and judge an organization's success in terms of the fairness of its employment practices. There are in developed societies a large number of such public agencies. Other external bodies which accord material resources to organizations, such as financial institutions, thereby contribute to the definition of other organizational success criteria such as earnings per share. Social and material resource dependencies of this kind undoubtedly have an influence on the formulation of organizational intentions with respect to the innovations and changes which are contemplated. External bodies on which organizations depend for their survival are in a position to exercise a significant influence on the goals that are set for internal organizational learning and adaptive processes.

Strategic choice analysis offers two particularly useful contributions to the understanding of the process of accommodating to these external performance expectations. First is the recognition that people in organizations often belong, or have access, to both intra- and extraorganizational social groups. Specialists may belong to professional societies. Managers may be members of governmental working parties or commissions. Companies may share directors with relevant financial institutions. Second is the possibility that, through connections such as these, the members of an organization may be able to influence the success criteria applied to it by external bodies. In other words, through the social connections between organizations and environmental bodies, members of the former may be able proactively to influence the formulation of criteria imposed by the latter, as well as to generate a sympathetic climate under which the criteria are activated. The salient aspect of this process is lobbying, but it occurs in many less visible ways.

The relationships between organizational members and those of external bodies are likely to exhibit characteristics of social exchange (Blau, 1964). These social networks facilitate the acquisition of knowledge and other resources by organizations and the offering back of goods and services to the outside world. The same networks also permit exchanges of information relevant to the formulation of goals for organizational development and learning. The plurality of these networks, which is especially marked in larger organizations diversified across technological and regional divides, adds grist to the mill of internal political debate and negotiation.

Strategic choice analysis regards such debate and negotiation as integral to decision making on organizational priorities, policies, structures and actions. In other words, the ways in which openness to new information and knowledge is achieved, an openness regarded by students of the subject as essential to learning in organizations, establish processes through which that knowledge is handled within an organization and which will impinge on the use made of it. These processes have on the whole been neglected by writers on organizational learning and they can only be appreciated when learning is regarded as a social rather than a purely individual phenomenon. The mapping of external diversity onto organizational pluralism through cross-boundary networks also qualifies the adaptive view of organizations found in evolutionary economics. It acknowledges that external bodies are significant in the evolution of organizations but, because of the indeterminacy of the internal politics which organizational pluralism is instrumental in sustaining, the path taken by such evolution cannot simply be predicted as a function of external forces.

Summary

The strategic choice perspective remains consistent with the original Aston Programme in locating organizational structure within its context. It deploys the concepts so meticulously developed by Derek Pugh and his team. The difference is that it brings human agency into the picture: agency of the kind that I found myself part of in industry.

In essence, the strategic choice perspective posits a double structuration process. This involves multiple cycles, insofar as organizational actors seek to work both upon existing internal structures and relatively internal contextual items such as technology (internal structuration) and upon environmental conditions (external structuration). These structures and conditions impose constraints upon the actions which are feasible at any one point in time, but they are also the objects of intended change to which action is directed. This presents the paradox of simultaneous choice and constraint, change and continuity. Moreover, the strategic choice perspective assumes that each stage of the cycle is accomplished through social processes within organizations and with external parties which are political in the sense that outcomes emerge through persuasion, negotiation or even imposition. This chapter has argued that this dynamic process is central to the ways in which organizational learning takes place and hence lies at the heart of an organization's evolution within its environment.

Strategic choice is an action-oriented concept which, however, only makes sense with reference to both proaction and reaction. In other words, it builds theoretically upon the mutuality of action and constraint and seeks to encourage exploration of the dynamic which this mutuality sets up. It therefore regards as misleading the polarization in organizational analysis of determinism and voluntarism, of contingency and action. Whereas the strategic choice perspective necessarily engaged with the determinists when it first appeared, today it has become rather more appropriate for it to engage with those who would deconstruct organizational life to untrammelled actions of sense-making individuals. Both determinism and voluntarism are impoverished by the extremism of their positions. They illustrate the inherent destructiveness of the single paradigm approach to organization theory.

Note

1   This work did, however, help to shape a chapter on the subject in my book, *The Business Enterprise in Modern Industrial Society*, which was published in 1969 (Collier–Macmillan).

References

Argyris, C. and Schön, D. (1978), *Organizational Learning*, Reading, Mass.: Addison-Wesley.

Astley, W.G. and Van de Ven, A. (1983), 'Central perspectives and debates in organizational theory', *Administrative Science Quarterly*, **28**, 245–73.

Blau, P.M. (1964), *Exchange and Power in Social Life*, New York: Wiley.

Blau, P.M. and Schoenherr, R.A. (1971), *The Structure of Organizations*, New York: Basic Books.

Boisot, M. (1986), 'Markets and hierarchies in a cultural perspective', *Organization Studies*, **7**, 135–58.

Bourgeois, L.J. (1984), 'Strategic management and determinism', *Academy of Management Review*, **9**, 586–96.

Burns, T. and Stalker, G.M. (1961), *The Management of Innovation*, London: Tavistock.

Burrell, G. and Morgan, G. (1979), *Sociological Paradigms and Organizational Analysis*, London: Heinemann.

Child, J. (1969), *British Management Thought – A Critical Analysis*, London: Allen & Unwin.

Child. J. (1972), 'Organizational structure, environment and performance: The role of strategic choice', *Sociology*, **6**, 1–22.

Child, J. (1973), 'Organisation: a choice for Man', in J. Child (ed.), *Man and Organisation*, London: Allen & Unwin.

Child, J. (1975), 'Managerial and organizational factors associated with company performance – Part II: a contingency analysis', *Journal of Management Studies*, **12**, 12–27.

Child, J. and Loveridge, R. (1990), *Information Technology in European Services*, Oxford: Blackwell.

Child, J. and Smith, C. (1987), 'The context and process of organizational transformation – Cadbury Limited in its sector', *Journal of Management Studies*, **24**, 565–93.

Donaldson, L. (1985), *In Defence of Organization Theory*, Cambridge: Cambridge University Press.

Donaldson, L. (1995), *American Anti-Management Theories of Organisation*, Cambridge: Cambridge University Press.

Douglas, M. (1987), *How Institutions Think*, London: Routledge & Kegan Paul.

Dussage, P. and Garrette, B. (1993), 'Determinants of success in international strategic alliances: evidence from the global aerospace industry', working paper, HEC, Jouy-en-Josas.

Giddens, A. (1984), *The Constitution of Society*, Cambridge: Polity Press.

Graham, P. (ed.) (1995), *Mary Parker Follett – Prophet of Management*, Boston, Mass.: Harvard Business School Press.

Hambrick, D.C. and Finkelstein, S. (1987), 'Managerial discretion: a bridge between polar views of organizational outcomes', *Research in Organizational Behavior*, **9**, 369–406.

Hannan, M.T. and Freeman, J.H. (1989), *Organizational Ecology*, Cambridge, Mass.: Harvard University Press.

Hrebiniak, L.G. and Joyce, W.F. (1985), 'Organizational adaptation: strategic choice and environmental determinism', *Administrative Science Quarterly*, **30**, 336–49.

Huber, G.P. (1991), 'Organizational learning: the contributing processes and the literatures', *Organisation Science*, **2**, 88–115.

Johnson, G. (1990), 'Managing strategic change: the role of symbolic action', *British Journal of Management*, **1**, 183–200.

Lawrence, P.R. and Lorsch, J.W. (1967), *Organization and Environment*. Boston, Mass.: Harvard Business School Press.

Levitt, B. and March, J.G. (1988), 'Organizational learning', *Annual Review of Sociology*, **14**, 319–40.

Lorange, P. and Roos, J. (1992), *Strategic Alliances*, Oxford: Blackwell.

Lu, Y. and Heard, R. (1995), 'Socialized economic action: a comparison of strategic investment decisions in China and Britain', *Organization Studies*, **16**, 395–424.

Merton, R.K. (1940), 'Bureaucratic structure and personality', *Social Forces*, **XVII**, 560–68.

Miles, R.E. and Snow, C.C. (1978), *Organizational Strategy, Structure and Process*, New York: McGraw-Hill.

Neergaard, P. (1992), 'Environment, strategy and management accounting', *Proceedings of the Second European Symposium on Information Systems*, Versailles: HEC.

Pawlowsky, P. (1992), 'Betriebliche Qualifikationsstrategien und organisationales

Lernen', in W.H. Staehle and P. Conrad (eds), *Managementforschung 2*, Berlin: De Gruyter.

Porter, M.E. (1990), *The Competitive Advantage of Nations*, New York: Free Press.

Powell, W.W. and DiMaggio, P.J. (1991), *The New Institutionalism in Organizational Analysis*, Chicago: University of Chicago Press.

Pugh, D.S., Hickson, D.J., Hinings, C.R., Macdonald, K.M., Turner, C. and Lupton, T. (1963), 'A conceptual scheme for organizational analysis', *Administrative Science Quarterly*, **8**, 289–315.

Scott, W.R. (1995), *Institutions and Organizations*, Thousand Oaks: Sage.

Selznick, P. (1949), *TVA and the Grass Roots*, Berkeley: University of California Press.

Smith, C., Child, J. and Rowlinson, M. (1990), *Reshaping Work: The Cadbury Experience*, Cambridge: Cambridge University Press.

Spender, J-C. (1989), *Industry Recipes*, Oxford: Blackwell.

Strauss, A. (1978), *Negotiations: Varieties, Contexts, Processes and Social Order*, New York: Wiley.

Weick, K.E. (1969), *The Social Psychology of Organizing*, Reading, Mass.: Addison-Wesley.

Whitley, R. (1992), *Business Systems in East Asia*, London: Sage.

Whittington, R. (1988), 'Environmental structure and theories of strategic choice', *Journal of Management Studies*, **25**, 521–36.

Woodward, J. (1965), *Industrial Organisation – Theory and Practice*, London: Oxford University Press.

5 The Aston Studies and Design Causality

CHRIS ARGYRIS, *Harvard Business School, Harvard University*

All of us conducting social science research study universes that we define and construct. The purpose of our studies is to describe the universe as completely and economically as possible. We seek to produce propositions that generalize beyond the immediate study in which they were generated. We test the generalizations as rigorously as possible, using such criteria as confirmability and falsifiability. Prediction is accomplished by specifying causal hypotheses and testing them. The causal hypotheses typically take the form of: 'under these conditions, if A then B'. The most common rules about testing causal claims in organizational research are based on Mill's (1949) concept of Methods of Difference. At the heart of these methods is the belief that the best way to describe the universe is to construct it as a set of variables and to study how they vary. The Aston Studies were largely based on this view of causality (Pugh *et al.*, 1963; Pugh 1981a, 1983).

Getting at Causality Through Variance

Central to this view of causality is the concept of 'variable'. Simon expresses this when he says that each value of variables X and Y, standing for cause and effect, defines a class of events and that each variable therefore 'comprises a set of classes of events' (quoted in James *et al.*, 1982, p. 15). On this basis, it becomes possible to say that the same variable, X or Y, may have the same or different values in different settings, a condition necessary for the discovery of general causal relationships among variables.

According to this view of causality, causal inferences may be made from data provided by either of two principal methods of empirical research. In the first, contrived experiment, the researcher creates a research setting separate from the practice setting (an organizational simulation, for example) and constructs experimental and control groups in order to apply Mill's methods of causal inference. The second principal method of empirical research is natural experiment, or 'quasi-experimental method', in the words of Campbell and Stanley (1963). Here the researcher observes a number of practice settings, identifying and measuring in each case the values of the relevant variables. Observations are distributed across many local contexts so that the researcher avoids being misled by the peculiarities of any particular one. As in a contrived experiment, the researcher analyses the resulting data to test whether the values of the effect variables are uniquely determined by the values of the cause variables.

In order to recreate the generalizations from such research, the practitioner would have to produce the conditions that led to the causal generalizations in the first place. It is unlikely, I suggest, that the practitioners can do so, for at least three reasons (Argyris, 1980, 1993). First, they may not have the control over the variables and the 'subjects' the researchers had when they conducted their research. Second, in order to recreate the propositions in the everyday world, the managers would have to have the time (and other resources) to carry out the required analysis. Third, it is not likely that the managers can deal with the substantive issues they are trying to solve and these issues of causality because of the finiteness of the processing capacity of the human mind (Simon, 1990) and often the finiteness of material and time resources.

All three reasons are related to the actionability of the findings. Actionability means that the generalizations can be used to create the phenomena of interest, not simply to understand and explain them. Actionability goes beyond external validity. The latter focuses on the relevance of research findings in the everyday world of action. The former make the relevance operational so that it can be implemented by actors. For example, there is much research to show that trust is a relevant variable in managing people (external validity). The same research says little about ways in which actors can create trust under everyday conditions in organizations (Argyris, 1980, 1993). Actionability is therefore a more robust scientific test of theory than is external validity.

Actionability also increases the likelihood that practitioners can use the knowledge. I should like to combine these two consequences and suggest the following objective of research in organizations: social scientists should seek to produce valid knowledge (propositions and generalizations) that, when used by practitioners or researchers in the everyday world, becomes a valid occasion for a robust test of that knowledge. Under this proposal actionability is a more powerful scientific goal than validity because it raises the standard for validity and, at the same time, it raises the standard for relevance and usability. To the extent that these two consequences are accomplished, the interdependence between science and practice is enhanced.

Design Causality

A core requirement for beginning to implement this recommendation is to develop a different view of causality, which can be labelled 'design causality'. In order to expand on the meaning of actionability, I should like to describe the relationship between knowledge and the production of action in an admittedly simplified manner. Let us think of two phases (see Figure 5.1).

Phase I is composed of diagnostic activities through which a problem is discovered. The next step, in the same phase, is the invention of a solution to the problem. The solution is in the form of a design for action. The design specifies a sequence of actions. Phase II is the actual production or implementation of the design. This occurs at a

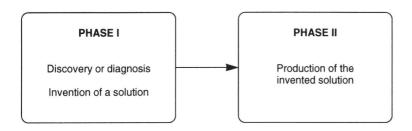

Figure 5.1 The relationship of knowledge to action

meeting and it is constrained in time. There are several key differences between thinking about, inventing solutions, and creating designs for action and the activities that produce the intended action:

- Producing the intended consequences requires knowledge that is storable, retrievable and producible by the human mind/brain within the allocated time (and other constraints).
- This knowledge should not only specify the sequence of actions in order to produce the intended consequences, it should specify the way to monitor the actual impact of the implementation.
- The way the mind/brain is used during phase II is different from the way it is used during phase I. Phase II depends on short-term memory and on on-line iterative learning because the human mind/brain is a limited processing system. It is difficult to augment these limitations with external memories such as notes, books and other relevant knowledge and use them in an on-line manner because they are likely to get in the way of the flow of events during the meeting.

It is features such as these that must somehow be incorporated in the scientific generalizations that we produce if they are to be actionable. Even with these challenges, we should take actionability seriously since the universe that we purport to study exists because actionability is crucial to those who inhabit it. Human beings, and the social entities that they create, are primarily concerned about effectiveness. Effectiveness is defined as achieving intended consequences (from individual to organizational) in such a way that they persevere and do so without harming the present level of effectiveness.

The universe that we describe is therefore a normative one because definitions of effectiveness are based on choices human beings make. These choices are related to whatever objectives they wish to achieve and values they wish to satisfice. There is no one imposing quasi-resolution of conflict, organizational defensive routines or unilateral control. The actors who choose to create the universe create the phenomena that we study. Our generalizations must contain the mechanisms by which they choose to create and by which they implement these choices.

The moment we accept as a key objective of scientific inquiry the need to specify how to create the phenomena that we describe, we must ask how actions are created. The answer is by human beings acting for themselves or as agents of their organizations. What do they use in order to act? Human beings use their mind/brain in order to produce actions. They design their actions and they design the implementations of their actions. Human beings are therefore first and foremost designing organisms. The social unities that they create are also created and managed by design (Argyris and Schön, 1974; Simon, 1965). Designs specify (1) an objective or intended consequence, (2) the behaviours and their sequences necessary to achieve the intended consequences, and (3) the values that are to be satisfied.

It is possible to identify two types of design: the design that is espoused and the design that is actually used. The degree of seamlessness between the two varies. For example, the espoused design to produce a balance sheet and the design-in-use to do so are highly similar. Indeed, it is the aspiration of most managerial functional disciplines such as accounting, finance, strategy and marketing to produce seamlessness between their espoused designs and designs-in-use (Argyris, 1990; Argyris and Kaplan, 1994). On the other hand, there is often a wide discrepancy between espoused designs and the ones in use when individuals deal with issues that are embarrassing or threatening (Argyris, 1984, 1990, 1993; Argyris and Schön, 1974, 1995). The discrepancy itself is designed so that the actors are unaware of the incongruity they are producing. If they are aware, they use another design that blames factors outside the actor.

No generalizable design (or master programme) is likely to be all encompassing so that it is able to deal a priori with the richness of the concrete case. Herein we have a dilemma. Human beings require designs in order to act, yet the designs that they store and retrieve are unlikely to deal with the richness of the individual case. The resolution of this dilemma is not simply to conduct more serious research, because the human mind/brain can only deal with a finite amount of information. One solution is to create master programmes that can be used in any situation, with the limits of the master programme being clearly defined ahead of time. Such a solution means that there will always be gaps. Since human beings are designing systems they will also require a design for gap filling. Argyris and Schön (1995) claim to have identified such a programme for dealing with any issue of embarrassment and threat. They call it Model I and claim it is found in all industrialized cultures. They also claim that, since organizations are populated overwhelmingly with individuals whose theories-in-use are Model I, these individuals naturally create organization-level factors that have similar features. For example, individuals, acting as agents for the organization, use Model I, which limits double-loop learning. These interpersonal limits are transformed into organizational processes such as organizational defences (Argyris, 1990). The mechanisms by which the limited learning processes are created are specifiable (Argyris, 1993; Argyris and Schön, 1995).

Finally, an effective design can be used in everyday life without requiring the actor to be in complete unilateral control, without requiring that intentions be kept secret and without requiring bypass of embarrassment or threat and cover-up of the bypass. Interestingly, most human beings are acculturated to act in precisely these ways when the issues are embarrassing or threatening. In the name of caring, concern, honesty and integrity, human beings produced hurt, distancing, dishonesty and mistrust and do so in way that can use societal norms to cover up the discrepancies and cover up the cover-up (Argyris, 1990, 1993; Argyris and Schön, 1995).

The framework just outlined briefly is based on the fundamental assumption that the way to understand causality is to identify the design or master programmes that individuals and organizations use. Such causal explanations will automatically describe what is going on, define the normative intentions and can be used to pre-scribe how to act. Such causal explanations can therefore be used to explain and to create the phenomena that they explain. Creating phenomena, to repeat, is the most fundamental activity of actors in organizations and must be accounted for if our generalizations are to be valid and actionable.

The Aston Studies

In this section I should like to examine two of the most fundamental concepts of the Aston Group in light of the comments about design causality. I refer to what they call 'activity variables' and 'structural variables'.

Activity Variables

Pugh *et al.* (1963) begin by noting that organizations are full of activi-ties at many different levels of analysis. The activity variables are fundamental in the sense that structure is derived from the activities. The Aston Group (1963) chose the organizational processes that Bakke and I developed to begin to organize their view of the complexity of activities that exist in any organization (Bakke, 1950, 1959). We ar-rived at these process variables by reviewing the literature, observing actual organizations and interviewing practitioners and scholars. We believed that these categories captured the essential processes, a be-lief that we knew would have to be tested through empirical research. Our methodology of testing was primarily qualitative. Our concepts, however, were not limited to such a methodology – witness the Aston Group's use of them to organize the processual features of their universe. An example of these processes is one we called 'per-petuation'. All organizations, we claimed, had to acquire, maintain, transform and develop their basic resources. Next, we claimed that organizations did so by personnel activities (people resource), services (material), finance (money) and cultivation (operational field).

Reflecting on our thinking, we created a basic organizational process (perpetuation) and illustrated the organizational or managerial functions in which it was primarily implemented. The concepts and the location of implementation were highly abstract precisely because we wanted the categories to be comprehensive. We created these categories primarily in the form of a list that we claimed could be used to understand organizations. We never focused on how to create them. Nor had we thought through the causal processes to create them or the causal processes of the way they affected each other. If we had done so, we would have begun to move towards design causality. Indeed, one might say that, because we did not transform these categories into causal designs, it made it possible for the Aston Group to use them, given their empirical methodology. Their assumption was that a careful and rigorous study of variance would get at causality as defined by research methods that assumed that was the way to get at causality.

There is an important problem with this assumption. It produces knowledge that is difficult to make actionable. For example, if we examine what they call their simple model of organizational functioning (Pugh, 1981a, p. 138) rigorous empirical research could produce, as Pugh points out, millions of statistical relationships. Clearly, that would be unwieldy. What is required is some second-order organization of knowledge. One such second-order organization is the use of models to organize meaningfully the many empirical relationships. The first difficulty with these models (ibid., p. 140) is that they are too complex to store in and to retrieve from the human mind to use in an on-line manner. At best, they have to be placed in some sort of book, chapter or sheets of paper, all of which are external memories. What are the actors to do when they wish to use these models? Do they pull out the chapter? Do they stop the flow of the dialogue? This is especially vexing when dealing with variables such as leadership, inter-group rivalries and groups with self-fuelling counterproductive processes.

The second difficulty, as illustrated by the Aston system model (Pugh, 1981a, p. 140) is that the variables are organized in a manner that hypothesizes causality without taking a causal position about effectiveness. As we have noted above, effectiveness is a core feature of individuals, groups and organizations. For example, we learn that the organizational environment (general and specific: each is specified, for example customers and suppliers) causally influences organizational aims and resources as well as structure and processes (again illustrated) which in turn influence aims and resources. All these causally influence efficiency, productivity and so on. The model is testable if the goal is to test the empirical interrelationships among the variables. But, left as they are, they are not helpful for testing the normative features of the universe such as increasing or decreasing efficiency, effectiveness and so on. The model is even less helpful in informing actors how to create or produce these consequences, yet these are the type of activities the actors are involved in that created the universe in the first place. Empirical propositions that can be used to create intended consequences are much more powerful for science than evidence that there is a significant statistical relationship among the variables.

The reason that such propositions are more rigorous and robust about causality is that in combination, specified ahead of time, they will specify the actions needed to produce the intended consequences. Claims about creation cannot be made or tested without making explicit the behavioural processes and causal mechanisms by which they are hypothesized to occur. These are the claims that are at the heart of design causality.

To summarize, Bakke and I and the Aston Group developed a set of categories to organize organizational activities. Neither group thought these through to the point that they could identify a priori the causality involved. If they had done so, both would have moved towards design causality. It is my hypothesis that no amount of empirical research of the kind Bakke and I envisioned (largely qualitative) or the Aston Group produced (heavily quantitative) would lead to knowledge that would make it possible simultaneously to describe and explain the normative features of our universe and that could be used to prescribe how to enhance (or reduce) effectiveness. When such knowledge is produced, the practitioners or the researchers can use their actions (the former, let us say, as a leader, the latter as an interventionist) as relevant tests of features of the design theory they used to create their respective actions.

Structural Variables

The Aston Group relied heavily on the work of Max Weber (1947) for their structural variables. Weber defined several features of all pyramidal organizations, private or public. The Aston Group took these features and translated them into dimensions such as specialization, standardization, formalization, centralization, configuration and flexibility. These were then operationalized. For example, specialization included a count of those functions performed by specialists, the ratio of line to staff personnel and so on. Formalization includes statements of procedures, rules, roles and operation of procedures (dealing with decision seeking, conveying of decisions and so on).

Rereading Weber, I now see that his causal reasoning was consistent with design causality. If his ideas were to be tested then the research would have to focus on testing the many statements of causality that he makes at different levels of abstraction. For example, Weber's bureaucracy is defined as having a fixed set of rules and regulations that are structured in fixed ways as official duties. There exists authority to give commands and to reward or penalize in order to compel performance. There also exist 'files' or policies intended to perpetuate or preserve the bureaucracy. From such features he defines the properties of authority, from which he distinguishes between the properties which attach to the formal position (power) of any official from their personal position.

These categories are more than logical boxes in which to organize observations. They specify what must exist in order to have a bureaucracy. In this sense an ideal–type is a design for compelling actions on the part of the participants if a bureaucracy is to function effectively. Weber describes bureaucracy as a hierarchy of causal sequences intended to achieve its objectives. This is the essence of design causality.

In the translation of Weber's work, Parsons comments on Weber's methodology of social science. He describes Weber's research strategy as being based on a subjectivist point of view where the universe of study is created or constructed by the social scientists. Weber's whole methodology is normatively oriented because actors are concerned with producing actions that are successful (read 'effective'). Actors are compelled to act consistently with the normatively ideal type: indeed, doing so is, according to Weber, the essence of acting rationally. 'Rational behaviour is following the dictates of the type [that is, design] because such action is oriented to a formulated goal, or to a set of values ... and the means chosen are ... adapted to the utilization of the goal' (Weber, 1947, p. 16). This definition is consistent with the concept of design.

The Aston Group chose to study these ideas by conducting research that identified the empirical relationships among them. This led to generalizations that are as abstract as their models and therefore are not actionable; or, at least, it is not clear how they can be actionable.

1 Comparative youthfulness of management and a lower level of structuring of activities appear to be linked with more rapid growth. The term 'linked' means that they are statistically associated. But what is the action meaning or causal meaning? Does one hire young managers and fire those who are old? Which structuring of activities do you lower since the operational definition of structuring included many variables (Pugh, 1981a)?

2   No overall relationship with centralization was found. It appears that production decisions are delegated to a greater extent in more successful companies in stable environments, while successful companies in variable environments have a greater tendency to centralize decisions concerned with finance and purchasing. How does one reconcile these results with the Burns and Stalker (1961) findings that decisions are delegated in successful companies in unstable environments and that that is true for manufacturing and engineering decisions (as well as) for finance and purchasing?

    Moreover, how different is the organic organization from the mechanistic? Is it not the case that the organic organizations also contained Weberian features of bureaucracy? True, they often by-passed them – hence the concept of organic – but an analysis of the few transcripts available in the book indicate that the actual dialogue was connected with Model I theory-in-use, a theory-in-use associated with mechanistic organizations (Argyris, 1980).

3   Specialization, standardization and formalization are highly interrelated in work organizations and trade unions but standardization is not related to formalization in local government departments. Why are there differences between public and private when Weber and Bakke and myself claimed that such differences would not exist? Where were we wrong? How are such questions to be answered when, for example, the scales like standardization contained 128 dichotomized items?

4   Child is quoted as arguing that centralization, 'scored negatively should be included in the same cluster as specialization, standardization, and so on, to form a Weberian dimension of bureaucratization which, as he shows, included decentralization' (Pugh, 1981a, p. 147). Pugh's response is that doing so would dilute the very high intercorrelation found between specialization, formalization and standardization, with a variable that correlated only –0.3 to –0.5 with them. Pugh respects the recommendation because of a concern for losing statistical significance elsewhere. The rejection is self-referential since it relies upon the logic used to create the data in the first place and not some test that is independent of that logic. It is not by chance, I suggest, that the discussion of how to interpret empirical results obtained in different studies is never informed by issues of actionability or the introduction of designs that could help to account for the differences (Pugh, 1981a, pp. 145–9).

Pluralism, Design Causality and Actionable Knowledge

In several papers Pugh (1981a, 1983) describes himself as a positivist working primarily within the functionalist paradigms as defined by Morgan and Smircich (1980). I suggest that his very use of this model assumes that pluralism in approaches is not only a good idea but that it is the researchers' prerogative to select their paradigm. I would like to question these assumptions. Elsewhere I have tried to show that, when researchers describe, explain and predict in order to produce generalizations that can be used to create phenomena, they will not find the 30 box matrix of Morgan and Smircich (1980) very helpful because they will be using almost all of them during different phases of intervention research (Argyris, 1993).

For example, Argyris (1993) reports that the pattern of a director group's defensive routines represents reality as a social construct. It is implemented in a realm of symbolic discourse. It is a contextual field of information. It is a representation of concrete processes and structures in the sense that these processes and structures exist 'out there'. It coerces different directors to behave in similar manners. The assumptions about human nature illustrated in this research also range from the extremes of subjectivism to those of objectivism. For example, the participants were symbol creatures, symbol users and actors using symbols. The research depended heavily on understanding them as information processors with limited capacity to deal with the environmental complexity. Many examples were described where the same individuals were primarily adapters and responders before and after the interventions.

Finally, the research methods ranged from explorations of pure subjectivity, to script and symbolic analysis, to contextual analysis, to historical analysis of the director's group and to the design and execution of many experiments. Moreover, the entire research project occurred over a period of five years before publication and it continues. History became increasingly important as the interventions became cumulative, but so did the testing and experimenting used to asses the extent to which the new pattern contained processes and structures that 'coerced' action in the service of learning and of reducing defensive routines at all levels.

Design causality requires that we include all the methodologies necessary to describe the normative features of the universe in order to create more effective organizations. This, in turn, requires developing prescriptions which will help the actors to implement. Models of pluralistic approaches, I suggest, are only possible when social scientists focus on describing, explaining and predicting. As long as they exclude actionability from being pre-eminent they can select whatever boxes in the Morgan–Smircich model they wish. They can claim 'freedom of choice' for researchers because they do not have to subject their choices to any criterion beyond the logic that they used to make the choice in the first place. This is self-serving and violates the core of scientific inquiry, namely, the testing of positions with logic that is independent of the logic used to create the position in the first place.

There is a second reason why a model that supports the idea of pluralism in research methods is to be questioned. Recently, I conducted an analysis of empirical research by a group of scholars who identified themselves as in the subjective, interpretative, humanistic domain (Argyris, 1995). I concluded that there was a substantial amount of research that was manipulative, that covered up features from subjects, that appeared to acquiesce in unilateral control over subjects, and that the researchers distanced themselves from becoming aware of this possibility. Indeed, a bit more attention to the positivist value of testing and disconfirmability would have helped to reveal the possibility that they were unwittingly kidding themselves and others. If we, as scientists, choose to support pluralism, we should test the degree to which taking this position bypasses realizing that we may be fooling ourselves and others about the validity and relevance of our research.

Starbuck (1981) in a thoughtful critique of the Aston work concluded, according to Pugh (1981b), with a question: was it worth doing? Starbuck, as Pugh sees it, suggests it was not because organization theorists already knew before 1960 the generalizations that the Aston programme established. I believe that Starbuck is correct if we think of organizational theorists such as Fayol, Follet, Gulick and Urwick. Yet none of these conducted rigorous empirical research of the kind the Aston Group conducted. I believe these organizational theorists would find the Aston empirical work bewildering and that it did not add to knowledge of the type that concerned them: the design and management of organizations. All these theorists were unabashedly normative, prescriptive and concerned with creating. All of them, especially Follet, used designed causality as their primary mode of inquiry.

For a final example, I return to the Aston Group's criticism of Weber's (1947) concept of the bureaucratic firm. They assert that Weber saw the bureaucratic firm as a particular 'type' rather than a variable: 'An organization is or is not a bureaucracy, rather than either more or less bureaucratic' (Pugh *et al.*, 1963; p. 296). Why should Weber have conceived of bureaucracy as a variable? Because the Aston perspective wishes that he do so? Presumably, they take this stance because they claim it is more scientific. How do they know it is more scientific? They know because that is the foundation upon which their research is based. The logic is self-serving. There is no attempt to test this requirement independent of their logic. What would happen if the concept of design causality was the basis for the research? Such a concept would require the researchers to identify and state more explicitly and rigorously (than Weber did) the causal relationships between the features of a bureaucratic structure and its consequences, for example, upon office and leadership.

A design causality perspective leads to viewing variance in a different light. An increase or decrease in the frequency or strength of the variables should not lead to consequences that are different from those stipulated in the design. If the consequences are different, the design inferred is wrong, or the entire idea of design causality is wrong. For example, a theory of action design perspective predicts that when individuals evaluate or attribute in the service of Model I governing values (for example, unilateral control, maximizing winning and minimizing losing) escalation of error and defensiveness will occur. The frequency of Model I evaluations and attributions could vary greatly, yet the consequences predicted a priori are the ones that should be observed. One empirically observed instance to the contrary would disconfirm the theory. The reason this is so is that the design leads to a priori specified consequences. You should not be able to observe a different set of consequences regardless of the variance of the actions.

Nor can the actors predict that they will alter their design and do so. They must first develop, for example, the Model II skills in order to alter the Model I consequences. Again this is easily testable. If individuals who use Model I as their theory-in-use decide to use Model II (and are free to do so) they should not be able to do so. They have to move from Model II as an espoused theory to a theory-in-use.

The learning seminars that we conduct to help the individuals move from here to there are explicitly designed around such objectives. For example, individuals who attend these seminars learn the extent to which they use a Model I theory-in-use. Next we teach them Model II. Often, most individuals decide they want to use Model II. They attempt to recraft the Model I cases that they wrote to be more consistent with Model II. In no case have they been able to do so without supervised practice (Argyris, 1984, 1990). In the case described above, some of the owner-directors decided to use Model II immediately. We predicted that they would not be able to do so without practice. We then tape-recorded the discussions questioning our predictions as well as many business meetings over a nine-month period. They were unable to use Model II (Argyris, 1993).

In Conclusion, a Proposal

I have learned much from Derek over the years and propose a way that we can continue the learning. How about finding a way to cooperate in a research project where the two forms of causality could be studied? It would be instructive to show empirically where and how they could be integrated and, at the same time, it would be of value to the world of practice.

References

Argyris, C. (1980), *Inner Contradictions of Rigorous Research*, New York: Academic Press.

Argyris, C. (1984), *Reasoning, Learning and Action*, San Francisco: Jossey-Bass.

Argyris, C. (1990), 'The dilemma of implementing controls: the case of managerial accounting', *Accounting Organizations and Society*, **15**, (6), 503–11.

Argyris, C. (1993), *Overcoming Organizational Defenses*, Needham, Mass.: Allyn Bacon.

Argyris, C. (1993), *Knowledge for Action*, San Francisco: Jossey-Bass.

Argyris, C. (1995), 'Knowledge when used in practice to test theory: the case of applied communication research,' in M. Kenneth (ed.), *Applied Communication in the 21st Century*, Cissna, NJ: Lawrence Erlbaum Associates, pp. 1–19.

Argyris, C. and Kaplan, R.S. (1994), 'Implementing new knowledge: the case of activity-based costing', *Accounting Horizons*, **8**, (3), pp. 83–105.

Argyris, C. and Schön, D. (1974), *Theory in Practice*, San Francisco: Jossey-Bass.

Argyris, C. and Schön, D. (1995), *Organizational Learning II*, Reading, Mass.: Addison-Wesley.

Bakke, E.W. (1950), *Bonds of Organization*, New York: Wiley.

Bakke, E.W. (1959), 'Concept of the social organization' in M. Haire (ed.), *Modern Organization Theory*, New York: Wiley.

Burns, T. and Stalker, G.M. (1961), *The Management of Innovation*, London: Tavistock.

Campbell, D.T. and Stanley, J.C. (1963), *Experimental and Quasi-Experimental Design for Research*, Skoki, Ill.: Rand McNally.

James, L.R., Mulaik, S.A. and Brett, J.M. (1982), *Causal Analysis: Assumptions, Models and Data*, Newbury Park, CA: Sage.

Mill, J.S. (1949), *A System of Logic*, London: Longman (originally published 1843).

Morgan, S. and Smircich, L. (1980), 'The case for qualitative research', *Academy of Management Review*, **5**, (4), 491–500.

Pugh, D.S. (1981a), 'The Aston program perspective', in A.H. Van de Ven and W.F. Joyce (eds), *Perspectives on Organization Design and Behavior*, New York: Wiley, pp. 135–66.

Pugh, D.S. (1981b), 'Rejoinder to Starbuck', in A.H. Van de Ven and W.F. Joyce (eds), *Perspectives on Organization Design and Behavior*, New York: Wiley, pp. 199–203.

Pugh, D.S. (1983), 'Studying organizational structure and process', in G. Morgan (ed.), *Beyond Method: Strategies for Social Research*, Beverley Hills, CA: Sage, pp. 45–56.

Pugh, D.S., Hickson, D.F., Hinings, C.R., MacDonald, K.M., Turner, C. and Lupton, T. (1963), 'A conceptual scheme for organizational analysis', *Administrative Science Quarterly*, **8**, 289–315.

Simon, H.A. (1965), *The Science of the Artificial*, Cambridge, Mass.: MIT Press.

Simon, H.A. (1990), 'Invariants of human behaviour', *Annual Review of Psychology*, **41**, 1–20.

Starbuck, W.H. (1981), 'A trip to view the elephants and the rattlesnakes in the garden of Aston', in A.H. Van de Ven and W.F. Joyce (eds), *Perspectives on Organization Design and Behavior*, New York: Wiley, pp. 167–98.

Weber, M. (1947), *The Theory of Social and Economic Organization*, trans. A.M. Henderson and Talcott Parsons, New York: Oxford University Press.

6 Never Mind Structure – What About Climate?

ROY L. PAYNE, *School of Psychology, Curtin University of Technology, Perth, Western Australia*

I had graduated with a degree in psychology just two years before I joined the Aston Group and a major intellectual influence during my undergraduate years was Kurt Lewin whose dictum that behaviour was a function of the interaction between the person and the environment ($B = fP \times E$) led me to the view that we had a set of concepts and measures that were useful for understanding people, but few that helped in conceptualizing and measuring the environment. I had already developed an interest in the concept of organizational climate,[1] but the Aston Group's work on organizational structure was clearly an approach that was potentially symbiotic with my interest. Indeed, what was particularly appealing about the Aston Group was the long-term plan it had to study behaviour in organizations at three levels of analysis – the organization, the group (within the organization) and the individual (within the group, within the organization). I was recruited along with Diana Pheysey and Kerr Inkson to study the group level, as by 1965 the conceptual work on the organization level was well established, all the fieldwork was done and the analysis was well on its way, though we all spent a considerable amount of time on the structural analyses, many of which never saw the light of day (examples include the attempt to create a measure of status of specialisms, and several variations of centralization).

The fundamental assumption of the group-level project was that the structure and behaviour (culture?) of groups would be influenced by the structure and culture of the organization in which they were embedded. To investigate this assumption, three organizations were selected which were assessed with the organization-level measures so that we knew they differed in certain ways. Thus two were of similar size (350–400 employees) but one was very structured, having a high level of specialization and standardization (Aston) whereas the other had very little of either (Brum). The third (Carrs) was much bigger (about 3000 employees) and had about the same degree of standardization and specialization as the more structured smaller one (Aston). From the organization data bank it was possible to conclude that the larger organization (Carrs) had about the degree of structure that would be expected for a manufacturing organization of its size, and that the smaller, structured organization (Aston) was much more structured than would be expected for a manufacturing company employing only 350 people.

The results of these and related studies on organizational climate can be found in the third volume of papers deriving from the Aston Studies (Pugh and Payne, 1977). Since they are much less widely known than the structure studies, they are briefly described below, but the main reason for introducing them is to indicate that they raised issues about organizational climate and team climate that continue to interest me personally, and also other workers in the field.

The Group-Level Studies: Rationale

Figure 6.1 details the variables studied and presents the relationships expected to occur in a mechanistic organization with high role prescription. The rationale for the relationships suggested in Figure 6.1 is as follows. First, *organizational structure and organizational climate*: a mechanistic structuring of activities, through division of labour, standardized procedures and written specification overprescribes the tasks of managers and is, therefore, not likely to produce a development climate where people are stimulated to be innovative. Secondly, the centralization and the high ration of superordinates characteristic of such organizations are likely to lead to an emphasis on control.

Second, *organizational structure and group structure*: at the group level, a mechanistic structure is likely to result in low task complexity, especially at lower levels, and in greater formality of relationships, with emphasis on memos, minutes, written instructions and agendas limiting the opportunity for spontaneous, informal communication. Lack of autonomy may accompany the formality, since authority in a mechanistic organization tends to be concentrated at the top of the hierarchy (Burns and Stalker, 1961). These characteristics are not always associated, however, as Pugh *et al.* (1968) showed. Their measure of structuring of work activities – which included formalization – was independent of centralization of authority.

Third, *organizational climate and group climate*: many writers have argued that top executives are likely to have great influence on the climate of the organization, and, once the top policy makers have

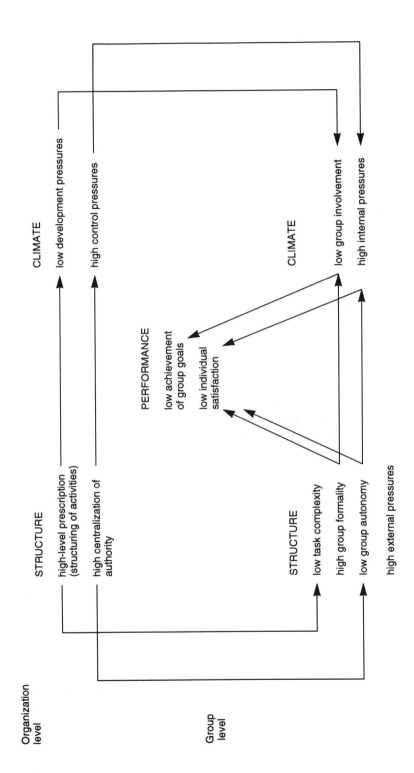

Figure 6.1 Relationships expected among structure and climate variables in a mechanistic organization

made decisions, they exert pressure on subordinates to execute then. Members under such pressure and control, who must execute decisions in which they have not participated, are not likely to have a high sense of involvement in the group's activities and goals, and therefore are not likely to take great satisfaction in their work.

Method

Procedures

The procedure for collecting the data in this study was as follows:

1 Information on organizational structure and context was obtained by interviews with senior managers.
2 A sociometric questionnaire was given to line managers and related staff personnel.
3 Interviews were held with members of the selected groups to collect data about their individual jobs, interdependence with other personnel, and individual job satisfaction.
4 Hemphill's (1956) questionnaire on group dimensions was left with members of the groups at the end of these interviews.
5 Further interviews were held with group members about the task structure of group, group atmosphere, perceived pressures on the group, group aims, and so on.
6 The business organizational climate index was left with members of the groups at the end of the interview.
7 Written reports were sent back to all participants.

The group measures used were as follows, with mean item-analysis values given in parentheses.

Work Group Structure

1 Task complexity: nine items, related to Shaw's (1963) dimensions, each rated for frequency of occurrence on an eight-point scale (0.54).
2 Formality: Hemphill's (1956) flexibility scale shortened to eight items and scoring reversed (0.63).
3 Autonomy: Hemphill's (1956) autonomy scale shortened to eight items (0.83).
4 External pressures: eight-point frequency rating of how often pressure was exerted on the group from five external sources (0.66).

Work Group Climate

1   Involvement: Hemphill's (1956) potency scale shortened to 10 items (0.67) and Hemphill's (1956) participation scale shortened to seven items (0.75).
2   Internal pressures: eight-point frequency rating in answer to the question, 'How often does the group come under pressure from people within the group itself?'

Work Group Performance

1   Achievement of subgroup goals: eight-point rating from very successful to very unsuccessful.
2   Satisfaction with individual members: Cornell job description index of satisfaction with work, pay, promotion, supervision and people (Smith *et al.*, 1969).

Findings

Organizational Structure and Organizational Climate

The development of the climate measure (the Business Organization Climate Index or BOCI) is described in Payne and Pheysey (1977) which includes a comparison of the three organizations described above. When comparing the two small organizations only some of the classical hypotheses about the effects of bureaucracy were strongly supported. The small structured, more bureaucratic organization (Aston) had a climate much higher on scales such as rules orientation, administrative efficiency and conventionality. Contrary to much of the literature, however, Aston had none of the negative, alienating effects supposed to exist in highly structured organizations. The climate for the Work Interest Scales such as industriousness, future orientation and job challenge was seen as much more positive. In addition, the climate was much more open to the questioning of authority, and leaders were seen as closer to the workforce. The only scales that were higher in the less structured organization were orientation to the wider community and altruism. When Aston was compared to Carrs (the large bureaucracy) its climate was still much higher on the climate measures of rules orientation, conventionality and so on, but again it also had the much more open and positive climate on the other measures. We concluded that Aston had managed to combine the positive features of specialization and standardization with the more communicative, close relationships that small size allows, always assuming the managers choose to use them. One other structural feature that benefited this company compared with the less structured small company (Brum) was that it had only five hierarchical levels, compared to eight.

What these results indicate is the need to have reasonably complex measures of structure because the effects of one feature of structure (standardization) might be counteracted by another (fewer levels) and that the relationship between dimensions of structure and dimensions of climate is complexly determined.

This complexity of relationships, and the naivety of the bureaucratic hypothesis, was further confirmed in a slightly larger study of structure and climate (Payne and Mansfield, 1977). On a sample of 14 organizations, only 10 per cent of the correlations relating structural variables to climate variables (180 in total) reached the 5 per cent confidence level, and most of these were with the contextual variable log of the size of the parent organization and log of size. The results of this study were summarized as follows:

> Organizational climate seems to be affected by organizational size and dependence (on a larger owning group). Each of these is associated with a climate that is relatively involved in matters surrounding work itself (i.e. high on scales such as future orientation, scientific and technical orientation, job challenge, readiness to innovate). This probably derives from the greater complexity that comes with greater size, and with the increased financial and professional resources of larger organizations, which are available even to the dependent, smaller organizations which are owned by them. Size has some negative effects on the social processes in the organization in that leaders are seen as more psychologically distant, emotional control is higher, and conventionality is higher. These are to some extent countered by the readiness to question authority, to innovate, and the higher concern of management for the involvement of their employees. Most of the negative social consequences are reversed with dependency. As size and dependency are almost independent of each other, perhaps some of the most attractive climates are found in large dependent organizations.

One of the other important results in this paper was the demonstration that perceptions of organization climate differed by hierarchical level for 15 out of 20 scales. In all cases the more senior people saw the climate more positively. This was one of the first papers to raise the issue of whether the mean score on organizational climate is a valid index of the climate, though in the same year Guion (1973) produced one of the classic papers on this topic. Payne and Mansfield (1977) attempted to take account of the problem statistically by comparing the overall mean score with a score weighted by hierarchical level. When the latter score on the 20 climate scales was correlated with scores on the nine structural/contextual variables it produced 67 correlations which accounted for more than 10 per cent of the variance, compared to only 47 using the straight mean score. This suggests the weighted mean is a more valid indicator of the climate. This issue about the extent to which members of organizations agree about the nature of the climate has become a major debating point in the climate literature and it is one to which we will return, but it is worth recording that the Aston Studies made an early contribution to it.

The Pheysey *et al.* (1971) paper reports all the main combinations of variables such as organizational structure and group structure, organizational climate and group climate, but we shall concentrate on the group structure and group climate results because they resurface the issue about consensus measures of the properties of collectives.

Group Structure and Group Climate

As indicated earlier, the measures of group structure were task complexity, formality and autonomy. The group climate measures were involvement, participation and internal group pressure. As at the organizational level, the assumption was that groups that had less complex tasks and more formality would have less involvement. In testing this hypothesis it was recognized that the group scores were aggregates of individual scores. It was therefore decided that each individual in the group should be given a group score so that correlations could be calculated across the group scores, and then the individual scores could be controlled by partial correlation. In the present example the zero-order correlation between formality and involvement was 0.82 ($p<0.05$, $N = 42$) but this dropped to a non-significant correlation of 0.60 when the individual scores were held constant. This positive correlation is in the opposite direction to the hypothesis and results from the higher levels of involvement in the more structured and more centralized organization (Aston). It is, of course, consistent with the relationships found at the organizational level.

It was further hypothesized that the combination of formal relationships, low group autonomy and high external pressures on the group would lead to higher felt internal pressures (Figure 6.1), but there was no evidence that these structural features of the group affected group climate.

Both the climate variables and the perceived structure variables were also correlated with group satisfaction, the latter being the aggregate of each of the five satisfaction variables (work, pay, promotion, supervision and co-workers) in the Job Description Index. It was hypothesized that structure and climate were likely to influence satisfaction with work and supervision, and possibly co-workers, but not pay and promotion. Once again partial correlation was used to look at the group-level variables while controlling the individual-level scores. None of the hypotheses was supported ($p < 0.05$), and where there was evidence for a relationship, it was inconsistent with the hypotheses. Thus both group formality and group involvement were correlated with satisfaction with promotion, whereas autonomy was not correlated with satisfaction with work or with supervision. The main point to be made about these results is that partialling out for the individual-level scores had a strong tendency to reduce the correlations at the group level. This is not a procedure that has been widely used, but there have been many studies of groups where it might well have been used and provided a better estimate of the true relationship between perceived measures of group structure and group climate variables. It is yet another example of the problem of using aggregate scores to represent a property of a social collectivity.

As the above studies were being published, Derek Pugh was invited to write a chapter on structure for the first edition of Marvin Dunnette's *Handbook of Industrial and Organizational Psychology* (Payne and Pugh, 1976). Derek in turn invited me to co-author it and we wrote a chapter entitled 'Organizational structure and climate'. The chapter has two conclusions. The first is a pessimistic conclusion which was written by me, to which Derek replied with an optimistic conclusion. This probably says more about us than the data, but my pessimism was based on the following facts:

- different operationalizations (objective and subjective) of each of the structure and climate measures have shown low correlations with each other;
- different positions in the structural hierarchy have shown systematic differences in measures of perceived organizational climate and structure (the aggregation problem);
- detailed case study work was required to capture this complexity and 'Idiosyncratic and time-consuming work of this kind makes comparative research on a large scale presently impossible. When thousands of such cases exist then we may again attempt comparative research.'

Derek's more optimistic interpretation was that both sorts of measures do still show different profiles across organizations, that climate had been shown to relate to satisfaction and performance, and that structure too had been shown to relate to performance (quoting Woodward, 1965), but of course the Aston group itself found little evidence to support Woodward's findings that structure relates to performance (Child, 1974). Finally, Derek argued that comparative and process approaches should be linked to complement each other, and the Aston work at the group level reported above is one model for attempting to do that. Sadly, I cannot think of any subsequent studies that have followed that sort of design and deliberately compared organizations which differ in known ways on structure and context as conceived by the Aston group, though there are examples of differences in technology and organization conceived in other ways (Miles and Snow, 1978; Wall *et al.*, 1986).

Some More Recent Studies of Climate

For about a decade I believed that my pessimistic conclusions had prevailed, for papers on climate were relatively rare during the late 1970s and early 1980s. However, the resurgence of interest in culture provoked by the Special Issue of *Administrative Science Quarterly* on organizational culture (1983) seemed to revitalize climate too. The last decade has seen a number of important papers and books on the following:

- the concept of climate – Glick (1985), Ashforth (1985), Schneider (1990), Pheysey (1992);
- the relationship of climate to other organizational variables including performance – Schneider (1990), Dennison (1990), Zammuto and Krakower (1991), West and Burningham (1995);
- the aggregation issue – Joyce and Slocum (1984), Jackofsky and Slocum (1988), Kozlowski and Hattrup (1992), James *et al.* (1993).

The papers by Joyce and Slocum (1984) and Jackofsky and Slocum (1988) rekindled my own interest in the aggregation issue, for their work was based on a suggestion put forward in Payne and Pugh (1976) that cluster analysis might be used to identify groups in organizations that do see the climate in a similar way, and this may be one way of getting around the aggregation issue. In both studies cluster analysis was used to identify such 'collective climates'. I criticized their approach on the grounds that such collectives could only represent the concept scientifically if the members had some other meaningful sociopsychological identity (for example, they were all in the same department, clique or team – see Payne, 1990). Such departmental identification was shown to exist in phase 1 of the Jackofsky and Slocum study, but this was not replicated some months later at phase 2.

As well as using cluster analysis to identify collectives, Joyce and Slocum followed others in using intra-class correlation as a means of estimating the degree of agreement within the clusters. However, there is disagreement about the most suitable formula and about the size of the coefficient which might indicate adequate levels of agreement for claiming the collective had a consensus view that indicated the existence of a distinctive climate. The use of different indices has led to a debate about the relative merits of different formulae and the size of the coefficient. The main protagonists have been James *et al.* (1984), Yammarino and Markham (1992), Kozlowski and Hattrup (1992), Schmidt and Hunter (1989) and James *et al.* (1993).

Despite this well known debate, studies of climate still appear which use the mean score without testing for degree of consensus, or, more commonly now, do test it and report the coefficients of agreement, but ignore them if they are lower than they should be, arguing that other studies have done the same, and/or that there is no real way of knowing how big the coefficient needs to be (for example, Zammuto and Krakower, 1991), although guidelines are offered (about 0.70). In the Zammuto and Krakower study, the average coefficient of the top 25 per cent in their sample of 332 colleges was 0.66. For the bottom 25 per cent it was only 0.2.

Using a revised and updated version of the Business Organization Climate Index (Payne, *et al.*, 1992), I, and colleagues, have explored the properties of the version of the intra-class correlation coefficient proposed by James *et al.* in 1984 and further justified in 1993, it being the most widely accepted formula. The studies are based on a sample of 56 organizations involving 2150 respondents, each of whom completed the 17 scales of the revised version of the BOCI. These unpublished papers were written by Padmore *et al.* (1993) and Padmore and Payne (1995). The organizations ranged in size from 70 to 7100; 24 were in manufacturing, 23 in service, nine in retailing/distribution. The number of respondents ranged from 12 to 56, with a mean of 38. The respondents were drawn from all levels of the organization and the numbers of respondents, in three broad hierarchical groups, were 163 at senior manager level, 803 at supervisory level and 1155 at the operational level.

In the 1993 paper, the purpose was to calculate the James *et al.* within groups coefficient $(r_{wg(j)})$ for each scale in all 56 organizations and to see what sorts of coefficients emerged under different assumptions. Initially, it was assumed that the response would show no systematic sources of variation other than true response variance. Thus responses to each item would follow a uniform distribution, leading to an expected variance of 1.25. Indices estimated using this value may be regarded as upper-bound estimates of the true level of consensus (Kozlowski and Hattrup, 1992). Two possible forms of systematic response bias were considered, both for moderately skewed distributions and having variances of 1.00 and 0.89, respectively. It was felt that these three hypothetical response distributions gave an adequate indication of the range of values over which actual indices of consensus would lie. The indices for each condition were displayed as box and whisker plots (Tukey, 1977) by scale and by organization.

It was clear that there are large variations in the indices of consensus by scale. Given the heterogeneous sample of organizations, it is perhaps not surprising that the scale of Scientific and Technical Orientation has great variation in its index of consensus. More importantly, however, the results show large numbers of organizations with low levels of consensus across scales. Using the lower estimate of variance (0.89), the organizations were examined individually to assess whether there was adequate consensus within them. Accepting 0.7 as a standard, it was decided that organizations could be retained if (1) more than 75 per cent of the scales (12 or more) scored higher than 0.7, and (2) no scale exhibited a value of less than 0.5 (already lowering the recommended standards, of course). On this basis, 35 out of the 56 organizations could be used in comparative studies of organizational climate. Many studies, including our own, have undoubtedly included organizations where the level of consensus was not high enough to justify the claim that the mean score accurately represents the climate.

The Bootstrapping Study

We recognized that the method just described is a relatively crude way of determining adequacy of consensus and in the 1995 paper we used bootstrapping (Efron, 1979) to help provide a more systematic way of deciding level of consensus and when organizations meet the appropriate criteria.

Bootstrapping has been developed to estimate the sampling distribution for a statistic in order to make inferences about a population parameter using limited information. Its essence is the simulation of relevant properties of statistical procedures with minimal model assumptions. The techniques centre around repeatedly 'resampling from the sample' in order to generate an empirical estimate of the entire sampling distribution of the statistic. Here bootstrapping was used to assess the degree of consensus within organizations. This was achieved by comparing those values of $r_{wg(j)}$ actually observed, with a bootstrap estimate of those that might be obtained under the assumption of no differences between organizations. This is achieved by treating all individuals as representatives of the population so that it is possible to simulate the drawing of samples of a given size from the population by resampling from the sample with continuous replacement. The values of the coefficient of consensus can be calculated for these facsimile samples and, ultimately, an estimate of the empirical distribution can be calculated, assuming no consensus within organizations. A comparison of the bootstrap statistics with the values obtained from real organizations provides a means of estimating the extent to which consensus exists in the real organizations.

Under the assumption of no interorganizational differences, 1000 facsimile samples were constructed using a variety of sample sizes, ranging from 10 to 60. For each sample and each of the 17 scales, the item index of consensus was calculated. The box and whisker plots of all these can be found in Padmore and Payne (1995) but the statistics for the sample size of 40 are presented in Table 6.1. The mean column shows that even, with randomly drawn groups, the consensus statistic is often around the 0.7 recommended as indicating adequate consensus. The boxplot in Figure 6.2 shows the actual data for the 17 scales assuming a variance of 0.89 and it shows clearly that scale 8 and scale 13 produce wide distributions within the 56 organizations studied here. Some of the other scales, however, have distributions which show much greater levels of consensus than expected by chance (for example, scales 2, 4, 9 and 14). When the actual values were compared to the upper 10 per cent cut-off point of the

Table 6.1   Summary statistics of bootstrap results ($n = 40$)

Scale	Minimum	Maximum	Mean	Standard deviation	Skewness	Kurtosis
1	0.00	0.87	0.696	0.116	−1.908	5.680
2	0.33	0.90	0.795	0.106	−1.556	4.987
3	0.00	0.87	0.686	0.069	−2.148	7.291
4	0.38	0.90	0.795	0.128	−1.701	5.161
5	0.00	0.89	0.729	0.062	−2.501	11.056
6	0.00	0.87	0.694	0.116	−1.978	6.430
7	0.00	0.87	0.685	0.113	−1.529	3.620
8	0.00	0.78	0.369	0.241	−0.340	−1.202
0	0.00	0.89	0.720	0.102	−1.811	5.643
10	0.00	0.86	0.656	0.140	−1.850	4.715
11	0.00	0.90	0.737	0.102	−1.948	6.761
12	0.00	0.87	0.521	0.211	−1.045	0.374
13	0.00	0.89	0.649	0.158	−1.793	4.169
14	0.36	0.90	0.756	0.073	−1.209	2.363
15	0.00	0.90	0.741	0.095	−2.253	10.091
16	0.00	0.88	0.680	0.135	−2.085	6.405
17	0.00	0.82	0.585	0.171	−1.603	2.613

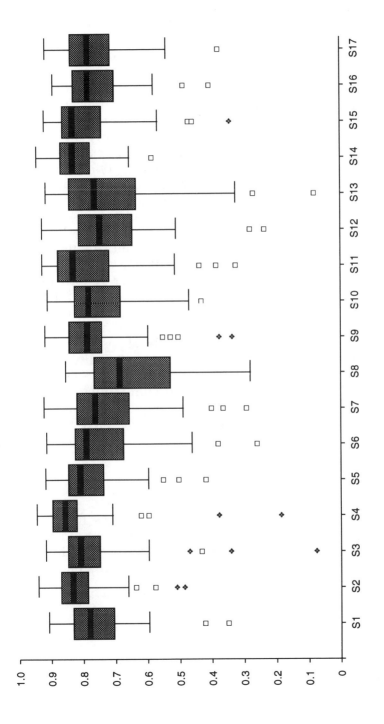

Figure 6.2 Boxplot of $r_{wg(j),\,0.89}$ by scale

bootstrapped critical values for the sample size of 40, three organizations were found in which all 17 scales were significant, 18
organizations had 12 scales or more which were significant and 24
organizations had over half of the 17 scales where the index of consensus was significant. These results indicate the presence of a
considerable degree of consensus within some of the organizations
investigated and, in general, the observed frequency distribution has
much higher frequencies in the upper range than might be expected
under the assumption of no intraorganizational consensus.

However, these results clearly demonstrate that within many organizations there is not enough consensus to justify the claim that
aggregation represents the existence of a particular kind of climate.
Out of the original sample of 56 organizations, only three contain
people who agree reasonably well across all 17 scales, and only 24
have values high enough to justify aggregation across nine scales.

While the positive message from these calculations is that there is
a method which provides a statistical and empirical way of determining level of consensus, the negative side must be that many of
the studies that have reported results predicting climate from structure (for example, Payne and Mansfield, 1977) or performance from
climate (for example, Dennison, 1990) must be treated with caution.

An obvious consequence of such findings is a search for the factors
which lead to diversity (or consensus). Some of the variation will be
due to differences in roles and hierarchical levels, as already reported
here, and some to individual differences in personality and values,
as well as affective variables such as job satisfaction. Others will no
doubt reside in aspects of structure and culture themselves. Some
cultures have strong norms about encouraging diversity of views
and values. Perhaps for all norms but that one, there may well be
lack of consensus.

Conclusion

The contribution of this chapter is, I hope, to show that the Aston
group made a contribution, and continues to make a contribution, to
the organizational literature which extends well beyond the confines
of structure and that Derek Pugh has played a significant role in
accumulating that body of research.

Note

1   'A molar concept reflecting the content and strength of the prevalent values,
    norms, attitudes, behaviors and feelings of the members of a social system

which can be operationally measured through the perceptions of system members or observational and other objective means' (Payne and Pugh, 1976, p. 1141).

References

Administrative Science Quarterly (1983), Special Issue on Culture, **28**.

Ashforth, B.E. (1985), 'Climate formation: issues and extensions', *Academy of Management Review*, **10**, 837–847.

Burns, T. and Stalker, G.M. (1961), *The Management of Innovation*, London: Tavistock.

Child, J. (1974), 'Managerial and organizational factors associated with company performance', *Journal of Management Studies*, **11**, 175–89.

Dennison, D.R. (1990), *Corporate Culture and Organizational Effectiveness*, New York: Wiley.

Dunnette, M. (1976), *Handbook of Organizational Psychology*, Chicago: Rand-McNally.

Efron, B. (1979), 'Bootstrap methods: another look at the jackknife', *Annals of Statistics*, **7**, 1–26.

Glick, W.H. (1985), 'Conceptualizing and measuring organizational and psychological climate: pitfalls in multilevel research', *Academy of Management Review*, **10**, 601–16.

Guion, R.M. (1973), 'A note on organizational climate', *Organizational Behaviour and Human Performance*, **9**, 120–25.

Hemphill, J.K. (1956), 'Group dimensions: a manual for their measurement', Columbus, Ohio State University Bureau of Business Research, research monograph no. 87.

Jackofsky, E.F. and Slocum, J.W. Jr. (1988), 'A longitudinal study of climate', *Journal of Organizational Behaviour*, **9**, 319–34.

James, L.R., Demaree, R.G. and Wolf, G. (1984), 'Estimating within-group interrater reliability with and without response bias', *Journal of Applied Psychology*, **69**, 85–98.

James, L.R., Demaree, R.G. and Wolf, G. (1993), 'r_{wg}: an assessment of within-group interrater agreement', *Journal of Applied Psychology*, **78**, 306–9.

Joyce, W.F. and Slocum, J.W. Jr. (1984), 'Collective climate: agreement as a basis for defining aggregate climates in organizations', *Academy of Management Journal*, **27**, 721–42.

Kozlowski, S.W.J. and Hattrup, K. (1992), 'A disagreement about within-group agreement: disentangling issues of consistency versus consensus', *Journal of Applied Psychology*, **77**, 161–7.

Miles, R.E. and Snow, C.C. (1978), *Organizational Strategy, Structure and Process*, New York: McGraw-Hill.

Padmore, J. and Payne, R.L. (1995), 'A pragmatic approach to the problem of aggregation in organizational climate research – Part Two', Sheffield University Management School, Working Paper Series.

Padmore, J., Gaston, K. and Payne, R.L. (1993), 'A pragmatic approach to the problem of aggregation in organizational climate research', Sheffield University Management School, Working Paper Series.

Payne, R.L. (1990), 'Madness in our method: a comment on Jackofsky and Slocum's paper – a longitudinal study of climates', *Journal of Organizational Behaviour*, **11**, 77–80.

Payne, R.L. and Mansfield, R. (1977), 'Relationships of perceptions of organizational climate to organizational structure, context and hierarchical position', in

Organizational Behaviour in its Context – The Aston Programme II, D.S. Pugh and R.L. Payne (eds), Aldershot: Gower, pp. 134–48.

Payne, R.L. and Pheysey, D.C. (1977), 'Stern's organizational climate index: a reconceptualization and application to business organizations', in Pugh, D.S. and Payne, R.L. (eds), *Organizational Behaviour in its Context – The Aston Programme II*, Aldershot, Gower, pp. 113–33.

Payne, R.L. and Pugh, D.S. (1976), 'Organizational structure and climate', in M. Dunnette (ed.), *Handbook of Organizational Psychology*, Chicago: Rand-McNally, pp. 1125–73.

Payne, R.L., Brown, A.D. and Gaston, K. (1992), 'Reliability and validity of an updated version of the business organization climate index (BOCI). A research note', Working Paper No. 227, Manchester Business School.

Pheysey, D.C. (1992), *Organizational Cultures, Types and Transformations*, London: Routledge.

Pheysey, D.C., Payne, R.L. and Pugh, D.S. (1971), 'The influence of structure at organizational and group levels', *Administrative Science Quarterly*, **16**, 61–73.

Pugh, D.S. and Payne, R.L. (1977), *Organizational Behaviour in its Context – The Aston Programme II*, Aldershot: Gower.

Pugh, D.S., Hickson, D.J., Hinings, C.R. and Turner, C. (1968), 'Dimensions of organization structure', *Administrative Science Quarterly*, **13**, 65–105.

Schmidt, F.L. and Hunter, J.E. (1989), 'Interrater reliability coefficients cannot be computed when only one stimulus is rated', *Journal of Applied Psychology*, **74**, 368–70.

Schneider, B. (1990), *Organizational Climate and Culture*, San Francisco: Jossey-Bass.

Shaw, M.E. (1963), 'Scaling group tasks: a method for dimensional analysis', working paper, University of Florida Technical Report No. 1.

Smith, P.C., Kendall, L.M. and Hulin, C.L. (1969), *The Measurement of Satisfaction in Work and Retirement*, Chicago: Rand-McNally.

Tukey, J.U. (1977), *Exploratory Data Analysis*, Reading, Mass.: Addison-Wesley.

Wall, T.D., Kemp, N.J., Jackson, P.R. and Clegg, C.W. (1986), 'Outcomes of autonomous workgroups: a long-term field experiment', *Academy of Management Journal*, June, 280–304.

West, M. and Burningham, C. (1995), 'Individual, climate and group interaction processes as predictors of work team innovation', *Small Group Research*, **26**, 106–17.

Woodward, J. (1965), *Industrial Organization: Theory and Practice*, London: Oxford University Press.

Yammarino, F.J. and Markham, S.E. (1992), 'On the application of within and between analysis: are absence and affect really group based phenomena?', *Journal of Applied Psychology*, **77**, 168–76.

Zammuto, R.F. and Krakower, J.Y. (1991), 'Quantitative and qualitative studies of organizational culture', *Research in Organizational Change and Development*, **5**, 84–114.

PART II
THE CHANGING NATURE OF
ORGANIZATIONS

7 Structural Change and the Role of Taxonomies

C.R. HININGS, DALE CUNNINGHAM,
University of Alberta and **TREVOR SLACK,**
De Montfort University

The original Aston Studies were developed in part from the ideas of Max Weber on bureaucracy (Weber, 1949). Starting from that base, one aim was to dimensionalize Weber's ideal-type of bureaucracy, something which is expressed in the original framework paper (Pugh *et al.*, 1963) and perhaps even more clearly in Hinings *et al.* (1967). Two aspects underlay this approach. One was to explicate the structural dimensions that underlay the concept of bureaucracy, in particular, the elements of specialization standardization, formalization and centralization. The second was to produce an empirically based taxonomy of bureaucracies, suggesting that it was necessary to go beyond ideal-type analysis.

The empirical output of what became known as the Aston Studies is found in four papers (Pugh *et al.*, 1968, 1969a; Pugh *et al.*, 1969b; Hickson *et al.*, 1969). One of these, Pugh *et al.* (1969b) dealt with the issue of taxonomies. That paper stated: 'The term "taxonomy" implies that the classification is based upon dimensions that are measurable and empirically established … A taxonomy is thus a multidimensional classification' (Pugh *et al.*, 1969b, p. 116). This taxonomic approach was followed at two levels. First, four 'clear' types were identified, namely, the Workflow Bureaucracy, the Personnel Bureaucracy, the Full Bureaucracy and the Implicitly Structured Organization. The names used show the basis of the studies in Weber's notion of bureaucracy.

The second level of analysis recognized that in using a taxonomy there are always cases that do not fit neatly into the 'pure' cases. Thus Pugh *et al.* (1969b) also recognized the Nascent Workflow Bureaucracy, the Preworkflow Bureaucracy, and the Nascent Full Bureaucracy. Not only do these names recognize the difficulties of dealing with marginal cases, they also indicate *movement*, in the sense that these marginal organizations are seen as being on their way to becoming bureaucracies. In fact, part of the paper is headed 'Developmental Sequences'. Again, to quote the paper:

> There is the line controlled, implicitly structured organization, initially small in size (relatively speaking) with a flexible technology. In the preworkflow bureaucracy there is a change from line to staff control ... With the nascent workflow bureaucracy there are the beginnings of structuring, the appearance of specialists and expansion of procedural control. With the workflow bureaucracy, specialists appear, producing more procedures and reinforcing control by the line with impersonal bureaucratic regulation. The same sequence of arguments would apply in regard to the development of nascent full bureaucracies into full bureaucracies. (Pugh *et al.*, 1969b, p. 124)

Interestingly, there was a debate within the research team as to whether this paper should be written, a debate which illustrates a significant, continuing theme in organization theory. On the one hand, there is the style of theorizing and research which emphasizes univariate and multivariate relationships between aspects of structure and between structure and context. On the other hand, there is an approach which favours examining the patterning of those relations in a holistic way. The original Aston research did both, but the aspects which have been taken up are those of examining relationships between variables. There is a sense in which the taxonomy lies forgotten and relatively uncited.

The argument of this chapter is that, given recent developments in the study of organizational change, taxonomies have an important role in identifying and analysing change. In particular, theoretical developments that have emphasized concepts of coherence, archetypes, inertia, momentum and institutional specificity are susceptible to such an approach. The idea of configuration has come to the fore again (Meyer *et al.*, 1993). These associated theories stress a holistic approach to understanding organization structure. They also underline the particular starting point of an organization in understanding its ability to change in either revolutionary or evolutionary ways. We argue that taxonomies are an important element in such theorizing because of their role in identifying and analysing structural patterns in change.

To do this, we examine the theoretical basis of theories of change that emphasize coherence and archetypes and patterns of evolution and revolution in change. We argue that such theorizing lends itself to a taxonomic approach and go on to consider those issues which have to be dealt with when using taxonomies in the study of change. We also deal with the importance of an institutionally specific approach to analysing change.

Configurational Theories of Structural Change

This chapter is concerned with organizational types in relation to what they will add to our understanding of change. In doing this it follows the recent literature on organizational transformations and reorientations (Miles and Snow, 1978; Starbuck *et al.*, 1978; Ranson *et al.*, 1980; Tichy, 1983; Kimberly and Quinn, 1984; Miller and Friesen, 1984; Pettigrew, 1985; Tushman and Romanelli, 1985; Child and Smith, 1987; Kimberly, 1987; Zucker, 1987; Hinings and Greenwood, 1988b). This literature deals with the way in which the existing structural patterning of an organization is crucially important to the ease or difficulty with which that organization can change. Starbuck *et al.* (1978), for example, argue that the current structural arrangements and modes of operating in an organization determine its responses to environmental pressures in such a way that it is only when a crisis is reached that most organizations change their fundamental structure. Kimberly (1987) introduces the idea of a biographical approach to understanding organizational change because of the strong impact of past, historical decisions on current structures and approaches. Kimberly and Rottman (1987) demonstrate the empirical validity of this approach.

An important part of this theorizing is that there are archetypes (Miller and Friesen, 1984) representing a limited number of configurations of structure, strategy and environment; there is *coherence*. Miller and Friesen (1984) showed that there were a limited number of such types. Because of this, they argue that a dominant organizational condition is momentum, the process whereby an organization exhibits incremental change which extends and elaborates its current archetype. There is also much inertia, as a result of which major change can only occur when there are strong and unavoidable pressures to change. Starbuck *et al.* (1978) demonstrate such organizational momentum and inertia in their work.

In a somewhat similar vein, Tushman and Romanelli (1985) suggest that organizations go through periods of convergence where organizational structures and systems become interlinked and coalesce into a mutually reinforcing whole. Change, other than incremental change, is made difficult because of this coherence and 'frame-breaking' change only occurs in response to, or in anticipation of, major environmental change. The emphasis on alternate periods of evolution and revolution suggests the importance of coherence, momentum and inertia.

The approach of Kimberly (1987) and Kimberly and Rottman (1987) also supports this particular position. They suggest that the initial decisions of a new organization about its domain, form of governance, organizational design and the nature of expertise required become templates for future decisions. That is, an archetype is set up which makes future strategic change difficult. The existing structural position, which is coherent, constrains change. Child and Smith (1987) and Pettigrew (1985, 1987) in their studies of Cadbury and ICI, respectively, also demonstrate the organizational coherence that comes from the historical templates and strategic recipes.

Greenwood and Hinings (1988) and Hinings and Greenwood (1988b) have taken this theorizing a stage further with the concept of a 'design archetype'. Following Ranson *et al.* (1980), they argue that 'organizational structures should be seen as embodiments of ideas, beliefs and values which constitute an overarching and prevailing "province of meaning" or "interpretive scheme"' (Greenwood and Hinings, 1988, p. 295). That is, organization structures are not purely instrumental, rational devices attuned to contextual pressures, but are endowed with meaning by their participants. It is these underpinning interpretive schemes that make major change difficult and reinforce processes of momentum and inertia because of their expression in organizational structures and systems. These values also lead to organizational coherence as structures and systems are 'tested' by organizational members for their relationship to valued meanings. A coherent set of values, structures and systems constitutes a design archetype.

There are a number of important theoretical propositions underlying these approaches. One is that organizations strive for coherence within a structural pattern which is valued by organizational members. A second proposition is that organizations are steered by this valued patterning on paths of inertia and momentum. A third proposition is that frame-breaking change involves moving from one coherent, archetypal position to a different coherent, archetypal position. A fourth proposition is that such change will only be set in motion when there are strong environmental forces in play. The need for a configurational, taxonomic approach is central to all of these propositions.

Structural Change and Institutional Specificity

In studying change, both Child (1988) and Pettigrew (1985, 1987) have argued for the importance of a more historical and substantive conceptualization of environment rather than current abstract images. As Child (1988) puts this problem of abstraction, 'in common with much organization theory, this accords a somewhat distant higher order status to environment rather than viewing it as a social domain of organizations themselves which regularly interact and share a common identity' (Child, 1988, p. 14). Child suggests that the more contextually sensitive notion of sector is important. Pettigrew (1985) develops a notion of contextual analysis which places strong emphasis on the particularities of institutional spheres. These positions suggest the need for more limited, institutionally based samples of organizations when studying change.

Organizational types are affected, not just by the nature of their general environment, but, more importantly, by their specific institutional environment. Institutional theory, starting with Selznick (1949) and firmly anchored in the work of Meyer and Rowan (1977) argues for an understanding of the particular *content* of externally imposed change and the processes of legitimation that accompany it. DiMaggio and Powell (1983) outline the three processes of normative, mimetic and coercive adoption which ensure the dissemination of institutionally legitimated values about organizations. These lead to coherent, homogenized organizational responses which have been empirically demonstrated by Galaskiewicz and Wasserman (1989) and Levitt and Nass (1989).

Hinings and Greenwood (1987) suggest that change between design types is subject to institutional definition. Such institutional limitations on organizational design arise because of 'what is defined as appropriate and inappropriate in domain, organizational form, and criteria for evaluation' (Hinings and Greenwood, 1988a). According to these authors, organizational design types may be specific to certain institutional settings. Similarly, Tolbert and Zucker (1983) show how a particular organizational design type, the 'reform' organization, was adopted by a large number of municipal governments as a response to institutional definition. That is, a particular way of organizing became legitimated because of its adoption and supposed effectiveness in a limited number of municipalities. As a result, it was widely adopted as the 'appropriate' organizational form.

All of these arguments lead to a conclusion that taxonomies aimed at understanding change should start from a basis of institutional or sectoral limitation (Child and Smith, 1987). This fits with the idea of middle-range theorizing, isolating key impact systems (and thus being aware of interorganizational differences), being able to deal with specific institutional effects and being sensitive to possible changes over time. It is also quite different from the initial thrust of the Aston Studies, which were aimed at producing highly general statements about organizations.

However, the literature we have reviewed *reinforces the importance of structural taxonomies*. On the one hand, the concept of coherence suggests that there are a limited range of organizational forms and that an understanding of the parts within an organization can be gained only by looking at the overall patterning. This is precisely the problem with which typological and taxonomic approaches to organizational structure and functioning have dealt. On the other hand, change is hypothesized to be difficult precisely because of the structural constraints that a current design type places on organizational movement. So 'understanding which archetype an organization is in, is crucial for understanding structural change and its difficulties' (Greenwood and Hinings, 1988, p. 294). The taxonomic starting point of an organization is vital as a major part of the analysis of how and why it will change or be stable. It also goes beyond the 'developmental sequence' idea of Pugh *et al.* (1969b) suggesting that being in a taxonomic class makes change difficult.

A taxonomic approach, relying on the holistic relationship between organizational elements, catches this much better than the more established contingency approach with its emphasis on individual dimensions of organization structure and their relationship to individual aspects of environments. The initial roots of much of this work lie in the typologizing of Burns and Stalker (1961) who showed the ability of organic organizations to change, as against the inertia and momentum of mechanistic organizations.

The creation of organizational classifications or taxonomies has been justified in organization theory in a variety of ways. On epistemological grounds, writers such as Haas *et al.* (1966) and McKelvey (1975, 1982) argue that to understand commonalties which exist across organizations a science of diversity must first be developed which would allow classification of organizations into homogeneous categories. McKelvey (1982), in particular, suggests that the identification of homogeneous groups is beneficial to organizational science in that solid findings about a narrower population are better than marginal findings of questionable generalizability to a broadly defined population. If this principle is repeated with other populations, scientific findings from one population can be replicated on other populations, thus building up a larger corpus of knowledge about generalizable principles of organizational function and process. Classification viewed in these terms is seen as an important and basic step in the conduct of scientific inquiry into organizations.

Other authors, having accepted the fundamental need for capturing organizational diversity in a systematic way, debate the utility of attempts at classification on the basis of what type of methodological approach is best used to capture this diversity. Carper and Snizek (1980) divide attempts to create organizational taxonomies into two categories: *theoretical works* are those which rely on deduction and heuristics and where data are gathered primarily in support of the theoretical categories being advanced; *empirical works* are those where data are analysed by using statistical techniques to actually produce taxonomies and not just to support existing conceptualizations.

Pinder and Moore (1979) suggest the use of taxonomies for generating theories of the middle range rather than seeking a unified, general set of theories of organizations. Universal theories sacrifice predictability at the detailed level of the single case in exchange for parsimony at the general level. In contrast, middle range theorizing attempts explanation and prediction for only a portion of organizational reality. Particular mid-range theories make different sets of assumptions, stress different parameters and prescribe unique applications (Pinder and Moore, 1979).

Structural Taxonomies and Organization Theory

A central thrust of organizational theory is the need to understand organizational diversity. The field has a research tradition rife with conceptual attempts at classifying organizations, as Carper and Snizek (1980) and McKelvey (1982) have documented. Greenwood and Hinings (1988, p. 296) suggest that classification has

> long been at the basis of organizational theorizing, from Weber's (1949) notions of charisma, traditionalism and bureaucracy, through Burns and Stalker's (1961) distinction between mechanistic and organic structures, to Mintzberg's (1979) distinctions between simple structure, machine bureaucracy, professional bureaucracy, divisionalized form and adhocracy.

The purpose of classification has been to abstract and more systematically explore what have been seen as key theoretical ideas, such as rationality, bureaucracy and control. Classes have been used to support a central proposition of organization theory that there are different kinds of organization and it is important to capture this diversity because it affects so many aspects of organizational functioning.

Greenwood and Hinings (1988) suggest that there are two very important principles underlying attempts to create classification systems. The first is the idea of *coherence* between organizational elements. Theorizing has suggested, and much empirical research has confirmed, that elements such as specialization, standardization and centralization correlate in understandable ways (Donaldson, 1986). This leads to the second principle, the *holistic* nature of organizational phenomena. It is the patterning of organizational elements that should be the focus of enquiry rather than 'bivariate or sharply circumscribed multivariate analysis' (Miller and Friesen, 1984, p. 15). We need to be careful not to atomize the essential interconnectedness of organizations.

In McKelvey's (1982) terms, producing a classification system such as a taxonomy involves both phyletics and phenetics. The phyletic method is an inductive one that hypothesizes classes a priori by tracing organizational lines of development. Phenetics involves the use of empirical taxonomic methods to test these classes deductively. The taxonomic concept allows the organizational researcher to test theoretical propositions made about organizational phenomena. As we have said, the Aston work was based on testing the bureaucratic type. Taxonomies, by identifying similarities and differences among organizational elements, can provide the basis for explanation, prediction and scientific understanding of a number of organizational phenomena (McKelvey, 1975). These include organizational structure, effectiveness, managerial behaviour, strategy and, our particular focus, organizational change.

It is mistaken and indeed impossible to carry out taxonomic work without a good theoretical basis for choosing the organizational elements on which to base a taxonomy. Organization theory has been particularly concerned with structural taxonomies with the usually implicit theoretical dynamic that

> the structure of an organization importantly influences the flow of information and the context and nature of human interactions. It channels collaboration, specifies modes of coordination, allocates power and responsibility, and prescribes levels of formality and complexity. (Miller, 1987, p. 7)

The rationale for the production of theoretically based, empirical taxonomies is the theorized impact of taxonomic position on a wide range of other organizational phenomena. This has been the classic issue of organization theory (the impact of structure on other aspects of organizational operation, process and performance). The historical emphasis on classification derives from the idea of generalizable, holistic, structural differences between classes of organization which are central to all aspects of organizational life. As a result, we argue that *organization theory should be less concerned with taxonomy, per se, than with taxonomies appropriate for dealing with particular issues.*

Our position is that theorizing about types, and the search for their existence in taxonomic classes, is important as the basis for a wide range of theorizing. The rationale for this search is the hypothesized impact of structural differences on aspects of organizational functioning. We have argued that the recent thrust of much theorizing about organizational change takes us back to the search for classes of organization and their empirical existence.

Issues in the Construction of Structural Taxonomies

The formation of taxonomies in the past has entailed certain commonalities. McKelvey (1975) notes that many early attempts were concerned with producing taxonomies from only one or two parameters (cf. Etzioni, 1961; Blau and Scott, 1962; Katz and Kahn, 1966; Perrow, 1967; Thompson, 1967). Pinder and Moore (1979) point out that much of the comparative approach to categorizing organizations (cf. Udy, 1965; Heydebrand, 1973) neglected *intraorganizational* differences by grouping whole organizations into categories on the basis of interorganizational similarities and differences stemming from parameters assumed to characterize the entire organization. The variables for the categorization scheme were treated as organization-wide attributes when in effect they often varied from subunit to subunit. Also Pinder and Moore (1979), as well as Miller and Friesen (1984), note that past classificatory attempts assume the constancy of variables over time, ignoring the possibility of these parameters varying across organizations at given points in time. Such classifications may not recognize the possibility of a given organization belonging to a specific category at one juncture but to another category at some later point in time, an observation which is very important when one is using a taxonomic approach in relation to change.

Of course, one of the major issues in constructing any taxonomy is that of the concepts to use as the basis for classification. McKelvey (1982) argues that large numbers of variables should be used covering as many aspects of organizational structure and functioning as possible. However, most proponents of the reawakening interest in organizational taxonomies have taken a rather different view. Hambrick (1984, p. 32) notes that such an approach would lead to 'extremely grand classes of organizations' and would thus 'prevent the taxonomy from providing real insight'. He suggests that the conceptual issue of what to classify should be solved by the use of variables with established theoretical merit for the organizations under study. Similarly, Carper and Snizek (1980), drawing on Haas *et al.* (1966), relate the advantages of taxonomy to their ability to elaborate on *existing* theory rather than to developing new, overarching classifications. That is, they argue for using taxonomies to refine hypotheses, as a means of examining the usefulness of existing typologies, and to serve as a basis for predicting other aspects of organizations.

We would argue that studies of organization structure tend to operate with a limited set of concepts, essentially centred around the structure of roles and responsibilities and decision making. Concepts which derive from these include specialization, standardization, formalization, centralization, complexity, differentiation and integration. There has been a wide measure of agreement about these as adequate descriptors of organizational design (Daft, 1988; Donaldson, 1986) and in order to build successfully on current theorizing any taxonomic approaches should be based on all, or a subset of them. A further issue in developing taxonomies is that of what organizations to use for the classification. Again, McKelvey (1982) takes the position of using as many organizations of as many different kinds as possible. Hambrick (1984), however, points out that work done so far in the social sciences using taxonomic methods typically yields only steady increments in cluster tightness and distinctiveness which suggests that, unlike the case of the biological sciences, strong natural clusters do not exist. Of course, this raises the whole issue of the best approach to comparative organizational research. Burns (1967) and Blau and Schoenherr (1971) argued for institutionally specific samples of organizations building up to ever wider kinds of organization. In the specific context of taxonomies, Pinder and Moore (1979) make the same suggestion. They argue that taxonomies should be used for generating theories of the middle range rather than seeking a unified general set of theories of organizations. Mid-range theories, they suggest, attempt to predict and explain only a subset of all organizational phenomena. Using a taxonomic approach to generate middle-range theories requires more limited sampling of organizations.

A further point of importance to the development of taxonomies in relation to change and design archetypes is the notion of primary or 'high impact' systems (Kanter, 1984). These are structural or systemic elements which particularly embody the values and meanings of either the existing design archetype or the one to which an organization is attempting to move. While organizations need to be approached holistically, some organizational elements are more subject to change than others because they are more peripheral to the particular design type. Changes within key systems or subunits may have an unduly profound affect on total organizational change. Which systems are crucial is likely to vary across organizational populations.

Following Kimberly (1987) and Hinings and Greenwood (1988b), such key impact systems will centre around past decisions and critical values, suggesting that any taxonomic approach has to have a good understanding of particular institutional settings. Also what is a key system may vary over time as organizations move from one archetype to another. Thus an important consideration for the development of taxonomies is the fact that classifications must be sensitive to the possibility of parameters not remaining constant over time, and therefore of organizations shifting between categories over time in relation to one or more parameters.

Taxonomies, Change and Voluntary Sports Organizations

In order to show the applicability of these arguments, illustrative material is provided from a continuing study of Canadian amateur sports organizations (for more information and analysis on this study, see Kikulis *et al.*, 1992; Kikulis *et al.*, 1995; Slack and Hinings, 1994; Hinings *et al.*, 1996). Prior to the early 1970s, this particular group of organizations operated with what has been termed a 'kitchen table' style of management (Rea, 1969). That is to say, for the most part they were literally operating off the kitchen table of their volunteer president. Their structural arrangements were characterized by 'undifferentiated task arrangements, low formalization of procedures and participative decision making' (Hinings and Slack, 1987, p. 186). Both policy and operational decisions were made by volunteers and these same people carried out the day-to-day operational tasks. The structural design of these organizations resembled what Mintzberg (1979) has called a simple structure.

As a design archetype, this form of organization was given meaning and coherence by a dominant set of values and beliefs that complemented these structural arrangements. Control was in the hands of volunteers who sought intrinsic rewards for themselves and the athletes who participated in their sport. Increased participation in the sport was the main focus and elite performances were to be a consequence of participation, not a specific goal. There was a coherence between structures and values, with this design type being the dominant way of organizing for the delivery of amateur sport (Hinings *et al.*, 1996).

In the early 1970s, a number of initiatives by the federal government provided initial pressures for these organizations to move away from this particular design archetype. These initiatives included the opportunity to acquire office space in a newly constructed National Sport and Recreation Center, the provision of clerical, computer and marketing support in the centre, and the opportunity for some organizations to receive financial support to hire professional staff to assist them with their day-to-day operations. The resultant organizational changes saw a shift in structural arrangements in the direction of a more professional and bureaucratic form.

This move has been increasingly legitimated by key individuals and institutions involved in the delivery of sport and it continued to develop incrementally through the 1970s. In 1983, further impetus was given to this type of organizational change with the introduction of a Quadrennial Planning Process by Sport Canada, a directorate of the federal government. This planning process was applied to all 'major' sports with the explicit aim of developing athletes for future international games. The planning process was externally driven and the allocation of federal government funds was tied to participation in the programme. Consequently, it had considerable potential to serve as a vehicle for introducing different goals, values, structures and systems in national amateur sport organizations.

As a result, there was a strong possibility that, rather than just a continued incremental movement towards a more professional and bureaucratic form, the planning system would become a means of producing a qualitative change in the speed of organizational change. In Tushman and Romanelli's (1985) terms, the introduction of the requirement of four-year planning was a major disturbance in the environment of these organizations and provided the potential for frame-breaking change. It is important to note that there is a considerable difference to be observed in organizations between a continuous process of incremental change and a relatively discontinuous event which may have the effect of a 'quantum change' (Miller and Friesen, 1984).

Table 7.1 summarizes the major difference between the two design archetypes in terms of basic categories of organizational structure and the Greenwood and Hinings (1988) conceptualization of interpretive schemes. It is important to note that we do not specifically address the question of the values and beliefs which underpin interpretive schemes in this chapter. Cunningham *et al.* (1987), Slack and

Table 7.1   The two design archetypes

		Archetype 1: kitchen table bureaucracy	Archetype 2: professional
1.	Interpretive scheme		
	A Domain	Recreation and participation	Elite, high-performance sport
	B Principles of organizing	Volunteer control	Professional, paid staff
	C Evaluation criteria	Athlete and volunteer satisfaction	Placings in international competition
2.	Organization design		
	A Structure of roles and responsibilities	Personally based task allocation; no formalization of activities	High differentiation of technical tasks; high specification
	B Decision making	Volunteer involvement in all aspects	High professional involvement; volunteers as policy makers

Thibault (1988) and Hinings *et al.* (1996) have shown the move to values underpinning the professional bureaucratic form for organizations in the Canadian sports system.

Central to recent theorizing about change is the idea that structural patterns are the outcome of archetypal beliefs. With the specification of the institutional values and their structural consequences, in an ideal typical form, a structural taxonomy can then be used to show how far a given set of organizations within that institutional sector exhibit archetypal status or are in a variety of transitional modes. In this chapter we are examining how a structurally based taxonomy may aid the development of theory concerning change. The set of Canadian national sports organizations has been under pressure to move from one dominant organizational design archetype, the simple structure, to another, the professional bureaucratic form. We are arguing that organizational taxonomies can provide a useful starting point for understanding the nature and process of change.

Given the theoretical position that the initial, starting structural position of an organization has an important impact on subsequent ability to change, it is first of all necessary to establish where a particular organization is. Also the emphases on coherence, momentum and inertia mean that this starting position has to be examined in a holistic way. This requires a taxonomic approach which is theoretically and institutionally informed. In the case of this particular study, it is theoretically informed through the concepts of archetype, bureaucratization and professionalization. It is institutionally informed by establishing what the particular archetypal pressures are for these organizations. Analysis thus links the specific issues in this sector with the general theoretical thrust of an important area of organizational analysis.

A taxonomic approach will then do a number of things. First, it will establish how the organizations are distributed between the given archetypes, showing how close some are to the desired, legitimated, professional bureaucracy and the degrees of distance that they all are from it. Also, working with the concept of archetype and having established what they are for this sector, one can see how far organizations exhibit coherence or how far they are in conceptually non-coherent positions. It allows one to have a measure of the distance that any particular organization has to travel in order to complete the desired changes. This is a key point, given the importance of the starting organizational structure in producing momentum rather than transformation. In examining a sample or population of organizations a taxonomy is necessary to understand the potential ease or difficulty of change, the existence of momentum or transformation.

For example, analysis of the 36 Canadian Olympic national sports organizations that were part of the planning process showed that, in

1984, the start point, only 10 organizations were anywhere close to the institutionally prescribed professional bureaucracy (Slack and Hinings, 1989); eight were closer to the proscribed archetype, the kitchen table or simple structure, and the remaining 18 were in a variety of transitional stages. This leads one to hypothesize that there would be considerable structural inertia in the system unless major transformational pressures and capacity were introduced (Hinings and Greenwood, 1988b). The role of the government directorate, Sport Canada, has been to push national sport organizations in the direction of the professional bureaucracy.

Second, a taxonomic approach which is informed by the idea of key impact systems can take the ideas of momentum and transformation a stage further by identifying whether the required archetypal changes are in such areas. While the twin processes of professionalization and bureaucratization are central to understanding the nature of change in this particular organizational population, the key impact system which epitomizes the meaning of the changes is decision making. The new interpretive schemes and organizational forms underscore the move from volunteer control to professional control. A taxonomy not only allows one to distribute organizations between the two archetypes, it also enables one to examine how far changes are required in key systems, as opposed to more peripheral ones.

Again, analysis of the Canadian national sports organizations shows that the organizational elements furthest away from the professional bureaucracy were those concerned with decision making. In 1984, most of these organizations had decision making in the hands of volunteers. By 1986, every one of them had increased the professional and bureaucratic component in their technical activities, but there was very little alteration in the patterns of decision making, something which limits a total organizational change in the prescribed direction.

Implications for Future Research

This chapter has argued that the real rationale of the continuing search for organizational taxonomies should be in their ability to explain other phenomena, such as the ability or inability of an organization to change, rather than as a search for enduring, definitive organizational 'species'. The latter are unlikely to occur. The study of macro-organizational change, in particular, has developed to a point with the concepts of convergence, holism, archetypes, inertia, momentum and transformation where a taxonomic approach is necessary. Organizations have to be categorized to establish the position at which they are beginning any process of change.

A structural taxonomy, when it is seen as an outcome of the pressures for coherence, inertia and momentum in relation to a design archetype, can then be used as an analytical description of the change state of an organizational sector. It allows the researcher to know the distribution of a set of organizations *in relation to* a desired change end point. It recognizes that there will be degrees of non-coherence, and hybrid organizations which will face change pressures and processes which are different from those in archetypically coherent situations. The illustrative material from Canadian amateur sports organizations shows not only that organizations face different change situations, but that the taxonomic approach allows a precise specification of the nature of that difference. This will allow much more precise hypotheses about the possibilities and difficulties of organizational transformations and transitions.

However, analysing such change involves a strong contextual understanding of the particular institutional setting. This enables the researcher to elaborate the particular organizational design archetypes which are extant and which are institutionally prescribed and proscribed (Hinings and Greenwood, 1988a). From this comes an understanding of the key systems that are expected to change and, through a taxonomy, establishing how far a particular set of organizations are in a position to undertake such change easily or not. That is, the pressures for inertia or transformation can be identified.

Working from a taxonomic starting point allows the researcher to identify the elements and pace of change. Hinings and Greenwood (1988b, 1989) have suggested that an important area of research is that of establishing the periodicity of change. The approach outlined in this chapter would allow a more accurate pinpointing of the sequencing of change in different organizational elements, the scope and depth of those changes, and the time periods over which such changes take place.

In summary, we have illustrated some of the arguments we are making for the use of taxonomies as a means to understand change through an initial, illustrative examination of a particular institutional set of organizations, namely, Canadian voluntary sports organizations and the pressures that have developed for them to move from one organizational design archetype to another. We suggest that the use of institutionally based taxonomies enables the researcher to better identify and chart processes of organizational change. Taxonomies based on theoretically relevant and institutionally specific concepts provide a method of categorizing organizations into types from which the mapping of changes can proceed.

References

Blau, P.M. and Schoenherr, R.A. (1971), *The Structure of Organizations*, New York: Basic Books.

Blau, P.M. and Scott, W.R. (1962), *Formal Organizations*, San Francisco: Chandler.

Burns, T. (1967), 'The comparative study of organizations', in V. Vroom (ed.), *Methods of Organizational Research*, Pittsburg: University of Pittsburg Press.

Burns, T. and Stalker, G.M. (1961), *The Management of Innovation*, London: Tavistock.

Carper, W.B. and Snizek, W.E. (1980), 'The nature and types of organizational taxonomies: an overview', *Academy of Management Review*, **5**, 65–75.

Child, J. (1988), 'On organizations in their sectors', *Organization Studies*, **9**, 13–19.

Child, J. and Smith, C. (1987), 'The context and process of organizational trans-formation: Cadbury Ltd in its sector', *Journal of Management Studies*, **24**, 565–94.

Cunningham, D., Slack, T. and Hinings, C.R. (1987), 'Changing design archetypes in amateur sport organizations', in T. Slack and C.R. Hinings (eds), *The Organiz-ation* and *Administration of Sport*, London, Ontario: Sports Dynamics Publishers, pp. 59–82.

Daft, R. (1988), *Organization Theory and Design*, New York: West Publishing.

DiMaggio, P. and Powell, W.W. (1983) 'The iron cage revised: institutional isomor-phism and collective rationality', *American Sociological Review*, **48**, pp. 147–60.

Donaldson, L. (1986), *In Defence of Organization Theory*, Cambridge: Cambridge University Press.

Etzioni, A. (1961), *A Comparative Analysis of Complex Organizations*, New York: Free Press.

Galaskiewicz, J. and Wasserman, S. (1989), 'Mimetic processes within an interorganizational field: an empirical test', *Administrative Science Quarterly*, **34**, 454–79.

Greenwood, R. and Hinings, C.R. (1988), 'Organizational design types, tracks and the dynamics of strategic change', *Organization Studies*, **9**, 293–316.

Haas, F.E., Hall, R.H. and Johnson, N.J. (1966), 'Toward an empirically derived taxonomy of organizations', in R.V. Bowers (ed.), *Studies on Behavior*, Athens: University of Georgia Press.

Hambrick, D.C. (1984), 'Taxonomic approaches to studying strategy: some concep-tual and methodological issues', *Journal of Management*, **10**, 27–41.

Heydebrand, W.V. (ed.) (1973), *Comparative Organizations*, Englewood Cliffs, NJ: Prentice-Hall.

Hickson, D.J., Pugh, D.S. and Pheysey, D.C. (1969), 'Operations technology and organization structure: an empirical reappraisal', *Administrative Science Quarterly*, **14**, 378–97.

Hinings, C.R. and Greenwood, R. (1988a), 'The normative prescription of organiz-ations', in L.G. Zucker (ed.), *Institutional Patterns and Organizations*, Cambridge, Mass.: Ballinger, pp. 53–70.

Hinings, C.R. and Greenwood, R. (1988b), *The Dynamics of Strategic Change*, Oxford: Blackwell.

Hinings, C.R. and Greenwood, R. (1989), 'Strategic Change Since the Dark Ages', unpublished paper, University of Alberta.

Hinings, C.R. and Slack, T. (1987), 'The dynamics of quadrennial plan implementa-tion in national sport organizations', in T. Slack and C.R. Hinings (eds), *The Organization and Administration of Sport*, London, Ontario: Sports Dynamics Pub-lishers.

Hinings, C.R., Pugh, D.S., Hickson, D.J. and Turner, C. (1967), 'An approach to the study of bureaucracy', *Sociology*, **1**, 61–72.

Hinings, C.R., Thibault, L., Slack, T. and Kikulis, L. (1996), 'Values and organizational structure', *Human Relations*, **49**, 885–916.

Kanter, R. (1984), 'Managing transitions in organizational culture: the case of participative management at Honeywell', in J.R. Kimberly and R.E. Quinn (eds), *Managing Organizational Transitions*, Homewood, Ill.: Richard D. Irwin.

Katz, D. and Kahn, R.L. (1966), *The Social Psychology of Organizations*, New York: Wiley.

Kikulis, L., Slack, T. and Hinings, C.R. (1992), 'Institutionally specific design archetypes: a framework for understanding change in national sport organizations', *Internationl Review for the Sociology of Sport*, **27**, 343–70.

Kikulis, L., Slack, T. and Hinings, C.R. (1995), 'Sector specific patterns of organizational design change', *Journal of Management Studies*, **32**, 67–100.

Kimberly, J.R. (1987), 'The study of organization: toward a biographical perspective', in J.W. Lorsch (ed.), *Handbook of Organizational Behavior*, Englewood Cliffs, NJ: Prentice-Hall.

Kimberly J.R. and Quinn, R. (eds) (1984), *Managing Organizational Transitions*, Homewood, Ill.: Richard D. Irwin.

Kimberly, J.R. and Rottman, D. (1987), 'Organization and effectiveness: a biographical approach', *Journal of Management Studies*, **24**, 595–621.

Levitt, B. and Nass, C. (1989), 'The line or the garbage can: institutional constraints on decision making in the technical core of college-text publishers', *Administrative Science Quarterly*, **34**, 190–207.

McKelvey, B. (1975), 'Guidelines for the empirical classification of organizations', *Administrative Science Quarterly*, **20**, 509–25.

McKelvey, B. (1982), *Organizational Systematics*, Berkeley: University of California Press.

Meyer, A.D., Tsui, A. and Hinings, C.R. (1993), 'Configurational approaches to organizational analysis', *Academy of Management Journal*, **36**, 1175–95.

Meyer, J.W. and Rowan B. (1977), 'Institutionalized organizations: formal structure as myth and ceremony', *American Journal of Sociology*, **83**, 340–63.

Miles, R. and Snow, C. (1978), *Organizational Strategy, Structure and Process*, New York: McGraw-Hill.

Miller, D. (1987), 'Strategy making and structure: analysis and implications for performance', *Academy of Management Journal*, **30**, 7–32.

Miller, D. and Friesen, P. (1984), *Organizations: A Quantum View*, Englewood Cliffs, NJ: Prentice-Hall.

Mintzberg, H. (1979), *The Structuring of Organizations*, Englewood Cliffs, NJ: Prentice-Hall.

Perrow, C. (1967), 'A framework for the comparative analysis of organizations', *American Sociological Review*, **32**, 194–208.

Pettigrew, A. (1985), *The Awakening Giant*, Oxford: Basil Blackwell.

Pettigrew, A. (1987), 'Context and action in the transformation of the firm', *Journal of Management Studies*, **24**, 649–70.

Pinder, C.C. and Moore, L.F. (1979), 'The resurrection of taxonomy to aid the development of middle range theories of organizational behavior', *Administrative Science Quarterly*, **24**, 99–118.

Pugh, D.S., Hickson, D.J. and Hinings, C.R. (1969a), 'The context of organization structures', *Administrative Science Quarterly*, **14**, 47–61.

Pugh, D.S., Hickson, D.J. and Hinings, C.R. (1969b), 'An empirical taxonomy of work organizations', *Administrative Science Quarterly*, **14**, 115–26.

Pugh, D.S., Hickson, D.J., Hinings, C.R. and Turner, C. (1968), 'Dimensions of organization structure', *Administrative Science Quarterly*, **13**, 65–105.

Pugh, D.S., Hickson, D.J., Hinings, C.R., Macdonald, K., Turner, C. and Lupton, T.

(1963), 'A conceptual scheme for organizational analysis', *Administrative Science Quarterly*, **8**, 289–515.

Ranson, S., Hinings, C.R. and Greenwood, R. (1980), 'The structuring of organizational structures', *Administrative Science Quarterly*, **25**, 1–17.

Rea, H. (1969), *The Report of the Task Force on Sports for Canadians*, Ottawa: Queens Printers.

Selznick, P. (1949), *TVA and the Grass Roots*, Berkeley: University of California Press.

Slack, T. and Hinings, C.R. (1989), 'A taxonomic approach to identifying organizational design', paper presented at the European Group for Organization Studies, West Berlin, July.

Slack, T. and Hinings, C.R. (1994), 'Institutional pressures and isomorphic changes: an empirical test', *Organizational Studies*, **15**, 803–27.

Slack, T. and Thibault, L. (1988), 'Values and beliefs: their role in the structuring of national sport organizations', *Arena Review*, **12**, 140–55.

Starbuck, W.H., Greve, A. and Hedberg, B. (1978), 'Responding to crises', *Journal of Business Administration*, **9**, 111–37.

Thompson, J.D. (1967), *Organizations in Action*, New York: McGraw-Hill.

Tichy, N. (1983), *Managing Strategic Change: Technical, Political and Cultural Dynamics*, New York: Wiley-Interscience.

Tolbert, P. and Zucker, L. (1983), 'Institutional sources of change in the formal structure of organization: the diffusion of civil service reform, 1800–1935', *Administrative Science Quarterly*, **28**, 22–39.

Tushman, M.L. and Romanelli, E. (1985), 'Organizational evolution: a metamorphic model of inertia and reorientation', in B.M. Staw and L.L Cummings (eds), *Research in Organizational Behavior*, Greenwich, Conn: JAI Press.

Udy, S.H. (1965), 'The comparative analysis of organizations', in J.G. March (ed.), *Handbook of Organizations*, Chicago: Rand McNally, pp. 678–709.

Weber, M. (1949), *The Theory of Economic and Social Organization*, Glencoe, Ill: The Free Press.

Zucker, L. (1987), 'Normal change or risky business: institutional effects of the "hazard" of change in hospital organizations, 1959–1979', *Journal of Management Studies*, **24**, 671–700.

8 The 'Why?' and 'How?' of Organization Design

TOM LUPTON

Introduction

In this short chapter, the main problem addressed is that of translating academic work in organization design into procedures for diagnosis and decision for use by those concerned with organizational effectiveness, mainly senior managers.

The chapter begins with a justification for focusing on one aspect of organization – structure – to the partial, but not complete, exclusion of others. Then follows a general discussion of the main issue in structural design (recognized by academics and practitioners alike) – to divide labour and to coordinate. At one level of abstraction, human organizations (like human beings) have many characteristics in common, and these are briefly touched upon. However, it is the differences that matter at the practical level. Differences in structure arise from differences in markets for products and services, differences in technology, even differences in political and economic philosophy. It is at this level that our presentation is located. Some selected examples from the author's experience as consultant/researcher and academic manager illustrate the consequences of inappropriate structures and show how solutions may be sought. The question posed and the answers sought are similar for both scholars and managers. However, the *process* of finding answers and learning from them are different and disconnected. The result is that a clear, usable procedure for structural design has not, as yet, emerged. A proposal for such a procedure is presented. Finally, there is a discussion of current ideas and controversies, touching on the organizational design issues arising from the global market, the rise of the mega-corporation, and the astonishing spread of electronic information transmission. It is argued that, in essence, the issues of organization design remain the same.

Why Structure?

In his book, *Organisations*, Child (1984) writes that 'Structure, however well designed, can only be expected to make a limited, but none-the-less significant contribution to organisational effectiveness.' Possible reasons for the limitations of structure include lack of will, skill and competence amongst those who occupy specialist roles or have responsibilities for coordination. Child also mentions the climate of morale and the power games that are played in organizations. Structure, he claims, cannot by itself resolve the behavioural distortions arising from organizational politics, personal ambition and management style, nor can it compensate for lack of competence or motivation. Structures may be the *outcome* of personal ambition and power seeking rather than of a rational analysis relating strategy and structure. If, for this or other reasons, employees perceive organization strategies as being at odds with their personal or specialist aims and ambitions, the structure may come to be regarded as an instrument of coercion and control, with the result of diminishing the will to cooperate. Finally, national and organization cultures may well influence the way that management structures and styles are perceived, for example as authoritarian, democratic, participative and so on.

However, despite the limitations cited by Child, the importance of finding appropriate designs of organization structures for effectiveness cannot be in serious doubt, as witness the considerable academic and popular output on the subject. The problem of structural design is seen as one of arriving at a pattern of specialization that is appropriate to the tasks faced by organizations in relating to their environment and in utilizing their technology and then superimposing structures and processes of coordination to offset the tendencies to disintegration inherent in specialist structures.

Much is known, but comparatively little is applied, in the sense that it is not easy for those for whom structural designs might be, or become, a practical problem – senior managers, for example – to find 'how to do it' procedures for diagnosing structural shortcomings and arriving at designs for structures of specialization, and structures and processes of coordination, that are appropriate in particular situations. Child (1984), Mintzberg (1983), Lawrence and Lorsch (1967) and Woodward (1965) give useful ideas that could be used, and Pugh (1979) has given some hints on the diagnosis of defects in structures and processes of coordination. My intention in this chapter is to attempt to pull together the ideas, the hints and the prescriptions, and develop a step-by-step procedure that can be used by the practitioner for diagnosis and decision.

Several years ago, working with members of executive courses at the Manchester Business School, I attempted to devise a systematic practical procedure for organization design, drawing on the litera-ture and my own research and consulting experience. However, the ideas and procedures in it remained undeveloped. The invitation to write this chapter, the existence of work done since I wrote the paper, and ideas emerging from my current research on transnational or-ganizations investing in Central Europe led me to look out my notes with improvement in mind.

The remainder of this chapter sets out a systematic, practical and rigorous procedure for designing organizational structures. For the manager, the design of the structure of his or her organization, or the part of it for which he or she is responsible, is of little interest until some difficulty arises which he or she suspects may be due to faults in the structure. Pugh (1979) has usefully defined six warning signs of structural defects relating to integration. These are (as I sum-marize them):

1   persistent conflict between departments;
2   proliferation of committees that obscure rather than resolve the issue of integration;
3   overloading of top management;
4   paperwork designed to integrate becomes 'red tape' ritual;
5   empire-building by coordinators – blocking more transparent in-tegrative devices;
6   complaints of clients, customers and so on who receive conflict-ing and confusing messages.

The issue of integration and coordination arises, of course, because organizations, as they are created or as they evolve, break up into specialized subunits, each with a tendency to pursue its own subgoals. As Mintzberg (1983) succinctly puts it:

> Every organized human activity ... gives rise to two fundamental and opposing requirements: the division of labour into various tasks to be performed and co-ordination of these tasks to be accomplished. The structure of an organization can be defined simply as the sum total of the ways in which labour is divided into distinct tasks and then co-ordination is achieved amongst those tasks.

Pugh (1979) points to two kinds of possible inadequacies in the operation of integrative devices: first, the structural design is faulty and, second, while the design may be well-suited for the purpose of integration, the purposes are subverted by groups and individuals. If, however, one examines the specialization aspect of Mintzberg's opposing requirements, it may well be that it is undue fragmentation of specialized departments or units which places too heavy a burden on the designed structural mechanisms and the social processes which activate them. The warning signals might lead one to investigate the division of labour as a first step.

Given these general and basic indicators of the design issues arising from the process of seeking an accommodation between fragmentation and integration, especially in situations where the imperatives for specialization are changing, it should be possible to develop a systematic design procedure to arrive at a satisfactory resolution of the conflict between the opposing forces. This is what I now attempt to do, building on the work already cited and referring generally to the sociotechnical systems ideas of the Tavistock researchers.

Characteristics of Organizations

What are the characteristics that all organizations share? They all procure inputs from an environment that includes other organizations. For example, a manufacturing firm buys raw materials and components from supplier organizations. It has relationships with banks to finance these purchases and to fund capital investment and work in progress. It obtains know-how from the environment of scientific and technical knowledge, and it engages human competences in the labour market. Every organization works on the inputs to transform them into outputs. Our manufacturing firm will have plant and machinery, and procedures for seeing that products are produced by using and maintaining the plant and machinery: procedures for planning, scheduling and monitoring, for example.

Organizations also have arrangements for getting products and services to consumers, who could be other organizations or individuals. It is also necessary, of course, to find out what present or potential users of outputs want. Finally, organizations are influenced by governments and public opinion. The law insists, for example, on minimum levels of safety and product quality; it specifies the conditions under which people may be dismissed and effluent disposed of. Public opinion can cause organizations to control atmospheric pollution, or to discontinue or modify the manufacture of certain products. We may call this the social/political context in which organizations work. For publicly owned organizations, this can be an especially potent influence.

Inputs and the costs of transforming them have to be paid for by income generated by the disposal of outputs. If they are not, the organization will not survive, or will have to be subsidized – as universities generally are. Although at one level of analysis organizations have common characteristics, they may differ from each other in the nature of their inputs, their transformation processes and their outputs, in their socio/political contexts and in their relations with financial institutions. They may also differ in size and in the degree to which their operations are geographically spread. This is why a structure appropriate to one organization may be inappropriate for another, and why a structure appropriate at one period in the history of an organization may be inappropriate at another.

The analysis of current structures of specialization and integration, and the measurement and the judgement of their appropriateness in a particular organization, begins by separating analytically (1) those activities which are specialized – in the sense that it is possible to recognize boundaries which mark them off from other specialist units, such as, for example, boundaries of expertise and space; (2) those which are specialized in the above sense, but also include an integrative component; and (3) those units whose sole function is integrative.

The reason for these distinctions rests on a belief that the specialisms under (1) above are prior to those under (2) and (3), in the sense that the need for integrative structures and processes arises logically from the process of structural fragmentation which takes place as the result of the need to adjust to environmental pressures and the exigencies of organizing work flow from inputs to outputs. The integrative structures may be put in place at the same time as specialized subunits are created – for example, when an experienced senior manager sketches on the back of an envelope a structural design for a greenfield site organization. This analytical sequence allows one in a particular case to address several questions.

1   Is the *pattern* or structure of specialization that exists an appropriate response to the pressures from environment and from the exigencies arising from the need to organize the sequences from inputs to outputs?
2   Is the *depth* of specialization that exists in each specialization too deep, too superficial or exactly right?
3   What is the cost and what are the other consequences of inappropriate structures of specialization or inappropriate depth of specialization?
4   Is the structure and depth of specialization that exists appropriate or inappropriate in the sense that they postulate costly structures and processes of integration?
5   What would be the cost of modifying a structure already identified as appropriate to reduce the costs of integration?
6   What needs to be done to make sure that, when environments, products and technology change, appropriate changes are made to structures of specialization and structures of integration?

Figure 8.1 below is a simple example of a typical structure of specialisms and coordinating devices in a manufacturing unit.

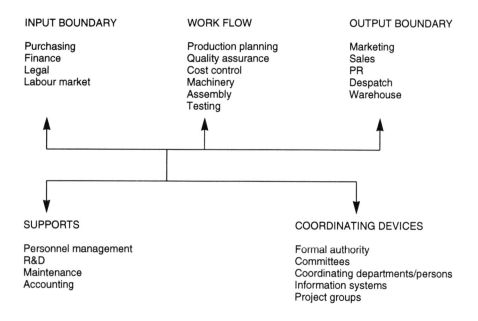

INPUT BOUNDARY

Purchasing
Finance
Legal
Labour market

WORK FLOW

Production planning
Quality assurance
Cost control
Machinery
Assembly
Testing

OUTPUT BOUNDARY

Marketing
Sales
PR
Despatch
Warehouse

SUPPORTS

Personnel management
R&D
Maintenance
Accounting

COORDINATING DEVICES

Formal authority
Committees
Coordinating departments/persons
Information systems
Project groups

Figure 8.1   Simplified example showing the structure of specialisms and coordinating devices in a manufacturing unit

The specialisms we have just listed are related to function, such as accounting, or to product, such as market/selling. Many large organizations, for example transnational companies such as Unilever, ICI, ABB and IBM, have manufacturing facilities or sales organizations in many locations in their country of origin and also in other countries. A very significant part of the environment of the subsidiaries is the parent company. In these cases, we might regard the activity of relating to the parent as one specialized activity, amongst many, of the subsidiary. From the point of view of the parent company, each unit becomes specialized by location, even though its products and services might be disposed of by a central or regional marketing and sales organization.

The specialized activities of a hospital, when compared with a manufacturing unit, are even more numerous. A superficial count gives five at the input area of the boundary, for example registration and liaison with general practitioners. In the work flow there are numerous medical specialisms, such as neurology, cardiology and psychiatry. Medical support systems include nursing, physiotherapy, radiology and so on. There are more general support specialisms such as portering, patient records, administrative and secretarial. Outputs include patient aftercare. My own quick count gives some 40 specialisms. The reader is invited to make his or her own list and to conjecture what may be the integrative structures and processes that might bind them together in pursuit of the primary tasks of the organization.

Fragmentation and Integration: Some Examples

Three examples from my experience as consultant/action researcher may be used to illustrate the relationship between requisite structure and integration. The first of these refers to events several years ago in a sizeable city in the north of England. As consultant and facilitator, I was personally involved in some of these events. The city (like many others in Britain) had an ageing population. The situation was aggravated by the exit of young people to seek employment as the city's traditional industries went into decline. The strain on the city's resources for the care of its elderly people was increasing and the organization of care was proving inadequate to the task.

Some of the services were provided by town hall departments, for example home help, housing, 'meals-on-wheels' and warden services. Others were provided by hospital doctors, general practitioners, visiting nurses and voluntary agencies such as Age Concern. The result of this weakly coordinated proliferation of agencies was the appearance of gaps in provision, complaints, conflict and recrimination. Concerned by this state of affairs, three influential people – a senior town hall official, the chairman of the local health authority and the head of nursing services at the local hospital – sought my advice. Arising from our discussions, representatives of the agencies involved and some local councillors were invited to a four-day retreat in a residential training centre on the outskirts of the town.

Using a process I had earlier proposed (Lupton and Tanner, 1987) the issues were exposed and addressed, conflicts brought into the open and solutions sought to problems commonly agreed to exist. Finally, a programme for change was agreed. First, there was a need for a common database, giving details of the number of elderly people, their ages, their location, their ethnic identity, state of health and

so on. The creation of this database and the procedures for its continual updating became a project for a group of second-year MBA
students at a local business school. Given this base, the second step
(the task of a small group selected from those who had attended the
retreat) was to divide the city into 'areas of provision' where all the
services available could be concentrated and coordinated. One result
(as I saw it) was that common concern for high-quality care overrode
specialist interests and created the will to act appropriately to provide it. This could be called 'integration by mutual concern', although
there was also, significantly, a major structural shift towards 'integration by task location'. The new structure resembled the multi-discipline
project teams that are used as integrative devices in complex manufacturing organizations, and to some extent it was, and is, a matrix of
tasks and specialisms.

My second example comes from a large, long-established commercial bank with international connections, faced by new competitive
pressures consequent on deregulation raising doubts on the ability of
the bank's structures and processes to meet the new challenges. Processes similar to those used in the first case involved senior managers
heading specialist departments. Their recommendations for change
and for the ordering of priorities for change were discussed with the
chief executive and the board of directors and were also tested, in the
survey feedback mode, amongst junior managers and supervisors.

In this case, the proposals for change were less concerned with the
structures of specialization, although these were not ignored. Indeed,
given the advent of new technologies, changes in work flow specialization were already under way. However, the main concern was
with the processes of integration. Traditionally, coordination by centralized formal authority, often fragmented in its operation by the
influence of powerful functional specialists at board level, had been
the only formally recognized and sanctioned process of coordination. At lower levels of management, this showed as a culture of fear
of taking initiatives.

The recommended priorities were to move towards a common
bank culture based on flexibility, grass-roots participation and soon
overriding and weakening the strong, and often conflicting and ster-
eotypical, subcultures of the operating divisions and functional
departments. The small organizational development unit reporting
directly to the chief executive was strengthened to become the driving force behind the changes. This is a case of integration driven
mainly, but not entirely, by culture change.

The third example is a general one, relating to the organization of
university business schools. The basic question of requisite specialization is difficult to answer in this case. The remark that a university
business school is 'a loose federation of self-starters' is certainly apt.

In fact, the discipline groups, such as operations management, marketing, finance and accounting, and behavioural science are themselves loose federations of subspecialists whose main reference points are subspecialists in other universities. Most, but not all, business schools have a primary grouping of discipline departments with a senior specialist at the head.

Business schools also put on courses, seminars and similar activities, all or most of which call on all or most of the discipline specialists. These activities must bring in money in fees or subventions to cover, or partially cover, the costs involved in designing, manning and running them. Usually, one course, or a group of similar short ones, will have a director. The director may be an academic specialist with another hat on, or an administrator. The director could be made responsible for publicizing the course(s), for recruiting participants and for designing the timetable, although the discipline specialists will certainly influence that.

There are, then, two specialist structures, specialization by discipline and specialization by product. The need to match the available time of discipline specialists with the timetables of the courses is a main integrative process. The discipline specialists will have certainly negotiated with the dean or director a teaching load of X hours per annual teaching session, based on the equation $x + y + z = b$, where y is time for research and publishing and z is time for consultancy, b is a notional annual working load which includes an allowance for committee attendance, administration and so on. Where there are heads of discipline departments they will be responsible for negotiating amongst themselves and with the course director the allocation of discipline specialists to courses, the outcome of which may sometimes be to distort the (less powerful) course director's search for marketable balanced designs and quality inputs.

It may be imagined that coordination could be achieved by the authority of the dean or director in these mostly small organizations via a chain of command but, as some unwary new directors have discovered in such collegiate institutions, formal command is resented and opposed. More likely there are no chains, only mazes of relationships replete with dead ends. Leadership is largely a question of delicate politicking.

The requirement for structural specialization is not too difficult to perceive, both between and inside the two specialist structures, although there could and can be variations. The requirement for integration is by nature a bottom-up matter, given the heavy professional biases, external affiliations and necessary academic freedoms of the many professional specialists in a business school. It is necessary, then, to engender a common concern as in the first case, that is the care of the elderly, and a common understanding of the *raison d'être* of the institution and the conditions for its survival and development. This, although difficult, can be achieved by structural arrangements and social processes, where the purposes of the various specialized individuals and department are reconciled with the purposes of the institution, in the formulation of which they are, themselves, involved.

Issues from the Practitioner Perspective

We can now recall the questions raised earlier, which must be answered in the search for what we may define as 'requisite specialization' and 'requisite integration'.

1 Given the need for a structured response to the environment and to organize the flow of work from inputs to outputs, are the structures of specialization optimal in the sense that resources are not wasted?
2 Following from that, having decided on the division of labour into specialisms, other questions arise:
   (a) Is the function of each of the specialized departments appropriately defined?
   (b) Are the specialists in each specialized department appropriately organized?
   (c) Is the depth of specialized knowledge and skill
      (i)   too profound (wasted resource),
      (ii)   too shallow (inefficiency),
      (iii) satisfactorily appropriate to the task?

Given that the requisite structure of specialization has been defined, it is then necessary to determine which of the specialized departments/locations need to be integrated, and to what extent; and what structures and processes would be appropriate in response to the first question? These are practical questions. They have been addressed, as we have seen, but mostly in an abstract way by academic researchers. The main, but not exclusive, emphasis of the academics is on the search for generalized, empirically testable knowledge. A less pressing concern is the way managers and employees might go about answering the questions posed above. It is apparent that academic researchers and managers frame problems differently and follow different procedures for solving them. It is, perhaps, worth exploring briefly the reasons and outcomes of this difference.

The university-based researcher begins by scanning the state of knowledge in his discipline to find a puzzle yet awaiting a solution. For example, in the early 1960s, Derek Pugh saw the lack of a rigorous general method of organizational analysis capable of describing and comparing organizations as diverse as hospitals and engineering companies. Having identified the gap in knowledge, it was necessary to elaborate the method and, guided by it, to collect data that would begin to fill the gap – and to publish so that the results of the conceptual thinking, the measurements and data, would be exposed to the plaudits and/or criticisms of specialists in the field. There are two outputs from work of this kind. First, although a gap is partly filled, the need for further work is signalled, perhaps to elaborate conceptual schemes, to devise new measures and new tests of the robustness of the research processes and their outputs. This starts the process all over again, either by the original researcher, or by others. The cycle is continuous and eternal. The second output has to do with the recognition of the researcher/writer's reputation in the discipline, and his or her career prospects in academia.

By contrast, the manager starts the process of defining a problem and a method of problem solving, usually by being faced with a practical difficulty demanding urgent attention. The case of the care of the elderly in a northern town described above illustrates this well. The next stage in time and in logic is to find out what kind of problem arises from the difficulty – is it a problem of structure, of personal cussedness, of misunderstanding? Is it a technical problem, a problem of misused resources? Or a combination of these and others? It is possible that the question 'What is and where is the problem?' cannot be answered without reference to other employees. Pressure of time and cost will sometimes lead to faulty diagnosis and, in consequence, a costly solution to the wrong problem and/or the persistence of the original difficulty or another one. Once a problem *has* been identified, relevant information can be collected, decisions taken and followed by action. In the best case, this could be a process of organizational learning, where competence in overcoming difficulties is enhanced by the analysis of successful and unsuccessful problem definition and resolution. In the worst case, the reasons for success or otherwise remain unanalysed. Relief that the difficulty has passed is more likely and failure may be followed by recrimination rather than analysis.

Business school teachers faced with senior managers whose experience is deeply rooted in practice quickly learn that the overlap between the two problem-solving cycles is anything but obvious. For this reason, there is no clear answer in a particular case to the managers' problems of diagnosis, decision and action. It is perfectly true, of course, and a comfort to the academic worker, that a close and continuous study of academic research outputs and controversies would be very helpful to managers. However, managers, it seems, are not generally inclined towards this kind of pursuit, even if time were available. More likely, they will be influenced by popular interpretations and current fashions and the boiled-down inputs of short courses.

Problems and the Search for Solutions

We now enter the manager's cycle at the stage where his or her difficulty has been diagnosed as a problem of structure. The difficulty could be a boundary dispute between two specialist departments, which could signal either that the boundary may be badly drawn *or* that, although the boundaries may be well-drawn but inherently conflict-prone, the coordinating structures and processes are inadequate to the task of mediation. A classic case of this is reported by Sykes and Bates (1962) where a conflict between sales and production was resolved by a structural method of mediation. However, our task here is not the identification and resolution of a particular difficulty, but to propose a method for comparing the existing structure of an organization with the *requisite* structure and to ascertain what integrative structures and processes are necessary to 'glue' the separate parts together so that the whole works in as reasonable a harmony as is possible in pursuit of success and survival in the environment.

If we consider a small company with one product, serving one customer – a supplier of quality fasteners to a car assembly plant and employing, say, 20 machine operators and packers on the production line –the pattern of requisite specialization is easy to map.

1   A person – or small department – to be in contact with the customers' purchasing department.
2   A person or persons buying the materials out of which the fasteners are made.
3   A production department transforming the materials into fasteners to meet the customers' requirements as to quality, quantity and delivery.
4   A person or department keeping accounts – preparing paying of wages and salaries.
5   A maintenance fitter (or fitters) servicing the building and the machines.

In this simple example we can say that the requirements for coordination between the specialism in contact with the customer (call it 'sales') and the production department will be great. Coordination between purchasing and sales will also be necessary, but perhaps not so continuous. The maintenance service needs to coordinate with production, but not so much with sales and purchasing. There is a need for coordination of all departments with accounts.

In such a small organization of low complexity of product markets and technology, where all employees are under one roof, coordination can be effectively done via personal contact across boundaries or by the personal authority of the owner/manager. This is a case of low fragmentation, simple integration. We can see from this example the following possibilities.

1   In the search for requisite specialization there are (limited) choices – for example, the maintenance function may be placed with good reason inside the boundary of the production specialism – with possible displacement of conflict, for example when the office roof is leaking and a machine breaks down at the same time.
2   A score could be allocated to 'need for coordination' and, if a particular pattern of specialization scores high on need and another low, the latter alternative should be adopted because it reduces the necessity of allocating resources to the task of coordination.
3   In a small organization with a simple technology producing a simple product for a single customer under a single roof given the requisite structure (the one scoring lowest on coordination need), the coordination can be done through personal contact and, in case of difficulty, in interpersonal resolution of conflict by the owner/manager.

These principles of search for requisite structure and the identification of the need for co-ordination can readily be transferred to much more complex organizations. Child (1984) demonstrates a survey method, adapted from a study of an airline, where respondents were asked to allocate a score to the state of relationships between seven operating units on a scale ranging from 1 (sound relationships) to 7 (could not be worse), plus 8 (relations not required) (see Figure 8.2).

This exercise was based on the existing structure of specialisms: the higher the score up to 7, the more perceived problems of coordination. However, the pattern of scoring in the matrix suggests that a search could be made for alternatives with less overall coordination need; the high score, for example, between 'in-flight services' and 'flight operations' could have arisen because in-flight services were part of the marketing specialism and pilot scheduling part of flight operations, suggesting that consideration might be given to reallocation of specialisms within existing boundaries, or a redrawing of boundaries.

The first part of our procedure, then, is the search for the requisite structure of specialized activities, being defined, other things being

Scoring of relationships
Relations between these two units are:
1. Sound – full unity of effort is achieved
2. Almost full unity
3. Somewhat better than average relations
4. Average – sound enough to get by, even though there are many problems of achieving joint efforts
5. Somewhat of a breakdown in relations
6. Almost complete breakdown in relations
7. Couldn't be worse – bad relations – serious problems exist which are not being solved
8. Relations are not required

Matrix of relations between operating units

	Sales	Airport services	In-flight services	Scheduling adjustments	Operational control	Flight operations	Maintenance	Relations between regional divisions
Airport services	3							
In-flight services	4	3						
Scheduling adjustments	3	4	2					
Operational control	3	2	2	1				
Flight operations	3	3	6*	1	1			
Maintenance	8	2	4	2	1	2		
Regional divisions/offices	2	2	3	2	1	2	2	1

*   In-flight services scheduling is part of marketing while pilot scheduling is part of flight operations, which creates frequent conflicts between two groups.

Figure 8.2   Example of a method to assess perceptions of integration within an organization

equal, as the structure predicating the minimum allocation of resources to coordinating. This search can be aided by the kind of survey of employees' perceptions in the survey cited by Child. The comparison of the existing pattern and the requisite pattern indicates where changes should be considered. It might also suggest that the tasks and objectives of the organization may have changed, leaving a misfit between primary tasks and organization structure.

When the requisite structure has been identified, so also has the extent of the need for coordination, which can be measured in a similar way, that is, on a scale as shown in Figure 8.3, which indicates

Example: A residential university business school			Products			Support units							
			1	2	3	A	B	C	D	E			
			MBA	Doctoral programme	Short courses	Library	Disciplines	Computer services	Hotel catering	Reception	Totals	Need quotient	
Products	1	x Coordination req.^{t}	▨	5	2	9	10	8	3	8	45	65	.46
		y Difficulty of coord.^{n}	▨	2	1	3	8	4	1	1	20	140	
	2	x	5	▨	0	10	9	3	3	3	33	44	.31
		y	2	▨	0	2	4	1	1	1	11	140	
	3	x	4		▨								
		y	5		▨								
Supprt units	A	x				▨							
		y				▨							
	B	x					▨						
		y					▨						
	C	x						▨					
		y						▨					
	D	x							▨				
		y							▨				
	E	x								▨			
		y								▨			

Notes:
1 X scores for coordination requirement: 0 = no requirement, 10 = very high requirement. Y scroes for difficulty of coordination: 0 = no problems, 10 = very difficult.
2 Coordination need quotient, $\dfrac{X+Y}{\text{Possible total score}}$, indicates degree of attention needed for coordination structures and processes.
3 The scores in each box indicate both need and difficulty of coordination between pairs of specialized units.
4 This matrix does not include all possible specialisms and leaves out relationships with the university, local community, professional groups and other environmental entities.

Figure 8.3   Measuring coordination requirement

need by the scores between pairs. Summing these scores gives an indication of organization complexity of, for example, markets, products, technology, processes, locations and environmental influences. With increasing complexity, not only does the need for coordination increase, but the types of coordinating structures and processes increase also. To measure the coordination need and to identify the 'connection' between degrees of complexity and types of coordination is the second part of our procedure.

By following the two stages of our procedure, we are able (1) to delineate the structures of specialized units already existing and also the problems of coordinating; (2) to establish the requisite patterns of specialization; and (3) to note structural/cultural differences that require special attention where coordination need exists.

As an aid to the allocation of scores in Figure 8.3, especially the row 'X_t difficulty of coordination', one may refer to an idea of Lawrence and Lorsch (1967). They argued that problems of coordination arise significantly from differences in the level of uncertainty in which specialist departments operate. Departments operating in highly uncertain environments will tend to develop flexible structures and routines and the attitudes and values that go along with them. An example from a large bank may be taken to illustrate this point. The merchant bank division of the bank was characterized by a free-wheeling, buccaneering, risk-taking spirit. The branch banking division was almost exactly the opposite. On the measures of environmental uncertainty proposed by Lawrence and Lorsch – rate of environmental change, timespan of feedback of results, predictability of outcomes and reliability of information – they were miles apart. Such coordination as was needed between these divisions would therefore be somewhat hampered by differing attitudes and perceptions. In fact, the need for coordination in this case was low.

If each pair of specialized departments resulting from the requisite specialization procedure was allocated a score on a scale from very low to very high on the four indicators of environmental uncertainty, it might be assumed that, if the differences between the departments are high – and the coordination need is also high – then special procedures of coordination may be required to deal with difficulties arising in the meeting of different structures and cultures.

It remains now to show the kinds of coordination that are known and in what circumstances they may be regarded as appropriate. As a general rule, the move from low complexity of requisite structures of specialization to high complexity is associated with a move through structural and processual to cultural modes of integration. A scale can be constructed at one end of which we can place the small organization with a stable environment and a simple structure of specialization and coordination by personal command and control.

At the other end we can place the multinational corporation, with units of production or service in locations scattered around the world and competing in world markets, such as Philips, Nissan, Pilkington, ABB, Procter and Gamble, GE and smaller ones such as Nokia. These are seen as the emerging organizations of the future in the now extensive semi-popular literature: Drucker (1990) and Handy (1989), for example. Organizations such as these, it is argued, operate in complex and changing environments and success for them is measured by their capacity for flexible and appropriate response to change.

We know, from research and from recorded experience (Warmington et al., 1977) that, as environments and technologies become more complex and changeable, the possibilities of structural fragmentation increase also, as do the accompanying strains on the structures and processes of coordination. We also observe that the (or one) response is to put in place committees, integrating persons, matrix structures, task forces, inter-discipline project teams, organizational development units, change agents and so on.

Using our method of allocating scores based on survey material (see Figure 8.3) it is possible to measure coordination difficulty given the existing structure of specialist departments and activities. If the scores are high, indicating that coordination will probably be costly, alternative structures of specialization might be examined. The scale of complexity referred to, the two ends of which have been exemplified, is exhibited in Table 8.1 and can be laid alongside a scale showing coordinating structures and processes found to be appropriate for each part of the scale.

From point 2 onwards, the structures and processes are laid on top of one another so that organizations that score very high will cer-

Table 8.1   Responses to increasing structural complexity

Level of structural complexity	Typical cumulative coordinating structures and processes
Low	Boss command
	Hierarchical authority, committees
	Formal liaison roles
	Liaison departments
	Cross-cutting linkages (Likert, 1961)
	Matrix structures
	Inter-discipline task/project teams
	Culture building ⎫ leaders as
High	Corporate philosophies ⎰ exemplars

tainly have formal authority hierarchies (possibly flattened by 'delayering') and committees and control procedures – and, as things become more complex and uncertain, they will create roles and departments to mediate, coordinate and handle conflict. Then, as experience shows, come project teams, task forces, team working at all levels, devolved authority and responsibility, then organizational development processes designed to heighten commitment to organizational purposes and building a common vision and shared values.

In the current wisdom, the common vision is shared by a permanent core of managers and management professionals – flexible response being engineered by subcontracting and laying off or taking on full-time or part-time employees, as and when required, and sometimes moving operations from high-cost to low-cost locations.

Conclusion

This attempt to translate the thoughts and findings of academia and the experience of managers into practical procedures for organizational diagnosis and design is clearly far from being the complete answer to all the questions practitioners could legitimately ask of academics, yet the logical steps to an answer to some of them are surely now apparent and capable of further elaboration.

As the structures of hierarchy and specialization become more complex and dispersed, the integrative 'glue' of structure and command gives way to the development of cultures which stress commitment, adaptability and shared values with all the means for the training, socialization and development of the 'core' employee. Oddly, but on reflection perhaps a corollary of this, and encouraged by the wizardry of information technology, cultures of bottom-up management, employee empowerment and so on, which are common and increasingly fashionable responses to complexity, are counterbalanced by centralized financial control and often mobilization around the charisma of a powerful figure personifying the organization, expressing a unifying vision and mobilizing commitment in the competitive struggle, for example, Timmer of Philips, Barnevik of ABB, Smith of GE, Weinstock of GEC. More and more, the popular management literature attributes organization success or failure to personal leadership. This tendency, in my view, obscures rather than illuminates the issues I have tried to clarify.

The flexible organization needs adaptable and multi-competent people to man it – or so the latter-day wisdom proposes. The much cited, but rarely sighted, multinational manager is an example, multilingual, multiskilled, multicultural. Such people, it is said, may move easily across the boundaries from geographical location to location, from organization unit to organization unit, and in the process become an ingredient in the coordinating 'glue', or alternatively perhaps an unwelcome and puzzling stranger amongst locals and entrenched (probably essential) unskilled specialists.

I stress again that the proposals for discovering requisite specialization and requisite integration can only rest on the considered judgement of experienced and responsible people. The matrixes and tables of my procedure are informed by these judgements, which means that there are no general principles of organization design, not even span of control, which has long since gone into the delayerer's rubbish bin, along with unity and command. But there are choices, and one must monitor and learn from the outcomes of choosing. It is through the involvement of the actors in the participative processes of diagnosis design and subsequent change that the political and cultural obstacles to discovery and change can be uncovered and dealt with.

For many reasons already discussed, the personnel specialism has been dressed in new clothes and relabelled Human Resource Management. The management of complexity has led to the belated and welcome discovery by the great and the powerful of that eternal truth, 'people are our greatest asset'. That being so, the competences of people become a strategic resource, like money and machinery, and *that* being so, they need to be carefully husbanded, pointed in directions compatible with organizations' purposes and trained and developed to achieve them, and above all involved and listened to. Perhaps, as I advocated a long time ago (Lupton, 1966), the personnel (HR) manager may now begin to develop a role as the organization's applied social scientist and the one who might initiate the processes of diagnosis decision and change as set out in this chapter, and perhaps improve them and the theory behind them. I am not too optimistic. In this connection, as Legge (1995) points out, there is as much rhetoric in these matters as there is reality.

Finally (and although it will be fairly obvious), I have to acknowledge my debt to my erstwhile colleagues of the Aston Studies, especially Derek Pugh and John Child and members of my research team at the Manchester Business School, particularly the late Dan Gowler, Alan Warmington, Karen Legge and Angela Bowey.

References

Child, J. (1984), *Organisations*, London: Harper & Row.
Drucker, P. (1989), *The New Realities*, London: Mandarin.
Handy, C. (1989), *The Age of Unreason*, London: Arrow Books.
Lawrence, P.R. and Lorsch, S.W. (1967), *Organisation and Environment*, Cambridge, Mass.: Harvard University Press.

Legge, K. (1995), *Human Resource Management: Rhetorics and Realities*. London: Macmillan Business.

Likert, L. (1961), *New Patterns of Management*, New York: McGraw-Hill.

Lupton, T. (1996), *Industrial Behaviour and Personnel Management*, London: Institute of Personnel Management.

Lupton, T. and Tanner, I. (1987), *Achieving Change*, Aldershot: Gower.

Mintzberg, H. (1983), *Structures in Fives: Designing Effective Organizations*, Englewood Cliffs, NJ: Prentice-Hall.

Pugh, D. (1979), 'Effective co-ordination in organisations', *Advanced Management Journal*, Winter, 28–35.

Sykes, A. and Bates, J. (1962), 'A study of conflict between formal company policy and the interests of informal groups', *Sociological Review*, November.

Warmington, A., Lupton, T. and Gribbin, C. (1977), *Organisational Behaviour and Performance*, London: Macmillan.

Woodward, J. (1965), *Industrial Organisation: Theory and Practice*, London: Oxford University Press.

9 The Coevolution of Contexts and Structures: the N-Form[1]

VINCENZO PERRONE, *Department of Business Administration, University of Cassino*

Introduction

One of the most important findings of the original research conducted by Pugh and his colleagues was that the structure of an organization is strictly connected with the context in which it operates. Much of the variation in organizational structures is explained by contextual factors. Contextual variables in the model developed by the Aston Group were origin and history of the organization, ownership and control, size (in terms of both employees and net assets), charter (that is, the purpose of the organization and the value system present in it), technology, location, resources (human, ideational, financial and material elements available for the organization) and the degree of interdependence with suppliers, customers, competitors, labour unions, management organizations, and political and social institutions (Pugh and Hickson, 1976, pp. 35–9).

These factors have an impact on three structural dimensions:

> (1) *structuring of activities*; that is, the degree to which the intended behaviour of employees is overtly defined by task specialization, standard routines, and formal paper work; (2) *concentration of authority*; that is, the degree to which authority for decisions rests in controlling units outside the organization and is centralized at the higher hierarchical levels within it; and (3) *line control of workflow*; that is, the degree to which control is exercised by line personnel instead of through impersonal procedures. (Pugh and Hickson, 1976, p. 78)

Studies conducted by the Aston Group have shown that size and structuring of activities are positively related. Large organizations tend to have more specialization, more standardization and more formalization than smaller ones. Aston researchers also showed that organizations that are highly dependent upon other external units have a higher concentration of authority and less autonomy in decision making.

In the final part of their study, Pugh and his colleagues induced from their data a taxonomy of organizational work structures, by combining the three structural dimensions mentioned above. They identify seven types: full bureaucracy, nascent full bureaucracy, workflow bureaucracy, nascent workflow bureaucracy, preworkflow bureaucracy, personnel bureaucracy and implicitly structured organization. They are able to demonstrate with their research that *'bureaucracy takes different forms in different settings'* (Pugh and Hickson, 1976, p. 127; emphasis added).

In this chapter we start from the same contingent view. We explore how current changes in the context of organizations are influencing the development of organizational configurations. Furthermore, we conclude that it is possible to identify an organizational form which has characteristics that are different from those of the organizational types defined by Pugh and his colleagues. This exploration is mainly theoretical. In fact, though there is increasing evidence concerning the existence of the organizational form that we will examine (Nohria and Eccles, 1992), we do not have the same large and solid amount of data upon which the Aston Group developed its classification. We believe that, since the Aston research was conducted, some of the contextual variables studied have changed in a revolutionary way. In particular, we focus on the evolution of competition towards hypercompetitive environments (D'Aveni, 1994) and on the evolution of technology towards what has been called the 'information age'. We argue that these changes affect the organizational characteristics of a firm in ways that will be different from those discovered by Pugh and his colleagues. Technology has reduced the need for coordination through formalized, standardized and hierarchical control. In the past, only large and structured organizations were in a position to use these organizational devices for managing the enormous amount of information that is generated by complex activities (Chandler, 1962). Over time, technology has been able to reduce this competitive advantage that large and bureaucratic organizations have had over small and entrepreneurial organizations (Reich, 1991; Williamson, 1975). In connection with this change, hypercompetition has made the costs associated with structuring, formalization and bureaucratic control (that is, the cost of organizing) a target for cost reduction strategies. These in turn were designed to improve efficiency and flexibility while maintaining effectiveness. The combination of these two pressures has resulted in an organizational innovation which we term the Network Form or N-Form.

The Context of the N-Form

Firms that belong to developed economies have faced important changes in recent times. Technological revolution on one side and globalization on the other have created the conditions for the unfolding of a hypercompetitive environment. The fact that every 18 months the computational capacity of new machines doubles while their cost is cut by half is now part of technological legend. Technological innovation and diffusion processes occur at a rate never experienced before. These changes are propelling companies into the 'information age' where organizational environments are 'information-rich, computation-rich and communications-rich' (Bettis and Hitt, 1995, p. 9). New technologies affect not only those companies that produce them, like those in computer or biotechnology industries, but also firms that use technology, such as industries in the service sector like banking or consulting. The consequences of the development, adoption and use of new production technologies, such as robots and automated production lines, and of new information technologies, like computers and telecommunications, are relevant. On the one hand, new products are developed more rapidly, produced and distributed on a larger scale and in a greater variety, as the concept of *mass-customization* suggests (Kotha, 1995). Their life cycle is also shortened. On the other hand, new production and information technologies, coupled with organizational innovations, yield increases in productivity while reducing the need for human labour (Freeman and Soete, 1994). The high costs of product development and the need to absorb the huge investments made in new technologies and in new processes force companies to aim at the largest possible markets. For this reason, firms are struggling to become global competitors (Ohmae, 1991).

This scenario describes in quite a realistic way the working conditions of firms that operate in industries as diverse as motor cars (Womack *et al.*, 1990), software development (Cusumano, 1991), electronics (Bauer *et al.*, 1992) and fashion clothing (Perrone, 1987). These conditions might be summarized as follows:

1   The firm has to react to the behaviour of a small group of 'visible' competitors. However, the number of firms in the market is large enough to avoid collusion, which is also difficult to achieve because of the 'global' dimension of the market. The relative permeability of industrial boundaries makes markets 'contestable' (Baumol *et al.*, 1982) providing a further incentive for strategic behaviours focused on efficiency. Competitive pressure establishes the *survival domain* within which the organizational arrangements compatible with the economic survival of the firm are set (Tosi, 1992, pp. 55–8). Moreover, firms that operate in such conditions

have to discover as soon as possible where the survival boundaries are. Companies also have to monitor whether and how these boundaries move over time.

2   Technology is decomposable. There are different phases in the production process. The final one is generally the assembling of a number of standard components, accomplished in different ways according to the needs of the market.

3   The focus of the competitive strategy of the firm is based on differentiation. Differentiation is broadly implemented in order to improve the capacity of the firm to build and sustain a unique relationship with customers. The aim is to promote customer loyalty by increasing their dependency upon the firm. All the known sources of differentiation are simultaneously relevant: cost, quality, service and innovation. The degree of differentiation, as much as the uniqueness of the relationship with customers, tends to decrease rapidly over time, the reason being hypercompetition. This rapid sequence of creation and then erosion of competitive advantages creates the need for a huge and steady flow of resources.

4   The need to have resources available and to reduce risks connected with their use creates incentives for:
   (a)   sharing the burden with other firms;
   (b)   trying, even in cooperation with other firms, to slow down the pace of the erosion process;
   (c)   enhancing the productivity of each resource used in the process; such increases in productivity are due more to economies of scope than to economies of scale (Panzar and Willig, 1981);
   (d)   enhancing the capacity to deal with complexity;
   (e)   increasing flexibility in the use of resources, in particular human resources.

Companies have reacted to these conditions by developing an innovative type of organization. They have developed a form of organization enabling them to manage know-how development, maintenance and combination, to reduce risk and to maximize dynamic efficiency. This organizational innovation is the N-Form.

The N-Form Defined

The N-Form is a combination of coordination processes, of structures of positions, of relationships between those positions and of contracts, designed, interpreted and acted by a focal firm, in order to attain simultaneously objectives of dynamic system efficiency and of output variety on a large scale of activities. The form operates in dynamic, unstable and competitive environments.

The N-Form is articulated on two levels: the *focal firm* (Baker, 1990; Thompson, 1962) and the *organization-set* (Aiken and Hage, 1968; Aldrich and Whetten, 1981; Evan, 1966). The relationship between these levels is both strategic and organizational. It is strategic from the moment that there are common goals that favour cooperation among independently owned units (Luke *et al.*, 1989) and it is organizational because specific internal characteristics of the focal firm are coherent with the management of the external set of inter-organizational relationships (Aiken and Hage, 1968). The N-Form is therefore defined as a multi-level and multidimensional concept.

The basic characteristics of the N-Form are illustrated in Figure 9.1. The focal firm (Thompson, 1962) is defined in structural terms as *the most central unit* in a network of organizations that share a common strategic goal. The existence of such a central unit in a network is what contributes a distinction between the N-Form and other organizational forms. In strategic terms, the focal firm is defined as the unit which has been able to *focus* the set of activities performed internally on those segments of the value chain that provide the highest added value, that are the most consistent with the specific competencies of the firm, that allow the firm to have *control over the entire value chain*, and that provide the most valuable information for learning about the functioning, the results and the evolution of the chain. The formal, legal boundaries of the focal firm are defined by the time and space limits of the direct ownership of resources (that is, ownership rights).

The organization-set (Evan, 1966; DiMaggio, 1986; Scott, 1994) is defined as the *set of relationships* with other organizations, relatively autonomous from the point of view of ownership, in which the focal firm is involved, plus the relationships among its counterparts. Central among these connections are those with customers, suppliers and competitors. Relationships in the organization-set of the N-Form are characterized by the strong presence of cooperation rather than competition. From the point of view of the focal firm, the limits of the organization-set are the limits of its capacity to have access to resources and of the possibility of influencing the behaviour of individuals and of organizational units that have to match their preferences with those of the focal firm (access and influence rights).

Figure 9.1 indicates that the N-Form has three key dimensions: coordination processes, network structure and contractual regulations. These dimensions apply to both the focal firm level and the organization-set level. These are discussed in turn below.

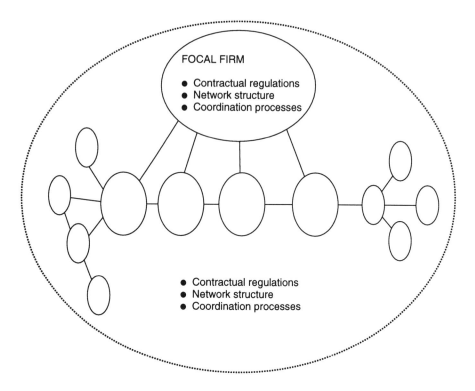

Figure 9.1   Levels and dimensions of the N-Form

Coordination Processes

The N-Form is characterized by the fact that coordination between parties, both internal and external to the focal firm, is obtained through a combination of many coordination processes which include signalling, communicating, negotiating, hierarchical authority and so forth. Communication supported by technology and cooperation based on trust and upon the internalization of shared cultural values and norms are also prominent processes in the mix that specifically applies to the N-Form. In comparison with other management processes, they require a longer time span to develop but are less expensive to use when established. In the N-Form, hierarchical authority and formal rules and procedure are less relevant compared to other forms. Therefore the degree of structuring of activities and of concentration of authority is low.

Network Structure

The second dimension is the structural properties of the network. Organization forms can be viewed as networks, that is as systems of objects, like individuals, units or companies, joined by a variety of relationships (Lincoln, 1982; Tichy *et al.*, 1979). This view is useful because players and their actions are viewed as interdependent rather than independent and relational ties (linkages) between actors are channels for the transfer of resources, either material or non-material like trust, obligations and affect (Mitchell, 1969; Wasserman and Faust, 1994). We do not assume that networks are 'non-hierarchical by definition' (Alter and Hage, 1992), neither are they only spontaneously built and based on friendship or trust. They are in fact influenced by rational design and formal rules and can be coordinated using hierarchy as well as other processes. However, networks cannot be limited to the formal ordering of units and positions into organizational ranks and departments, as was suggested by the 'configuration' structural variable defined by Pugh and colleagues (Pugh and Hickson, 1976, pp. 33–4). The properties of the links and of the web that they design are relevant for the functioning of a specific organizational form. In the N-Form, ties tend to be strong (that is, the flows are frequent, intense and protracted in time) and multiplex (that is, the same tie is a channel for the exchange of different contents such as resources, information, advice and friendship). The overall network structure of the N-Form has different properties when observed at the level of the focal firm or the organization-set. Centralization is low in the first case and relatively high in the second (owing to the centrality of the focal firm), while density and cohesiveness are higher inside the focal unit.

Contractual Regulations

The final dimension that has to be considered in analysing a form is contractual regulations (Noorderhaven, 1992). Contractual norms, legally enforced by a society's justice system, affect the intensity and kind of cooperation at both levels of the form. We consider contracts to be an interface between the local characteristics of relationships in a specific social system such as an organization, and society at large (Lowry, 1976). Thanks to the role of the other two dimensions, coordination processes and network structure, contracts alone cannot explain the dynamic of an organization form. However, they constrain and enable those dynamics. For example, the fact that at some point in time and in a certain society licensing or franchising agreements can be legally enforced favours the spreading of these organizational arrangements. On the internal organization side, the same can be said about new contractual regulations of the employment relation that permit part-time work and other forms of flexibility. The literature on business transactions has suggested distinguishing between formal and informal contracts (Macaulay, 1963). It is certainly true, for instance, that internalized cultural norms might work as well as an interface between local conditions and general society in regulating relationships. We prefer, though, to limit the notion of contract to the idea of legally enforced norms, from the moment that other informal norms of behaviour can be better captured by analysing coordination processes based on authority or on trust.

The structure, processes and contractual constraints of these patterns of relationships and the characteristics of the nodes determine the *performance* of the focal firm and of the entire form.

The N-Form Compared to the Aston Taxonomy of Organization Structure

Having defined the basic characteristics of the N-Form, which are represented in Figure 9.1, we are now in a position to assess the major differences between what we propose and the original taxonomy developed by the Aston Group. We suggest extending and slightly modifying that taxonomy in order to take into consideration the evolution of context. If we could measure the N-Form using the scales designed by Pugh and his colleagues, we would probably find low levels of structuring and centralization and mainly impersonal forms of control of the work flow. The organizations that were found to possess these characteristics were labelled 'preworkflow bureaucracies' in the Aston model. Implicitly structured organizations showed lack of structuring and decentralization, too, but distinguished themselves by a greater reliance on personal control mechanisms. Preworkflow bureaucracies were organizations characterized by small size and integrated technology. They were relatively independent of external organizations. Companies with these organizational traits were found in industries such as metal components, motor components, railway carriages, engineering tools and food manufacturing (Pugh and Hickson, 1976, pp. 119–20). In contrast, with the N-Form we are suggesting that informality and debureaucratization can be found in combination with a large scale of activities. Two components of size should be distinguished: number of employees and total net assets. If in fact we could measure these variables at the level of the focal firm, we would find low values for the former and high values for the latter. The reason is that size in our model is no longer part of the context but a result of a deliberate organizational strategy of the focal firm. In particular, externalization strategies and the reliance upon the organization-set allow for the combination of reduced personnel and a large scale of economic activity, coupled with an increased variety of outputs and throughputs, at the level of the focal firm. Such an attribute of the form that we are describing points up a second important difference in comparison with the Aston model: interdependence with other organizations is again not a contextual datum but a result of an organizational decision and part of the structural design of a form. From the moment that external interdependence is designed and managed by the focal firm, we do not expect to find it in association with high centralization of authority in its internal organization, as was common in the organizations studied by Pugh and his colleagues. Aston researchers correctly acknowledged the possibility of reversing the direction of causality between their structural dimensions and the contextual variables by recognizing the limits of their cross-sectional study (Pugh and Hickson, 1976, p. 108). However, they could not observe, at the time of their study, what is apparent today. The organization-set and the characteristics of the focal firm have to be assessed simultaneously if we want to understand how economic activities are organized in conjunction with them. We now turn to these.

The Organization-set and Management of External Relations

The environment of a firm might be conceived as a set of relationships with other organizations (Emery and Trist, 1965; Terreberry, 1968; Thompson, 1962, 1967). Moving from role theory, Evan (1966) has developed an 'organization-set' model comprising the network of interactions or linkages of a given organization with various organizations in its environment. By balancing cooperation and competition in its organization-set, the focal firm in the N-Form is able to meet the needs of a hypercompetitive and rapidly changing environment, remaining at the same time lean, flexible and efficient (Galbraith *et al.*, 1993; Kanter, 1989). The performance of the N-Form depends upon:

1 the structural properties of the network defined by the organization-set;
2 the effective use of coordination processes in the management of each relationship and the availability of contracts that favour the development of cooperative relationships by reducing their risk;
3 the overall effectiveness and efficiency of the focal firm in managing its organization-set.

With regard to the first point, the focal firm is highly central. Centrality gives the focal firm the power to control the value chain. Centrality is a matter of *degree*: the focal firm has the highest number of ties with other organizations in the form. It is also a matter of 'betweenness', meaning that, if two organizations, for example, two suppliers, in the form want to interact, in most of the cases they can do it only through the focal firm (Wasserman and Faust, 1994).

A question arises: how can these structural characteristics be a base for competitive advantage and for positive performance? A possible answer stems from recent developments in network analysis. To be effective, the focal firm has to be able to link with 'interesting' partners, that is partners who are 'port of access to clusters of people beyond. … these ports should be nonredundant so as to reach separate, and therefore more diverse, social worlds of networks benefits' (Burt, 1992, p. 21). Efficiency therefore might come from the fact that several secondary contacts are managed through only a few primary connections. This solution reduces the costs of managing relationships for the focal firm. It also has a positive impact on effectiveness. By being connected with a few but very diverse 'worlds', worlds divided by structural holes, the focal firm is able to acquire valuable information about opportunities (the development of a new technology, a change in customers' habits and needs, a new institutional regulation and so on) and threats (such as a competitor's investment decision, a supplier's move of downward integration or a sign of political instability) present in its environment. Linkages are therefore a door open to possibilities (Granovetter, 1973) and the social structure in which a focal firm is embedded becomes a vehicle for the organization of economic activities (Granovetter, 1985). In contrast, highly cohesive and dense networks imply redundant links which are expensive and even dangerous. In such webs, since everybody ultimately gains access to the same data, the richness of the information is reduced and members end up 'binding and blinding' each other and exposing themselves to dangerous strategic surprises (Grabher, 1993). A good example of the search for non-redundancy is the attempt of focal firms in N-Forms operating in the motor industry to change the structure of the system of relationships with suppliers (Lyons *et al.*, 1990). The decision to deal only with first-tier suppliers and to prefer single sources for core components of specific car models (McMillan, 1990) is a decision to reduce the number of links while increasing their intensity and their value, which in turn reduces coordination costs and increases effectiveness. The organization-set works as an *information multiplier* for the focal firm, and for the entire N-Form. Each node in the network may in fact learn by interacting with other organizations; each node may modify its expectations regarding future evolutions of the environment based on what other organizations are able to forecast and to plan; each node may complement internal strategic planning with external strategic learning, increasing its ability to cope and survive in an uncertain environment (Mintzberg, 1993).

The use of a balanced mix of coordination processes at the organization-set level is another source of organizational effectiveness for the N-Form. The management of external relationships in an N-Form is not only a matter of contract-regulated exchange and of negotiation (Williamson, 1975). Units that belong to an N-Form expect their relationship to last in the future and to be stable. These expectations create a positive incentive for waiving potential short-term gains deriving from opportunistic behaviours, such as cheating, hiding useful information, unilaterally reducing the quality of performance or missing important deadlines. Organizations will look instead for the higher value that it is possible to extract from repeated exchanges in a long-term relationship (Klein and Leffler, 1981; Telser, 1980).

Research has recently pointed out the importance of trust in developing and maintaining cooperative interorganizational relations (Sako, 1992; Smitka, 1991). Trust favours learning through collaboration (Buckley and Casson, 1988; Dodgson, 1993), enhances the comprehensiveness of joint decision-making processes (Mishra, 1992) and reduces conflict and negotiation costs (Zaheer *et al.*, 1995). Buyers and suppliers involved in the joint development of new products and in common strategies to reduce time and costs will benefit from these positive consequences of trust.

Intense communication is also useful for integrating relatively independent nodes into the N-Form. In this regard, technology is playing a crucial role, as recent applications of EDI (electronic data interchange) testify. A common operation performed by EDI is the automatic issuing of purchasing orders, based on some previously established criteria (for example, when stock levels at the buying organization's plant fall below a certain level). This way of managing the purchasing process significantly reduces the costs of negotiation and coordination.

It is possible to recognize coordination processes based on authority, rules and procedures in the context of relationships at the level of the organization-set. The focal firm might use its authority, based on the resources it controls, in coordinating the Form. For example, it might force its partners to hire and to pay managers that the focal firm has chosen. In the fashion industry, designers who own the focal firm often select product managers that are then hired by those companies to which designers outsource the production of clothes. There are other ways of creating 'bureaucratic' integration *between* organizations. It is possible to find joint decision-making processes performed by units where buyer and supplier representatives work together, as in the case of developing a new product. In other cases we have observed the development of a joint training programme, which members from most of the organizations in the network were supposed to attend.

Formal contracts perform important functions in regulating the behaviour of the N-Form at the level of the organization-set. For instance, contracts that regulate exchange, as long as the enforcement of rights and obligations is economical and punctual, make coordination based on trust less risky and provide a frame of reference for continuing negotiation between different nodes, reducing the likelihood of conflict. But other kinds of contract are crucial for the N-Form: the legal agreements that define the characteristics of a relationship between parties rather than just the 'simple' content of an exchange. Joint venture, franchising, licensing and consortium contracts belong to this category. Legal and social systems that do not provide firms with these types of contracts are not a favourable context for the development of the N-Form. However, formal characteristics of contracts do not define by themselves the organizational dynamics of a form. In order to appreciate those dynamics and to distinguish one form from another, it is necessary to assess contracts together with the characteristics of the mix of coordination processes used in conjunction with the structural properties of the network.

We are looking at the N-Form from the unifying point of view of the focal firm at its centre. We are therefore not interested in the optimal matching of the most efficient governance mode with the characteristics of a specific relationship in the organization-set. We prefer to concentrate our attention upon the organizational and managerial problem of combining different ways of governing relationships between the focal firm and the entire organization-set in a frame that is understandable, manageable and effective. We believe that research efforts are needed for the analysis of the balancing process between different relationships. Our contribution consists of an exploration of the potential sources of efficiency that stem from the fact that most of the relationships we observe in the N-Form have a party in common: the focal firm. This fact, of having the same actor across different relationships, might be an advantage for the form if:

1   the focal firm is able to *transfer efficient innovations* developed with regard to a specific relationship to other similar links;
2   it is possible to *control the costs* (due, for example, to the risk of potential opportunistic behaviour) of a specific relationship, through variations in the organization of similar ones;
3   a reduction in uncertainty and complexity is obtained by *transferring the information* gained by managing a specific relationship into the management of others;

4   the same link can be used for the development of different relationships; this is a property of links that is known as *multiplexity*
in network analysis (Wasserman and Faust, 1994).

Three examples of synergies in the management of the organization-set in the N-form may be considered. The first is based on
Versace's (fashion clothing) distributive structure. A few shops in the
most important cities such as Milan and New York are owned while
the others are franchised. The former are used as sensors for monitoring the evolution of final customers' needs and taste and for
assessing the impact of collections. They are also useful for controlling the costs of distributing the products of the company. Having
acquired this information, it is then easier to govern all the relationships with relatively independent franchisees, where negotiated
exchange together with some weak form of bureaucratic integration
are mainly used for coordination. This is a good example of the
interaction between contracts and coordination processes and of the
effects described above in points (2) and (3).

The second example refers to the strategy of differentiating the
relationships between counterparts in an outsourcing process. In this
case a strong and stable tie with one of the subcontractors, where
coordination is based on intense communication and trust, is a source
of valuable information that can be used for reducing the cost of
managing the relationships with other counterparts (Smitka, 1991).

Finally, there is an example of multiplexity. In a case we have
studied, an Italian company which produces 'getters' (small metallic
devices that absorb any kind of gases, thereby producing a vacuum)
was able to gain access to the knowledge of its Japanese buyer. An
optimal level of trust was established in the context of a buyer/
supplier relationship, allowing a new relationship to develop with
the same counterpart in the form of a joint venture contract for the
production and distribution of a new product: a gases super-purifier.

All three examples point out the importance of considering simultaneously the focal firm *and* the organization-set. Such an approach
leads to new questions: is it possible to manage an external network
the way we have described here, without developing adequate internal networking structures, systems, capabilities and aptitudes? What
then should be the internal organization of the focal firm?

The Internal Organization of the Focal Firm

The aforementioned context within which the focal firm evolved has
a profound impact on the characteristics of that firm's internal organization. Information technology has made it possible to *decompose*

the organization (Bettis and Hitt, 1995). Where one might expect to find a high level of structuring, of formalization and of centralized authority, because of the large scale of operations performed by the organization, one observes instead flexible, informal and efficient organization. It is important to underline the fact that flexibility and adaptability in the form we are describing are not obtained at the expenses of efficiency. A company functioning in a hypercompetitive market cannot afford slack resources, such as oversized corporate staffs or a huge supervisor to worker ratio. Furthermore, the N-Form is not supposed to work effectively only in situations where innovation is critical and rewarded enough to cover the costs of flexibility. These were the conditions identified as necessary for the development of organic systems (Burns and Stalker, 1961). In the context of the N-Form, instead, a strong thrust towards efficiency has favoured the diffusion of joint organizational and technological innovations.

The internal organization of the focal firm is shaped as a federation of quasi-autonomous units (Charan, 1991). These organizational units can be modules in the production process, special units that mediate between the internal network and the external organization-set, or teams responsible for the management of a firm's core processes, such as new product development or incoming orders processing (Hammer and Champy, 1993). The tendency to disintegrate the organization induced by new technologies and by organizational innovations creates a highly dense (i.e., many links between the nodes) and low centralized (i.e., a few nodes of great importance) network of relations between internal nodes (Dess *et al.*, 1995). The internal network is a result of organizational strategies oriented towards improving efficiency by simplifying the organization, by reducing its size in terms of the total number of employees and by redesigning the boundaries of the original functions in a more rational and process-oriented way (Keidel, 1994). The need to achieve objectives of effectiveness and of mass-customization by operating according to the evolution of relationships in the organization-set leads to a greater flexibility in production and, generally speaking, towards a reduction in the level of technical core insulation (Nemetz and Fry, 1988). For this reason, when an N-Form is characterized by a focal firm that has maintained internally some core production processes, it is at production plants level that the most advanced organizational innovations can be found.

The 'Double-net' Hypothesis

The most important features of the N-Form are summarized in Table 9.1. The three dimensions of contracts, network structure and coordi-

Table 9.1   A synthesis of the N-Form's characteristics

Dimensions levels	Focal firm	Organization-set
Contracts	Variety of employment contracts for achieving flexibility (temporary work; part-time; mobility; etc.)	Variety of contracts. Long-term orientation and emphasis on the nature of cooperative relationships between parties rather than on the content of exchange (e.g. joint venture; franchising; licensing; etc.)
Network structure	High density	Cliques and structural holes
	Low centralization	High centralization
	Multiplexity	Multiplexity
	Nodes: modules and empowered decisional nodes	Nodes: organizations
Coordination processes	Negotiated exchange in internal markets	Negotiated exchange
	Cooperation based on reputation and trust	Cooperation based on reputation and trust
	Intense communication supported by new technologies	Intense communication supported by new technologies
	Authority based on competence and network centrality	Authority based on know-how and network centrality
	Internalization of social norms and values	

nation processes are described at both the focal firm and the organization-set levels. These two levels have strategic and organizational connections that produce a coherent and consistent form. One of the main characteristics of the N-Form is that it is based on a double network of relationships. The coordination processes are different, from the moment that they have to adapt to the specificity of each relationship, but at the same time integrated, from the moment that they share homogeneous cognitive orientations and certain organizational arrangements. They are also supported by management systems that are designed to fit the entire N-Form.

The network is double because it develops both within the boundaries set by the property rights owned by the focal firm and within the limits of the focal firm's influence upon other units in the organization-set. Decentralized decision making, the development of empowered boundary-spanning units, a process-oriented organization based on semi-autonomous modules, coordination processes based on trust and on exchange and substitution, specific contracts for personnel employment and policies for its management are among the distinctive traits of the focal firm organization. At the organization-set level, we find contracts that regulate cooperation between independent units, coordination based on intense communication and on trust, and a learning process that exploits the multiplicity of relationships and the information available in the network and that favours an inductive and interactive strategy-making process. By balancing the flexibility of the focal firm with the richness of the organization-set, that allows access to differentiated resources when they are needed, the N-Form performs well in the context of a rapidly changing and hypercompetitive environment, where relentless technological innovation is the rule (Powell, 1990). The N-Form is a complex concept (Powell and Smith-Doerr, 1994). We are not saying that this is a new form of organization (Lammers, 1988). We believe instead that a precise and extensive definition of this configuration was missing and is useful in order to appreciate organizational innovations determined by changes in the context and to explain dissimilarities in performance between companies competing in the same unstable environment.

Concluding Remarks

A central tenet of the Aston programme of research is the relationship between context, organizational structure and performance. In this chapter we have addressed two questions: what should be the characteristics of an effective organization in a context characterized by hypercompetition and rapid technological evolution; and which kind of performance will be crucial for a firm's survival? The answer to these two questions is a particular organizational configuration that we have termed the N-Form (Network Form). The N-Form is a multidimensional and multi-level organizational concept. The di-

mensions of contracts, network structures and coordination processes at the focal firm and organization-set levels are consistently
developed to reduce risks, increase efficiency and recreate competitive advantage over time. Furthermore, the N-Form is an
organizational configuration designed to transform social capital into
competitive advantage. The characteristics of this form still need to
be tested empirically. We hope that the definition of its properties,
together with some of the hypotheses we have developed in this
chapter about its functioning, will encourage future research.

Note

1   I am most grateful to Henry Tosi, Anna Grandori, Enzo Rullani, Jerry Hage,
    Larry Cummings, Andy Van de Ven, Derek Pugh and Timothy Clark for their
    insightful comments and suggestions. Clearly, they are not responsible for the
    contents of this manuscript.

References

Aiken, M. and Hage, J. (1968), 'Organizational interdependence and intra-organiz-
ational structure', *American Sociological Review*, **33**, December, 912–30.
Aldrich, H.E. and Whetten, D. (1981), 'Organization-sets, action-sets and networks:
making the most of simplicity', in P.C. Nystrom and W.H. Starbuck (eds), *Hand-
book of Organizational Design*, New York: Oxford University Press.
Alter, C. and Hage, J. (1992), 'Organizations working together', *Coordination in
Interorganizational networks*, Newbury Park, CA: Sage.
Baker, W.E. (1990), 'Market networks and corporate behavior', *American Journal of
Sociology*, **96**, 589–625.
Bauer, R.A., Collar, E. and Tang, V. (1992), *The Silverlake Project. Transformation at
IBM*, New York: Oxford University Press.
Baumol, W.J., Panzar, J.C. and Willig, R.D. (1982), *Contestable Markets and the Theory
of Industry Structure*, New York: Harcourt Brace Jovanovich.
Bettis, R.A. and Hitt, M.A. (1995), 'The new competitive landscape', *Strategic Man-
agement Journal*, **16**, 7–19.
Buckley, P.J. and Casson, M. (1988), 'A theory of cooperation in international busi-
ness', in F.J. Contractor and P. Lorange (eds), *Cooperative Strategies in International
Business*, Lexington: Lexington Books.
Burns, T. and Stalker, G.M. (1961), *The Management of Innovation*, London: Tavistock.
Burt, R.S. (1992), *Structural Holes*, Boston, Mass.: Harvard University Press.
Chandler, A.D.J. (1962), *Strategy and Structure*, Cambridge, MA: MIT Press.
Charan, R. (1991), 'How networks reshape organizations for results', *Harvard Busi-
ness Review*, September–October, 104–15.
Cusumano, M.A. (1991), *Japan's Software Factories: A Challenge to U.S. Management*.
New York: Oxford University Press.
D'Aveni, R.A. (1994), *Hyper-competition. Managing the Dynamics of Strategic
Manoeuvering*, New York: Free Press.
Dess, G.G., Rasheed, A.M.A., McLaughlin, K.J. and Priem, R.L. (1995), 'The new
corporate architecture', *Academy of Management Executive*, **9**, 7–18.

DiMaggio, P.J. (1986), 'Structural analysis of organizational fields: a blockmodel approach', in B.M. Staw and L.L Cummings (eds), *Research in Organizational Behavior*, Greenwich, Conn.: JAI Press, pp. 335–70.

Dodgson, M. (1993), 'Learning, trust and technological collaboration', *Human Relations*, **46**, 77–95.

Emery, F.E. and Trist, E.L. (1965), 'The causal texture of organizational environments', *Human Relations*, **18**, 21–31.

Evan, W.M. (1966), 'The organization-set: toward a theory of interorganizational relations', in J.D. Thompson (ed), *Approaches to Organizational Design*, Pittsburgh: University of Pittsburgh Press, pp. 173–91.

Freeman, C. and Soete, L. (1994), *Work For All or Mass Unemployment?*, London: Pinter.

Galbraith, J.R., Lawler III, E.E. and Associates (1993), *Organizing for the Future: The New Logic for Managing Complex Organizations*, San Francisco, CA: Jossey-Bass.

Grabher, G. (1993), 'The weakness of strong ties: the lock-in of regional development in the Ruhr area', in G. Grabher (ed), *The Embedded Firm: On the Socioeconomics of Industrial Networks*, London: Routledge, pp. 255–77.

Granovetter, M. (1973), 'The strength of weak ties', *American Journal of Sociology*, **78**, 1360–80.

Granovetter, M. (1985), 'Economic action and social structure: the problem of embeddedness', *American Journal of Sociology*, **91**, 481–510.

Hammer, M. and Champy, J. (1993), *Reengineering the Corporation: A Manifesto for Business Revolution*, New York: Harper Business.

Kanter, R.M. (1989), *When Giants Learn to Dance: Mastering the Challenges of Strategy, Management and Careers in the 1990's*, New York: Simon & Schuster.

Keidel, R.W. (1994), 'Rethinking organizational design', *Academy of Management Executive*, **8**, 12–28.

Klein, B. and Leffler, B.K. (1981), 'The role of market forces in assuring contractual performance', *Journal of Political Economy*, **89**, 615–41.

Kotha, S. (1995), 'Mass customization: Implementing the emerging paradigm for competitive advantage', *Strategic Management Journal*, **16**, (Summer Special Issue), 21–42.

Lammers, C.J. (1988), 'Transience and persistence of ideal types in organization theory', in S.B. Bacharach (ed.), *Research in the Sociology of Organizations*, Greenwich, Conn.: JAI Press, pp. 203–24.

Lincoln, J.R. (1982), 'Intra- (and inter-) organizational networks', in S.B. Bacharach (ed.), *Research in the Sociology of Organizations*, Greenwich, Conn.: JAI Press, pp. 1–38.

Lowry, S.T. (1976), 'Bargain and contract theory in law and economics', *Journal of Economic Issues*, **10**, 1–22.

Luke, R.D., Begun, J.W. and Pointer, D.D. (1989), 'Quasi firms: Strategic interorganizational forms in the health care industry', *Academy of Management Review*, **14**, 9–19.

Lyons, T.F., Krachenberg, A.R. and Henke, J.W. (1990), 'Mixed motive marriages: What's next for buyer–supplier relations?', *Sloan Management Review*, (Spring).

Macaulay, S. (1963), 'Non contractual relations in business: a preliminary study', *American Sociological Review*, **28**, February, 55–69.

McMillan, J. (1990), 'Managing suppliers: incentive systems in Japanese and U.S. Industry', *California Management Review*, Summer, 38–55.

Mintzberg, H. (1993), *The Rise and Fall of Strategic Planning*, New York: The Free Press.

Mishra, A.K. (1992), 'Organizational responses to crisis: the role of mutual trust and top management teams', working paper, School of Business Administration, The University of Michigan.

Mitchell, J.C. (1969), 'The concept and use of social networks', in J.C. Mitchell (ed.), *Social Networks in Urban Situations*, Manchester: Manchester University Press, pp. 1–29.

Nemetz, P.L. and Fry, L.W. (1988), 'Flexible manufacturing organizations: implications for strategy formulation and organization design', *Academy of Management Review*, October, 627–38.

Noorderhaven, N.G. (1992), 'The problem of contract enforcement in economic organization theory', *Organization Studies*, **13**, 229–243.

Nohria, N. and Eccles, R.G. (1992), *Networks and Organizations: Structure Form and Action*, Boston, MA: Harvard Business School Press.

Omhae, K. (1991). *The Borderless World*, New York: Harper & Row.

Panzar, J.C. and Willig, R.D. (1981), 'Economies of Scope', *American Economic Review*, **71**, 268–272.

Perrone, V. (1987), 'Notes toward an organizational analysis of the textile-clothing industry', working paper, CRORA-Universita' Bocconi, Milan, Italy.

Powell, W.W. (1990), 'Neither market nor hierarchy: network forms of organization', in B.M. Staw and L.L. Cummings (eds), *Research in Organizational Behavior*, Greenwich, Conn.: JAI Press, pp. 295–336.

Powell, W.W. and Smith-Doerr, L. (1994)., 'Networks and economic life', in N.J. Smelser and R. Swedberg (eds), *The Handbook of Economic Sociology*, Princeton, N.J.: Princeton University Press, pp. 368–402.

Pugh, D.S. and Hickson, D.J. (1976), *Organizational Structure in its Context, The Aston Programme I*, Aldershot: Gower.

Reich, R.B. (1991), *The Work of Nations*, New York: Alfred K. Knopf.

Sako, M. (1992), *Prices, Quality and Trust: How Japanese and British companies manage buyer–supplier relations*, Cambridge: Cambridge University Press.

Scott, W.R. (1994), 'Conceptualizing organizational fields: linking organizations and societal systems', in U. Gerhardt, H-U. Derlein and F.W. Scharpf (eds), *Systems Rationality and Partial Interests. A festschrift to honor Renate Mayntz*,

Smitka, M.J. (1991), *Competitive Ties. Subcontracting in the Japanese Automotive Industry*, New York/Oxford: Columbia University Press.

Telser, L.G. (1980), 'A theory of self-enforcing agreements', *Journal of Business*, **53**, 27–44.

Terreberry, S. (1968), 'The evolution of organizational environments', *Administrative Science Quarterly*, **12**, 590–613.

Thompson, J.D. (1962), 'Organizations and output transactions', *American Journal of Sociology*, **LXVIII**, (3), November, 309–24.

Thompson, J.D. (1967), *Organizations in Action*, New York: McGraw-Hill.

Tichy, N.M., Tushman, M.L and Fombrun, C. (1979), 'Social network analysis for organizations', *Academy of Management Review*, **4**, 507–19.

Tosi, H. (1992), *The Environment/Organization/Person Contingency Model: A Meso Approach to the Study of Organizations*, Greenwich, Conn.: JAI Press.

Wasserman, S. and Faust, K. (1994), *Social Network Analysis: Methods and Applications*, New York: Cambridge University Press.

Williamson, O.E. (1975), *Markets and Hierarchies*, New York: The Free Press.

Womack, J., Jones, D. and Roos, D. (1990), *The Machine that Changed the World*, New York: Rawson.

Zaheer, A., McEvily, B. and Perrone, V. (1995), 'Does trust matter? Exploring the effects of interorganizational and interpersonal trust on performance', working paper. Carlson School of Management, University of Minnesota.

10 Organization Structure and the Transformation of Careers[1]

KERR INKSON, *Department of Management and Employment Relations, University of Auckland*

In tracing my ancestry through my mother's family in Aberdeen, Scotland, I recently came across some notes written by an elderly relative, concerning my great-uncle, Allan Wilson, who was born in 1862.

> Allan was at Ramage's school in Schoolhill. Book-keeping was his line and he was in the office of the comb works in Forbes Street in his teens. At around twenty he went to Ogston & Tennant soap and candle works in the Gallowgate where he remained for 50 years until he retired. He became cashier after he was there about 10 years. He died in 1948 aged 86.

So, a career lasting nearly 60 years, with perhaps three jobs, two employers; the same general occupation for nearly 60 years, the same employer, in the same building, for 50 years, the same job for 40 years. Today's student, looking forward to a career of continuous upward mobility, or constantly changing experiences, or the continuous development of new skills and challenges, would find it hard to endure the prospect of such a career. Yet great-uncle Allan appears to have been a man who knew how to be loyal to his employer and his trade, with an employer and a trade which knew how to be loyal to him. As a result, he may well have lived a life of relative security and perhaps even, within the mini-world of the Ogston & Tennant soap and candle works, challenge and responsibility. At all events, it apparently provided him with 50 years' uninterrupted employment. How many of today's fast-changing organizations would be able to do the same?

What were the forces governing great-uncle Allan's career? Why did he remain for so long in the same organization, in the same occupation? Two contrasting explanations can be put forward. Perhaps the social structure of Scotland in the late nineteenth and early twentieth century, or the organization structure of Ogston & Tennant, were so rigid that no other movement was possible; great-uncle Allan may have lived his career as no more than a helpless cog in a much greater organizational machine. Alternatively, he may have been the executor and controller of his own career, consciously remaining at Ogston & Tennant long-term because he found that his work in the organization satisfied his needs (for security, social interaction, challenge, or whatever else it might be) better than employment elsewhere might have done.

The first of these views considers careers as organizational phenomena (a sociological explanation), the second states that they are products of individual behaviour (a psychological explanation). In a seminal work, Pugh (1966) urges us to study organizational phenomena from both a sociological and a psychological perspective. If we view great-uncle Allan's career as simply a by-product of wider societal and organizational forces – for example, the market for soap and candles, the system of production and record-keeping set up by Ogston & Tennant to exploit the market – and fail to consider his own contribution to that career through his own behaviour, we are, according to Pugh, saying that these possibly important individual forces are of no account. If, alternatively, we believe that great-uncle Allan's career was explained totally by what he did, his work motivation and behaviour over a lifetime – and fail to consider the structures of organization and opportunity at Ogston & Tennant and elsewhere – we are saying that these possibly important sociological forces are of no account. In studying careers, as with other organizational phenomena, we need to pay attention both to broad economic and social (especially organizational) structures and to individual behaviour within and between these structures.

Careers, then, have an interesting duality (Hughes, 1937; Barley, 1989; Gunz, 1989). From the individual perspective, the one which great-uncle Allan most likely applied to his own experience, the career consists of a sequence of specific jobs, whereby the person can 'construct' his or her own pathway towards a desired pattern of status, wealth and fulfilment. But from an organizational perspective, such as that of the Ogston & Tennant soap and candle works, careers are seen as a way of obtaining, retaining, building and utilizing the skills and commitment which the organization needs.

In this chapter, I seek to consider how the careers of individuals, and the organizations within which careers develop, affect and interact with each other. My general thesis is that both organizations and careers are undergoing massive changes in their nature at the present time, and that these changes are closely related. In essence, organizations are becoming more fragmented and unstable, and careers are becoming less predictable, plannable and organizationally oriented.

From a sociological viewpoint, we might say that, as organizations become less structured, hierarchical and monolithic, new forms of career are created: continuous organizational and occupational careers transmute into, and are replaced by, interorganizational, transoccupational careers and other discontinuous careers. From a psychological point of view, we might say that individuals increasingly seek careers based on more demanding motives than those of status in, and loyalty to, the employer: in constructing these careers in the pursuit of variety, responsibility, autonomy and excellence, they destabilize old organizational forms and generate new, organic ones.

Bureaucratic Structure and Organizational Careers

Much of our thinking about careers is derived from, and sustained by, the assumed predominance of large bureaucratic organizations in our society. As Max Weber (1958) correctly predicted, bureaucracy has been the dominating form of social institution in the twentieth century.

The influential research of Pugh and his associates – the 'Aston Group' – edited in Pugh and Hickson, 1976; Pugh and Hinings, 1976; Pugh and Payne, 1977, has been well informed by the bureaucratic perspective. In their work specifying and operationally defining the key parameters of bureaucracy the Aston researchers refined descriptions of the anatomical form of organizations. They created a 'blueprint' for the bureaucratic form and at the same time showed that a bureaucracy is indeed an organization managed by blueprint, that is, one whose functioning is predetermined by explicit and implicit plans of operation. Bureaucracy typically involves formal recruitment and selection procedures to place suitable people in jobs; job descriptions rationally written so that all work is covered but no jobs overlap; standardized procedures so that things are done in standard, appropriate and manageable ways; and definitions of authority restricting decision makers to decisions they are competent to make. Bureaucracy has been immensely successful. Most of the business and public service organizations which dominate Western economies have a substantially bureaucratic form.

Pugh and the Aston Group defined the bureaucratic model in terms of a set of structural dimensions (Pugh *et al.*, 1968). Thus organizations might develop a system of highly specialized functions and roles (specialization), a set of formal descriptions of the way particular jobs and procedures were to be performed (standardizaton, formalization) and a hierarchical structure of authority for organizational decision making (centralization). They showed that an organization's structure, thus defined, was determined in part by 'contextual' factors such as its size, ownership and technology, and in part by its own choice. Organizations faced dilemmas in deciding the extent to which they would impose bureaucratic structure. Therefore both the context of the organization and the discretion of management led to a range of different types of organizational form within which individuals might build their careers.

The Aston researchers concluded from their study of these bureaucratic dimensions that the different aspects of the bureaucratic model were not necessarily perfectly correlated: they concluded, 'the concept of *the* bureaucratic type is no longer useful' (Pugh and Hickson, 1976, p. 51). Nevertheless, it is instructive to consider how the Aston dimensions – the different aspects of bureaucracy – are likely to affect career forms and career behaviour. The hierarchy of authority creates clear linear career paths which individual employees typically seek to ascend as their careers progress. The attractiveness of the path may depend on the centralization–decentralization aspect and the gradient of organizational power which one ascends. Specialized roles define the jobs which form the building-blocks of the career, and create opportunities for individuals to commence their careers by becoming 'expert' in a relatively narrow range of skills. As they ascend the organization they must progressively broaden their expertise so that they can take responsibility for the coordination and control of ranges of related roles, or for whole functions such as finance or marketing. Like specialization, standardization and formalization constrain individual discretion in the initial career stages. More broadly, employees build organization-specific expertise and improved understanding of a complex system as they remain within it and ascend through it. Taken together, the characteristics of bureaucratic organizations might be expected to encourage those who seek security, stability and certainty in their developing career, and to discourage, at least in the short term, those who seek autonomy, variety and challenge.

Another aspect of organization which was considered by the Aston researchers was 'configuration' or organizational shape (Pugh and Hickson, 1976, p. 53). In shape, formal organizations are often thought of as triangles, representative of an organization chart, with the hierarchy being indicated by the vertical dimension of the triangle, and the 'spans of control' or number of subordinates directly supervised by each manager determining the triangle's width. A 'tall' organization will have a long hierarchy and narrow spans of control, whereas a 'flat' one will have few hierarchical levels and wide spans. Again, configuration is determined in part by contextual variables, in part by management choice. In terms of careers, the narrow spans in tall organizations suggest that a new employee starting at the bottom might reasonably anticipate a career with relatively regular promotions to higher levels; the beginner in a flat organization may feel closer to the top, but may also find that it takes a frustratingly long time to make any 'vertical' career progress.

Without people and their energy, an organization structure is of course no more than a skeleton without flesh. Whether or not the work of the organization is predetermined by bureaucratic specification, it must attract qualified people and motivate them to perform. One of the characteristics of bureaucracy described by Weber (1958) designed to bring this about was the *career system*. That is, the positions in the organization were to be arranged in a hierarchy of increasing responsibility, status and formal rewards. Employees' direct work efforts were, of course, to be confined to the jobs they held; but at the same time, their growing expertise gained through doing their work equipped them for ever more senior roles.

Individuals were expected to develop loyalty and commitment not just to the position they occupied but to the whole organization. Thus the individual's commitment to the organization was based on a mutual understanding between employer and employee that a long-term contract was being made, and that enduring loyalty by the individual to the organization would be reciprocated by enduring loyalty of the organization to the individual. The employee was virtually assured of job security and steady promotion to the end of his or her working life, and quite possibly a comfortable pension beyond that. The 'organizational career' was a key component of the pyramidal post-war businesses characterized in William H. Whyte's (1957) *The Organization Man*.

'Organizational careers' depend on a *commitment* model of human resource management (Beer *et al.*, 1985). Employees are encouraged to commit their long-term allegiance to the employer. While this allegiance is based on guarantees of security of employment and of continually increasing status, the organization can do much more. 'Enriched' jobs, good pay and responsibility help employees to 'feel good' about the company. Company-sponsored opportunities for further training and development equip employees for their future roles in the company. Corporate social amenities and the cultivation of a strong 'corporate culture' increase employees' identification with the organization. 'Perks' for status, membership of a company pension fund and company health care encourage a growing dependence by the employee on the organization. Welfare and social provisions may even result in the employee's family being dependent on the company. All these encourage a long-term relationship between the individual and the organization and the building of organizational careers.

For the company, the organizational career system creates a corps of skilled and motivated staff whose long-term loyalty can be counted on and who are constantly developing expertise relevant to the company. For the individual, the benefit is predictability, continuous work in a familiar setting and the opportunity to perform, to progress and to develop new skills unhindered by anxiety about the future. Modern prescriptions for the management of human resources advise organizations to use the enticements of secure careers to acquire, retain and develop the competencies on which competitiveness is thought to be based. The well-known Harvard framework of human resource management (HRM) advocates that the organization must build commitment, competence, congruence (of employee efforts with organizational objectives) and cost-effectiveness (Beer *et al.*, 1985).

The success, in the post-war era, of the large Japanese manufacturing companies such as Toyota and Matsushita is often attributed to their ability to offer 'lifetime' employment and career systems offering total career security, with the additional benefits of a wide variety of jobs, the constant accrual of greater status and extensive medical, educational and social support for workers and their families. In other respects, these organizations departed somewhat from the bureaucratic model, for example by developing collective rather than individual forms of responsibility and decision making (Ouchi, 1981). But their hierarchies were rigid, their progressions seniority-based, their recruitment to all but entry-level jobs always from within the organization. The hierarchical structure of these companies was reinforced by a culture emphasizing loyalty, teamwork and collective success, and by the usual inducements of salary, security, welfare and pension. Their remorseless growth provided an ever-expanding hierarchy of roles through which careers could develop.

Individual Career Theory and Occupational Careers

If we try to understand careers, not from the perspective of those interested in organizations (the sociological perspective), but from the perspective of those interested in individual people (the psychological perspective), a very different picture emerges. For the organization, careers may be a means of mobilizing human energy and developing human skills towards organizational goals. For the individual, careers are much more likely to be seen as a means of meeting personal needs as diverse as security, social contact and personal fulfilment, over the period of a working life. Career theories have often taken this individual perspective, which is a foundation of modern practices of career guidance (Montross and Shinkman, 1992).

Individual theories attribute a much more proactive role to the person in constructing his or her own career. It is assumed that, rather than being a pawn in the grip of powerful organizational and managerial forces, the individual is an autonomous decision maker choosing career moves and constructing the career to his or her best personal advantage, for example deliberately moving through the organization as an exercise in personal development and self-fulfilment rather than being transferred around to ensure organizational needs are met.

Career theories often have pragmatic objectives. They seek to 'match' people and careers (Betz *et al.*, 1989). It is assumed that people will be more productive and more satisfied if their abilities, personality and interests are in some way suited to the work they do, and if they can see a path ahead towards the fulfilment of long-term goals.

Assessment of people's characteristics may assist us to determine their suitability for particular organizations or types of organization. For example, Schein's (1978) 'career anchor' theory suggests that career behaviours are mediated by relatively enduring clusters of values and interests: one may, for example be oriented towards 'security' or 'autonomy' or 'technical proficiency'. Self-knowledge or appropriate guidance may well enable one to choose an organization whose activities, structure and culture are in sympathy with one's orientations.

More commonly, however, these theories, and the prevailing conventional wisdom about how careers work, are based less upon the concept of 'organization' than upon that of 'occupation'. 'Person-fit' career theories relate people's characteristics to specifiable types of work role. Abilities, interests and values are more easily related to particular types of job than to particular organizations. We can assess individuals' abilities and their vocational interests (such as 'technical', 'numerical', 'artistic') in order to help – through vocational guidance or personnel selection – to improve the fit. Various 'systems' exist to test one's make-up and assist one to make appropriate career choices (Strong, 1943; Holland, 1985). There is evidence that a good fit does indeed assist career adjustment (Betz *et al.*, 1989). On the basis of this theory, careers are built around occupations – for example, bricklayer, hairdresser, nurse, accountant – rather than organizations.

In thinking about their careers, people tend to identify with occupations rather than organizations: 'I'm a computer programmer' rather than 'I work for IBM'. Parents and teachers encourage children to enter a trade or profession which can be practised sequentially in a variety of different organizational settings. For all the acknowledged dominance of big organizations as institutions in our society, they are not seen as the location of careers, except, presumably, by those who are building careers closely allied to particular organizations.

Occupational careers develop their own bureaucratic tendencies. They are assisted by the specialization of roles and of functions in organizations described in the Aston research (Pugh and Hickson, 1976) and also by the bonds of common interest that tend to develop among disparate members of a particular occupational group. Educational and training institutions, professional and trade associations, and trade unions become gatekeepers to the occupation. Certification as a medical practitioner, lawyer, physiotherapist or cabinet maker provides the individual with a basis to build a 'boundaryless' career (Arthur, 1994a); that is, one that is interorganizational rather than intraorganizational.

Individuals cultivating occupational careers will have a self-identity based on specialist skills and interests. They will seek to develop their careers by adding to these skills, practising them to a higher standard, taking up new challenges and more responsible work within their occupational area, and gaining in reputation rather than in organizational status. Which organization they work in will be a matter of indifference, except insofar as the organization values and enables them to develop their occupational skills.

The Limitations of Organizational and Occupational Careers

Organization and occupation therefore represent two alternative institutions around which we are encouraged to think about and structure our careers. They provide focus, mechanisms for protecting security and a means of providing, potentially, ever-increasing accomplishment and seniority. They can also be easily integrated, or moved between. Many individuals train for an occupational career, but later find a niche within a particular organization where they can broaden their skills from the specialist base, an example being a cost accountant who rises in one organization to become the senior financial executive. Others use the expertise they acquire in one organization to pursue occupational careers elsewhere: for example, a member of the IBM organization eventually becomes a self-employed analyst–programmer.

Many careers, including those of great-uncle Allan, of the writer and of Professor Pugh in whose honour this book is written, have been built on the twin organizational and occupational career systems: acquiring occupational expertise and then (eventually) using it in long-term loyal service to a single organization. However, as the twentieth century draws to a close, over-reliance on such a picture of careers as being prototypical involves dangerous conservative biases and is increasingly out of kilter with the changing nature of organizations and of work. For example, an accountant qualified in the early 1960s in accountancy, auditing and company law. He pursued his career as a professional accountant, moving between different companies to utilize his different skills (an occupational career), but also endeavouring to gain status within each company (an organizational career). He confidently expected to become, in due course, either a chief accountant, a company secretary, or a partner in an accounting firm. But as he went on, the finance-related skills needed by companies changed, and the organizations he joined restructured or went out of business. In 1995, in an economic boom, he had, at the age of 55, been virtually unemployed for 10 years. Can organizations and occupations be relied on, as great-uncle Allan was able to rely on them, to provide a secure basis for one's career?

A new MBA programme was started by a university in a major city. It was 'executive' in style; that is, it was limited to local managers of substantial experience who studied part-time while continuing to pursue careers in local companies. The university believed that, by enabling these managers to add a general business education to the specialist occupational qualifications they already possessed, it could help them to increase their breadth and value to their organizations and thereby enable them to gain merited promotion. The qualification was therefore promoted, not only to the prospective students, but to their employing organizations as a means of increasing their organizational expertise. To the embarrassment of the university and the chagrin of the employing companies, nearly all the students used the opportunity to move into some completely new line of work, in many cases in self-employment, and nearly always in different organizations. Do individuals any longer seek, as great-uncle Allan sought, to spend their careers within one organization or one specialist field?

It seems likely that, at least since the Second World War, the stability of careers and their adherence to organizational and occupational forms has been seriously overestimated. For a start, the concept of 'career', with its connotations of security, focus, progression and planning (Inkson, 1995), is a very middle-class idea. Many people still pursue 'jobs' or 'employment' on a continuing basis, without having any concept that these are linked meaningfully as a career.

Among professional and managerial staff, too, career stability may be overemphasized. In our consciousness of the secure, career-building Japanese 'salaryman' in his loyal relationship with the large corporation, we tend to forget that Japan has a huge small-business sector, that large Japanese corporations outsource much of their work through temporary contracts from smaller contractors, and that only a minority of Japanese therefore enjoy the secure organizational careers described earlier.

Nicholson and West (1989) found that, of a large sample of job changes reported by British managers in the early 1980s, nearly half involved a change of employer (not good evidence for organizational careers) and over three-quarters involved changing to a different function (not good evidence for occupational careers, though admittedly people defined as 'managers' would be more likely to shift functions than other, more specialized groups). Since the managers in this study were changing jobs approximately once every three years, it is likely that few of them were experiencing smooth linear careers. Cawsey and Inkson (1993) replicated these results in New Zealand.

Careers are often interrupted. Economic cycles, new technology, changing public fashions and differential business and entrepreneurial skills mean that some organizations flourish, multiplying the career opportunities they provide, whereas others shrink, restructure, reduce their size or close down, casting career makers out into an uncertain world. Those who base their careers on occupations find that their qualifications and their definition of what the occupation is may quickly become obsolete. In the British recession of the late 1980s and early 1990s, and the organizational restructuring that accompanied it, many linear careers were disrupted by redundancies, demotions and unwanted transfers (Inkson, 1995), resulting in disillusion, cynicism and reduced motivation (Goffee and Scase, 1992).

Both occupational and organizational career systems depend on the continuing existence of 'jobs', usually meaning full-time jobs. Jobs are the building-blocks of careers, the stopping-places between the transitions to organizational or occupational success. Jobs are an artificial invention of the nineteenth and twentieth century whereby, for the convenience of employees, work is divided up into packages of related duties, each package if possible being about 40 hours' worth per week, accomplished during weekdays. But such formulations carry fatal inflexibilities. Part-time, temporary and contract forms of employment are increasing, and full-time 'jobs' are declining. 'Jobs' as we commonly understand them are disappearing, and we are increasingly having to make our way in a 'de-jobbed' world (Bridges, 1995).

Even in large corporations, individuals are being encouraged to move beyond a defined job and to treat the work they do as part of a team achievement, broadening their contributions and seeing work from a more social perspective. The employee does not have a clearly defined 'job' but is expected to be able to turn their hand to the changing needs of the team. If careers are seen as life-long sequences of defined 'jobs', how do we understand careers when jobs no longer exist?

Organizational and occupational career systems also tend to ignore the relationship of one's career to one's wider life. Health issues, marriage, bearing and rearing children, the development of family life and its demands upon the career maker, the interacting career of one's spouse, leisure interests and location preferences may all interrupt the smooth accrual of organizational status or occupational skills. Historically, career theories have been formulated with men in mind (Marshall, 1989). In particular, careers are viewed as being continuous where only men find continuous employment possible. Organizational and occupational career systems are often incompatible with the need of most women – and an increasing number of men – to spend long periods with the work career in suspension while family life is given priority.

The Dissolution of Boundaries

What we appear to be witnessing in our developing organizational and non-organizational life is the gradual dissolution of *boundaries*. A boundary is a division between two definably different things. This is France, that is Germany – the boundary can be precisely defined. You cannot be in both France and Germany simultaneously (though one day you will be able to be so, when the European Union removes the boundary). In traditional organization theory, organizations are considered to have clear boundaries. An individual or an activity is either in the organization or outside the organization. In the Aston studies, Pugh and his colleagues defined the organizational boundary very carefully so that the organization could be measured. Employees were inside the boundary and could be counted precisely at any given time. Suppliers were outside the boundary, part of the 'context'.

The Aston system of organizational measurement is also a means of describing the degree of definition of the organization's *internal* boundaries – boundaries around hierarchical levels, boundaries around departments, boundaries around jobs, boundaries around the way things are to be done. Occupations have boundaries, too, defined in requirements for previous qualifications and experience, or for professional membership.

Boundaries have their value. They tell us where we are and where we should be. They enable us to know who is 'us' and who is 'them'. They keep intruders off our turf, they protect our privacy. They provide structure and certainty in an uncertain world. They give us a clear map upon which we can plan our lives, including our careers. But if ever a trend was apparent in the latter stages of the twentieth century, it is that boundaries are dissolving. Modern organization theory increasingly regards boundaries as being permeable and arbitrary (Quinn, 1992). When an organization involves itself in a series of joint ventures, collaborates rather than competes with same-industry companies, outsources critical componentry or replaces some of its core long-service employees with temporary contractors, it becomes harder to see where its external boundaries are. When it reduces its number of status levels, gets its managers to do their own personnel management rather than relying on a central department, and replaces individual job descriptions with statements of team or company goals, then its internal boundaries also fade.

Students of management are familiar with the popular different forms of traditional organization: functional, divisionalized and matrix. These develop as a firm grows, integrates vertically and seeks to acquire dominance in an increasing range of markets. Each form provides the firm with particular advantages, but each also requires a different mix of skills from employees: technical skills in functional organizations, commercial and governance skills in divisionalized organizations, collaborative skills in matrix organizations. As organizations strive to adapt their forms to the new international, technological, competitive environment, they increasingly focus on their own core areas of excellence, relying for the accomplishment of other necessary work on outsourcing, joint ventures and external networks. This fundamentally alters the mix of required skills, putting an emphasis on collaborative, cross-boundary skills such as referral, partnering and relationship management (Miles and Snow, 1996).

Handy (1989) has suggested that, in place of the clearly-bounded triangular hierarchies described in the Aston Studies, we can expect that future organizations will resemble three-leaf 'shamrocks': with one leaf representing the 'core' permanent staff, and the others representing respectively the 'contractual fringe' – short–term contractors – and 'the flexible labour force' of part-time and temporary employees. Many contractors and others will also work for other organizations. Both the external and internal boundaries of the organization become increasingly hard to define. The dissolution of structure is necessary because of the exigencies of the competitive situation and the necessity of adapting with speed (Peters, 1990). When the structure, especially the external boundary, becomes sufficiently blurred, it is legitimate to ask whether we should still be talking about 'the organization' as a definable entity, rather than 'organization' as a continual process (Arthur and Rousseau, 1996). We may also ask how organizational careers can develop without a structure for them to develop along.

The boundaries of occupations, like those of organizations, are increasingly threatened. Like the accountant referred to earlier, one may acquire skills in an occupation, and membership of it, only to find that its protective boundary dissolves or is redrawn by economic circumstance. The career blacksmith, once common, is nowadays rare. While professionals such as lawyers and accountants are better protected, continued professional membership nowadays is dependent on the constant upgrading of skills, as dictated by governing professional bodies, as the profession redefines itself in the face of technical and scientific developments. Even in large corporations, employees are encouraged to develop themselves outside their specialist occupational boundaries and to become multi-skilled 'team players' (Casey, 1995).

There are plenty of other examples of disappearing boundaries. A new employee of W.L. Gore and Co, an organization which attempts to define itself as a 'lattice' rather than a hierarchy, arrived on his first day and asked what his job was. The manager's answer was: 'Why don't you look around and find something you'd like to do?' (Shipper and Manz, 1992). In such a system, control through job definition is replaced by encouraging energy through personal commitment: one's only boundaries are self-imposed.

Information technology destroys, not only organizational boundaries, but also the boundary between work and home: when an accountant or a plumber acquires a cell-phone, he or she is knowingly making a choice which means that customer service may intrude on 'production', and also that work may intrude on home life, and home life on work. An employee of a company in Sydney may serve it from her at-home terminal in Singapore.

The boundaryless organization can be portrayed as exciting and glamorous: the abolition of pettifogging rules and regulations, the replacement of hierarchy and seniority by opportunity, the promise of easier escape from stultifying employment, a fuller integration and expression of oneself – these make a seductive picture. On the other hand, 'boundarylessness' is often not voluntary: workers in reduced organizations are suddenly made redundant; lower-status workers are put on temporary contracts, lose their security and become marginalized; those who remain become alienated through restructuring as the boundaries they have trusted for years are redrawn or disappear; their job descriptions disappear and are replaced by abruptly changing sequences of project assignment (Heckscher, 1995). Those who survive, those who build careers, will, it seems, be the multi-skilled and the flexible, but also perhaps the disloyal and the opportunistic, while those in difficulties will be the poorly educated and the rigid, but also the specialist and the loyal.

Boundaryless Careers

Kanter (1989) notes that there are three different career forms: the bureaucratic form, based on a logic of advancement (the 'organizational' career); the professional form, based on a logic of developing reputation within a specialist field (the 'occupational' career); and the entrepreneurial form, based on a logic of ownership and adding value. These are 'pure' types: most likely, few individuals have careers that are purely organizational, or purely occupational, or purely entrepreneurial, but the types help us to understand shifting forces acting on behaviour as the individual moves through the career. The logics underlying the forms come partly from social and organizational forces such as manner of production, the demand for skills and organizational and interorganizational structures, and partly from the individual's own changing circumstances and aspirations.

The 'new' type of career form suggested by Kanter is the entrepreneurial. She points out that entrepreneurial careers are not restricted to the owners of organizations or to the self-employed: other examples of people pursuing entrepreneurial careers might be commission-paid salespeople with high autonomy to develop their territory; contractors paid for the achievement of results and not employed by the contracting organization; experts employed for the duration of a single project; and leased executives. The entrepreneurial career maker owns his or her skills, and directs effort into gaining a personal return on this piece of capital and into increasing its value. As a capitalist, the career maker seeks to make business contracts, whether as an 'internal' employee or as an 'external' contractor, which best protect and develop his or her resources. He or she may of course choose to conduct the entire career, or a major part of it, within a single organization or occupation. But the logic of the career will be quite different than in an organizational or occupational career. If organizations and occupations are to embrace such careers, they will have to change drastically.

Of the three forms, the entrepreneurial career appears best suited to flourish in a boundaryless world. As boundaries dissolve, work is done more and more by people in these entrepreneurial roles. A major challenge for career theory is to go beyond the understanding of the roles themselves and to define a logic of role-to-role advancement or progression. A second challenge is to determine practical principles whereby organizations can develop new patterns of human resource management practice to reflect the growing reality of entrepreneurial careers. A third is to teach career makers to adapt their career planning and skill acquisition strategies to the new realities.

In response to the disappearance of boundaries, particularly boundaries around and within organizations, Arthur (1994a) and Arthur and Rousseau (1996) have stimulated and developed a new literature on boundaryless careers. In a boundaryless career, according to Arthur (1994b, p. 296), the career may:

- move across the boundaries of separate employers;
- draw validation from outside the present employer;
- be sustained by extraorganizational networks of information;
- break intraorganizational boundaries, especially hierarchical;
- be independent of traditional organizational career principles.

A key feature of boundaryless careers is their dependence on informal networks, both social and informational. Every career is to some extent sustained by networks. For example, in a high proportion of cases where individuals move to new positions, they obtain them through a connection in a personal network (Inkson *et al.*, 1995). Those seeking to build organizational careers seek to cultivate appropriate relationships with the powerful and the well-informed in their organizations. Those pursuing professional careers seek to acquire and develop a good reputation in the eyes of their professional peers outside their employing organization: in Kanter's (1989) terms, 'Have reputation, will travel'. But these networks are cultivated within constraining (organizational or occupational) boundaries. Furthermore, as Raider and Burt (1996) show, they tend to contain too many redundant and overlapping connections to enable the individual to develop a strong 'social capital'. Individuals will inreasingly turn to communities and networks beyond their regular ones – communities based on industry, region, and non-work for example – if they are to acquire the information, contacts and reputation to enhance a boundaryless career.

Although boundaryless career theory has been developed largely as an alternative to organizationally bounded concepts of career, boundaryless career concepts may help us to see how the work/non-work boundary might also be made more permeable. The inapplicability to women's careers of 'continuous' career models, and the failure of these models to allow for the transferability of non-work experience to work roles, have been much criticized (Marshall, 1989). An alternative career theory would see the individual's career as involving a continuing sequence of overlapping and developing social roles, including non-work as well as work roles. Present attempts to break down the barrier are limited by the common managerial assumption that work roles and non-work roles are not just mutually exclusive but adversarial (Fletcher and Bailyn, 1996).

In boundaryless careers, collaborative skills such as those developed in family settings are increasingly valued. In boundaryless careers, work is increasingly arranged in temporary projects, employees are accountable for results rather than nine-to-five presence and linear ascent is devalued as a marker of career success. Under these circumstances, discontinuous work careers become more possible. It is arguable that the move to boundaryless careers restores some equity to women, who are socialized to expect the necessity of career discontinuity and may be more flexible in their consideration of opportunities.

Boundaryless careers have been described as 'repositories of knowledge' (Bird, 1994). On this view, the underlying principle of career development is to develop expertise through continuous new challenges. It is of course possible to interpret organizational and occupational careers in the same way, but the type of knowledge developed in these careers would be, as we have seen, restricted by boundaries. In the new environment, knowledge is built across organizations and across occupational boundaries. Thus a young accounting graduate, finding herself stereotyped as an accounting specialist, deliberately gained experience in marketing in various marketing roles in a major corporation; but her objective was not to secure promotion or to become an expert in that organization's specific marketing problems, but to gain marketing expertise on a broad front which would enable her to develop her career elsewhere. So, even during the five years she worked for the corporation, she was indulging in boundaryless behaviour: when the right opportunity arose – as marketing manager for a much smaller company – she left.

Conceptualizing careers as boundaryless helps us to see that influence effects between organizations and employees are not all one-way. The organizational career system emphasizes the effects of organizations on people. Careers are seen as sequences of organizationally induced moves between organizationally defined 'jobs'. Individuals pursuing boundaryless careers reverse this cause and effect, enacting their wish to pursue knowledge in 'collective improvisation' (Weick, 1996) with other career makers. They thus replace the logic of permanent hierarchy with a logic of transitory collaboration. Rather than seeing the career as a logical long-term by-product of organization structure and functioning, we may see the organization as a shifting nexus of interacting career behaviours.

Careers and Human Resource Management

In recent years, the focus in strategic management has shifted from the external to the internal: from the analysis of the market and the company's competitive environment (for example, Porter, 1985) to the company's internal resources, particularly human resources (Lado and Wilson, 1994), to enable it to meet the market demands and sustain a competitive advantage. But how are appropriate human resources to be acquired, maintained and adapted to changing demands? Some maintain that it is essential to have human resource management strongly focused in the company's strategic planning

(Schuler and Jackson, 1987; Boxall, 1994), thereby developing competencies which are 'firm-specific, embedded in a firm's history and culture, and generating tacit organizational knowledge' (Lado and Wilson, 1994); 'HR practices ... can be levers to develop the human capital to behave in ways congruent with firm goals, the "essence" of strategic human resource management' (Wright *et al.*, 1994).

Commitment-building practices are appropriate to traditional corporate forms and organizational careers. They place the responsibility for the individual's career development in the hands of his or her employing organization. They require the organization to specify required skills ahead of time and to develop these skills in current staff. They involve the inculcation of the firm's culture as part of development. They limit the individual's autonomy, and arguably constrain his or her long-term employability. They may not appeal either to tomorrow's boundaryless organization, with its requirements for flexibility, renewal and external engagement, or to tomorrow's 'boundaryless career maker' who will seek a career of increasing cross-company employability through unfolding project-to-project transitions.

Waterman *et al.* (1994) argue that employers and employees can build a 'career-resilient workforce' by developing a new covenant of shared responsibility for maintaining and developing the individual's longer-term employability, including his or her employability outside the organization. However, even this model may involve a degree of organizational dependence incompatible with the boundaryless career model in its pure form. Jones (1996), in detailing the decline of the large studio system of film-making and its replacement by a system of one-off projects staffed by itinerant professionals building reputational careers, provides an alternative template for the meshing of business goals with individual careers. On this model, the short-term acquisition of human resources by the organization becomes the critical human resource function, and the responsibility for the development of competencies and reputation is devolved to individuals.

Individual Career Planning

Finally, let us consider the implications of this chapter for the individual career maker, such as the student reader of this book. It is evident that the business environment in which people build their careers is changing rapidly. Recent academic thinking and research has enabled us to plot these changes and understand their significance, but, I suggest, public and managerial stereotypes based on obsolete models remain dominant. As a result, many systems of human resource management continue to be based on outmoded expectations of career behaviour; and many individuals enter their careers and attempt to advance them on the basis of false expectations. The false rhetoric is colluded in by the corporations continuing to encourage organizational careers, occupational bodies and trade unions, and schools, tertiary institutes and guidance bodies promoting traditional careers.

A theme in careers research, which harks back to the issue of sociological versus psychological explanation explored by Pugh (1966) is, 'Who is in charge?' Are careers imposed on individuals by their organizations or wider forces, or do individuals choose and create their own destinies? The labour market is important: in times of skill shortage, skilled people dominate the market and create their own futures; in times of surplus, they are at the mercy of the organization – their 'boundarylessness' is involuntary (Inkson, 1995).

Knowledge and skill are the human capital of career builders. No longer able to rely on organizations or professional bodies to guide their knowledge acquisition, they must take responsibility for their own careers and choose opportunities which are not only rewarding in their own right, but also result in accumulation of capital in a currency with future value. Every job or project must be evaluated not only in terms of its material rewards and job satisfaction but also in terms of its potential learning, social as well as cognitive, and the likely relationship of that learning to possible future developments.

Career makers need to have a keen awareness of their own aptitudes and values ('knowing-why', Arthur *et al.*, 1995); a developing portfolio of skill and knowledge informed by good information about the future ('knowing-how') and a far-reaching network of contacts and sources of information ('knowing-whom'). They need to avoid, in general, the blandishments of the large corporation view of their development. They should also avoid being hung up on security, status and salary as the markers of career success. They should be willing to accept short-term project work from which important career-relevant learning will come. They should be alert to new opportunities and active – even during periods of relatively secure employment – in gathering information about them, and in building external networks. If the watchwords of past careers were 'organization' and 'occupation', that of the future will be 'opportunity'.

Conclusion

Careers have been described as the threads of which organizations are woven (Arthur and Rousseau, 1996). The excitement of the new age of careers in the twenty-first century is the thought that, more and more, the work can be done, not by a gigantic organizationally controlled loom, but by thousands of individual career builders, spinning their own lives and finding for themselves new patterns to weave into an ever-richer texture of organizational life.

Note

1 The author wishes to thank Michael Arthur and David Brock for their helpful comments on a first draft of this chapter.

References

Arthur, M.B. (ed.) (1994a), 'Special Issue: The boundaryless career', *Journal of Organizational Behavior*, **15**, 295–381.

Arthur, M.B. (1994b), 'The boundaryless career: a new perspective for organizational inquiry', *Journal of Organizational Behavior*, **15**, 295–306.

Arthur, M.B., and Rousseau, D.M. (eds) (1996), *The Boundaryless Career: A New Employment Principle for a New Organizational Era*, New York: Oxford University Press.

Arthur, M.B., Claman, P., and DeFillippi, R. (1995), 'Intelligent enterprise, intelligent careers', *Academy of Management Executive*, **9**, 7–20.

Barley, S.R. (1989), 'Careers, identities, and institutions', in M.B. Arthur, D.T. Hall, and B.S. Lawrence (eds), *Handbook of Career Theory*, Cambridge: Cambridge University Press.

Beer, M., Sector, B., Lawrence, P.R. and Walton, R.E. (1985), *Human Resource Management*. New York: The Free Press.

Betz, N.E., Fitzgerald, L.F. and Hill, R.E. (1989), 'Trait-factor theories: traditional cornerstone of career theory', in M.B. Arthur, D.T. Hall and B.S. Lawrence (eds), *Handbook of Career Theory*, Cambridge: Cambridge University Press.

Bird, A. (1994), 'Careers as repositories of knowledge', *Journal of Organizational Behavior*, **15**, 325–44.

Boxall, P. (1994), 'Placing HR strategy at the heart of business success', *International Journal of Human Resource Management*, **4**, 645–64.

Bridges, W. (1995), *JobShift: How to Prosper in a Workplace without Jobs*, London: Allen & Unwin.

Casey, C. (1995), *Work, Self and Society After Industrialism*, London: Routledge.

Cawsey, T. and Inkson, K. (1993), 'Patterns of managerial job change: a New Zealand study', *New Zealand Journal of Business*, **14**, 13–25.

Fletcher, J.K. and Bailyn, L. (1996), 'Challenging the last boundary: re-connecting work and family', in M.B. Arthur and D.M. Rousseau (eds), *The Boundaryless Career: A New Employment Principle for a New Organizational Era*, New York: Oxford University Press.

Goffee, R. and Scase, R. (1992), 'Organizational change and the corporate career: the restructuring of managers' job aspirations', *Human Relations*, **45**, 363–85.

Gunz, H.P. (1989), 'The dual meaning of managerial careers: organizational and individual levels of analysis', *Journal of Management Studies*, **26**, 225–50.

Handy, C. (1994), *The Empty Raincoat.: Making Sense of the Future*, London: Hutchinson.

Heckscher, C. (1995), *White-Collar Blues: Management Loyalties in an Age of Corporate Restructuring*, New York: Basic Books.

Holland, J.L. (1985), *Making Vocational Choices*, Englewood Cliffs, NJ: Prentice-Hall.

Hughes, E.C. (1937), 'Institutional office and the person', *American Journal of Sociology*, **43**, 104–43.

Inkson, K. (1995), 'The effects of economic recession on managerial job change and careers', *British Journal of Management*, **6**, 183–94.

Inkson, K., Arthur, M.B., Pringle, J. and O'Shea, K. (1995), 'Third millennium economies and boundaryless careers', paper given at Australian and New Zealand Academy of Management Annual Conference, Townsville, Queensland, December.

Jones, C. (1996), 'Careers in project networks: the case of the film industry', in M.B. Arthur and D.M. Rousseau (eds), *The Boundaryless Career: A New Employment Principle for a New Organizational Era*, New York: Oxford University Press.

Kanter, R.M. (1989), 'Careers and the wealth of nations: a macro-perspective on the structure and implications of career forms', in M.B. Arthur, D.T. Hall and B.S. Lawrence (eds), *Handbook of Career Theory*, Cambridge: Cambridge University Press.

Lado, A. and Wilson, M. (1994), 'Human resource systems and sustained competitive advantage: a competency-based perspective', *Academy of Management Review*, **19**, 699–727.

Marshall, J. (1989), 'Re-visioning career concepts: a feminist invitation', in M.B. Arthur, D.T. Hall and B.S. Lawrence (eds), *Handbook of Career Theory*, Cambridge: Cambridge University Press.

Miles, R.E. and Snow, C.C. (1996), 'Twenty-first century careers', in M.B. Arthur, and D.M. Rousseau (eds), *The Boundaryless Career: A New Employment Principle for a New Organizational Era*, New York: Oxford University Press.

Montross, D. and Shinkman, C.J. (eds) (1992), *Career Development: Theory and Practice*, Springfield, Ill.: Charles C. Thomas.

Nicholson, N. and West, M.A. (1988), *Managerial Job Change: Men and Women in Transition*, Cambridge: Cambridge University Press.

Ouchi, W.G. (1981), *Theory Z: How American Business Can Meet the Japanese Challenge*, Reading, Mass.: Addison-Wesley.

Peters, T. (1990), 'Prometheus nearly unbound', *Academy of Management Executive*, **4**, 70–84.

Porter, M. (1985), *Competitive Advantage: Creating and Sustaining Superior Performance*, New York: The Free Press.

Pugh, D.S. (1966), 'Modern organization theory: a psychological and sociological study', *Psychological Bulletin*, **66**, 235–51.

Pugh, D.S. and Hickson, D.J. (eds) (1976), *Organizational Structure in its Context: The Aston Programme I*, Aldershot: Gower.

Pugh, D.S. and Hinings, C.R. (eds) (1976), *Organizational Structure: Extensions and Replications: The Aston Programme II*, Aldershot: Gower.

Pugh, D.S. and Payne, R.L. (eds) (1977), *Organizational Behaviour in its Context: The Aston Programme III*, Aldershot: Gower.

Pugh, D.S., Hickson, D.J., Hinings, C.R. and Turner, C. (1968), 'Dimensions of organization structure', *Administrative Science Quarterly*, **13**, 65–105.

Quinn, J.B. (1992), *Intelligent Enterprise*, New York: The Free Press.

Raider, H. and Burt, R.S. (1996), 'Boundaryless careers and social capital', in M.B. Arthur and D.M. Rousseau (eds), *The Boundaryless Career: A New Employment Principle for a New Organizational Era*, New York: Oxford University Press.

Schein, E.H. (1978), *Career Dynamics: Matching Individual and Organizational Needs*, Reading, Mass.: Addison-Wesley.

Schuler, R. and Jackson, S. (1987), 'Linking competitive strategies with human resource management policies', *Academy of Management Executive*, **1**, 207–19.

Shipper, F. and C.C. Manz (1992), 'Employee self-management without formally designated teams', *Organizational Dynamics*, **20**, 48–61.

Strong, E.K. (1943), *Vocational Interests of Men and Women*, Stanford, CA: Stanford University Press.

Waterman, R.H., Waterman, J. and Collard, J. (1994), 'Toward a career-resilient workforce', *Harvard Business Review*, (July–August), 87–95.

Weber, M. (1958), *The Protestant Ethic and the Spirit of Capitalism*, New York: Scribner's (originally published in Germany, 1905).

Weick, K.M. (1996), 'Enactment and the boundaryless career: organizing as we work', in M.B. Arthur and D.M. Rousseau (eds), *The Boundaryless Career: A New Employment Principle for a New Organizational Era*, New York: Oxford University Press.

Whyte, W.H. (1957), *The Organization Man*, London: Cape.

Wright, P., McMahan, G. and Williams, A. (1994), 'Human resources and sustained competitive advantage: a resource-based perspective', *International Journal of Human Resource Management*, **5**, 301–26.

11 Rethinking Organizations

CHARLES HANDY

In the late 1960s, I went off to the Sloan School of Management at MIT to learn the theory of what I had been practising as a manager in an oil company for the previous ten years. It was there that I first came across the words 'organization behaviour'. Strangely, I had not, until then, thought of organizations 'behaving', but the more I learnt the more interested I became. It was when I came back to London, to manage executive programmes at the new London Business School, that I first met Derek Pugh who was shortly to become Britain's first ever Professor of Organization Behaviour at the School. I was clearly going to be in the right place at the right time!

Amid all the shifting sands of speculation about the ways of organizations, at that time, the work of the Aston Group stood out as some sort of sure rock of reliability. Where others relied for their propositions on the cooperation of reluctant students or on overdesigned and artificial experiments, the work of the Aston Group was based on reality, it could be measured, and it could be compared and contrasted across different types of organizations. To me, a novice in the area, it was a beacon of enlightenment and good sense, buttressed by good measures and sound research. I learnt much from Derek at that time, not only about organizations and how to look at them, but about the processes of research, about the education of managers and the strange ways of universities and business schools.

We both moved on, I from educating managers to speculating about the likely futures of organizations and their people in a changing world, and Derek to yet another innovative educational venture, the Open University and, in due course, the Open University Business School, where he ended as Professor of International Management, the right title, I suspect, for the times. Organizations, too, have changed and it is those changes that I want to address in this chapter. No longer, in my view, are organizations discrete entities which can be described and measured in the ways the Aston studies once did. No longer can we predict correlations as surely as we used to do, or neatly prescribe for managers how they should design and structure their institutions. We have to rethink *what* an organization is, conceptually, and *why* it exists, for what and for whom.

This is a task for a philosopher more than for a researcher, for philosophers pose questions which have yet to be asked and suggest answers which are often too new to be studied in action. I write, therefore, as a self-styled social philosopher intrigued by the future, its possibilities and its problems.

Virtuality and the New Science

Margaret Wheatley (1992) has written of the danger of believing in Newtonian organizations in a quantum age. Newton was not wrong. He just was not right enough to cope with the dilemmas of science now. Similarly, the old way of looking at organizations was not wrong; it just does not capture the real essence of what it means to organize today. Organizations are not the visible, tangible, obvious places that they used to be. No longer, for instance, do you have to have every-one in the same place at the same time in order to get things done. Place and time are now independent of one another. Global organizations will pass a project to a chain of groups around the world to keep pace with the time zones. More mundanely, people can work together connected only by their phones, fax or e-mail. If information is the raw material of the work, there need be no common space at all. Already the office blocks of our cities are being turned into apartments as their previous inhabitants find it too expensive to keep an asset available for 168 hours a week and yet have most of their people do their work elsewhere: on the train, in the plane, with the client, in their homes or on assignment.

More importantly, organizations no longer feel that they have to own all the people needed to get the work done, let alone have them where they can see them. Partnerships, outsourcing, flexible labour and interim managers are a way of keeping risks within bounds, and of exporting the slack needed to cope with the peaks or the emerg-encies. $1/2 \times 2 \times 3$ is now a favoured formula, meaning half as many people employed in future as there are now, paid on average twice as well (and working twice as hard) but producing three times as much. Some organizations are, in reality, little more than 'boxes of con-tracts', contracts with suppliers, agents and specialists of one sort or another, with no visible presence at all. The new library created in Dubrovnik, to replace the one destroyed in the fighting some years back, is tiny, but it is computer-linked to all the libraries in the world. It has few books or journals of its own and needs no large acres of shelves to satisfy its readers, who do not need, in fact, to go near the place at all if they have the necessary technology in their own homes. It is not so very different, in fact, from the Open University in Britain, which is, for its students, only a conceptual space, not a physical one.

Such organizations are increasingly 'virtual': you can describe what they do but cannot see them. What, then, is this thing called an organization? It seems more of a verb, these days, than a noun, a means of organizing instead of a thing or a body. And how does one manage something one cannot see, or people whom you never meet? For many a manager, these new organizations are something to be kept as far away as possible for as long as possible. Most of us prefer to walk backwards into the future, a posture which may be uncomfortable but at least allows us to keep on looking at things familiar as long as we can. Many will feel about the new organizations as the scientist Erwin Schroedinger felt about quantum theory: 'I don't like it, and I'm sorry that I ever had anything to do with it.'

Unfortunately for our comfort, neither quantum theory nor the new order can be ignored. We have to try to understand it so that we can live with it and use it, as we do with science. In the new science, matter is not something fixed, it is a mix of particles and waves, a mix which can never be completely captured because the two can never be measured at the same time. In the same way, organizations are more properly viewed, I suggest, as patterns of relationships, an ever-changing mix of particles – or people – and waves – or transactions. Physicists speak of particles as 'bundles of potentiality'. I see that as quite a good description of the people we want in the new organizations, no longer role occupants in prescribed boxes but would-be butterflies, as in chaos theory, capable of starting perturbations which ripple out to cause a thunderstorm across the world.

Prediction and uniformity are no longer, now, possible in any detail. Just as Heisenberg pointed out that the very act of observation changes the thing observed, so, too, the way we see someone affects the way they behave, while our own actions often help to create the environment which we think we are responding to. Power, in the new organizations, comes from relationships, not from structures. Those who have established reputations acquire authority which was not handed down from above, while those who are open to others create positive energy around them, energy which did not exist before. Love or, to give it a more corporately respectable title, 'unconditional positive regard', may not make the world go round, but it can certainly release unsuspected potential. This makes for an untidy world, but one with its positive side. Unlike physical systems, and older models of organizations, the new organizations do not obey the Second Law of Thermodynamics with its relentless downwards drag, but have a capacity to find new sources of energy and so to renew themselves. They contain within them the real clue to a so-called 'learning organization'.

To heighten the unpredictability, isolated events can cause unanticipated major changes, as they do in science; a customer enquiry, for example, a mistake or an unexpected experimental result can lead to a whole new product range. There is order, of a sort, in the world, or daily life would be impossible, and there has to be order in its organizations, but order no longer implies control. The new organizations are, in fact, always tending to be slightly out of control, their structures flexing, their people innovating. Non-linear systems, a concept which includes people, tend to feed back on themselves, creating unforeseen results, rather like what often happens in marriage. In these new organizations, therefore, some older ideas, such as management hierarchies, spans of control, grading systems, job descriptions or career planning, can seem as time-bound and out-of-place as trying to send a telegram in the world of e-mail, nostalgic but unreal. Instead, a new language is emerging, a language which would seem strange and weird to the old order, a language of metaphor and simile, low in definition but rich in suggestion.

The New Language

How then does one govern such places? Once again, we might be tempted to borrow our metaphors from science. Field theory is one appealing idea. Electrical fields, for instance, are real, their effects can be seen, measured and, within limits, predicted, but the field itself is invisible, intangible and unmeasurable. These fields create energy, activating inert points and holding the whole together. I believe that the metaphor can usefully be carried over to the organization, if we think of the 'fields' being such things as culture, values, ethics, beliefs or vision.

These words are now commonplace in organizations as they fumble for ways to hold the thing together, to give it a common thrust when a tight plan is no longer feasible, a central ethic in place of control, and norms of behaviour instead of rules. The field I particularly favour is that of *trust*. Francis Fukuyama (1995) has argued recently that societies of high trust do better economically. I would extend his idea to organizations. Organizations who rely on trust as their principal means of control are more effective, more creative, more fun and cheaper to operate.

Trust, however, imposes its own constraints and has its own rules. I can list ten by way of illustration, but there could be more.

1 Trust is limited. How many people can one person trust, and how long must that person have known them and worked with them? It is unlikely to be more than 20 or 30 at the most, with shared experience extending over two or three years at least. This constraint requires a structure of small, long-lasting groups and a core group of long-serving managers. Trust does not grow in a culture where short-term contracts are the norm.

2 Trust has boundaries. The extent of discretion must be clearly identified. Where there is trust there can be no uninvited supervision or inspection. Clear boundaries limit the risk of trusting someone beyond their capacity or of betting the company on one person's decisions.

3 Trust implies choice. It is unrealistic to expect a manager to trust someone imposed upon them or inherited by them. Only if the individual is personally chosen will they be personally trusted. Since it is not only the leader who has to trust people but their colleagues as well, this rule requires new appointments to be made collectively, by the team as a whole, rather as some Japanese companies do now.

4 Trust needs purpose. Without a knowledge of, and a commitment to, the purpose of the activity, trust can become misdirected. A well-defined and agreed set of goals is essential. Without a real sense of ownership of those goals, the energy contained in trust will not be released.

5 Trust needs information. Trust does not operate to the best advantage in the dark. A knowledge of results is essential, particularly if one is privy to those results oneself in the first instance, giving one time to rectify any errors before they are picked up by one's superiors. More generally, a truly open information system carries the message that there are no secrets, that you are trusted to use whatever information you find useful and to share your data with anyone who wants them. The modern information systems allow much more freedom of data and are to be welcomed on that score alone.

6 Trust needs reinforcement. Rewards and thanks for results achieved give point to the responsibility that goes with being trusted. Celebration creates energy. Similarly, the occasional reaffirmation of one's trust and confidence in a person is necessary if that person is to take full responsibility for what he or she does. Only if this positive reinforcement is done will any criticism be heard, if any is needed, however well-intentioned.

7 Trust demands learning. Semi-permanent groups must be broadly-skilled groups if they are not to become out-of-date. The members, too, must be able to turn their hands to different roles as the nature of the work develops. This will only happen if the

members are able and willing to invest in their own development, and if the organization makes proper provision for it. A
field of trust does, however, allow for mistakes as a necessary
part of learning, provided always that one learns from those
mistakes, and that the mistakes do not take one over the permitted boundary of discretion.

8   Trust needs touch. It is hard to trust people whom you never or
very seldom see. Even if the work of the group can be carried on
separately and at a distance, the occasional get-together acts as a
bond. Hi-Tech, as Ronald Naisbitt once put it, needs Hi-Touch.
'Away-days' are as much about bonding as they are about content, but should not be discounted because of that.

9   Trust needs standards. If all are to work together without supervision or too much bureaucracy, there has to be a well-understood
and accepted set of standards, ethical, cultural and behavioural.
It needs to be clear how 'things get done around here', how
people behave to one another, what is acceptable and what is
not. Some organizations have what they call their 'bible', which
lays down the basic 'commandments' of the culture.

10   Trust is tough. If someone constantly proves unworthy of the
confidence and trust placed in them, then they will have to
leave. The organization cannot carry someone who cannot be
relied upon. One bad apple spoils the heap. Lifetime jobs are not
on offer in advance these days; loyalty has to be earned before it
is given.

Provided these rules of trust are kept, trust can be a major source
of energy. It is exciting to be trusted. It is also good for one's self-
worth. People then try to live up to, even to exceed, the expectations
that others have of them, so that trust makes possible new levels of
achievement. It is, however, lonely at the centre. I asked one vice-
president, who was in charge of administration in the centre of one
large multinational, how it felt to be in charge of so many people
who were out of sight but hardly out of his mind. 'It is worrying,' he
said, 'but all that one can do is to watch the herd, and to observe,
with some relief, that in general it is heading in a westerly direction!'

I once jokingly accused a project team of resembling nothing so
much as a rowing eight on the river: 'eight people going backwards
as fast as they can without talking to each other, steered by the one
person who can't row!' I thought it quite witty, but I was rebuked by
one member of the group who introduced himself as an Olympic
oarsman: 'How do you think that we could go backwards so fast
without talking to each other *unless* we had (a) total trust in each
other and complete confidence in each other's ability to do the job
they were supposed to do, including the person who doesn't row,

and (b) we were all aware of where we were trying to get to, of how important it was and were dedicated to do our best to get there as quickly as possible? It is,' he went on, 'the perfect recipe for a team.' I could only agree and I noted, then, how carefully, although instinctively, they followed all the rules of trust, living and working together, constant feedback, celebrations when they won, the dropping from the crew of those that did not make the grade and, above all, total commitment to one goal.

'But', I asked the oarsman, 'who is the leader of this team?' 'We have several,' he replied. 'There is, of course, the captain of the boat – he is responsible for choosing the team, for setting the goal and for discipline, feedback and congratulations, but on the task, on the river, he just does his thing, pulls his own oar. On the river it is the cox who is in command, because only he, or she, can see where we are going and how we compare with the competition, while the rate, the standard, is set by another leader, the stroke. Then, in training, there is the most important leader of all – the coach, who never gets in the boat at all.' Interesting, I thought, a multiplex and flexible hierarchy, fine-tuned to the needs of the changing task, just as it should be in the project teams and groups of the new organizations.

Trust is one example of the way a 'field' can be used as a way of obtaining some leverage on the new disaggregated organization. It works best, however, if the field theory is combined with another metaphor from the new science, that of the 'strange attractor' which, in chaos theory, becomes the organizing focus of the emerging patterns, the way out of chaos, the thing which gives meaning to movement. Chaotic, energetic but uncontrolled organizations will exhibit movement without motion unless they have found their 'strange attractor' which gives them point and purpose. Some have called this the 'soul' of the organization, another soft but pregnant word which fits the new language of organization. It is, I now believe, the principal task of leadership to find the strange attractor which will give meaning to movement, around which a field of trust can be built which will allow the organization to devote most of its energies to its product instead of to its own entrails. No one is saying that the task is easy, but it is often very rewarding.

The New Contract

Under the old order, instrumentalism ruled, OK. The organization was the instrument of its owners, particularly if it was a business, and the workers were the instruments of the organization. The managers were there to see that the organization delivered what the owners wanted and that the workers did what the organization needed. The contract was clear; the organization was not only an instrument but a piece of property to be disposed of if the owners tired of it.

But if the organization is a changing mix of people and relationships, not a building with plant and machinery, it makes less sense to talk of the people who put up the money 'owning' it, for how can one morally or practically 'own' other people or their relationships? If the organization is largely virtual, a box of contracts, there is, in any case, nothing tangible at all to 'own'. If there is a building it is probably on a short lease, and any computers are likely to be leased as well. To add complication to complication, the workers are now the principal assets of the organization: if they walk out, they take their skills and know-how with them. Assets are more than instruments; assets are things to be cherished, guarded and invested in as well as used.

Self-directing assets are a new phenomenon in organization behaviour. Karl Marx would be amused. He longed for the day when the workers would own the means of production. Now they do. He meant, of course, that the workers would, through revolution, become the financial owners. They are instead the literal owners because the means of production in most organizations these days reside in the heads and the hands of the workers themselves – if they leave, there is almost nothing left.

We need a new contract, a new way of spelling out the responsibilities of financiers, workers and managers and of their relationship to each other. In the process we shall probably rediscover that a 'company', if the organization is a business, is in law much more than a mere instrument of the owners: it is equivalent, in English law, to a person. It can be sued as a person, charged as a person with criminal offences, held responsible for good behaviour and required to conform to regulations. A company has always been more than a piece of property, although common usage tended to forget that, and so let instrumentalism pervade our way of thinking, turning people into things or, at best, into human resources.

A new contract will probably forgo the language of property and property rights in favour of talking of membership, associates and investors. Members belong to a company, as they would to any association or club. No one owns a voluntary association; no one needs to, but members have a feeling of psychological ownership which becomes crucial when they are themselves the principal assets. Members have rights, which need eventually to be defined by law, but so should investors have rights, although not as all-embracing as they are at present, as well as associates such as suppliers or agents. No one, for instance, should have the right to dispose of the company over the heads of the members any more than a club could be sold along with its members.

A membership contract along these lines would redefine the role of the management. The managers now become the agents of the members rather than their bosses. They manage because they are, in a sense, willed to manage by the workers. They draw their authority from the people over whom it is to be exercised. That is already the way it is in many organizations as they struggle to find a way to harness the talents and skills of the people who are also now their principal assets rather than their instruments. It makes the job of the manager more difficult but much more legitimate.

It makes it more legitimate, for instance, for the managers to question what should be the driving purpose of the organization, the strange attractor that will give it meaning. No longer will it be possible to evade the question by maintaining that the sole purpose of the business is to enrich its owners, for there will be no owners, only investors. Clearly the business, any business, needs to reward its investors and to provide for its future, but that has always begged the question – what future? For what and for whom does the organization exist? Under the new contract, there will be no evading that crucial question. There will be no standard answers, just as there will in future be no standard organizations. It will be for each to determine their own destiny, their own strange attractor.

I have no doubt that the new organizations will be less easy places than those of old, they will certainly be less predictable, less measurable, less amenable to the disciplines of the Aston Group of old, but we cannot reject the future just because it is uncomfortable. What we have to do is to find a way to understand them so that we can make them work for us. The first step to that understanding is a new conceptual vocabulary and a new way of defining these strange creations. We need, maybe, to reinvent the Aston Group for this new age.

References

Fukuyama, F. (1995), *Trust, the Social Virtues and the Creation of Prosperity*, New York: The Free Press.

Wheatley, M.J. (1992), *Leadership and the New Science: Learning About Organization from an Orderly Universe*, San Francisco: Berrett-Koehler.

PART III
ORGANIZATION AND MANAGEMENT WORLDWIDE

12 Linking Structure to Culture

GEERT HOFSTEDE, *Institute for Research of Intercultural Co-operation, University of Limburg*

The Europeanization of Aston

The 1970s were a productive decade for European cooperation in organization studies. Representatives from different European schools rather suddenly discovered each others' existence. EGOS, the European Group for Organizational Studies, was founded in 1974. The decision to publish *Organization Studies*, our own European journal, was taken in 1977; the first issue appeared in 1980.

In those days I taught at INSEAD, the international business school in Fontainebleau, France. At INSEAD an American visiting professor, Sami Kassem, suggested we should bring the senior European organization scholars together. Kassem is an Egyptian by birth and initial education, and he found the European developments more relevant to his cross-cultural experiences than what he had learned in America. Kassem and I got INSEAD's executive school, CEDEP, to sponsor a European seminar on Organization Theory. This seminar was held at INSEAD in May 1975.

The purpose of the INSEAD seminar was to present a state of the art. The proceedings appeared in *European Contributions to Organization Theory*, which was published at the beginning of 1976. Contributors were the leading scholars in organization studies of those days, a remarkable list of names: Derek Pugh and Eric Miller (Great Britain), Alain Cotta and Michel Crozier (France), Niklas Luhmann and Renate Mayntz (Germany), Franco Ferraresi and Gianni Gasparini (Italy), Gunnar Hjelholt (Denmark), Einar Thorsrud (Norway), Dick Ramström (Sweden), Cornelis Lammers and Mauk Mulder (Netherlands), Tadeusz Pszczolowski (Poland), Eugen Pusic (Yugoslavia), Jermen Gvishiani and Gavriil Popov (Soviet Union). Derek Pugh's contribution, of course, dealt with the Aston Studies. To take a few examples from the others, Eric Miller covered the Tavistock Institute legacy, Michel Crozier the functioning of a bureaucracy, Niklas Luhmann his theory of power and Eugen Pusic Yugoslav worker self-management.

At that time the Aston Programme had been running for more than a decade. Its unique and novel characteristic was the sociological approach of comparison at the level of organizations, rather than – as was the case in the American tradition – at the psychological level of managers or employees. But the project's aspirations, as Derek Pugh described them in Fontainebleau, went beyond that:

> to establish general conclusions pertaining to work organizations, by studying simultaneously or stepwise:
>
> – the context in which an organization operates,
> – certain dimensions of the organization's structure and functioning,
> – group composition and interaction of organization members,
> – individual personality and behaviour,
> – and, finally, processes of stability and change in the organization.
> (Pugh, 1976, p. 62)

Thus the Aston project had a truly multi-level agenda. At the time of Pugh's lecture, the first three of the five points mentioned above had been addressed. Of these, of course, the second, dimensions of organizational structure and functioning, had had the strongest impact on the state of the art of organization studies. Factor analysis of quantitative measurements of organization structure across several hundred organizations had revealed the three underlying structural dimensions: structuring of activities, centralization of decisions (later called 'concentration of authority') and line control of work flow.

Of the other Fontainebleau contributors, only Michel Crozier referred to the Aston Studies. It should be said that the number of cross-references among the various speakers was generally low – for many, this was the first time they had met, and anyway they had been asked to talk about their own theories rather than others'. Crozier, having described the historical tradition of studying organizations via single case studies, wrote a comment about the Aston Studies which I will quote at length:

> The sixties have seen the emergence and progressive predominance of a hard-headed, supposedly more scientific approach; intended to produce evidence by measuring hard facts bearing specifically on the organizational phenomenon, i.e., on organizations as units. For this purpose, the main effort has been toward producing data on samples of organizations and on using statistical analyses of these data for proving or disproving hypotheses. This has meant a sharp break with

social psychology and anthropology and the development of new questions that were compatible with the new evidence; what kind of variables do affect organizations' characteristics and what kind of impact do those characteristics have on an organization's results? Behind these questions, a new paradigm emerged, which I see developing around the problem of structure: some environmental variables or problems determine the structure of an organization, and the structure of an organization or the fit between the structure and the problem determine its effectiveness.

This paradigm has led to innumerable demonstrations of the influence of diverse sets of variables on organizational performance, but most of the time this has been mediated by the basic problem of structures, and very often with a normative orientation: which structure is the best? While very promising at first, with a welcome and much clearer view on the importance of the environment of organizations and especially technology, this paradigm has led to more and more formalistic studies with less and less meaningful results.

It was suffering from three very strong biases. First, it was very deterministic in an old-fashioned, simplistic way which was not adequate for a phenomenon of high order complexity such as organizations; second, *it was incapable of dealing with the cultural variable and tended to overemphasize a universalistic one best way* [my italics]; third, it never questioned the implicit assumption it made of equating structure (and practically formal structure) with all other organizational characteristics since it made structure the only mediating link between the environment of an organization and its output. True enough, the theoretical view was much more complex, but the necessity of measurement forced most authors to this reductionist position at the operational, that is, at the crucial level. (Crozier, 1976, p. 195)

Crozier then goes on to introduce his own approach of comparing organizational 'games', leading to a different research agenda: 'What are the different systems of games that can solve the same problems – i.e., the meeting of the same contextual constraints? What kind of capacities do they require from the members concerned? How do such capacities develop and how do new games and new systems of games become possible?' (ibid., p. 205).

The value of Crozier's elaborate comment is that it places the Aston approach on the international agenda; theories developed in one country should expose themselves to criticism from abroad, otherwise they remain parochial. Crozier also raises the fundamental issue of culture. Of course, the existence of country-linked intellectual traditions is in itself a strong manifestation of national cultural differences.

The Aston Studies and National Cultures

The Aston data Pugh referred to came mainly from the UK, although he mentioned some studies in other countries. A more complete analysis of the cross-national extensions of the Aston Studies was published several years later (see Hickson and McMillan, 1981). By then, data had become available from manufacturing organizations in 10 countries, but the different studies had not been coordinated and the results therefore lacked coherence (ibid., p. 187). A basic proposition had been formulated as early as 1974: the 'culture-free context of organization structure'. It predicted – originally on the basis of a comparison of the USA, Britain and Canada only – that relationships between variables of organization context and of organization structure would hold for work organizations in all societies: 'Even though Indian organizations might turn out to be less formalized or less autonomous than American organizations, bigger Indian units would still be more formalized than smaller Indian units, and dependent Indian units will be less autonomous than relatively independent ones' (Hickson *et al.*, 1974, reprinted in Hickson and McMillan, 1981, p. 16).

After inspecting the data from 10 countries, Hickson and McMillan (1981, p. 194) conclude: 'Size and dependence therefore become the bases for explanations of broad features of organization. Indeed, they appear to be of more importance for how an organization is set up in these ways than its national location. In this, context is primary and country is secondary'. But the authors do signal the need to have a further look at culture – with a respectful reference to my just-published *Culture's Consequences* (Hofstede, 1980) of which they had seen the manuscript.

Culture's Consequences describes how data from a huge cross-national database on work-related employee values collected by the multinational IBM were analysed for country-to-country differences. Across matched samples from, first, 40, and later on more than 50 countries, the analysis identified four dimensions of differences in national culture, in the sense of 'the collective programming of the mind which distinguishes the members of one human group from another' (p. 25). The first two were called 'power distance' and 'uncertainty avoidance'. Power distance is 'the extent to which the less powerful members of institutions and organizations within a country expect and accept that power is distributed unequally' (Hofstede, 1991, p. 262). Uncertainty avoidance is 'the extent to which members of a culture feel threatened by uncertain or unknown situations' (ibid., p. 263).

Relative scores of matched respondent samples on these dimensions were computed for 50 countries, plus three multi-country regions. In a power distance × uncertainty avoidance score plot, Latin and other Mediterranean countries, plus Japan and Korea, are found in the large power distance, strong uncertainty avoidance quadrant. All other Asian countries combine large power distances with medium to weak uncertainty avoidance. German-speaking countries, plus Israel and Finland, combine small power distances with medium to strong uncertainty avoidance, and English-speaking countries, including Jamaica but not India, Scandinavian countries, and the Netherlands combine small power distances with weak uncertainty avoidance.

Culture's Consequences contains a section on 'Power Distance, Uncertainty Avoidance and Organizations' (pp. 318ff). The following is a slightly edited version of its arguments. In their impact on the structure and functioning of organizations, power distance and uncertainty avoidance interact. In cultures where power distances are large, power is the leading principle which keeps the organization together and which protects it against uncertainty. In addition, the level of uncertainty avoidance determines to what extent formalization is sought. In cultures where power distances are small, there are two possibilities: if people have an inner need for living up to rules (strong uncertainty avoidance), the leading principle for keeping the organization together can be formal rules; if people do not have an inner need for living up to rules (weak uncertainty avoidance), the organization has to be kept together by recurrent ad hoc negotiations.

Power distance and uncertainty avoidance, I argued, can be logically associated with the first two main dimensions of organization structure revealed by the Aston Studies: power distance with 'concentration of authority' and uncertainty avoidance with 'structuring of activities'. From Pugh's work (1976, p. 70) a fourfold typology of organization structures can be read, with high and low concentration of authority and high and low structuring of activities. In Table 12.1, this typology has been applied to indicate the type of organization that fits best in a certain group of countries.

We should read Table 12.1 in such a way that, task, size of organization and so on being equal, the countries in the fourth quadrant would tend more towards creating 'implicitly structured' organizations and, for example, those in the second quadrant would tend more towards creating 'full bureaucracies'. In the full bureaucracy, the relationships both among people and between people and the work processes tend to be rigidly prescribed, either in formal rules and laws or in traditions. In the personnel bureaucracy, relationships among people are prescribed but not the work processes; in the work flow bureaucracy, the opposite is the case. Finally, in the implicitly structured organizations, neither the relationships among people nor those between people and the work processes are strictly prescribed.

Table 12.1   Connotations of the four combinations of power distance and uncertainty avoidance levels

(4) Small power distance Weak uncertainty avoidance	(1) Large power distance Weak uncertainty avoidance
Countries: Anglo, Scandinavian, Netherlands	Countries: Asia
Organization type: implicity structured	Organization type: personnel bureaucracy
Implicit model of organization: market	Implicit model of organization: family
(3) Small power distance Strong uncertainty avoidance	(2) Large power distance Strong uncertainty avoidance
Countries: German-speaking, Finland, Israel	Countries: Latin, Mediterranean, Japan, Korea
Organization type: work flow bureaucracy	Organization type: full bureaucracy
Implicit model of organization: machine	Implicit model of organization: pyramid

Source: Adapted from Hofstede (1980, Figure 7.5).

Table 12.1 also contains references to 'implicit models' of organizations in different countries which derive from an unpublished study
by Owen James Stevens, an American who was my colleague at
INSEAD. Stevens compared French, German and British MBA (Master of Business Administration) students at INSEAD. In one of a
series of different experiments, he let students of the three nationalities individually analyse the same case study of an organizational
conflict. The majority of the French tended to resolve the problem by
referring to the hierarchy; the British, by horizontal negotiation; the
Germans, by the establishment of procedures. Stevens therefore identified the implicit model of a well-functioning organization for the
French as a pyramid; for the British as a (village) market; for the
Germans as a (well-oiled) machine. This fits the types of full bu-

reaucracy, implicitly structured organization and work flow bureaucracy, respectively. Stevens did not have Asian students available, but, inspired by some Indian colleagues, I chose the 'family' as the implicit model for an Asian organization. The 'personnel bureaucracy' means that relationships among people are strictly determined by the hierarchical framework, but that the work-flow is not at all codified to the same extent. China belongs in the same quadrant, and the main continuous principle of Chinese administration has been described as 'government of man' in contrast to the Western idea of 'government by law'.

Culture, Aston and Mintzberg

It has been the merit of Henry Mintzberg from Canada to reformulate the state of the art in the study of organization structures into a comprehensive framework that lends itself very well to purposes of teaching and to use by consultants and practitioners (Mintzberg, 1979, 1983). To Mintzberg (1983), all good things in organizations come in fives.[1] Organizations in general contain up to five distinct parts: (1) the operating core (the people who do the work); (2) the strategic apex (the top management); (3) the middle line (the hierarchy in between); (4) the technostructure (people in staff roles supplying ideas); and (5) the support staff (people in staff roles supplying services). Organizations in general use one or more of five mechanisms for coordinating activities: (1) mutual adjustment (of people through informal communication); (2) direct supervision (by a hierarchical superior); (3) standardization of work processes (specifying the contents of work); (4) standardization of outputs (specifying the desired results); and (5) standardization of skills (specifying the training required to perform the work).

Most organizations, according to Mintzberg, show one of five typical configurations: (1) the simple structure; in this case, the key part is the strategic apex, and the coordinating mechanism is direct supervision; (2) the machine bureaucracy; key part: the technostructure; coordinating mechanism: standardization of work processes; (3) the professional bureaucracy; key part: the operating core; coordinating mechanism: standardization of skills; (4) the divisionalized form; key part: the middle line; coordinating mechanism: standardization of outputs; (5) the adhocracy; key part: the support staff (sometimes with the operating core); coordinating mechanism: mutual adjustment.

Mintzberg's typology has taken the national culture factor into account even less than did the Aston Studies. Implicitly, he has recognized the role of values in the choice of coordinating mechanisms, as in the following quotation:

> Organizations formalize behavior to reduce its variability, ultimately
> to predict and control it ... to co-ordinate activities ... to ensure the
> machinelike consistency that leads to efficient production ... to ensure
> fairness to clients ... . Organizations formalize behavior for other
> reasons as well, of more questionable validity. Formalization may, for
> example, reflect an arbitrary desire for order. ... The highly formalized
> structure is above all the neat one; it warms the heart of people who
> like to see things orderly. (Mintzberg, 1983, p. 34–5)

This, of course, implies the role of cultural uncertainty avoidance
in the formalization process. In fact, I had little trouble in linking
Mintzberg's typology of organizational configurations to national
cultural differences as pictured in the power distance × uncertainty
avoidance matrix (Table 12.1, see also Hofstede, 1991, pp. 150 ff). The
link means that, other factors being equal, people from a particular
national background will prefer a particular configuration because it
fits their implicit model, and that otherwise similar organizations in
different countries are likely to resemble different Mintzberg configuration types because of these different cultural preferences.

The link between Mintzberg's five configurations and the quadrants of the power distance × uncertainty avoidance diagram is
presented in Table 12.2. This diagram at the same time relates
Mintzberg's terminology to the typical organization types according
to Aston and the implicit models of organization according to Stevens,
as listed in Table 12.1. One adaptation was made: Mintzberg used the
term 'machine' in a different sense than Stevens (and I) did: in his
'machine bureaucracy', Mintzberg stressed the role of the
technostructure, that is the more highly educated specialists, but not
the role of the highly trained workers who belong to his 'operating
core'. Therefore Mintzberg's machine bureaucracy corresponds, not
to Stevens' machine, but to his pyramid. In order to avoid confusion,
I have replaced Mintzberg's machine bureaucracy with the Aston
term, 'full bureaucracy'.

From the other quadrants, the simple structure corresponds to the
Aston personnel bureaucracy and to Stevens' family model; the professional bureaucracy corresponds to the work flow bureaucracy and
the well-oiled machine; the adhocracy corresponds to the implicitly
structured Aston type and to the village market. Finally, the
divisionalized form takes a middle position on both culture dimensions, with elements of all four models. A typical country near the
centre of the power distance × uncertainty avoidance matrix is the
USA, where the divisionalized form originated and enjoys great popularity.

Table 12.2 explains a number of national characteristics known
from the professional and anecdotal literature about differences in

Table 12.2   Mintzberg's configuration of organizations projected onto a power distance × uncertainty avoidance matrix

(4) Small power distance Weak uncertainty avoidance	(1) Large power distance Weak uncertainty avoidance
Typical country: Britain	Typical country: China
a: Adhocracy b: Mutual adjustment c: Support staff	a: Simple structure b: Direct supervision c: Strategic apex

(5)
Medium power distance
Medium uncertainty avoidance

Typical country: USA

a: Divisionalized Form
b: Standardization of Outputs
c: Middle Lane

(3) Small power distance Strong uncertainty avoidance	(2) Large power distance Strong uncertainty avoidance
Typical country: Germany	Typical country: France
a: Professional bureaucracy b: Standardization of skills c: Operating core	a: Full bureaucracy b: Standardization of work processes c: Technostructure

Notes: a = preferred configuration; b = preferred coordination mechanism; c = key part of organization.

organizations between countries; these are especially clear in the 'preferred coordination mechanisms'. *Mutual adjustment* fits the market model of organizations and the stress on ad hoc negotiation in the Anglo countries. *Standardization of skills* explains the traditional emphasis in countries like Germany and Switzerland on the professional qualification of workers, and the high status in these countries of apprentice systems. *Standardization of work processes* fits the French concept of bureaucracy as it is pictured, for example, by Michel Crozier in his classic *The Bureaucratic Phenomenon* (1964). *Direct supervision* corresponds to what we know about Chinese organizations, also outside mainland China, which emphasize coordination through personal intervention of the owner and his relatives. *Standardization of outputs* is very much the preferred philosophy in the USA, tried even in cases where outputs are difficult to assess.[2]

Structure and Organization Culture

The original purpose of the Aston Studies was cross-institutional comparison within Britain: comparing organizations from different spheres of life. In addition to manufacturing organizations, service organizations, government bureaucracies, schools, labour unions and churches were also studied. At the time of the Aston Programme (1960s and 1970s) the term 'organization culture' had not yet become popular; this only happened in the early 1980s. But the programme as Pugh described it in Fontainebleau included aspects that would later be considered part of the organizations' cultures: work roles, behavioural variables and a 'climate index'.

Thus I found myself on the Aston track with a cross-institutional research project carried out between 1985 and 1987 under the auspices of IRIC, the Institute for Research on Intercultural Co-operation, now at the universities of Brabant at Tilburg and of Limburg at Maastricht in the Netherlands. It made intensive use of the experience collected from the cross-national IBM project as described in *Culture's Consequences*. Paradoxically, the cross-national research in IBM did not reveal any direct information about IBM's corporate culture: all units studied shared the same corporate culture, and there were no outside points of comparison. IBM's pronounced corporate culture did contribute to the reliability of the cross-national comparisons, because it excluded one source of variance from the data: samples of IBMers from different countries were better matched, on characteristics other than nationality, than almost any other population that could be imagined.

The cross-national study served as a model of the way a cross-organizational or cross-institutional study could be designed. Instead of one corporation in many countries, the new study should cover many different organizations in one or at least few countries: a similar approach, but replacing national with institutional differences. The cross-organizational study (Hofstede *et al.*, 1990) covered 20 organizational units in Denmark and the Netherlands, with a variety not unlike the original Aston sample in Britain. The units were engaged in the following activities:

Private manufacturing companies (electronics, chemicals, consumer goods)

total divisions or production units	6
head office or marketing units	3
research and development units	2
Private service companies	
(banking, transport, trade) units	5
Public institutions	
(telecommunication, police) units	4
Total number of units studied	20

Unit sizes varied from 60 to 2500 persons. The number of 20 units was small enough to allow studying each unit in depth, qualitatively, as a separate case study. At the same time, it was large enough to permit statistical analysis of comparative quantitative data across all cases.

The first, qualitative phase of the research consisted of in-depth interviews with key informants for each unit; a total of 180 interviews were conducted. These served both to get a qualitative feel for the whole (the 'Gestalt') of the unit's culture and to collect issues to be included in the questionnaire for the ensuing survey.

The second, quantitative phase of the project consisted of a paper-and-pencil survey with precoded questions, administered, contrary to the first phase, to a strictly *random* sample from the unit. This sample was composed of 20–25 managers (or as many as the unit had), 20–25 college-level non-managers ('professionals') and 20–25 non-college-level non-managers. All in all, we collected 1295 usable questionnaires, an average of 65 per organization. The questions in the survey included those about work-related values used in the cross-national IBM study, plus a number of later additions; most, however, were developed on the basis of the interviews of the first phase. The new questions in particular dealt with many perceptions of daily practices, which had been missing in the cross-national studies.

For the values questions, differences among organizations were found to be smaller than differences among countries that had been in the IBM studies. It was the practices questions, not the values questions, that showed large differences among organizations. A key conclusion from the research project was that organizational cultures differ mainly in their practices, while national cultures differ mainly in their values.

A factor analysis of the mean scores for the practices questions (61 questions, 20 organizational units: this is a so-called 'ecological' factor analysis) produced six orthogonal dimensions of organization cultures, based on differences in practices, labelled (1) process versus results-oriented, (2) employee versus job-oriented, (3) parochial versus professional, (4) open versus closed system, (5) loose versus tight control and (6) normative versus pragmatic. Dimension 1 contrasts process-oriented organization cultures, dominated by technical and bureaucratic routines, with results-oriented cultures, dominated by a common concern for outcomes. Dimension 2 contrasts employee-oriented cultures assuming a broad responsibility for their members' well-being, with job-oriented cultures assuming responsibility for the employees' job performance only. Dimension 3 opposes parochial cultures in which members derive their identity from the organization for which they work, with professional cultures in which the (usually highly educated) members identify primarily with their profession. Dimension 4 refers to the common style of internal and external communication, and to the ease with which outsiders and newcomers are admitted. Dimension 5 deals with the amount of internal structuring and with the degree of formality and punctuality within the organization. Dimension 6 describes the prevailing way (rigid or flexible) of dealing with the environment, in particular with customers and/or clients.

In contrast with the four dimensions of national culture found in the IBM project that belonged to anthropology, the six dimensions found in the organizational culture study belong to sociology and to management theory. Related concepts in the literature are, for dimension 1 (process/results): mechanistic versus organic solidarity (Burns and Stalker, 1961); for dimension 2 (employee/job): consideration versus initiation of structure (Fleishman *et al.*, 1955); for dimension 3 (parochial/professional): local versus cosmopolitan (Merton, 1968); for dimension 4 (open/closed): communication climate (Poole, 1985); for dimension 5 (loose/tight): control theory (among others Hofstede, 1967); and for dimension 6 (normative/pragmatic) customer orientation (among others Peters and Waterman, 1982).

The Aston Studies related dimensions of organizational structure to aspects of the context in which an organization operates. In the IBM studies, a national culture's antecedents and consequences were shown by correlating the country scores with all kinds of external data, such as the country's per capita gross national product, political measures, such as an index of press freedom, and demographic data, such as the population growth rate. Comparisons were also made with the results of other surveys covering the same countries but using different questions and different respondents. The IRIC cross-organizational study followed the Aston Studies and the IBM studies by including a similar validation of the dimension scores against context data. The informants for the context data were the top manager, the chief personnel officer and the chief budget officer. They were presented with written questionnaires, followed up by personal interviews.

Examples of the context data collected are total employee strength, budget composition, economic results and the ages of key managers. For structure we relied on Aston: three simplified scales were used, based on the Aston questionnaires, to measure centralization, specialization and formalization. Both specialization and formalization were significantly negatively correlated with dimension 1, results orientation: more specialized and more formalized units tended to be less results-oriented, more process-oriented. Specialization was also associated with dimension 3, with a professional (as opposed to a parochial) culture. Formalization was also associated with dimension 5, tight as opposed to loose control, which validates the objective against the subjective measure. No correlations with any of the dimensions were found for centralization.

These – and many other – relationships with context data showed which objective conditions of organizations were associated with which particular culture profiles. They point to the things one has to change in order to modify an organization's culture. The way to change culture may be to redesign structure.

From Collective Culture to Individual Personality

The fourth point in Derek Pugh's aspirations in his Fontainebleau speech was individual personality and behaviour: 'Study of the work behaviour of individuals or groups should be related to study of the characteristics of the organization in which the behaviour occurs ... Later (after studying groups, GH) we study individual behaviour and personality in relation to context, structure and group behaviour' (Pugh, 1976, pp. 63–4).

Pugh's paper at that time did not report any results of studies at the individual level. I imagine the individuals the Aston team would be particularly interested in would be the chief executives or other key actors. But in the field of organization studies in general I have seen very few studies, other than single case studies, that succeeded in relating individual personalities to organizational phenomena in any systematic way. In this respect I can report on one rather unplanned outcome of the IRIC research project into organization cultures. It led from the sociology of the organizations into the psychology of the actors, although these were the members of the organizations, not their leaders or heroes. In 1990, with the help of my Hong Kong colleagues Michael H. Bond and Chung-Leung Luk, I reanalysed the existing database of the 1985–7 organizational cultures study, which so far had only been studied at the organizations (ecological) level, at the level of individual respondents. We used an approach described by Leung and Bond (1989): we eliminated the interorganizational variance, only retaining the intraorganizational variance. From each individual's score on a question the organization's mean score on that question (which had been the basis for the ecological analysis) was deducted. Thus only the variance of individual responses around the organization's means remained. After this operation the answers of all individuals from all organizations were pooled.

Instead of 20 organizations, we now studied 1295 individuals, trying to explain what led different individuals to give different answers to the same questions about the same organizations. Separate factor analyses were performed on the 57 questions about values and on 61 questions about practices. The latter at the individual level measure *individual* perceptions of *common* practices in the organization. The two analyses yielded six factors each, and these combined the questions in ways very different from the ecological analyses. In the ecological analyses the 'values' factors had proved much weaker than the 'practices' factors, so that only the latter had been used for the dimensions of organization cultures. In the individual analysis the reverse was the case: the values factors were stronger than the practices factors, implying that, between respondents, differences in values were larger than differences in perceptions of practices (Hofstede *et al.*, 1993). This makes sense, because people's values were largely formed before they joined this organization, while perceptions of practices were obviously based on experiences within the organization that to a large extent were shared with other respondents.

Values and perceptions of practices had so far been kept separate in the individual analysis, but this does not mean that they are independent. A second-order factor analysis of the factor scores for the 1295 individuals on the six values factors and the six practices factors produced six overall factors. Five of these were remarkably similar to the 'big five' dimensions of personality. In the area of personality research there has been a recent move towards simplification. Secondary research across a large number of earlier studies looking for dimensions of personality has led to the identification of five universal dimensions of individual personality which turn up in almost any study (Hogan, 1992). These were labelled (McCrae and John, 1992) as follows:

O: openness (key words: imaginative and original, as opposed to conventional);
E: extraversion (active and energetic, as opposed to passive);

C: conscientiousness (organized and efficient, as opposed to messy);

N: neuroticism (anxious and hostile, as opposed to relaxed);

A: agreeableness (altruistic and modest, as opposed to cold).

All five were found in the individual variance of our organizational culture questionnaire answers. This shows that different individuals report different values and different perceptions of the same organizational realities because they have different personalities. This may not be surprising, but it is still remarkable that, starting from a sociological study of organizations, a jump from the ecological to the individual level of analysis has put us right into the heart of personality psychology. Our study also offers an independent confirmation of the 'big five' metatheory.

This confirmation is the more remarkable because the data analysed were from Danish and Dutch respondents, while most of the studies in the 'big five' secondary analysis used US subjects. However, our study yielded an unmistakable sixth dimension, which we labelled 'authoritarianism'. It is somewhat surprising that the big five research did not reveal a personality factor related to dependence on authority.

Structure and Culture in Multinationals

Organization studies are always inspired by two motives – intellectual curiosity, and the search for rules and laws – apart from any personal motives the researchers may have, like earning a living. Intellectual curiosity leads to understanding, insight, empathy and to publications aimed at scholars; the search for rules and laws leads to a normative position, and to publications aimed at consultants and practitioners. One of Crozier's misgivings about the early Aston work was that it 'tended to overemphasize a universalistic one best way', which is one of the dangers of becoming normative, and a reason why normative publications have a short half-life. In the light of history, Aston's contribution to understanding organizations has been more important than its contribution to rules for managing them.

The same can be said of my own work, although it may have inspired others to try normative approaches, as in cross-cultural training. One of the few times I have tried to become normative myself was in an article (Hofstede, 1989) originally written for the think tank of a multi-business multinational corporation that wanted guidelines for the development of its organization structure. Being multinational meant the structure would have to cope with differences in national cultures; being multi-business implied internal differences in business cultures. Business cultures are the traits different companies in the same business have in common: examples are the business culture of banks, of software houses and of armed forces. Business cultures are somewhere in between organizational and occupational cultures. Some of my normative conclusions for organizing multi-business multinationals follow. They are based on both my cross-national and my cross-institutional research experiences. They refer to the 'business unit' as the smallest cell: a business unit is the entity conducting one type of business in one country.

The purpose of any structure is the coordination of the corporation's activities. The design of a corporate structure always reflects three choices for each business unit, whether explicit or implicit. First, which of the unit's inputs and outputs should be coordinated from elsewhere in the corporation? For example, only financial results, or also production volumes, or also personnel policies? Basically, coordination is desirable in case of interdependencies: connected flows of materials, exchange of ideas, exchange of people, exchange of currencies, operation within the same markets. Coordination is imperative for those aspects of the unit's functioning which directly affect the corporation's results, such as major investments, profits and losses.

Second, where should the coordination take place ? This means the choice of a level in the organization and of a location, for example, a country, regional or divisional head office, or the corporate office. The obvious answer to the 'where' question is that coordination should be located where the necessary knowledge for coordination is. In the case of interdependencies among units, the point of optimal coordination is the lowest level from which the interdependent streams (of materials, ideas, people, currencies and markets) can be viewed. However, the choice of a coordination level can also be shown to be influenced by cultural preferences. In corporations from larger power distance countries, there is a strong tendency towards centralization of coordination decisions beyond the level of optimal knowledge; in small power distance countries, this tendency is weaker. Besides national culture, corporate culture idiosyncrasies also play a role in determining the actual levels of co-ordination.

Third, what mechanisms will be used for co-ordination? We can imagine a tight–loose scale for coordination mechanisms, rather similar to dimension 5 of the organization culture study. Tight coordination means detailed prescription by another agency within the corporation, for example a central planning department or head office functional staff office. Loose coordination means leaving the unit largely to itself, assuming that market forces will guarantee an optimal result. In the extreme case, the corporation acts as a distant owner, managing the unit at arm's length through some seats on the unit's board of directors. The only possible intervention by the corporation in this case is the replacement of the unit's top manager, or ultimately the divestment of the unit as a whole. Research – other people's and mine – has shown that the choice of the appropriate degree of tightness or looseness of coordination mechanisms is to a large extent a cultural one, affected by both national and corporate cultural traditions. Other factors being equal, corporations from weak uncertainty avoidance countries will have more sympathy for coordination through market mechanisms; those from strong uncertainty avoidance countries will tend to favour direct prescription. These national preferences are modified, however, by the idiosyncrasies of particular corporations, often influenced by the personalities of top leaders. Famous examples are shoe pioneer Thomas Bat'a as a protagonist of control through market forces, and ITT's Howard Geneen as a champion of control through detailed prescription.

For a multinational, multi-business corporation there is an innate conflict between factors favouring coordination along geographical lines and those suggesting following type of business lines. Matrix structures are an imperfect answer: they are costly, often meaning a doubling of the management ranks, and their actual functioning may raise more problems than it resolves. A single structural principle is unlikely to fit for the entire corporation: in some cases the business structure should dominate, in others geographical coordination should have priority. This means a patchwork structure which may lack beauty, but it does follow the needs of markets and business unit cultures. Variety within the environment in which a company operates should be matched by appropriate internal variety. Too often, top managers look for uniform principles in structuring their entire corporation. These may satisfy their need for simple solutions, but they are bound to violate the needs of some parts of the organization. The diversity in structural solutions advocated is not only one of place, but also of time: optimal solutions will very likely change over time, so that the periodic reshufflings which any large organization knows should be seen as functional.

The Hofstede (1989) article cited goes on to discuss the common problem of how to incorporate a new acquisition in one country into the multinational's corporate structure: whether to make it report to the national head office or to the international corporate office, and whether to place corporation people at key positions in (but not necessarily at the top of) the new business unit. The key questions to be asked in a case like this are (1) What interdependencies exist between this company and other business units in the country (materials, ideas, people, currencies, markets) and (2) where is the necessary business and cultural knowledge for coordination best available?

Where no interdependencies exist, and business knowledge is not available within the rest of the national subsidiary, it may be a wise protective device to avoid interference with a successful acquisition and to run it at arm's length from the international corporate office. Whether corporation people should be implanted in the new subsidiary depends primarily on the availability of suitable persons. The transferees should be able to function in at least two cultures: the culture of the new unit and the corporate culture. If suitable people for this role are not available, this supports the 'arm's length' alternative. If the corporation intends to follow an active acquisition programme, it actually needs a corps of corporate diplomats, consisting of home country or other nationals impregnated with the corporate culture, multilingual, from various occupational backgrounds and experienced in living and functioning in various foreign cultures. These people are essential for making multinational structures work, as liaison persons in the various head offices or as temporary managers for new ventures. Timely recruiting of future managerial talent from different nationalities, career moves through planned transfers in view of acculturation in the corporate ways and cultural awareness training for business experts who will have to operate in foreign territories can all contribute to having the proper people available when they are needed.

Other dilemmas dealt with in the article are whether or not to maintain a national head office in each country, and choosing strategies for entering new countries and/or businesses: mergers, acquisitions, joint ventures, strategic alliances or starting from scratch (the 'greenfield' option). All of these were part of the original advice I gave to the multinational in question. Unfortunately, my contact person in the corporation think tank told me later that, when my advice arrived, the corporation's top management had just introduced a new structure which in many respects was exactly the opposite of what I had suggested. Therefore my contact had judged it more expedient not to submit my advice!

All professors know, or should know, G.B. Shaw's aphorism: 'He who can does. He who cannot, teaches.' And researches, I would add. I guess Derek Pugh will have as few misgivings about this division of labour as I have.

Notes

1   In *Mintzberg on Management* (1989), Mintzberg has added a 'missionary configuration' with 'standardization of norms'. To me, this is an aspect of the other types rather than a type by itself. It deals with the strength of an organization's culture.
2   Examples are Management by Objectives for university professors, and PPBS – Program Planning Budgeting System – for the federal government. The latter

was introduced in the early 1960s by Secretary of Defense Robert McNamara who came from the Ford Corporation; it is generally considered a failure.

References

Burns, T. and Stalker, G.M. (1961), *The Management of Innovation*, London: Tavistock.

Crozier, M. (1964), *The Bureaucratic Phenomenon*, Chicago: University of Chicago Press.

Crozier, M. (1976), 'Comparing structures and comparing games', in G. Hofstede and M.S. Kassem (eds), *European Contributions to Organization Theory*, Assen, Netherlands: Van Gorcum, pp. 193–207.

Fleishman, E., Harris, E.F. and Burtt, H.E. (1955), *Leadership and Supervision in Industry*, Columbus, OH: Ohio State University, Bureau of Educational Research.

Hickson, D.J. and McMillan, C.J. (1981) (eds), *Organization and Nation; The Aston Programme IV*, Aldershot: Gower.

Hickson, D.J., Hinings, C.R., McMillan, C.J. and Schwitter, J.P. (1974), 'The culture-free context of organization structure', *Sociology*, **8**, 59–80.

Hofstede, G. (1967), *The Game of Budget Control*, Assen, Netherlands: Van Gorcum; and (1968) London: Tavistock.

Hofstede, G. (1980), *Culture's Consequences: International Differences in Work-related Values*, Beverly Hills, CA: Sage.

Hofstede, G. (1989), 'Organizing for cultural diversity', *European Management Journal*, **7**, 390–97.

Hofstede, G. (1991), *Cultures and Organizations: Software of the Mind*, London: McGraw-Hill.

Hofstede, G. and Kassem, M.S. (eds) (1976), *European Contributions to Organization Theory*, Assen, Netherlands: Van Gorcum.

Hofstede, G., Bond, M.H. and Luk, C.L. (1993), 'Individual perceptions of organizational cultures: a methodological treatise on levels of analysis', *Organization Studies*, **14**, 483–503.

Hofstede, G., Neuijen, B., Ohayv, D.D. and Sanders, G. (1990), 'Measuring organizational cultures', *Administrative Science Quarterly*, **35**, 286–316.

Hogan, R. (1992), 'Personality and personality measurement', in M.D. Dunnette and L. Hough (eds), *Handbook of Industrial and Organizational Psychology*, 2nd edn, ch.17, Palo Alto, CA: Consulting Psychologists Press.

Leung, K. and Bond, M.H. (1989), 'On the empirical identification of dimensions for cross-cultural comparisons', *Journal of Cross-Cultural Psychology*, **20**, 133–51.

McCrae, R.R. and John, O.P. (1992), 'An introduction to the five-factor model and its applications', *Journal of Personality and Social Psychology*, **60**, 175–215.

Merton, R.K. (1968), *Social Theory and Social Structure*, rev. edn, New York: The Free Press.

Mintzberg, H. (1979), *The Structuring of Organizations*, Englewood Cliffs, NJ: Prentice-Hall.

Mintzberg, H. (1983), *Structures in Fives: Designing Effective Organizations*, Englewood Cliffs, NJ: Prentice-Hall.

Mintzberg, H. (1989), *Mintzberg on Management: Inside our Strange World of Organizations*, New York: The Free Press.

Peters, T.J. and Waterman, R.H. (1982), *In Search of Excellence: Lessons from America's Best-Run Companies*, New York: Harper & Row.

Poole, M.S. (1985), 'Communication and organizational climates: Review, critique and a new perspective', in R.D. McPhee and P.K. Tompkins (eds), *Organizational Communication*, Beverly Hills, CA: Sage, pp. 79–108.

Pugh, D.S. (1976), 'The "Aston" approach to the study of organizations', in G. Hofstede and M.S. Kassem (eds), *European Contributions to Organization Theory*, Assen, Netherlands: Van Gorcum, pp. 62–78.

13 Bureaucracy in Socialist Economic Organization and Management: the East German Experience[1]

ARNDT SORGE, *Work and Organization Research Centre, Tilburg University*

Introduction

One of the most topical and scholarly stimulating predictions of Weber during 1918 was that socialism would have to be built on bureaucratic domination and organization. This generated much discussion and controversy at the time and later. As socialist regimes in Europe have collapsed, more independent and richer retrospective research on the way socialism worked has been produced. This allows a more detailed and sober examination of Weber's proposition and the evidence. This chapter attempts such an examination with reference to the case of East Germany. The chapter begins by sketching Weber's proposition, to show the ramifications of his argument, and then goes through the evidence from recent studies. This examination leads to both a qualified acceptance and a rejection of the proposition.

I suggest that this examination not only holds lessons for the diagnosis of how socialism worked, but also a more general theoretical lesson. It leads to the conclusion that the societal embeddedness of organizational forms and modes of coordination implies dialectical effects. These signify an inevitable subversion of organizational forms and the modes of coordination which they contain. As a society comes to embody a specific form of domination and organization, this necessarily becomes subverted and contorted. But it also becomes stabilized by countervailing types of domination and organization.

Weber's Analysis of Organizational Tendencies Under Socialism

In 1918, towards the end of the First World War, Max Weber addressed a meeting of Austro-Hungarian military officers in Vienna, to give them some ideas on what to expect from socialist tendencies. The paper for this address was not a rigorous academic paper. It was written in the style of 'social comment' on the occasion of topical developments. Although Weber did not mention it, defeat in the war must have appeared imminent to the audience. Those who heard the paper were, in experience and intellectual posture, far from a social science audience. They were worried about the recent Socialist Revolution in Russia, and what this and other possible political changes in their home country might imply. They were probably thinking about the spillover effects of the new Soviet Empire on Austria–Hungary. Weber aimed his speech specifically at this audience, beginning and ending it by dealing with what socialism might imply for governmental authority and the role of the professionalized military in a new order.

A large part of the paper is thus an exercise in political sociology and social stratification. It is concerned with the architecture of society and, in particular, the construction of rule and domination, including the use of physical force. For the Austro-Hungarian officers, Weber's analysis must have been meant to be reassuring. He more or less told them that a socialist regime, despite syndicalist or anarchist tendencies, would have a vested functional interest in a stable governmental and military bureaucracy. However, this stability was contingent: 'the more the ranks are secure in their impression that only the *factual* interest in maintaining discipline and *no* party or class interests determine the behaviour of military authorities, that therefore only what is *factually* inevitable in war happens, the more unshakeable will military authority remain' (Weber, 1988, p. 518; my translation here and in the quotations to follow).

Earlier in the paper, Weber had observed that, in his experience with the German army, despite dislike for some status- and class-specific behaviour in the officer corps, the authority of officers had remained stable throughout the war, and that it could do so because it was a functional authority arising from factual competence within a bureaucratic order, the way he had described it in his own ideal-typical way. Weber also remarked that 'the German army for at least two-thirds of its strength was recruited from rural areas, and for a further sixth from the lower bourgeoisie, to whom roughing up workers or whoever else would make such revolutions would mean great fun' (1988, p. 515). This turned out to be a very good prediction, as the end of the war showed. The functional base of authority in the military, it has to be added, had been greatly strengthened during the war, since promotion to officer rank from the non-commissioned officers had become frequent and the officer corps had become a great melting pot of aristocratic, upper and lower middle-class people. Just as the Second Empire in Germany had been formed through 'revolution from above', so relative social equality of advancement, particularly in the wartime army, had been constituted by populist mobilization from above. This surely helped to legitimize a social definition of authority in bureaucracy as based on factual competence, as Weber saw it.

However, the prediction did not turn out to be that good for Austria–Hungary. The problem probably lay less in the factual competence and 'democratization' of the officer corps than in the ethnic, cultural and linguistic rifts that also became sociopolitical ones and deprived the Austro-Hungarian army of its homogeneity. Towards the end of the war, desertion, mutiny and passivity became endemic. Ethnically or culturally, German–Austrian and Hungarian officers lost control over regiments whose ranks were Czech, Slovak, Croatian, Polish, Slovenian, Bosnian and so on. The factual competence of the officer corps helped little and, in terms of our present-day sociology, we can imagine that the sociocultural foundations of authority were in no way near those in the German army, which is why Weber's ideal type of functional authority (Hartmann, 1964) worked reasonably well in the latter, whereas it did not work at all in the Austro-Hungarian army. Maybe the officers that Weber addressed grasped this, and felt less comfortable after his speech than he anticipated.

Lest readers think that all this is anecdotal and beside the point, let me stress that it is the first glimpse that we get, in the material under discussion here, of the importance of seeing organizational functioning in a wider societal perspective. Weber generally cannot be accused of having neglected the wider societal setting of organizations. It was he who made the classic point that modern bureaucratic organization is an outflow of rational–legal forms of domination (Weber, 1964, pp. 160–66, 703–38). In the paper, Weber (1988) discusses and compares organizational modes from different societies, but, when he gets to the point, he seems curiously to overestimate the extent to which rational–legal domination can be taken for granted or approximated in a modern state, in this case Austria–Hungary, and he neglects what, in his own theory, must boil down to the perseverance and reconstruction of traditional and charismatic forms of domination. This is a side-line, but it helps to focus the argument on factors which Weber had incorporated into his own theory, but which he shunted aside in the analysis of specific events or developments.

Back then, to the specific argument about bureaucracy and socialism, the way Weber presented it. Surprisingly, he first makes a detour via democratic government and public administration in Switzerland and the USA. This serves to make the point that non-bureaucratic, therefore elected or politically appointed, and in either case dilettantish administrators are either unpaid or in unstable jobs, dependent on political tides, and therefore less professional and effective although they may be democratically very legitimate. As regards the USA, he says that the country will emerge from the war a different society, much more bureaucratized, that is with a more stable public service and economic bureaucracy that recruits according to meritocratic criteria, after relevant education and training, people who are thought to hold a secure and politically neutral position, for the duration rather than until the political tide is reversed. Weber calls this the 'Europeanization' of the USA, and he sees it occurring together with the 'Americanization' of Europe. One would add that the best confirmation of this prediction happened after the Second World War, when the USA finally established the biggest bureaucracies the world has seen, in government and in the economy, focused upon the 'military–industrial complex'.

For Weber (1988, pp. 497–8), the reason was simple:

> Modern democracy, wherever it is a large state's democracy, becomes a bureaucratic democracy. And it has to be like that, for it replaces noble or other honorary functionaries with paid functionaries … . This is inevitable, and this fact is the first and foremost one with which socialism has to reckon, too: there is a necessity for long years of professional schooling, progressive professional specialization, and management by a specialized profession of functionaries, trained in that way. There is no other way of managing the modern economy.

With a big stride, Weber thus leaves the USA behind and lands in the territory of socialism. But for him, the step is a safe one, because there is an inevitable tendency for all societies that arrange solutions for specific problems 'on a large scale', 'in a uniform way' – Weber regularly uses such phrases when he explains the context under which bureaucracy is both legitimate and effective – to bureaucratize the organization and management of various public and private activities. Socialism cannot help but succumb to such tendencies.

Interestingly, Weber's reasoning for the pervasive and universal rise of bureaucracy is not as absolute as is often thought. He has a persistent habit of linking the argument for the advent of bureaucracy to the geographical and population size of a society, its amount of social integration, the concentration of authority in the hands of a few 'masters' that control an organization, and pressures for identical, reliable and equitable solutions throughout that larger society. This is contingency theory in a nutshell, for the amount of bureaucratization is seen to depend on size factors, and on the relative stability of organizational tasks, targets, standards and routines. Much later, we learned that there is in fact more than one way of organizing bureaucratically (Pugh and Hickson, 1976) and we learned to understand the variation of organizational forms in relation to the variation of organizational contexts and environments. But Weber already had the germs of this contingency theory in his hands, when referring to the most prominent contextual and environmental contingencies.

Later, we also gradually came to understand that the evolution of modern and capitalist societies brings with it not only a continuous increase in salient sizes, standardization and routinization of tasks, but also a uniformity and stability of contexts and environments. Modern capitalism may, depending on the time period and location, also effect a reduction in salient size factors, favour unpredictable adaptation of tasks and put a premium on organizational structures which are less bureaucratic, or bureaucratic in a different way than simply across-the-board. But Weber, and we cannot really blame him for this, did not see in 1918 such countervailing tendencies, which is why his prediction of the rise of bureaucracy looks more absolute than its theoretical roots.

The point that what is inevitable will also be inevitable under socialism would have been rather crude. This is not an argument to which Weber limited himself. He proceeded with a careful analysis of socialist doctrines, and with an analysis of how a change-over to socialism would happen in the real world. He discarded the more ambiguous or romantic socialist doctrines, about 'associations of producers', or cooperatives, or syndicalist organization. He also pointed out that a change from capitalism to socialism was not to be expected because of the manifest and increasing misery of the people, and the concomitant illegitimacy of the economic and political order. According to pre-war experience, that was definitely not on the cards (and how right he was) since the beginning and proliferation of socialist revolutions were invariably due to the breakdown of a political order, after a ruling elite was discredited by dramatic defeat in war or was too weak to win a serious power struggle in a civil war.

In the country he was most concerned with, his native Germany rather than the Austria–Hungary of his audience, Weber observed socioeconomic shifts towards socialism which owed little to misery, but a lot to the changing institutional order of capitalism. For one thing, capitalists formed cartels and associations and increasingly started to 'organize' capitalism, following a logic that obliterated the anonymous forces of the pure market, which had been held responsible for exploitation and the foreseeable inability of the capitalist order to provide for the bare essentials of civilized survival. Never mind the attention given to 'disorganized capitalism' later, according to Weber, we had not seen much of pervasive disorganized capital-ism in Germany since the end of the nineteenth century, at least. The economic historians proved him right.

Furthermore, the war production and mobilization effort, Weber says, brought with it an organized coordination between the govern-ment and economic actors which was much more bureaucratic and planned and remotely approached some sort of collective and delib-erate resonsibility that socialist thinkers must have had in mind. For Weber, socialism was likely to take on the shape that could be pre-dicted from the earlier experience which the population had known: cartellized capitalism, big enterprise capitalism, managerial capital-ism and 'state-monopoly capitalism' during the First World War together demonstrated the way in which socialism would also work. It would rest on a professionalized planning and management bu-reaucracy that bridged private–economic and public functions, and which was already there, as well-tried machinery. Weber could even have claimed to be close to Marx in this type of argument. Was it not Marx who had seen the – then – novel joint-stock company (*Aktiengesellschaft*) as one step towards socialism which happened while bourgeois ownership of the means of production still applied?

It is this, revisionist, view of the advent of socialism which Weber develops, roughly following earlier pre-war social democratic think-ers such as Bernstein. It might be contended that this change-over to socialism did not in fact happen, and that the change-over that did happen was indeed revolutionary. But, referring to early Soviet tech-nocratic concepts and reiterating that socialist organization could be inspected at home, Weber suggested that socialist economic organ-ization would have to be carried out by a class of trained specialists, within a larger bureaucracy. After all, what was a bureaucracy but a disciplined body of people, oriented towards the achievement of an organizational purpose and divested of the owership of the means of production. With reference to such functionaries, Weber used the word *Stand*, a term which is best translated by 'estate' and denotes a category of people with a specific status and situs, and corporatively associated rights and obligations with regard to the wider society.

Such an argument is an important specification of Weber's basic approach to the societal foundations of organization. If bureaucratic organization arises with the concentration of legitimate authority, and of the legitimate exercise of physical violence, if it originates out of the will to administer identical solutions to identical problems in a uniform and reliable way, and if what socialism intends is to give control over the economic fate of society to legitimate authorities rather than anonymous markets, then socialism had to intensify a mode of social coordination which inevitably was bureaucratic. To Clausewitz, war was the continuation of politics by means of force.

To Weber, socialism was the continuation of bureaucracy under new ownership of the means of production. Hence the prediction that socialism, whatever its proponents suggested, would have to go hand-in-hand with bureaucratic organization, and that it would reinforce the establishment of a bureaucratic service class.

Had Weber lived longer than he did, he certainly would not have been surprised by the course that socialism took in the Soviet Union. Particularly under Stalin and his successors, everything that happened would have appeared to him as a splendid confirmation of his earlier prediction. Observers of socialism also must have come to that conclusion. Probably, in his typical sobriety, Weber would have pointed out that, never mind the atrocities, tyranny and killings under Stalin, he probably had no other choice but to erect this gigantic governmental bureaucracy, by means which appear excessively severe, in order to make the bureaucratic control of such a far-flung society reliable and efficient in the hand of the 'master'. But let us not examine the evidence for Weber's thesis in the case of the Soviet Union. The social, economic and political preconditions for Russian socialism are specific to Russian history, with its long-standing tyranny, absence of private ownership and civic society, radical concentration of formal and symbolic authority and underdeveloped private capitalism. According to Marx, it certainly did not qualify for a pioneering role in socialism. Let us turn to a societal setting which was the same as the setting which Weber mainly had in mind: Germany.

Socialist Organization and Management in East Germany

It has almost become a cliché that economic organization in socialist East Germany, following the Soviet model, was bureaucratic through and through. This impression is founded on governmental planning, concentration of firms under the umbrella of publicly owned and very large enterprises, notably highly vertically integrated industrial and service combines (*Kombinate*), subordination of enterprises to governmental ministerial authority, economic governance by international agreements within COMECON and other institutionally pervasive structures of the societal and economic order. Where the behaviour of economic actors is concerned, there are countless episodes of experience that illustrate the rigidity with which centrally devised policies and plans were put into operation. Decades of anecdotes and jokes from East Germany and former East Germans have thus highlighted the association of socialism with bureaucracy. The reputational standing of both of these has suffered from the association, becoming even more tied up with inflexibility, sloth, waste of resources, wilfulness and shoddy output.

On the other hand, there also emerged a counter-joke which I heard in England. This had it that the East Germans were the most effective people in the world because they had succeeded in making socialism work. On the whole, the comparative reputation for efficiency and effectiveness of East German socialism after the collectivization of agriculture, the replacement of private with national and cooperative ownership of the means of production, the erection of the Berlin Wall in 1961 and the economic boom period during the 1970s was not bad, either at home or internationally. Is this another brilliant vindication of Weber's prediction? Of course, Weber had used the term 'bureaucracy' in an evaluatively more approving manner than colloquial language. Who knows, maybe he would have pointed out, in the 1970s, if he had lived to see the day, that socialism in East Germany owed its relative performance and legitimacy to bureaucracy.

At present, we are probably only beginning to see the more detailed evidence for and against the systematic association between bureaucracy and socialism, and between this association and either sloth or performance, but let me try a first, limited summary of the evidence that has surfaced so far, leaving out the negative and positive performance aspects and concentrating on the elementary bureaucracy–socialism interaction effect. It is illuminating to start with a frequent impression, in East Germany after 1990, that economic life under the institutional set-up in the Federal Republic is *more* bureaucratic than it was in the past. Although I am not aware of systematic survey data, I am convinced that they would point in this direction.

To make a more differentiated test of the 'bureaucratic socialism' hypothesis, let us distinguish the following larger substantive domains. On the one hand, under what is called *economic and corporate governance*, we look at organizational mechanisms that institute and modify key objectives, strategies and decision makers, both within enterprises and at higher levels, in government and in the sphere of stakeholders. On the other hand, we have to consider the *organization and management of enterprises*, which are focused on the way that key objectives and strategies are transformed into, or linked with, everyday performance in direct and indirect operative work roles.

Related to this dichotomy is another. On the one hand, we have characteristics related to the *population of organizational forms and modes of coordination* that we find in a society and its economy. Essential types, of organization forms and modes of coordination, have been suggested by, for example, Pugh (1984, pp. 72–7) and Mintzberg (1983). They are framed in such terms as full bureaucracy, work flow bureaucracy, personnel bureaucracy and so on, by Pugh, and as machine bureaucracy, professional bureaucracy, adhocracy and so on, by Mintzberg. Types of coordination across individual focal organizations are, of course, markets, networks, relational contracting and vertical or horizontal integration. The latter is, in much of the going literature, improperly confined to 'hierarchy', which is in fact only one of the possible coordination modes within organizations (Douma and Schreuder, 1992, pp. 36–9).

Distinct from the population of organizational forms and modes of coordination, we have the actual *organizational and work behaviour practice*, of individuals and groups, which is formally less explicit but socially very often highly regularized and legitimated. Such practice may conflict with the organizational forms and types of coordination under which it is deployed, or it may give such forms and types a particular nuance. And it may be rooted in other aspects of organization which are highly formalized. Formalized rights of employees, to participate, to enjoy employment security and so on, are for instance an important basis for the cultivation of an organizational and work behaviour practice which conflicts with formally instituted management prerogatives. This conflict may occur both in the sphere of organization and management within enterprises and in the sphere of economic and corporate governance.

First, let us take a look at what happened in the economic and corporate governance of the East German economy, specifically how it embodied organizational forms and types of coordination. Various analysts concur that hierarchical coordination under governmental agencies, by plans and programmes, had driven out market mechanisms (Heidenreich, 1992; Schmidt, 1993; Schmidt and Lutz, 1995). Employment was concentrated into large and very large enterprises; these were subordinated to national plans, and enterprise objectives and strategies were centred around the fulfilment and overfulfilment of plans. Enterprise concentration and the bureaucratization of economic activity went hand-in-hand with an emphasis on product and service standardization. Production regimes were oriented by the achievement of economies of scale. There were abundant organizational staff to plan and administrate activities. Functional and professional specialization of work roles was high. With a large industrial sector, with well over 50 per cent of employment in the society, and with this sector mainly consisting of large enterprises producing large volumes of standardized products, it is no exaggeration to say that East German economic activity was mainly governed by bureaucratic and hierarchical coordination, and that this was focused on the institution of large-scale, mass and continuous production regimes. Indeed, it was the deliberate aim of government policy, with the nationalization of enterprises, to obtain large and integrated units that would lend themselves to rationalization more easily.

Accordingly, what we learn from the literature about the organization and management of enterprises boils down to the theme that something like the Astonian 'full bureaucracy' or the Mintzbergian 'machine bureaucracy' was prevalent, to all intents and purposes. A 'full bureaucracy' is characterized by 'high' scores on all the classic Astonian dimensions of bureaucratization; it is centralized, has an impersonal control of work flow and shows extensive structuring of activities (Pugh, 1984, p. 75). We also learn that East German enterprises, in a way, seem to have been made to select that form of organization and coordination which, according to standard contingency theory, is well adapted to respective contextual and environmental conditions: that is, large unit size, dependence on concentrated ownership and external interests, uniform, stable or unproblematic demand for products and services, standardization of products and services, and production or service provision on a large scale. The 'administrative component' of industrial enterprises was notoriously large, work systems and work roles were rather segmented, despite a comparatively very high incidence of formally certified basic vocational qualifications (from apprenticeship) and shift work was more extensive than in West Germany.

A conclusion which seems to be well accepted is that the more classical rationalization strategies and forms of organization abounded, and that their domination was so institutionalized that it forestalled a change-over to 'diversified quality production' (Sorge 1993). It has also become accepted that this imbalance was at the root of economic problems and crises of enterprises after German unification, along with the vanishing of established customers in the former COMECON countries (see Wittke *et al.*, 1993; Gebbert and Gebbert, 1993; Voskamp and Volker, 1991). But on the other hand, the literature has also demonstrated that the rise of full and machine bureaucracy in East Germany, as in other COMECON countries, was limited by a much higher degree of input uncertainty than in the West. Whereas, in the East, sales never were a problem for enterprises, obtaining the right material inputs and investment goods on time was a perennial problem. This problem had to be met by various methods, ranging from continuous expediencies, that is rescheduling, reworking, flexible use of labour and so on to more strategic behaviour in the form of maintenance of very large inventories, backward integration and networking, or political orchestration of supplier relationships.

Thus it appears that the very system of bureaucratic planning which was to reduce uncertainty could not help but generate increasing uncertainty on a specific count, which limited the practicability of bureaucracy and virtually every organizational form or type of coordination that was built on the assumption of largely predictable or reliable information. This dialectic of bureaucracy, that the phenomenon and tendency itself would to some extent annihilate its own paperwork, was not anticipated by Weber. But it is well within the theoretical range of Weberian organization theory, which had come to highlight the degree of environmental stability and predictability as the most important predictor of full bureaucratization.

Remember also that another classical author of contingency theorizing, Burns (1984), pointed out that mechanistic management systems may become entrenched to such an extent that organizations react bureaucratically to environments becoming volatile, which can be considered a source of organizational pathology that is similar to the 'downward spirals' of enterprise economic decline, demonstrated by Voskamp and Wittke (1991). Contingency theory had tended to see organizational performance as related to the degree of 'fit' or congruence between environmental and contextual properties and organizational forms. Misfit or incongruence between these sets of factors occurred after the unification of Germany pushed towards environments, contexts and organizational forms that favoured diversified quality production for volatile markets. This conflicted with institutionalized organizational forms and types of coordination, which matched contexts and environments that had the opposite properties. This diagnosis implies a contingency theory argument, and it again turns out to be pertinent in the analysis of problems after the collapse of socialism. To that extent, post or neo-Weberian theorizing, of which Aston has been one of the most eminent examples in organization theory, is still very influential. One might even argue that limits to bureaucratization under socialism, while they were not yet conceived by Weber, are compatible with the theory which he had sparked off.

On the other hand, it also emerges that there were limits to bureaucratization under socialism which were neither conceived by Weber nor successfully explained by the classical authors in contingency theory who succeeded him. These emerge very clearly from an examination of the results of research on prevalent organization and work behaviour practice under East German socialism. First, with regard to economic and coporate governance, it turns out that this was highly politicized and influenced by personal relationships and networks. Authors such as Marz (1993) and Kreißig (1993) make it very clear that both enterprise targets and material and personal resources were very much influenced by the political connections, within the socialist SED party and in the state apparatus, that enterprise top management was able to build up and cultivate. Contrary to the logic of bureaucracy, economic planning and corporate governance was thus to an important extent personalized and reputational rather than matter-of-fact – *versachlicht* as Weber would have termed it. It was built on the exercise of charismatic and traditional authority, rather than rational–legal authority.

The logic of this phenomenon is beguilingly simple. Where economic shortage is decoupled from pricing mechanisms, there will be alternative mechanisms to determine the allocation of factors such as finance, qualified workers, capital goods and supplies to enterprises – these mechanisms of a political, relational, personal and reputational nature. In addition, it has to be remembered that, under socialism, enterprise performance was not evaluated according to functionally rather specific criteria alone. Next to fulfilment of national plans and achievement of certain quality standards, enterprises were also confronted by other criteria of success, from absorbing excess labour, promoting sports and making volunteers available to the armed forces, down to electric energy generation and a wide range of other services for the local or regional environment. An enterprise under socialism thus had the broad scope of an encompassing microcosm of society (Etzioni, 1961), rather than being a functionally specific ingredient of society, as under capitalism.

By that token, economic and corporate governance under socialism was not much less than the management of societal segments in the Durkheimian sense, where segments are functionally encompassing units that might even be called quasi-autonomous. This had to signify a much more political character of management, not only in the party political sense. The politicization of any whichever social unit's management will be a function of the scope and variety of the unit's goals. Where goals are wide and differentiated, and where differentiated goals are not ordered hierarchically but compete, the organization and management will be more politicized. Pluralism of goals is unmanageable on a rational-legal basis alone. It cries out for the politicization of decision-making. This kind of extensive pluralism of goals is unmanageable on a rational–legal basis alone. It cries out for the politicization of decision making. The deviation from rational–legal principles leaves no option but recourse to tradition – the tradition of socialism, to be sure – and charismatic – the charisma being that of socialist leaders – criteria. Expressed in a Weberian form, but going beyond Weber's analysis of 1918, once socialism had opted against the functional differentiation of society and therefore against functionally specific enterprise objectives, it was set on a path that reduced rational–legal economic and corporate governance to a superficial, formal role, and it had to evolve towards personalized networking, much more so than under 'relational contracting' in capitalism. Socialism thus turned out to be an almost ideal-typical haven for relational, often tacit, contracts. To this extent at least, socialism had to become postmodernism *avant la lettre*.

There were endeavours to increase enterprise responsibility for its own value-added, as a more specific and focal goal, since the deleterious effects of a wide lateral pluralism of goals, and of rigid planning, were acknowledged. First, in the second half of the 1960s, the 'New Economic System' (NÖS) was put forward. At the beginning of the 1980s, there were similar efforts to make enterprises more specifically responsible. However, the conclusion is that such efforts proved fruitless (Edeling, 1992, pp. 327–9), since the planning machinery targets remained in place and retained their overriding importance. It also emerged that institutionalized rules and forms of adhocratic 'coping' had generated rather robust clienteles that had to be kept acquiescent. This was put forward by my colleagues Ettrich and Lohr, in a seminar. There were, thus, not only formally ordained and enforced but popularly buttressed limits to change. This was probably less a matter of doctrine and domination than of vested interests shared by a large part of the population.

A similar picture emerges when we take a closer look at the actual behaviour of actors in the organization and management of enterprises. The central findings can be summarized by saying that neither a reliable control of work flow and quality of output nor a reliable control of the workforce was ever obtained. This has to do with the unpredictability of material inputs, but, in the internal organization, the most outstanding factor seems to be a lack of legitimate and effective control over work performance and labour mobility. Tolerance of absence from work for a variety of reasons was high, and it was very difficult to discipline workers at any level. Employment security was very high and truly punishing redundancies were more or less reserved for cases where the political loyalty of a worker was questionable. Likewise, positive sanctions were largely ineffective. The financial returns to promotion were usually small, and sometimes even negative. Fringe benefits, such as advantageous access to holiday resorts, good accommodation, specific consumption goods and better old-age pensions were tied either to specific occupations or objective criteria (marriage, number of children and so on) or they required particular non-work efforts in mass organizations (party, trade union, youth organization, society for German–Soviet friendship and the like), sports or the armed forces, including the enterprise militia (*Betriebskampfgruppe*) which many work organizations had to have.

Almost paradoxically, socialist work systems, which had been devised with a view to implementing a collective will in the most efficient way possible, thus turned out to be ill-disciplined and hard to manage (see Marz, 1993; Kreißig, 1993; Pohlmann and Schmidt, 1995). Fairly secure rights of workers not to be dismissed, or to escape internal transfer, and to participate in decisions via the enter-

prise union organization implied not only autonomy in job performance, but also a considerable softening of classical rationalization
concepts and, in conjunction with the vicissitudes of the socialist
planning system and the requirements for in-job flexibility, some
leeway for the building up and exercise of job, group, departmental
or functional privileges (Bluhm, 1992). Socialist planning sought a
specific legitimacy that undercut the authority of local management
and stylized the responsibility of the working-class grass roots.

In its everyday practice, socialist enterprise management was thus
a continuous and painful process of bargaining with other management, individuals and collectively organized workers, with hardly
any stick and a rotten carrot in hand. To the extent that authors
mention reasonably effective mobilization campaigns, they address
collective rather than individual incentives. Very often there were
implicit 'plan fulfilment pacts' (*Planerfüllungspakte*) between management and the workforce, but they were concerned with primarily
quantitative output goals and they centred upon advantages for larger
work collectives. In the economy at large, apart from some specific
enterprises that produced for Western markets, such pacts had the
function of ensuring a minimum of development, production and
service delivery, rather than mobilizing workers to pursue more innovative projects.

One of the authors in particular, Marz, has deployed a remarkably
vivid inside view of the systemic aspects of deficient work flow and
workforce control in East Germany. The essence of this is that, where
quantitative adaptation of employment to the workload is illegitimate and does not pay economically, and where qualitative
enterprise-led adaptation to perceived market opportunities is similarly illegitimate and ineffective, in view of institutionalized
diseconomies to diverging from ordained goals, poor work flow control and poor workforce control reinforce each other, via far-reaching
feedback cycles. Unpredictable deliveries, in shops and in manufacturing establishments, lead to intermittent underutilization of
resources and spasmodic bursts of both work and shopping or other
procurement activities. Since management acknowledges that workers who are also consumers have to adapt use of their time, not only
to prescribed working times but also to unpredictable time requirements and opportunities in the family and the sphere of consumption,
it grudgingly tolerates absence from the workplace. It also allows
some time for rest and recovery, at work, from politically sanctioned
meetings, demonstrations and 'societally useful' weekend activities.

Management cannot guarantee smooth operation, maintenance,
investment in physical capital and supplies, nor can workers guarantee dedicated and attentive work performance. Part of the story relates
to objective fluctuations, part to cynicism and demotivation, and

part to the rigidity arising from the protection of vested interests, residing in the job and in the privileges attached to collectives. All the parts of the story illustrate a vicious circle leading to suboptimal achievement of both work and consumption goals. In such a system, bureaucratic planning is revealed as window-dressing, as a camouflage for organizational pathologies. Workers and managers learn to bend the formalized system, to subvert it, in order to make it work and satisfy personal wishes and requirements to some extent.

This sheds light on the way East Germans experienced bureaucracy, and how this is different from the West German experience. East German bureaucratic rules and plans were very much in evidence, but they were uniform and straightforward, political and other connections were used to bend them, and they could be subverted. The West German experience is radically different on most counts. West German regulations are much more complex and differentiated, and the drive to stylize them as politically neutral means that it takes makes much more effort and diligence to bend them. Hence it is not astonishing that East Germans experience the new Germany as more bureaucratic. This reflects their experiental difficulty of manoeuvring in, and bending, a more complex, differentiated and resistant web of rules. Interestingly, bureaucratic coordination apparently became less contested and more developed and respected in a society where it also had to compete with market and political mechanisms. This was in West Germany.

The irony is that bureaucracy became delegitimated in East Germany, through being encompassing but rather crude, built on plans and absolute programmes, simple to understand and easy to evade in both political and informal but socially legitimate ways. In West Germany, bureaucracy became ever more fine-grained and adjusted to minute differences, built on contingency programmes, which kept it relatively more viable, despite manifest derision of bureaucratic tendencies. Enterprises in East Germany were styled as full bureaucracies but made to work as adhocracies, and the gulf between the two types was bridged by the personalized and political manufacturing of bona fide consensus. Enterprises in West Germany, however, combined professional bureaucracy and adhocracy, which minimized the conflict between countervailing types of organization (Sorge, 1991). People in East Germany learnt to beat the system in order to make it work, and people in West Germany refined the system in order to make it work as one consistent whole. Whereas the clash between the full or machine bureaucracy and everyday adhocracy in East Germany was stark, the difference between the professional bureaucracy and the adhocracy in West Germany was less conflictual to start with, and this allowed for a subtle attenuation of the conflict.

Conclusions

On balance, the evidence for bureaucracy under socialism in East Germany is thus rather mixed. There has been a tendency to bureaucratize society and the economy systematically, and to set up full bureaucracies, but this brought about the subversion of bureaucracy. Interestingly, this subversion did not happen in a society that inadvertently weakened the applicability of bureaucratic organization. East Germany did its utmost to *create* stable and predictable environmental conditions for enterprises, thereby approximating Weber's and, more explicitly, Aston's ideal-type of fully bureaucratic organization. One explanation is that full bureaucratization across the board, with the elimination of market and price mechanisms, possibly increases rather than decreases environmental turbulence and unpredictability, more than the organizational capacity of full bureaucracies permits. As a consequence, there is a counter-bureaucratic tendency, the systematic cultivation of everyday 'coping' by adhocracy.

This is the dialectics of full bureaucratization, already mentioned above. It may hold a lesson that is theoretically valid, even after the demise of socialism. It means that the stability of bureaucracy, or of a more specific type like Astonian full bureaucracy, is to some extent assured by the deployment of countervailing organizational types and their associated coordination mechanisms. Apparently, even the drive to create the appropriate environmental and contextual conditions for the full bureaucracy turns on its head and has the opposite effect. It makes the task of environment more turbulent, the effects of which can be explained by contingency theory, but not how turbulence is created despite pervasive efforts to make the environment predictable. The twist to the argument around organizational types is that the promotion of a specific type is linked to the deployment of a countervailing type, or to its amalgamation with a countervailing type.

This point needs some explanation. It is uncomfortable to contingency theorists, imbued with positivism. Dialectics often excites horror in positivists. Note that I am not using either dialectics or positivism in a derogatory or laudatory manner. Both of them are perfectly consistent approaches and, in the explanation of organizational phenomena, we cannot escape either approach. Positivist contingency theory has conceived organizational configurations as approaching an ideal-typical form, through the matching of related contextual and organizational phenomena. It has not considered that the expansive crystallization of any particular set of contextual and environmental phenomena, in this case the contextual properties matching the full bureaucracy or the machine bureaucracy, may lead to the development of opposed contextual phenomena, in this case those matching the adhocracy. This is dialectics at work: the deployment of contextual properties matching the full bureaucracy itself is necessarily linked, at some stage, to the rise of countervailing contextual properties, in this case those making for adhocracy. By that token, it may be said that the deployment of one specific configuration has the effect of undermining the foundation of this configuration.

This is so even though actors contrive to prevent a lack of fit by promoting bureaucracy and its contextual and environmental conditions. It would therefore appear that even the pursuit of an organizational type like full bureaucracy bounces actors back to countervailing types. For what it is worth, this can be formulated as a law-like statement: *promotion of a specific organizational type, in an individual organization and in a larger population of organizations, leads to adverse task environmental effects that favour alternative types.* This explanation works via dialectic effects in the task and the general environment in particular through the general environment, the wider society and political factors are central to this explanation. For present purposes, it has two major components. One is the encompassing scope of enterprises in a socialist society, the fact that it stretches over domains and functions that are allocated to separate spheres in capitalist market economies. In East Germany, an enterprise was typically very large, catered for both work and non-work roles of its members, had an internal labour market that was highly self-contained by Western standards, provided services for the wider community, was used to ensure social security and full employment, and even played a part in the state monopoly of physical violence. It was more of a *Gemeinschaft* than a *Gesellschaft* type of collectivity.

The other component of this explanation is a distinction between the polity which society has and the focal microcosm of society under socialism, the enterprise. This distinction appears to be characteristic of socialism, most certainly its East German variant. While the polity was a locus for either the suppression of civic rights or the manufacturing of superficial consensus, the enterprise was a place that safeguarded individual rights and tolerated, not only the manifestation of rights, but also the violation of obligations. Whereas most Westerners are likely to experience the polity as tolerant and the enterprise as either demanding or repressive, East Germans must have seen the contrast the other way round, even if the polity also used the enterprise as its microcosm.

No larger society can effectively function, in the long run, without generating some elementary legitimacy for its basic order. This is a profoundly Weberian assumption and it tallies with the classic statement of Talleyrand, foreign minister in France under different regimes, that you can do a lot with bayonets, but they are thoroughly uncomfortable to sit on. Socialism generated relative legitimacy by a specific bargain with individuals and organized groups. Far from mainly relying on repression alone, East German society was organized to derive relative mass loyalty or conformity from the assurance of stable employment and veto or participation rights in the work sphere. In addition, the immediate work environment also offered a substantial amount of personal intimacy and solidarity. And the enterprise constituted the port of entry into other social rights and opportunities.

This peculiarly 'pre-modern' construction, not only of the enterprise but also of wider society, was part of the socialist legitimatory bargain, and it counterbalanced political repression and mechanical conformity. Another part of the bargain was the relative stability of consumer prices for basic goods. It was a bargain which the DDR government and SED party did not fully devise originally, but learned to heed 'the hard way'. The popular revolt of 1953, incidentally the first one to take place against socialist government outside the Soviet Union, had been sparked off by a strike and demonstration of the workers building the Karl-Marx-Allee (formerly Stalinallee), as a showcase of new socialist architecture. The grievance was, in the first instance, that work norms had been tightened. The demonstration quickly escalated towards widespread political rebellion and would have swept the government aside, had it not been for the Soviet forces. The SED drew the most evident but partial conclusion: that mass loyalty is a function of work norms, employment security, other working conditions and prices. This bargain was apparently required in order to legitimize that concentration of power and domination which was euphemistically referred to as 'democratic centralism'. It can be seen that one and the same event, 17 June 1953, led to both entrenchment of rights at the place of work and a huge state security apparatus. Democratic centralism was, in turn, required structurally to achieve a coherent, non-pluralist management of all the different aspects of life in society. And both democratic centralism and coherent management of society were foundations for the full bureaucratization of society and the economy.

Bureaucratization was thus dependent on a political construction that undermined it: it was interdependent with strong status rights in the enterprise that helped to weaken, deflect, bypass or render impossible full bureaucratic control (see also Lutz, 1995). The political undermining of the full bureaucracy is not separable from the undermining which is due to the mentioned dialectic effect in the task environment. It is both an ingredient of political pacification and one of everyday coping through adhocracy. Quite simply, full bureaucracy could not do the job it was supposed to be cut out for, according to contingency theory.

This could not be anticipated by Weber, or his successors in organizational contingency theory. Socialism did not amount to a climax of rational–legal domination; it became an untidy compromise between full bureaucratization and adhocracy. Although that is so, it should be pointed out that Weber did elsewhere consider dialectical effects in the wider society. After the fall of the German Empire of 1871–1918, for instance, he argued for the strengthening of the position of the president of the (Weimar) Republic. No matter whether this was a good or a bad idea, his argument is interesting. He had suggested that a charismatic president is necessary to counterbalance rational–legal rule by ministerial and parliamentary government. Rational–legal rule was insufficient to organize society and it had to be complemented by countervailing structures, resting on charismatic and traditional principles. Here Weber proved himself a more dialectical theorist than he was later often made out to be. Dialectical relationships, by which a type of domination or of organization is interdependent with its conceptual opposite, were certainly not unknown to him.

Such dialectical effects fully emerge only when we see organization as embedded in the construction of wider society. The most striking dialectical effects are societal effects (Maurice *et al.*, 1982). One example of a striking societal effect in West German society is the case of *Handwerk* (artisanal smaller) firms (Streeck, 1992, pp. 105–36). These have been protected from competition by large firms through corporatist organization and privileges, as long ago as the nineteenth century. This had rendered the small firm sector institutionally distinct from other industrial and commerce enterprises. It boiled down to the creation of a safer niche for an organizational form that Mintzberg called the 'simple structure'. But this institutional separation also made possible the evolution of *Handwerk* firms towards more modern and innovative products and services, rational organizational methods and satisfactory economic performance. The dialectical evolutionary twist of this effect is that *Handwerk* firms have come to be corporatively distinct, but more contiguous with large firms than in other societies, in terms of organizational practice, effectiveness, training standards and industrial relations coverage. The encouragement and institutional isolation of the 'simple structure', rather than one-sidedly preserving its own properties, were instrumental in infusing it with more bureaucratic properties.

Such societal effects have to be considered if we want to understand why and how societies become populated by organizational types, and what these look like. The societal context of organizing produces societally distinctive organizational types and populations of organizations. To explain how this happens, contingency theory is useful, but we need more than that. Otherwise, we will not understand how task environments become undermined in the way described, and how what is called the 'general environment' works and affects organizing.

Note

1   For helpful comments and suggestions, I am very grateful to Karin Lohr. I am also in debt to the East German friends, colleagues and neighbours, in whose midst I have lived and worked since 1992, as a West German who 'came in from the cold' (that is, the Netherlands) and listened to their oral history.

References

Bluhm, K. (1992), 'Vom gescheiterten zum nachholenden Fordismus?', in E. Senghaas-Knobloch and H. Lange (eds), *DDR-Gesellschaft von Innen: Arbeit und Technik im Transformationsprozeß*, Bonn: Friedrich-Ebert-Stiftung, pp. 44–56.

Burns, T. (1984), 'Mechanistic and organismic structures', in D.S. Pugh (ed.), *Organization Theory: Selected Readings*, 2nd edn, Harmondsworth: Penguin, pp. 40–51.

Douma, S. and Schreuder, H. (1992), *Economic Approaches to Organizations*, New York: Prentice-Hall.

Edeling, T. (1992), 'Organisationssoziologische Ansätze in der Industriesoziologie der DDR', *Berliner Journal für Soziologie*, **2**, 323–32.

Etzioni, A. (1961), *A Comparative Analysis of Complex Organizations: On Power, Involvement and their Correlates*, Glencoe Ill.: The Free Press.

Gebbert, C. and Gebbert, V. (1993), 'Neuanfang oder Niedergang? Transformation probleme der ostdeutschen Bekleidungsindustrie', in Schmidt (ed.) (1993), pp. 215–29.

Hartmann, H., (1964), *Funktionale Autorität*, Stuttgart: Enke.

Heidenreich, M. (ed.) (1992), *Krisen, Kader, Kombinate: Kontinuität und Wandel in ostdeutschen Betrieben*, Berlin: Sigma.

Kreißig, V. (1993), 'Realsozialistische loetriebliche Machtstrukturen und industrielle Beziehungen im Transformationsprozeß zur Marktwirtschaft', in Schmidt (ed.) (1993), pp. 109–30.

Lutz, B. (1995), 'Betriebe im realen Sozialismus a/s Lebensraum und Basisinstitution: Erste Hypothesen und offene Fragen zur Transformationsforschung', in Schmidt and Lutz, (eds) (1995), pp. 135–158.

Marz, L. (1993), 'System-Zeit und Entökonomisierung. Zu Zeit/Machtdispositiven und mentalen Dispositionen in realsozialistischen Wirtschaften', in Schmidt (ed.) (1993), pp. 73–108.

Maurice, M., Sellier, F. and Silvestre, J.-J. (1982), *Politique d'éducation et organisation industrielle en France et en Allemagne: Essai d'analyse sociétale*, Paris: Presses Universitaires de France.

Mintzberg, H. (1983), *Structure in Fives: Designing Effective Organizations*, Englewood Cliffs, NJ: Prentice-Hall.

Pohlmann, M. and Schmidt, R. (1995), 'Management in Ostdeutschland', in Schmidt and Lutz (eds) (1995), pp. 217–44.

Pugh, D. (1984), 'The measurement of organization structures: Does context determine form?', in D.S. Pugh (ed.), *Organization Theory: Selected Readings*, 2nd edn, Harmondsworth: Penguin, pp. 67–86.

Pugh, D.S. and Hickson, D.J. (eds) (1976), *Organizational Structure in its Context: The Aston programme I*, Aldershot: Gower.

Schmidt, R. (1993), 'Einleitung', in Schmidt (ed.) (1993), pp. 7–26.

Schmidt, R. (ed.) (1993), *Zwischenbilanz: Analysen zum Transformationsprozeß der ostdeutschen Industrie*, Berlin: Akademie-Verlag.

Schmidt, R. and Lutz, B. (eds) (1995), *Chancen und Risiken der industriellen Restrukturierung in Ostdeutschland*, Berlin: Akademie-Verlag.

Sorge, A. (1991), 'Strategic fit and the societal effect: interpreting cross-national comparisons of technology, organization and human resources', *Organization Studies*, **12**, 161–90.

Sorge, A. (1993), 'Arbeit, Organisation und Arbeitsbeziehungen in Ostdeutschland', *Berliner Journal für Soziologie*, **3**, 549–67.

Streeck, W. (1992), *Social Institutions and Economic Performance: Studies of Industrial Relations in Advanced Capitalist Economies*, London: Sage.

Voskamp, U. and Volker W. (1991), 'Aus Modernisierungsblockaden werden Abwärtsspiralen: Zur Reorganisation von Betrieben und Kombinaten der ehemaligen DDR', *Berliner Journal für Soziologie*, **1**, 17–40.

Weber, M. (1964), *Wirtschaft und Gesellschaft: Grundriß der verstehenden Soziologie*, Cologne/Berlin: Kiepenheuer & Witsch.

Weber, M. (1988), *Gesammelte Aufsätze zur Soziologie und Sozialpolitik* (Collected Works in Sociology and Social Policy), Tübingen: J.C.B. Mohr Uni-Taschenbücher.

Wittke, V., Voskamp, U. and Bluhm, K. (1993), 'De Westen überholen, ohne ihn einzuholen?', in Schmidt, R. (ed.) (1993), pp. 131–54.

14 Children of the System: Management in Russia

MOSHE BANAI, *The City University of New York*

Introduction

It all started on my first visit to Russia in 1993. On the second day in Kazan, the capital of the Republic of Tatarstan, I was asked by Russian scholars and students about how long I thought it would take Russia to recover from the negative effects of the transition of the economy. My hosts wanted to know how long it would take for the Russian markets to behave in a style which is similar to the behaviour of the markets in Western countries. The correct answer to this question is that nobody knows how long it will take. However, this did not seem to be a satisfactory answer to this large audience and the national media. Hence, after a short pause for reflection, I replied that, in my opinion, the time which would be needed to introduce such a change is a generation. I have since visited Russia on two further occasions, living there for over seven months. I have used these visits to interview those in government, business and academe, as well as laymen, in order to find a more systematic answer to the question of Russian economic recovery.

The purpose of this chapter is to use Western concepts to explain current organizational behaviour in Russian public and private firms, and to identify tendencies that may enable us to predict how long it will take for the Russian economy to reach Western standards. The main thesis of the chapter is that the Russian economic and political system has engraved itself upon people's organizational behaviour over the last 70 years to the extent that, even though the system is now changing, people cannot change their old behaviour. It is up to the younger generation, those who are now 20 years of age or less, and who will assume powerful positions in their society in about 15–20 years, to introduce new role models and reward new patterns of organizational behaviour in the future.

Research Approach

A number of important studies have been published in recent years which attempt to describe the current management systems in Russia. However, most of these studies have been designed by US researchers who used Western theories of management to survey and observe behaviour in Russia. In my view these studies have failed to provide good descriptions or valid explanations, and for a number of reasons. First, the length of time of the actual field studies has been too short for the researchers to really understand the systems. Second, visitors to foreign countries tend to have a first impression of this country that may later prove to be inaccurate and in most cases is subject to change. Most US researchers had very little opportunity to gain second and third impressions. Third, Russian society is secretive. It takes a long period of time to develop interpersonal trust that may be used for the discovery of valid facts and data – and even then one cannot be sure if one is on the right track. Fourth, lying is not considered to be a negative norm in Russia. People and corporations may make up any story to satisfy the listener and at the same time to achieve their own objectives or maintain personal security. Thus it takes considerable cross-investigation and verification to arrive at some aspects of the truth.

For example, during a visit to one of the seven factories that were involved in this research study, a production manager was interviewed. At one stage, and without being asked, he disclosed his salary to be the equivalent of $200. Cross-validation from other sources revealed that the actual salary of the manager was the equivalent of $1200. The difference consisted of unofficial pay that may not have been disclosed to the tax agencies.

I have thus chosen a qualitative research approach because it is a powerful means of studying new trends. I used interviews and observation techniques because they are effective in exploring various attitudes and behaviours that may not be disclosed by surveys. It has been proposed by Johannessen (1994) that the three most effective processes of information gathering in Russia are trust, relationship and integration. These three processes can best be served by a qualitative, longitudinal study. The present chapter summarizes interviews and observations and, while lacking hard figures, is a result of an intensive information-gathering effort, cross-validated and checked for accuracy over a long period of time.

The Nature of Russian Management

Economic, political, social and organizational systems are very powerful in modifying people's behaviour. While personality traits, in addition to education and primary socialization, are usually regarded as the key influences on human behaviour, we use the present situation of Russian management to argue that institutional and organizational systems have an almost unlimited power in shaping human behaviour in organizations. Russia is a country in transition where management systems are moving from relying on a centrally controlled economy to a free market economy, but while the assumptions underlying market behaviour have changed, people's behaviour has not. Managers and workers are behaving as if the old rules which underpinned the previous business economic system still prevail.

The new 'desirable' free market economy is based on Western conceptions of the principles of bureaucracy, while the old system of central planning was based upon the interpretation by the Communist regime of Marx's conceptions of social effectiveness through conflict. The differences may be described as in Table 14.1 (adapted from Whyte, 1973).

Under the assumptions of communism, economic organization is a subsystem of the larger political system. The chain of command does not start with the general manager of the organization but rather with the political deputy assigned by the government (Hickson and Pugh, 1995). The free market model presents organizations that have the autonomy to make their own decisions within regulated boundaries. In contrast, the central market economy sets no clear boundaries between the economic organization and its political environment. It limits the organization's autonomy and therefore its members' contractual relationship with the organization. The nature of the contract is such that an organizational member's first loyalty is to the political system represented by their immediate boss.

While the Weberian model of bureaucracy has been ideologically replaced by contingency models of current Western scholars of management, the reality is that the principles of bureaucracy can still be found in one form or another in most organizations worldwide. They have been adjusted to domestic political and technological contingencies.

The following sections present a description of organizations in transition in Russia. Using the traditional categories of management behaviour – planning, organizing, leading and controlling – we examine the current management system and depict the behaviour of managers and workers in both the public and private sectors. This behaviour is later compared with the model of bureaucracy and the

Table 14.1 Western and Communist conceptions of management

Western conception	Communist conception
1 Use criteria of technical competence in personnel allocation	Use both technical and political competence
2 Promote organizational autonomy	Promote openness to outside political demands
3 Legal rational authority	Legal political authority
4 Informal social groups are unavoidable	Informal groups should be eliminated
5 Differentiated rewards for office and performance encouraged	Differentiated rewards de-emphasized
6 Varied compliance strategies applied by the organization	Coercion applied by the political system
7 Formalistic impersonality	Comradeship
8 Unemotionality	Political zeal encouraged
9 Partial inclusion and limited contractual obligations of office holders	Near total inclusion and theoretically unlimited obligation
10 Job security encouraged	Job security
11 Predictability through rules and regulations	Rules and regulations
12 Unity of command and strict hierarchy of communication	Collective leadership

Marxist model of conflict given above. Conclusions are drawn to support the argument that it is easier to make an administrative decision to change the principles of an economic system than to actually change human behaviour and thereby change the socioeconomic system. To achieve a significant market-oriented system through a desirable change in human behaviour may therefore take Russia a generation.

Planning

Planning is the management function of making decisions for the future. In Western organizations it involves strategic or long-range planning, tactical or short-range planning and operational or day-to-day planning. The planning process may begin with a SWOT analysis (a comparison of the organization's strengths and weaknesses with environmental opportunities and threats). This is followed by a formulation of the organization's mission, objectives and standards of performance. Then the means, responsibilities and timetable of the plan and its deployment are prescribed. As the plan is executed, it is constantly evaluated in terms of the standards set and corrected if necessary. All members of management are involved in one way or another in the planning process and are committed to the plan's success.

In Russia, the planning process up to 1991 was conducted centrally. Government offices based their production targets on some combination of past performance, national and international trends and political needs (Sanna, 1993). Thus the relevant office might have decided to produce more nails to meet the new building construction plans or to use the same facilities to produce metal wires that may be needed for security purposes. This plan was communicated to the plant. Since the consequences of not meeting the output standards were severe, the plant's management would make every possible effort to meet them. These efforts encompassed tactics such as renegotiating the standards with the relevant government office, employing special 'pushers' to identify possible sources of the raw materials and negotiate their procurement, compromising product quality, overworking or underworking the plant's personnel, stockpiling in an easy year for a difficult one, modifying the books to prove that more products had left the factory gates than was the case and bartering with other plants that found themselves overproducing a product in exchange for another product that was in shortage (May and Bormann, 1993).

Since government decision makers were exposed in the main to incomplete or faulty information, the plans had very little chance of being corrected to meet reality. Hence, in any given year, there was little match between the central plans and production schedules, with the consequence that the plans became administrative orders rather than a realistic assessment of what could be achieved.

In the new era of a market economy there is not much incentive for government businesses to change. They are still monopolistic and centrally controlled by the government. While the managements of private organizations have many incentives to try and adjust their planning patterns to those applied in Western countries, this has not happened. These managers can hardly plan their day-to-day activities owing to the high level of uncertainty in the environment.

One of the aspects of this uncertainty is the unreliability of the suppliers (Sanna, 1993). Companies are closing down every day and are unable to respect their commitments. There are many examples of this: a supplier that was supposed to deliver raw materials or components may not deliver because its supplier could not itself get the raw materials needed. A dishonest supplier may take advance payment for goods and then disappear. The old habit of stockpiling is widely employed to overcome this problem. A further example is of the owner of a private firm that produces plastic products. He was looking for a small amount of alcohol which was needed for the production process. He stumbled upon a supplier who wanted to sell one hundred times the quantity needed. The owner bought all this quantity in the hope that he would be able to resell most of it, but thereby ran into the difficulties of storing the alcohol, a problem that his organization could not cope with.

Credit is also haphazard. Privatized banks still have the state as their major stockholder. Other banks are wholly owned by the state. In the face of the great number of bad loans and the money extorted by illegal operators, banks are very hesitant to issue credit. Consequently, credits are issued on the basis of personal contacts and therefore socializing and networking become the primary functions of the managers.

Several solutions to this problem are attempted. The first is to charge the customer for the goods before delivery is completed. This practice, while solving the cash flow problem, does not allow for the expansion of the organization's production. A speciality shoe company that has been established by three young people faced this problem. The factory was located in a government building which enjoyed a high level of security, thus limiting the capacity of criminal forces to intervene. However, as in many other cases, the government demanded a stake in the ownership as a condition of giving credit for expansion. The owners of the shoe factory tried to maintain their independence by using the second available tactic: borrowing from the customers. Since the company exported its product to Western countries, the owners believed that the retail chain to whom they shipped the final product would come to their aid by issuing them with credit. However, this did not happen. The foreigners wanted securities for their loans that could not be given. Consequently, the owners split up, to create two separate organizations: one that continued to maintain a low level of production in the secured facility and a second that moved to a new location, applying the final tactic: getting the 'grey market' economy involved.

Workforce planning is difficult. One would expect that in a transitional economy many people would be looking for jobs. All those who were employed by the defence industry and those industries that have changed hands from the public to private ownership may be looking for new jobs. However, most of these job seekers lack the necessary skills and work ethic. Potential employees do not want to work for the meagre rewards offered, they are unable to master new technologies and, when employed, they do not show the motivation that would justify more training, promotion and better compensation (Gimpelson and Magun, 1993). Hence a vicious circle of undiscriminating recruitment takes place. The new employees are then subjected to a month's trial period which is most likely to end with a termination. Alternatively, the new employee may hop jobs to improve income slightly. Managers can only make sure that they have a steady influx of job candidates so that the production lines are never idle. As McCarthy *et al.* (1993), show new Russian entrepreneurs have identified employees' skills and attitudes as one of the core problems of their new businesses.

Work is not planned for a longer period than a month or two. Since management is unable to plan the production properly, a common practice for organizations is to have the finished good in hand before looking for a buyer. Once the buyer is identified, the producer will collect all payment in advance and only then will he ship the goods. This practice is a result of the bad payment ethics and lack of trust between the supplier and the customer. Again, the supply of raw materials or components is haphazard. Raw materials may become unavailable because of real supply and delivery problems or because the suppliers have found a customer who is willing to pay more for a certain batch. Signed contracts do not guarantee that a delivery at a certain price will take place. Replacements for broken tools and machinery cannot always be found and improvisation must take place in fixing broken equipment. In short, since orders are not stable and supply of components and replacement parts is not always available, managers can plan work only in a very limited way.

Organizing

Organizing is the creation of a structure of relationships among employees that will enable them to carry out management's plans and meet overall objectives. In addition it requires the formulation of procedures that integrate the activities performed by separate groups in an organization.

Organizational structures in Russia resemble those in the West. Enterprises have a single head who bears responsibility for the firm's results. The most common departmentalization principle has been the functional one: organizations were commonly broken down into production, operations and administration departments. Functions such as finance, accounting and human resource management (HRM) were included in the administration department. The function of marketing did not exist as such but rather in the form of shipping and handling (Shama, 1993). Financing was all organized through the state central planning function and therefore was handled as an administrative issue, as was accountancy, which was not used to calculate cost and profit, but rather to monitor the in-and-out flow of resources such as labour, cash and products in a form of book-keeping. This function was used in a limited manner because there was no need for a more sophisticated use. Organizations had never been profit-oriented, even though they were productivity-oriented. Thus profit was not calculated and productivity had no meaning when no real competition existed between organizations. Lack of competition did not allow for comparison and hence for any realistic measurement of productivity. The yardstick was decided by the central planning office on the basis of historical measures.

The shift to a free market economy has presented managers with organizing problems unfamiliar to them. Suddenly, the need has arisen for departmentalization that will result in efficient management and control. One organization has taken the initiative. The book-keeping department has been split into three departments: one became the accountancy arm of the organization, the second became the finance unit and the third became the human resource department. The production department was broken down into production, maintenance and engineering. The administration was restructured into facilities management, transport, security and an employees' restaurant. The shipping and handling department became the marketing unit and was broken down into product design, sales and shipping. Since there was only one major supplier of raw materials, the general manager took it upon himself to handle this critical bottleneck.

While these moves may have the potential to solve some of the organizing problems of the firm, the reality is that there are no trained managers to perform some of the more advanced functions such as finance, accountancy, HRM and marketing. Moreover, there are a number of reasons why the owner of the company, who serves as the general manager, will not relinquish authority to the department managers. First, Russian organizations were run in a very paternalistic manner under the communist regime and managers still adhere to the old system, in order to preserve their power. Second, the hired employees and managers are used to the old system in which they did not have to take responsibility or justify their existence on a daily basis. Jobs were secure regardless of the individual's efforts. So the general manager feels that he cannot delegate major responsibility to these people and put the fate of his own organization in their hands. Third, even if managers are dedicated, they still lack the necessary management and professional skills, so that the general manager cannot fully rely on them. Fourth, a great part of the general manager's job is networking – identifying and securing raw materials, components, financing and, most of all, customers. The process of networking is essential in present-day Russia because the market is not efficient. Government officials who still control some major resources are purposely obstructive with the consequence that illegal enterprises dominate a great part of the market. Under these conditions the general manager feels that, if other managers get involved in critical aspects of management, they may establish their own networks and eventually steal the business from him.

The following examples illustrate these problems. A US businessman who was dealing with oil barters developed an operations office in the Ukraine. He identified a young local and trusted person and trained him over a year to take charge of the subsidiary. Once the employee was ready for the job, he opened his own barter firm, taking with him all major customers. A Russian manager who decided to prepare a marketing manager for his business convinced a loyal and bright employee to apply for a marketing job with a US subsidiary. The individual infiltrated the US organization, learned as much as possible, identified major suppliers and customers, and returned to the original organization to be appointed as a marketing manager. Under such circumstances, and to avoid such situations, general managers prefer to train their managers to do only a small part of the job, keeping in their own hands the keys to critical aspects of the organization.

Paternalism and centralization mean that the coordination of the organization is done by very few people, sometimes by the owner alone. There are no management meetings. All managers meet the general manager individually. Sometimes, a third manager may be called to participate in a meeting to resolve a specific problem or conflict. This style of coordination is very inefficient. For example, when the general manager is not on the premises the operations will continue as long as there is no need to make a critical decision. However, once a non-routine decision is called for, the activities grind to a minimum, sometimes halting altogether

Human resources are managed in a very haphazard way. No real recruitment efforts are exerted (Shekshnia, 1994). Potential employees apply to the organization on the basis of acquaintances, referrals or personal contacts with managers or employees. Selection of all employees needs the final approval of the general manager. People are selected according to their level of education, some past experience and foreseeable potential. There is no documentation of the employees' selection process. Once an employee has been offered a job, a personal file is opened carrying the employee's basic background information. This file is then updated on a regular basis with information about the employee's attendance and sickness record. Compensation is distributed on the basis of equity with all others in

the same job classification. There are some mechanisms for providing special cash awards for extraordinary accomplishments. Bonuses
at all levels of the corporation are widespread. Typically, all employees receive a thirteenth month's pay as a bonus at the end of each
year (Hermann, 1994).

Employees who have proved to be personally loyal to the general
manager may be promoted to a supervisory, and later to a managerial, position. In one case, a manager promoted his driver/guard's
wife from the management of the kitchen to the management of
human resources. A translator who has command of several foreign
languages and who attended many business meetings with customers was promoted to the position of sales manager. Formal
performance evaluation does not exist. Direct supervisors make occasional oral reports to the manager. In private corporations, and
with the absence of unions, compensation is negotiated in person
between the employee and the general manager. Rewards are meagre in Western terms. The average salary for a worker in 1994 was
about $50 per month. Managers may make more. A great portion of
the salary is paid 'under the table' to avoid taxes. Labour and safety
laws exist, but not much attention is paid to them, as is the case in all
aspects of life in Russia.

Trade unions are left over from the Soviet Union. In public or semi-
private corporations, the unions are to some extent involved in
managerial decisions. In the private sector, there are no unions.

Leading

Leadership in organizations is the ability to influence, motivate and
direct others in order to attain desired organizational objectives. Western management literature has for many years preached the use of
the democratic/participatory leadership style as the preferred and
most efficient. This literature has also emphasized the combination
of a people-oriented and task-oriented leadership style as having the
potential to achieve the best organizational results. While in practice
many Western managers do not necessarily resort to this style, they
mostly agree about its desirability.

In comparison, the common Russian style of leadership could be
described as paternalistic, if not authoritarian. Since Russian enterprises have legally been required to follow the one man management
principle, managers do not tend to share authority. Consequently, a
more participative management style has not been shown to increase
Russian employees' performance (Welsh *et al.*, 1993). It may be a
result of the Russian value system which is anchored in Russian
history, of the functional behaviour which has been dictated by real

life circumstances, or of the high level of uncertainty involved in the current Russian economy. Whichever is the case, the fact is that Russian managers treat their employees as if they are immature adults, continually instructing and directing them. Verbal and even physical abuse are not uncommon in this style of leadership. Employees are not highly impressed by this extreme behaviour.

For example, an engineer in a plant that served the defence industry had lost his job as a result of staff reductions. He found a job as a shift manager on a manufacturing production line. The engineer, who has a degree from a respectable Russian higher education institution, has to work and direct line workers who, in the best case, may possess high school diplomas. Some of the subordinates may come to their shift drunk and unable to perform. The shift manager is not able to achieve the daily production target. The general manager calls him to his office and verabally abuses him in front of guests and others. The shift manager first tries to explain the situation. When the general manager continues with the abuse, the shift manager answers back. Since Russians are expressive by nature, both managers tend to forget the incident in a few minutes and go back to their activities until the next incident happens. The general manager knows that the engineer is overqualified for the job and is poorly paid ($100 per month) and he also knows that the engineer will not leave the job because of the scarcity of this type of job. The engineer knows that the manager will cool down and he also knows that the manager cannot replace him with a more obedient shift manager. Thus the manager and the engineer may be colluding in the same game.

Extrinsic rewards seem to be more influential in motivating Russian workers than intrinsic rewards. Since the reward and punishment power of management is limited, and the legitimate power is considered to be very weak in a society that generally does not abide by the legal system, managers will resort to the application of expert and referent powers. Managers will use their contacts in the higher echelons of government, their professional knowledge and their authority to convince people to comply with their instructions. In the absence of a great number of formal extrinsic rewards, managers are engaged in a 'favour for favour' exchange process (Puffer, 1994). The manager releases the driver early on Friday just to make sure that the same driver is available for the manager's personal use over the weekend. This barter method is probably a residual effect of the communist regime, when formal rewards were supposedly equally distributed. The only way to give someone preferential treatment was by the application of the informal method of bartering. One of the common beliefs in Russia is that 'if you have friends, you do not need money'.

Communication is based on a top-down approach, with very little effort to initiate horizontal communication. It is done by face-to-face meetings. Memos and other documents are reserved only for special occasions when a formal contract is being formulated. Whether it is a result of the old times, when people were afraid to commit themselves to anything that might eventually backfire on them, or of the high price of paper, the fact is that managers prefer to communicate with other managers and employees by using face-to-face interaction. Directives and timetables are transmitted in a downward information channel and very little feedback is transmitted upwards. Taking into account the confidentiality of the financial and other reports, communication might be minimized on purpose. The less the managers know about the financial operation of the organization, the less they can report it to external agencies. Lateral communication is scarce since the leadership style is very centralized. Under these circumstances, it is not surprising that informal communication is prevalent in Russian organizations. In the absence of formal communication, and in the face of the high level of uncertainty in Russia today, the vacuum in communication is filled with rumours and stories.

Though workers are rewarded individually, they tend to see their fate as being a collective one. Whether as a result of a long history of collective suffering, of communism or of a cultural value system, Russian workers tend to define themselves as 'we' and management as 'they' ('we pretend to work and they pretend to pay us'). This social categorization is likely to result in negative norms of work behaviour. Since decisions are dictated by management, there is very little for the workers to do in terms of decision making. However, those few decisions made by workers tend to be group decisions rather than individual ones. This seems to be aimed at risk reduction. In the absence of clear information and in view of the severe consequences of mistaken decisions in the past, it is not surprising that workers tend to share the risk involved in their decisions by consulting colleagues and those who seem to be experts in the matter in question.

Controlling

Controlling is defined as the methods and mechanisms used to ensure that behaviours and performance conform to an organization's objectives, plans and standards. Preventive control mechanisms are aimed at reducing errors and corrective mechanisms are intended to change unwanted behaviours.

Public organizations in Russia are still controlled by government. Although private business claims to be autonomous, it also is to a large extent controlled by government. Private companies' stocks held by government companies, licences, facilities leasings and monopolized services are all used by the government to force itself on private business. A private firm will not get a licence unless it complies with government officials' requirements – mostly to share profit. A private firm will not be able to use the public heating system unless it shares some of its profit with the government heating company. The deputies that headed government companies in the past do not want to relinquish power now that they are heading the same semi-privatized companies. Rather than getting their rewards from government, they now assign their own rewards to themselves. This is how the new Russian 'Nouveau Riche' group has come about.

Preventive control is applied concerning people's behaviour, machinery, products and financial resources. Behaviour is controlled by laws, by rules and regulations and by strict discipline. Workers who miss too many days of work, or are caught drunk on the job, are reprimanded. In the public sector, the union may support such an action. In the private sector, there are no unions and the government's laws are supposed to provide employees with protection against unfair and greedy owners.

In the absence of efficient accounting systems in Russia (Rosenbloom, 1994), the corrective measures of control used are mostly applied after a crisis has struck. It is not surprising, therefore, that crisis-handling skills were ranked highly by Russian managers who were asked about management skills and qualities needed in a free market Russia. Machines not well maintained can only indicate unskilled maintenance workers after they have broken down. Defective products are likely to be identified only after they come out of the production line or when returned by unhappy customers. The loss of money may sometimes not be detected until there is an acute cash flow shortage.

Security measures are prevalent in the current business environment. Security against internal theft and damage, combined with security against external 'hooligans', is important and organizations cannot function without it. Every manufacturing and service organization must have some type of security system. Most security is provided by government agencies or by ex-government agents who have become private operators. Also illegal agencies extort money for security. The lines between these three types of security providers is not always clear.

Since the total tax for organizations may reach the absurd level of 93 per cent (Nicandros, 1994) and since extortion rates vary between 10 and 30 per cent, in order to survive businesses have to maintain three cash flow books: one for the stockholders or owners, one for the government and one for the illegal agencies. Paying taxes is a matter of individual choice, and there is a saying in Russia that 'only fools and foreigners pay taxes'.

Machine maintenance is based on service instructions. The supervisor's job is to ensure that the instructions and the service schedules are met. In the past, a machine failure was attributed to the worker's lack of discipline, which was a consequence of the supervisor's leniency. Both might have been severely punished for such a failure. Today, workers still carry on the same value system, even though severe penalties cannot now be applied. Thus workers and supervisors will give priority to the maintenance over production unless otherwise instructed.

Lack of incentives to be efficient and to produce quality products is inherent in the centralized state system. Continuous shortage of raw materials and finished goods and products has taught the Russians to use everything and to minimize waste (Kornai, 1980). Hence quality control, while existing in manufacturing businesses, and claimed by some to have improved over previous years (Birch and Pooley, 1995), does not approach Western standards. The control is applied at the end of the production line. Products' quality is inspected and those items that seem to fail a preset standard are picked out by a quality control supervisor who is usually an experienced worker. The substandard products are then sold in a secondary market, or distributed among managers and employees for a marginal price. Service organizations apply internal quality standards but not external ones. Customer satisfaction is not used as a measure of quality in the manufacturing and the service sectors.

Accidents and injuries are common (Caras and Harvey, 1990; Kublin, 1990). Medical treatment is given free of charge to sick and injured employees by the public health system. The public system will also provide benefits to the disabled worker. However, it is rare for a worker who takes his employer to court to receive significant damages or compensation. The legal system is designed in such a way that it gives more protection to the government than to individuals. Violators of pollution and other ecological infractions are rarely punished. When punishment does occur, the penalty is usually a fine paid out of the enterprise's funds. Consequently, air and rivers are polluted, prohibited chemicals are used in agriculture and industry, and hazardous materials are dumped without control (Kublin, 1990).

Western-style accounting systems do not exist. Books are being used to monitor cash flow and employees' attendance, and as machine service logs.

Conclusion

Behaviour in organizations in transitional Russia may be used as a basis for the comparison of current Russian management systems with the bureaucratic and the Marxist models of organizations described earlier. Personnel allocation, even in the private sector, is still based on technical and political competence, except that the political criterion has now a different meaning: it is not a party membership that makes the difference, but rather an association with a government power group. A worker whose friend or family member has an influential position within a government agency is more likely to get an office than someone who does not enjoy the same networking. Officially, private organizations are encouraged to be autonomous. In reality, government officials will do anything in their power to get involved in private business. In the past, the motivation to do so was power. Today, the motivation is financial.

In contrast to the West, where emotion is not encouraged in organizational life, Russians are very emotional people and they bring their feelings to the workplace. Workers still have theoretically an unlimited obligation to the organization. Even managers in private business see their employees as their 'convicts'. They may ask them to do things that are not job-related and that are beyond the official call of duty. Workers may have mixed feelings about these demands, but in the face of a lack of alternatives they will most likely comply. Jobs are considered to be secure so long as the company has the resources to pay salaries. Employment may only be terminated by the organization in cases of workers' extreme negative behaviour.

Rules and regulations are at the core of Russian management. However, they are interpreted very informally and not in the legalistic manner in which they are applied in the West. Leadership style cannot be described as collective, or as hierarchical. Most managers, both in the private and in the public sectors, use a paternalistic and centralized style of management.

This profile of Russian managerial behaviour does not resemble the Weberian model of bureaucracy, or the Marxist model. It is a style of organizational behaviour which could be found in other parts of Eastern Europe such as Poland and the Ukraine (Sood and Mroczkowski, 1994) and is probably a result of the political history and the culture in this part of the world. Economic systems have tremendous power over individuals' behaviour. However, even these economic systems cannot influence value systems that have been shaped and reinforced over a very long period of time. Thus shifts in economic systems cannot successfully be achieved without a similar shift in people's values.

Adults' values can hardly be changed. It may take a long time and much effort to change a voter's behaviour from voting for one political party to voting for another. It is easier to convince a young person to vote for any of them. In the same way, it would be a waste of time to try and change Russian adults' values regarding organizational and business behaviour, when most of them suffer from the negative effects of the change. It would be much more effective to educate young people from a very early age and teach them the value of democracy and the free market economy, before they have any vested interests in the system. Thus it is my estimate, supported by others who have similar views on the topic (for example, Ivancevich *et al.*, 1992), that it will take Russians at least a generation, or 20 years, to change their value systems. Without this change, a Russian capitalistic revolution cannot be properly accomplished.

References

Birch, N. and Pooley, J. (1995), 'Changes in Russian quality management practices from 1989 to 1992', *Management International Review*, **35** (3), 219–39.

Caras, and Harvey S. (1990), 'Sizing up the Soviet system', *Personnel Journal*, (December), 38–43.

Gimpelson, V. and Magun V. (1993), 'Russian workers' strategies in adjusting to unfavourable changes in employment', *Economic and Industrial Democracy*, **14**, 95–117.

Hermann, E. (1994), 'Post Soviet HR reforms', *Personnel Journal*, (April), 41–9.

Hickson, D.J. and Pugh, D.S. (1995), *Management Worldwide*, Harmondsworth: Penguin.

Ivancevich, J.M., DeFrank, R.S. and Gregory, P.R. (1992), 'The Soviet enterprise director: an important resource before and after the coup', *Academy of Management Executive*, **6** (1), 42–55.

Johannessen J.A. (1994), 'Seeking information in Russia', *European Management Journal*, **12** (3), 338–45.

Kornai, J. (1980), *Economics of Shortage*, Amsterdam, North Holland.

Kublin, M. (1990), 'The Soviet factory director: a window on Eastern Bloc manufacturing', *Industrial Management*, (March–April), 21–6.

May, R.C. and Bormann, C.J. (1993), 'Managerial practices in the former Soviet Union', *Multinational Business Review*, (Fall), 66–73.

McCarthy, D.J., Puffer S.M. and Shekshnia, S.V. (1993), 'The resurgence of an entrepreneurial class in Russia', *Journal of Management Inquiry*, **2** (2), 125–37.

Nicandros, C.S. (1994), 'The Russian investment dilemma', *Harvard Business Review*, (May–June), 40.

Puffer, S.M. (1994), 'Understanding the bear: a portrait of Russian business leaders', *Academy of Management Executive*, **8** (1), 41–54.

Rosenbloom, A.H. (1994), 'The Russian investment dilemma', *Harvard Business Review*, (May–June), 42.

Sanna, M. (1993), 'Public management in Russia: failures of the old system', *The Public Manager, The New Bureaucrat*, (Summer), 35–8.

Shama, A. (1993), 'Management under fire: the transformation of managers in the Soviet Union and Eastern Europe', *Academy of Management Executive*, **7** (1), 22–35.

Shekshnia, S. (1994), 'Managing people in Russia: challenges for foreign investors', *European Management Journal*, **12** (3), 298–305.

Sood, J. and Mroczkowski, T. (1994), 'Human resource management challenges in Polish private enterprise', *International Studies of Management and Organization*, **24** (4), 48–63.

Welsh, D.H.B., Luthans, F. and Sommer, S.M. (1993), 'Managing Russian factory workers: the impact of US-based behavioral and participative techniques', *Academy of Management Journal*, (February), 58–77.

Whyte, M.K. (1973), 'Bureaucracy and modernization in China: the Maoist critique', *American Sociological Review*, **38**, 149–63.

15 The Emergence of Ethnic Chinese Business Groups in Pacific Asia

GORDON REDDING, *The Poon Kam Kai Institute of Management, University of Hong Kong*

The comparative study of organizations has only recently begun coming to terms with the significance of networks, commodity chains and strategic alliances. This coincides with two trends in the world of business practices. First, Western organizations are experimenting much more with looser structures and more innovative forms. Second, there is the emerging significance of Asian organizational forms as legitimate bases for the exercise of competitive alternatives to Western capitalism. The Asian forms are still relatively little understood by Western scholars and practitioners and two of them in particular, the Korean *chaebol* and the large Chinese family business, are developing at such speed as organizational types that it has been difficult to capture their essence reliably in organization theoretical terms.

The work of Derek Pugh and the Aston Group was highly significant in establishing an early understanding of the Chinese family business form in comparative terms. Derek's presence in Hong Kong in the mid-1980s, as part of a project which came under the title 'Beyond Bureaucracy' at the University of Hong Kong Business School, was instrumental in bringing both a rigorous method of data collection on organization structure and a depth of knowledge on the comparative study of organizations. The major outputs of the programme in book form have been a study of Chinese capitalism (Redding, 1990) and the extension of business systems theory into the Asian context (Whitley, 1992). But all of the conceptual work rests on the foundation of the Aston work with which the project began and which owes so much to Derek Pugh.

The research began in descriptive mode. It was necessary to understand the nature of the Chinese family business in comparative terms and to fill in a gap in the literature. Prior to that time, most descriptions of the form had been anecdotal or ethnographic, an excellent example of the latter being Silin's classic study of a Taiwanese factory (Silin, 1976). In the 1980s and 1990s, however, the phenomenal economic growth rates in Pacific Asia have fostered the emergence of much larger enterprises among the ethnic Chinese of the region. This has brought to the forefront a new and significant question: are we seeing the emergence of a new form of large-scale enterprise to compete in world terms alongside the *chaebol*, the Japanese *keiretsu* and the Western multinational? Another facet of the same question is: are these new forms of large-scale enterprise stable or does their dependence on an owning entrepreneur constitute a long-term weakness? To examine this question, the chapter is divided into six sections. In the first section, the historical background to Chinese capitalism is discussed The second section examines the regional impact of the ethnic Chinese. In the third section, the major players are identified, as well as the nature of their networks. In the fourth section the characteristics of the ethnic Chinese large business groups are highlighted. The fifth section examines the implications of these business groups for China. In the sixth and final section, a number of implications for organization theory are discussed.

Historical Background

China has always been a totalitarian state and has not yet made the transition to a 'modern' condition. If China were to follow historical precedents in other developed countries this would require (1) the introduction of a political authority structure based on abstract principles widely espoused by free individuals rather than on charismatic leadership, (2) the espousal of rationality as a means of escape from the personalism now used as a vertical and horizontal coordinating principle and (3) the encouragement of much greater degrees of specialization. In all three of these long-term historical changes to societies elsewhere, the role of the institutions of civil society has always been crucial. Such institutions have not yet appeared in China and the traditional intervention of the state in all areas of economic and social life has not changed. Whether under imperial rule or Marxist rule, the state apparatus has maintained power by seizing a monopoly on the right to interpret the state ideology and using force to maintain that position.

One of the consequences of keeping this traditional form of society is that the forms of organization able to operate comfortably within it are adapted to its constraints. The principal constraint is the inability to trust others outside a certain personally known network. The commitment of strangers in business transactions is not credible as there are no supporting institutions such as reliable commercial law, accountancy, professions or government encouragement, to make it so. And credible commitment among strangers is crucial for the intensive kinds of economic exchange reached in modern societies (North, 1994).

In societies such as this, economic activity tends to fall into two polarized camps. On the one hand, the state itself takes a strong position in large-scale business, a phenomenon clearly visible in Korea, Taiwan, Indonesia, Singapore and, historically, in Japan, as well as being very evident in China itself in the state-owned enterprise sector. On the other hand, the small and medium enterprise (SME) sector operates on a continually small scale, although by a proliferation of individual enterprises, and by networking to transcend its scale limitations. The SME sector is able to contribute significantly to national performances in economic development. The significant feature has been the gap in the middle, in other words the absence of large corporations free of government and managed in ways which lead to internationally competitive efficiency. This gap is now being closed in the Chinese case, but by organizations which still display their origins in a totalitarian context. The legacy of Chinese social history to the modern-day ethnically Chinese entrepreneur is seen by such recipients in terms of three components: paternalism, personalism and insecurity (Redding, 1990).

Paternalism is a moral code which serves to legitimize the power structures of society and business. Its Chinese version is founded in Confucianism and contains the notion of family as the model for relationships. Thus a boss behaves as a father figure and accepts responsibility for the welfare of subordinates in exchange for deference, loyalty, obedience and discipline. These processes are exercised on a continuum running from benevolent to harsh, depending on personality and on the surrounding circumstances affecting relative bargaining powers. In such a context, high scores for the centralization of decision making in organizations are predictable, and strategy making as well as much operational decision making remains a family and often an individual monopoly.

Personalism is a belief system which has emerged in conditions where the establishing of trusting relationships has not been fostered by societal institutions. In Chinese society, you trust those you know, especially family and those specific individuals with whom trust bonds have been built on the basis of the reciprocal exchange of obligations, or *guanxi*. You cannot trust others because the rules of such a society are essentially mutually exploitative. A society built of self-supporting families, and where the sense of community is weak, becomes minimally integrated and utilitarian (Lau, 1982). Again, a set of moral codes surrounds this field of interaction and the significance and value of friendship is heightened by ethical principles, again derived from Confucianism, which introduce severe sanctions of public odium for the breaching of bonds of personal trust. One's reputation for trustworthiness is important personal capital in the world of Chinese business and this serves to counteract the anarchic tendencies noted in other familistic societies which find coordination of economic exchange processes so difficult, for instance those of southern Italy (Putnam, 1993; Banfield, 1958) or South America (Harrison, 1985).

Insecurity is a natural outcome of totalitarianism especially for the businessman, because the accumulation of wealth makes business a target for unpredictable state interference. Officials have to be coopted in some way and such security may well be temporary when political succession is unpredictable. This can apply both at state and local levels, and thus on a large and small scale, and it has played a part in explaining the absence of large stable corporations free of government interference noted earlier. China's pre-modern condition tolerated rather than fostered small business and commerce, and fostered state business. But it also inhibited, until the Deng reforms of 1979, the rational pursuit of economic efficiency. In consequence, and especially during the nineteenth century when allied to conditions of overpopulation, political decadence and isolationism, the effects upon the population were severely negative and many sought to leave.

Many emigrants left to form the body of people known earlier as the Overseas Chinese but now more properly termed the ethnic Chinese of Pacific Asia. The reason for this retitling is that they are now in the main long-established citizens of Indonesia, Malaysia, Thailand, Philippines and so on, and their 'Chineseness' is a delicate and controversial question which deserves to be treated discreetly.

The Regional Impact of the Ethnic Chinese

The number of people of Chinese descent in Pacific Asia with a history of emigration from China in the past 200 years is approximately 40 million. That includes a large portion of the population of Taiwan, made up both of early immigrants across the straits from Fujian and of the nationalist waves of the late 1940s.

In Taiwan, Hong Kong and Singapore, the societies are overwhelmingly Chinese by population number. In Malaysia, the ethnic Chinese make up 37 per cent of the population. Elsewhere, their proportions are small: in Indonesia, 4 per cent, in Thailand 8 per cent and in the Philippines 1 per cent. Their economic significance, however, is great and out of all proportion to their population numbers, which pays great tribute to their business acumen.

Nine of the 10 largest business groups in Thailand are ethnically Chinese-owned (Mackie, 1992). In Indonesia, for the 300 largest corporations in the economy, ethnic Chinese control 80 per cent of assets. In the Philippines, ethnic Chinese control 68 per cent of the sales volume in commerce among the top 250 companies (Hicks and Redding, 1982). They are by far the largest investors in China and Vietnam and their accumulations of capital at the national level make the foreign reserves of Taiwan, Singapore and Hong Kong respectively the second, fifth and sixth largest in the world currently.

The Major Players and their Networks

There are several organizational forms which have emerged among the ethnic Chinese capitalists of Pacific Asia. The most common is the small or medium-sized family business. Another is the state-influenced or controlled business group, with examples clearly visible in Singapore, Taiwan and mainland China. A third is the emerging private sector in China and especially the town and village enterprise alliances between local officials and outside Chinese capitalists. Lastly, and of special concern in this chapter, are the large business groups still dominated by their owning families. These latter, although each has a main base in one country, are regional players. The principal ones and their network of alliances are illustrated in Figure 15.1.

To understand the pattern of alliances, it is necessary to take account of certain subethnic bases for trust which operate in the case of the ethnic Chinese who have family histories of migration to the region known as the Nanyang or the countries surrounding the South China Sea. A study of Singaporean Chinese family origins identified eight distinct subgroups along the coast of southern China from which most emigrants came. They have distinct language dialects, often mutually unintelligible, and retain a strong sense of loyalty to place-of-origin. The subgroups, running in a sequence from east to west along the southern coast, are Foochow, Hokchia, Henghua, Hokkien, Teochew, Hakka, Cantonese and Hainanese. In a society where trust is a limited but critical facilitator of business dealings, and an important means of reducing transaction costs, the availability of a social context in which another person's trustworthiness may be judged becomes important. Hence the tendency remains for business ties to reflect subethnic connections. This is not of course an absolute rule, but it is a significant tendency.

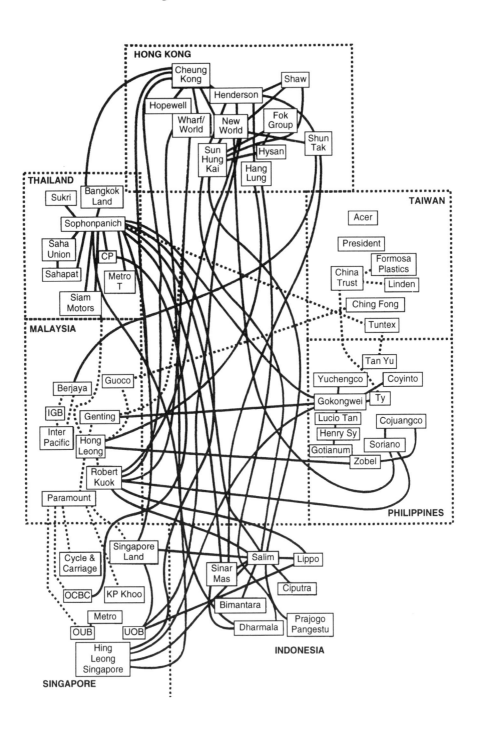

Figure 15.1   Overseas Chinese business webs

The business ties illustrated in Figure 15.1 are commonly a result of joint investments in projects. A typical pattern is for a large-scale entrepreneur in one locality to know of an opportunity for a viable investment. He will then invite a contribution to be made to the funding of a project by a friend in another locality, thus cutting him in on the deal and on the future benefits. This also hedges risk. In each case the investment may range from small, say 1 per cent to 5 per cent, to large – perhaps a third. What this then does is to open up the probability of the same happening in reverse. This is crucial because of one significant environmental characteristic. These environments are extremely difficult to read from the outside: they are both uncertain and volatile; information is rare and unreliable, and where it is reliable it is secret, and where it is secret it is a strategic possession of the firm and more specifically of the owner/entrepreneur. In this manner the opportunity spaces in very unlevel playing fields are sought and exploited by coalitions of entrepreneurs using trust bonds founded in ethnicity.

The lowering of transaction costs which occurs in this context is fostered by one distinct characteristic of this business system, namely the extreme concentration of decision-making power in the hands of the chief executives. This occurs because of an overriding concern with the retention of corporate control, even at the very large scale, through the careful structuring of firm ownership and governance. Thus deal makers act with full authority and require little in the way of permission seeking. It is also likely in this scenario that the information about opportunities, the fine judgement as to their viability, and the coopting of government permission where necessary to pursue the opportunity, are dependent on a single individual. The Achilles heel of these large corporations is that dependence, and it is clearly a source of long term instability for the firm.

Characteristics of the Large Business Groups of the Ethnic Chinese

The nature of the industries in which the large ethnic Chinese business groups operate varies geographically. In Hong Kong, there is an overwhelming tendency for the core business to be property, supplemented by diversification into service industries such as telecommunications, hotels and transport. In Thailand, the core businesses have tended to be banking, natural products processing and distribution, and property. So, too, in Malaysia and Singapore. In Indonesia, there is in addition a strong element of manufacturing or heavy industrial processing as, for example, with cement. In the Philippines, agribusiness, service industry and processing dominate. In Taiwan, there is a more even balance of manufacturing and service sector industry, such as insurance.

What is striking in this list is the relative insignificance of large-scale manufacturing industry (as opposed to natural products processing). Allied to that is the absence of globally recognized brand names. The solitary exceptions are *Acer* and *Tiger Balm*. There are three possible reasons for the tendency to avoid heavy manufacturing industry. First, as observed earlier, the political context in many states is uncertain and often potentially hostile. Even though coopting the support of the government regime is an important strategy for the firm in most countries in this region, this does not provide security against the behaviour of future regimes. Industrial investment is normally heavy and long-term and in risky environments will be avoided. The second feature is a corollary of this: government-supported firms may well be in place to handle crucial industries such as car manufacturing, if necessary with foreign technical inputs.

The third feature is connected with the structure and inner workings of the firms in this category. Here the overriding feature is tight central control of strategy and the retention in the centre of detailed control of operations. Adoption of these two principles is a source of efficiency under two conditions: firstly the divisions of the firm can operate largely as machine bureaucracies with standardized repetitive operations, as in property management, shipping, hotels, insurance and retail banking. These may then be safely left in the hands of professional managers responsible for daily operations but under strict conditions of central reporting. The firm can then divide into operating units. But the overall effectiveness of the firm is dependent on the second condition, which is that the chief executive/owner makes the correct strategic decisions applying to each specialist field. This requires the CEO either to share strategy making or to fully comprehend several industries. It is these latter requirements that are the most testing for such organizations and which arguably underlie most of the strategic failures.

As an illustration of the type of organization under consideration here, Table 15.1 presents data about the CP (Charoen Pokphand) Group of Thailand. This company, arguably one of the most successful in the category, has grown from 15 000 employees in 1979 to 70 000 in 1994, and over the same period from a network of 80 to 200 affiliated companies, with revenues in 1993 of over US$ 5 billion (*The Economist*, 1994). The corporate structure of the group is extremely complex, including 185 privately held companies plus others listed on stock exchanges in Bangkok, New York, London, Hong Kong, Jakarta, Taipei and Shanghai.

Having originated with the emigration of two brothers from southern China in 1917, and having specialized for decades in agribusiness,

Table 15.1   CP's listed companies, 1994

CP's listed companies	Main operations	Stock exchange	Market capitalization Nov. '94 ($USmn)	Ownership share of CP (%)
Telecom Asia	telecommunications	Bangkok	9 030	29
Orient Telecom and Technology Holdings	China property; telecoms in Thailand	Hong Kong	896	51
Siam Makro	warehouse distribution	Bangkok	875	15
CP Feedmill	agri-industrial	Bangkok	839	39
C.P. Phokphand	agri-industrial, motorcycle/car manufacturing	HK, London	622	56
Ek Chor China Motorcycle	motorcycle manufacturing	New York	360	72
CP Indonesia	animal feed, poultry operations	Jakarta	234	71
CP Prima	prawns, animal feed, poultry breeding	Jakarta	198	92
Shanghai Dajing	—	Shanghai	141	44
CP Enterprise, Taiwan	animal feed, poultry breeding	Taipei	132	30
Bangkok Agro-Industrial Products	agri-industrial	Bangkok	118	73
Hong Kong Fortune	China property	Hong Kong	107	64
CP Northeastern	agri-industrial	Bangkok	60	59
Bangkok Produce Merchandising	import and exports of animal feed inputs	Bangkok	49	37

Source: © *The Economist*, London (November, 1994).

especially feedstock and then chicken farming, the group has now returned to China with a wide range of investments. These now include agribusiness, beer, property, retailing, telecommunications and motorcycles, in this latter case holding 15 per cent of the China market (Semkow, 1995). Much of its success in China has been built on political cooptation at the local and regional government levels via joint ventures. In the CP Group there is extensive use of managerial professionalism and formal structure, so that many operations compare organizationally with equivalents in Western firms. At the same time, however, family control at the centre remains strong. The influence on strategy of the family head, Dhanin Chearavanont, is undeniable, and so too is the presence of family members in the boardroom.

Another example is the Cheung Kong group, of Hong Kong, headed by Li Ka Shing, and illustrated in Figure 15.2. Again, this group has grown explosively over three decades from the most modest of beginnings in plastic flower making. Its concentrations are in property, the obvious cornerstone in rentier capitalism, and in retailing, power generation and fuel, container handling, telecommunications and, more recently, hotels. Plans are in hand for expansion into insurance.

The non-property components of the group, originally a Western-led group, gathered under the corporate umbrella of Hutchison Whampoa Ltd, were rescued from bankruptcy in 1976 and grew under a regime of intense rationalization prior to takeover by Li in the early 1980s. In consequence, their systems of management remain reflective of a standard Western divisionalized multinational run by professionals. Since the takeover, however, there has been a recentralization of strategy making into a dominant coalition, the key power holders in which are family members. This logically reflects the weight of equity in family control. It was accompanied by a reduction in formalization as the previously elaborate system which diffused strategy making was dismantled. Whereas the strategic acumen of K.S. Li is a byword in Asia, and the source of much loyalty by the shareholding public, the apprenticeship via a succession of larger and larger deal making by his two sons and likely successors continues. This form of grooming (Redding, 1986) is undeniably both testing and revealing and it may well yield two new business empires in the longer term, as the group subdivides. This does not, however, alleviate the very high dependence of the structure on the family itself, and the risks that entails.

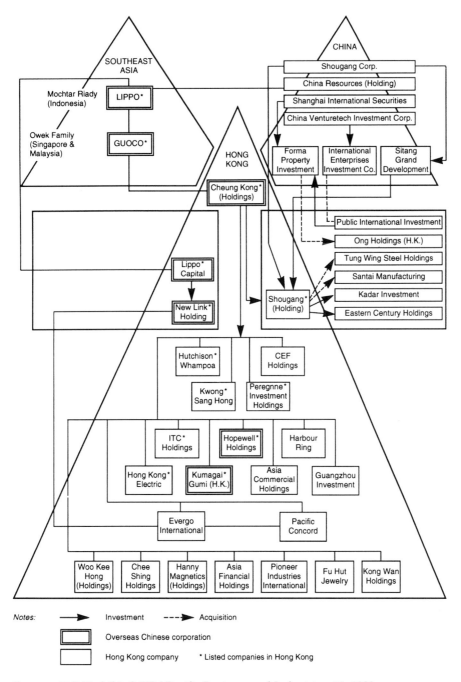

Notes:

→ Investment   ---→ Acquisition

Overseas Chinese corporation

Hong Kong company   * Listed companies in Hong Kong

Source: D.S. Tachiki, © RIM Pacific Business and Industries, **21**, 1993.

Figure 15.2   Investment alliance networks among NIEs and ASEAN transnational corporations

Investment Alliance Networks Among Newly Industrializing Economies (NIEs) and ASEAN Transnational Corporations

The evident success of such new large Chinese family groups in Pacific Asia rests upon three features. First, they are adept at coopting the political support needed in environments where government intervenes extensively in the economy. This is the case in Taiwan, Indonesia, Thailand, Malaysia, China and the Philippines, and is true also in Hong Kong in property, telecommunications and energy. Such cooptation is based on long-term courtship of sound relationships with a wide variety of people in the administration. This may be boosted by a series of gestures of good citizenship. In some countries it may involve the exchange of favours.

The second feature is that such firms are designed for opportunity seeking and taking. This arises because of the extreme concentration of decision-making power in the hands of single individuals, often dealing in alliance with other equally powerful individuals. Hence response rates are very fast. This is reinforced by access to large volumes of capital if a pattern of successful deals can strengthen a reputation for reliability.

The third feature is the network of collaborators, co-investors and providers of information and judgement about opportunities. This allows for the spreading of risk, but in particular the spotting of opportunity. It is especially potent in conditions of uncertainty such as those of the region. Here information is scarce and unreliable, business environments are complex and volatile, and potential inter-ference is endemic and unpredictable. Having emerged with such conditions as normal, the Chinese family business group is well adapted to cope and thrive. Western multinationals find such environments particularly challenging and they commonly seek local alliances with the ethnic Chinese companies as means of entry (Redding, 1995).

Implications for China

The economy of China is changing rapidly and radically as external standards of efficiency drive their way in. In 1980, the state-owned enterprise sector accounted for 75 per cent of the national product and the collective sector the rest. By 2000, it is likely that the state-owned sector will have declined to 25 per cent. Of the remainder, 25 per cent will be private and 50 per cent will be 'town and village enterprise'. The significance of this latter category in the context of this chapter is that it is increasingly taking on the characteristics of the private sector. Its behaviour is increasingly capitalist (Shaw and

Woetzel, 1992). This means that, at the turn of the millennium, China will, on present trends, be largely capitalistic in its economic instruments. Deng Xiao Ping, the 'capitalist roader' with his revolution of 1979, may have achieved more than he intended.

Although such an account does little justice to the complexities of the Chinese political economy, and although centralizing tendencies will be a very long time changing, the direction of movement is clear and so too are the implications for organization. One strong guarantor of that momentum is the national fear of unemployment on an unimaginable scale if the economic progress is reversed or even halted.

The ethnic Chinese of the region outside are the heaviest investors in China by a long margin (Crédit Lyonnais, 1994; East Asia Analytical Unit, 1995), with heavy concentrations of new business in Fujian from Taiwan, in Guangdong from Hong Kong, and in Shanghai. Movement into the interior is now proceeding from these coastal areas. The major investment fields by dollar volume have been property and infrastructure, but industrial investment is now following as the experience gained in small-scale operations provides more incentive to increase commitment.

In many ways, an older pattern is re-establishing itself, of a kind in which enterprises polarize into two types. At one end of the spectrum are small and medium enterprises, run paternally and with relatively low levels of structure. At the other end, large organizations exist at the behest, with the permission, or with the active involvement, of government, the role of the latter being to reduce risk. An argument explaining this polarization has been proposed by Fukuyama (1995), who predicts that, in societies where mistrust is endemic between strangers, and where in consequence the institutional fabric of society is weak, it will be difficult to achieve the stable coordination of economic action on a large scale in a voluntary, free-market mode. This arises, in his argument, because of a shortage of 'social capital', one of the key elements of which is a willingness by the individual to engage in collective purposes such as business enterprise, in ways other than the purely utilitarian. This prevents the managers of large organizations from tapping sources of creativity, talent and commitment to act on behalf of the company, and so limits the competitive efficiency of larger firms.

Mistrust and insecurity in China remain problems and are a legacy of a totalitarian structure using fear to preserve order, combined with a social philosophy based on familism. Change in this dimension is likely to be slow as it rests on the possibility that civil society might constitute itself from the base and create new institutional fabric to support trust. In the meantime, trustworthiness remains a powerful ethical principle, but paradoxically so because of the general inability to take it for granted. It is the glue which holds the functioning of

Chinese society together, known as *guanxi* (connections), but its structure is essentially interpersonal. It cannot be used to integrate complex action at the social or organizational level.

Implications for Organization Theory

It was argued some time ago (Lammers and Hickson, 1979) that the comparative study of organizations would benefit from the regular iteration between idiographic and nomothetic enquiry. In this way the progress of detailed description would be enhanced by better theories of determinacy and those theories would be strengthened by being better grounded. An example of this progression is visible in the use of the Aston data to fix more clearly, in comparative terms, an understanding of the Chinese family business (Pugh and Redding, 1986; Redding, 1990), followed by its incorporation into the development of a more general theory of the sociology of organizations by Whitley (1990, 1992).

In this larger theory, an argument is made that business systems, or in other words viable alternative systems of capitalism, are definable in terms of three components: the size and growth pattern of the kinds of firms which most typify the system; the nature of the bonding between the firms, if any; and the nature of the social glue which typically holds together the cooperative fabric of the firm itself. These features are themselves strongly influenced by the surrounding institutional fabric of society, and especially the structures it designs to handle the disposition within it of access to capital and to skills. These institutions are creatures of a society's particular experience of modernization, its distinct political economy and its governmental traditions. Important here also are the social inventions occurring during development, such as the joint stock company, systems of banking, trades unions and educational responses to needs in the economy. In turn, these institutional features of development are embedded in older traditions and societal norms, governing three influences especially: trust, identity, such as individualism or collectivism, and the ethical bases for legitimate authority.

This complex set of determinants and reciprocal connections constitutes a large single unit of analysis containing and explaining the firm, its structure and behaviour. It is the comparison of such large units, together with progress towards the understanding of their internal dynamics, which now constitutes the most fruitful mode of enquiry into the nature of organizations in the economic world of free market capitalism.

References

Banfield, E.C. (1958), *The Moral Basis of a Backward Society*, Chicago: The Free Press.

Crédit Lyonnais (1994), *Capital to China*, Research Report, Hong Kong.

Economist, The (1994), 'Emerging multinationals: A bruiser from Bankok', *The Economist*, 26 November, 79.

East Asia Analytical Unit (1995), *Overseas Chinese Business Networks in Asia*, Canberra, Dept. of Foreign Affairs and Trade.

Fukuyama, F. (1995), *Trust: The Social Virtues and the Creation of Prosperity*, New York: The Free Press.

Harrison, L.E. (1985), *Underdevelopment is a State of Mind*, Cambridge, Mass.: Harvard University, Center for International Affairs.

Hicks, G.L. and Redding, S.G. (1982), 'Culture and corporate performance in the Philippines: the Chinese puzzle', in R.M. Bantista and E.M. Pernia (eds), *Essays in Development Economics in Honor of Harry T. Oshima*, Manila: Philippine Institute for Development Studies.

Lammers, C.J. and Hickson D.J. (1979), 'Towards a comparative sociology of organizations', in C.J. Lammers and D.J. Hickson (eds), *Organizations Alike and Unlike*, London, Routledge & Kegan Paul.

Lau, S.K. (1982), *Society and Politics in Hong Kong*, Hong Kong: Chinese University Press.

Mackie, J. (1992), 'Changing patterns of Chinese big business in Southeast Asia', in R. McVey (ed.), *Southeast Asian Capitalists*, Ithaca, NY: Cornell University Southeast Asia Program.

North, D.C. (1994), 'The evolution of efficient markets in history', in J.A. James and M. Thomas (eds), *Capitalism in Context*, Chicago: University of Chicago Press.

Pugh, D.S. and Redding, S.G. (1986), 'The formal and the informal: Japanese and Chinese organization structures', in S.R. Clegg, D. Dunphy and S.G. Redding (eds), *The Enterprise and Management in East Asia*, Hong Kong: University of Hong Kong, Centre of Asian Studies.

Putnam, R.D. (1993), *Making Democracy Work: Civic Traditions in Modern Italy*, Princeton, NJ: Princeton University Press.

Redding, S.G. (1986), 'Developing managers without management development: the overseas Chinese solution', *Management Education and Development*, **17**, 271–81.

Redding, S.G. (1990), *The Spirit of Chinese Capitalism*, New York: De Gruyter.

Redding, S.G. (1995), 'Overseas Chinese networks: understanding the enigma', *Long Range Planning*, **28**, 61–9.

Semkow, B.W. (1995), 'Chinese corporate governance and finance in the ASEAN countries: some implications for Europe and European firms', working paper, Euro Asian Centre, Insead.

Shaw, S.M. and Woetzel, J.R. (1992), 'A fresh look at China', *McKinsey Quarterly*, **3**.

Silin, R.H. (1976), *Leadership and Values*, Cambridge, Mass.: Harvard University Press.

Tachiki, D.S. (1993), 'Striking up strategic alliances: the foreign direct investments of the NIE's and ASEAN transnational corporations', *RIM Pacific Business and Industries*, **21**, 22–36.

Whitley, R.D. (1990), 'Eastern Asian enterprise structures and the comparative analysis of forms of business organization', *Organization Studies*, **11**, 47–54.

Whitley, R.D. (1992), *Business Systems in East Asia*, London: Sage.

PART IV
THE FUTURE OF
MANAGEMENT RESEARCH

16 The Double Hurdles for Management Research[1]

ANDREW M. PETTIGREW, *Warwick Business School, University of Warwick*

The theme of this chapter is the social production of knowledge. It is fitting that this essay on knowledge production should be published in a book celebrating the career of a distinguished scholar. In a recent autobiographical account of his career, Derek Pugh outlines some of the cornerstones of his practice (Pugh, 1996). Central to his self-concept as a scholar is his identity as an 'unreconstructed positivist'. Derek has held to this 'realist, determinist approach to analysis' in a world where notions of objective truth have increasingly faced the combined assault of relativists, constructivists, postmodernists and mediativists. A further consistency in Derek's intellectual life has been his 'great scepticism about academic disciplines: in particular about the arbitrariness of their boundaries' Pugh (1996). This has led him to a career of open association with many disciplines, to team-based research on problems not containable within the myopia of any single discipline and to a sustained belief in the potential of an interdisciplinary approach to the behavioural aspects of management.

Recent writing on the natural sciences by Webster (1994) and Ziman (1994) and on the natural and social sciences by Gibbons *et al.* (1994) indicate some fundamental changes in the way knowledge is produced. The changes include who is involved in the production of knowledge, the process of knowledge production and types of available knowledge, and new settings and opportunities for knowledge production, dissemination and use.

The title of Ziman's book, *Prometheus Bound: Science in a Dynamic Steady State* (1994), indicates his scepticism about the trends he so sharply describes. He comments in the preface to his book that many scientists and scholars look back with nostalgia to a more relaxed and spacious environment for academic research. In this bygone era, scientists had social space for initiative and creativity, and time for ideas to grow and mature. There was an atmosphere receptive to debate, criticism and innovation, and respect for specialized expertise. However, Ziman's pragmatism outweighs the 'fruitless sentiment' of nostalgia: 'The real question is not whether the structural transition [in knowledge production] is desirable or could have been avoided: it is how to reshape the research system to fit a new environment without losing the features that have made it so productive in the past' (Ziman, 1994, pp. vii–viii).

But what are the broad elements of this structural transition in science? For Gibbons and his colleagues (1994) the move is from a Mode 1 to a Mode 2 form of knowledge production, with the Mode 2 still emerging alongside Mode 1 and supplementing rather than supplanting it. Gibbons *et al.* characterize Mode 1 as discipline driven. Here the research problems are framed and solved within a disciplinary context, are set within a linear process of discovery and dissemination, involve teams homogeneous in terms of skills and experience and feature discipline-directed quality control. In Mode 2, the research problem is framed in the context of application. Here research is transdiscipline-driven, allows a process of diffusion to occur during knowledge production, is heterogeneous in terms of skills and experience and is more socially and politically accountable than the discipline-driven control process of Mode 1.

Eschewing an ideal type of analysis, Ziman observes similar trends to Gibbons *et al.* Thus Ziman's picture of modern science is a tapestry of more management, more evaluation, greater interdisciplinarity, more emphasis on application, more networking and collaboration, more internationalism and more specialization and concentration of resources. Although neither Ziman nor Gibbons *et al.* refer directly to the field of management research, it is clear that the trends they refer to bear on the conduct of research in management in the mid and late 1990s. As knowledge producers, we need to consider how we are to engage with the new production of knowledge, critically examine our practice of knowledge production and take advantage of all the new opportunities which this changing intellectual, social and political context is presenting to us.

This chapter has four sections. The first engages critically with the Pfeffer and Van Maanen debate about paradigm development in organization theory, and concludes that, in the face of major contextual changes in knowledge production, this interesting argument represents a side-show, a debate in a social echo chamber. The second section outlines elements of the changing context of knowledge production and puts forward the thesis that a new social production of knowledge is emerging in the natural and social sciences. The third section switches the argument back to the particular field of management and uses two research projects, one initiated in 1985 and the other ten years later, to indicate some of the directions of change in the conduct of management research. The final section draws together the challenges to our practice embedded in the double hurdles for management research, the simplest statement of which is, of course, the simultaneous concern for scholarly quality and relevance. However, we shall see that the new social production of knowledge in management is not just a double hurdle but a whole series of linked, simultaneous and sometimes contradictory challenges, which may require for some of us the breaking of significant scholarly routines.

Paradigm Unity and the Field of Management and Organization Research

Management research as a field of intellectual inquiry has a number of descriptive characteristics. It is relatively new as a social science field, its origins and development in UK higher education dating from the early 1960s. The field is certainly multidisciplinary, with many of its early practitioners receiving their training in anthropology, economics, mathematics, psychology and sociology. This early disciplinary diversity has ensured that, from the outset, the field of management has been paradigmatically and methodologically diverse (Whitley, 1984a; Tsoukas, 1994). The ontological, epistemological and methodological disputes within the management research community, and between management scholars and other social scientists, have not been helped by the failure of management scholars to develop a literature on the meaning and significance of their scholarly endeavours. There may be elements of a literature on the methodologies of management research, but there is hardly any literature on the ontology and epistemology of management research.

The field of management is also organized in a fragmented and diffused fashion. The early disciplinary scholars assumed other titles and intellectual identities as interdisciplinary teaching and research themes (for example, organizational behaviour and corporate strategy) and functional themes (such as finance and marketing), gained prominence. The institutionalization of these new subfields was assisted by the development of doctoral programmes in management. Further fragmentation has occurred as subfields such as international business, operations management and public sector management have appeared as mobilizing research and teaching themes.

Within the field of management research there is also evidence of interdisciplinary theorizing, often guided by empirical research exploring broad themes such as the management of change, the internationalizing firm and the management of technologies. Management research can be a distinctively interdisciplinary activity, driven by themes which are appropriately studied from the analytical synthesis emerging from and resulting in interdisciplinary theorizing and empirical inquiry. This process of knowledge development occurs in a dynamic and reciprocal way with the evolution of related disciplines such as economics and sociology, and with the emergence and decay of new research themes. Thus management research is embedded within the assumptions, ideas and methods of the social science community and yet the framing of its research agenda, interdisciplinarity and thematic character give it a distinctive place within that community.

Management is also a relatively open research field. Its openness is reflected in the variety of contributors, the diversity of interest in the outputs of the research, and the influence of managers and policy makers upon standards, research questions and assessments of value. Without doubt, the ambiguous and conflicting views about standards in the field are exacerbated by the demands made that management should be a practically oriented social science (Whitley, 1984b). An already fragmented field is asked to meet the dual demands of theory and practice; knowledge should be developed in the image of science, while also contributing to practice and policy making.

Not all management and organization theorists would, of course, agree with the above characterization. Indeed, over the last few years a provocative essay by Pfeffer (1993) and responses by Van Maanen (1995) and Cannella and Paetzold (1994) have focused the knowledge production issue in organization studies on the narrow area of paradigmatic unity. Pfeffer's (1993) article was indeed a plea for paradigmatic unity. He argued that a combination of the nature of the subject of study in organizations and values in the field which welcomed theoretical and methodological diversity had led to excessive fragmentation and a danger that organization studies would be ripe for a hostile takeover by better organized and more paradigmatically unified fields such as economics. Van Maanen (1995) in a fluent and robust reply asked us to beware of a Stalinist purge of our low consensus field by well-published elites within our ranks. He further asserted that Pfeffer's position was sour, pious, philosophically indefensible, naive as to how science actually works and autocratic. For Van Maanen, diversity was inevitable in our field and a prime source of creativity. He further contended that language was a critical factor in representing the world we seek to understand and that a prime source of our influence lay in our capabilities as expressive and clever stylistic writers. Karl Weick was cited as the current exemplar of persuasive theorizing through style.

The Pfeffer and Van Maanen debate rumbles on and has its European equivalent, which draws on different sources and appeals to additional tribal groupings (Jackson and Carter, 1991; Hassard, 1993; Willmott, 1993). Such debates are, of course, important especially within a field such as management which lacks a strong reflective and critical tradition. But important as these debates are, they may, in a changing external context, represent at best intelligent mumblings in a social echo chamber and at worst territorial infighting by transient and endangered academic tribal groups.

The most striking feature of the original Pfeffer provocation, and at this time all subsequent responses, has been their essentially inner-directed character. The only external points of reference in Pfeffer's argument were the economists and political scientists who presumably were the hungry predators awaiting the hostile takeover. But what of the wider set of stakeholders for management research who may yet be crucial as fundors, co-producers and users of organization and management knowledge? Given existing trends in the new social production of knowledge, such stakeholders are likely to play an increasingly important part in our working environment. Not to learn how to live with these fellow knowledge producers and users will indeed condemn us to increasingly isolated debates in the social echo chamber of our own voices.

The New Social Production of Knowledge

What are the central tendencies and trends in modern science? What is the evidence for a new social production of knowledge in the natural and social sciences? If there is evidence of change, what are the contextual forces driving such changes and what are some of the choices being made by scholars by way of response?

There is a difficulty in answering such broad questions. Even the advocates of a change thesis, such as Gibbons *et al.* (1994) and Ziman (1994), recognize that the process is still emergent, that the rate of change varies in different national and disciplinary communities and that responses are predictably customized to local institution, profession and resource conditions. A further problem is that most of the knowledge we have about trends in knowledge production is focused on the natural sciences, where there is a strong tradition of science policy studies. There is little empirical work on science policy or the sociology of science which focuses on social scientists and even less to report on trends in the field of management research.

This section of the chapter thus draws heavily on empirical evidence of the new social production of knowledge in the natural sciences.

It is always tricky looking at others and ourselves through the partisan fog of the present. Obtaining perspective on an issue invariably therefore means calling on the services of history. Recently Gibbons *et al.* (1994) have argued for three phases of science and technology policy since the Second World War. In the first phase, 'Policy for Science', the emphasis was on the growth of science itself and particularly the development of the major scientific disciplines. The second phase, 'Science in Policy', shifted the emphasis to the role of science in the diverse policy objectives of the state. In both of these first two phases, there was an assumption that science would provide potential benefits but it was not necessarily the job of science to contribute to national well-being. All this was to change sharply in the 1980s, with the arrival of phase three and with it a new concern for 'Policy for Technological Innovation'. Declining economic performances and increasing worldwide competition were now forcing policy makers to narrow their perspective and to hitch the scientific enterprise to the single goal of industrial innovation and competitiveness.

Woolgar (1994), Webster (1994) and Faulkner and Senker (1995) have all described the increasing application of free market principles to research and knowledge production. With the increasing commercialization of modern science has come a decline in the relative autonomy of traditional knowledge-producing institutions, a variety of pressures to link more effectively the producers of knowledge with exploiters of knowledge and a new rhetoric of science which freely trumpets the virtues of wealth creation, social welfare, impact, application, outreach, transfer and dissemination.

It is early days to identify the intended and unintended consequences of such changes. Faulkner and Senker (1995) are concerned that the new emphasis on relevance and near-market research will sacrifice industry's traditional aspiration for academia for new knowledge, ideas and instrumentalities. However, Webster (1994) argues that it is naive to see the unilateral imposition of relevance on hapless academics as an entirely new phenomenon. Were academic science to be freed from commercialism, it would hardly be conducted in a purely disinterested, curiosity-driven manner. Science has never been just a cognitive endeavour. It has always been shaped by the combined effects of macro social, political and economic forces and the micro politics of disciplinary communities. Academics are scientists and citizens. They are calculative agents involved in a multi-actor negotiation process in which research agendas have always been negotiated and contested rather than set unilaterally by professionals operating unidimensionally in cognitive processes.

As Gibbons *et al.* (1994) argue, it is misplaced to see the drive for a new, more socially produced, knowledge just as demand-led. Certainly, there are demand-side factors emanating from economic, competitive and funding pressures, but there are also important long-term supply-side considerations enabling the move to more socially distributed knowledge. The massive post-war growth of education has created successive generations of knowledge producers who cannot be contained within either traditional disciplinary boundaries or the universities where in the past it has been assumed the majority of knowledge producers would carry out their practice. The new rhetoric of science with its dispersion of knowledge producers, national and international networks of providers, and concern for interdisciplinary problem solving and impact is not just rhetoric. The following evidence of increasing business enterprise finance in the public sector research system in the 1980s, on the growth in the USA of university-industry research centres over the same period, and recent trends in UK scientific publication, all point to substantial change in the funding, production and outputs of scientific inquiry.

Table 16.1 shows the increase of business enterprise finance in the public sector research system (universities and government laboratories) in seven major economies over the period 1980–88. Webster and Etzkowitz (1991) are careful to acknowledge that these aggregate figures conceal the fact that elite universities are overrepresented as early beneficiaries of such funding. It is also the case that certain sectors, notably information technology, biotechnology and pharmaceuticals, are also overrepresented in funding public sector research.

Figure 16.1 shows very clearly the tremendous growth of university–industry research centres in the United States in the period 1980–89. The pie diagram in Figure 16.1 shows that, by 1990, 31 per

Table 16.1   **Business enterprise finance in the public sector research system (1985 Prices, $mn)**

	1980	1981	1982	1983	1984	1985	1986	1987	1988
Australia		7			9		14		
France		26	27	27	33	42	45	82	
Germany		52		147		159	176	201	170
Italy	9	25	23	5	8	20	16	16	26
Japan	64	67	78	88	117	125	137	158	
UK		51		57		77	126	119	
USA	305	344	372	413	486	561	698	763	816

Source: Webster and Etzkowitz (1991).

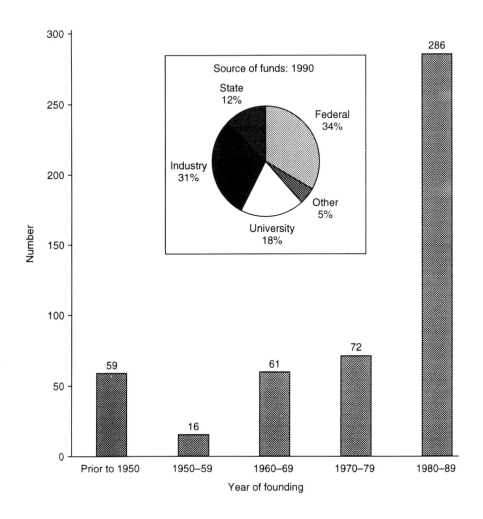

Notes: Data are for centres existing in 1990. Of an estimated 1058 centres, 458 provided funding data and 494 provided founding data.

Source: W. Cohen *et al.* (1993).

Figure 16.1   Growth in US university–industry research centres and sources of funds

cent of the funds for such university–industry research centres were coming from industry, while federal and state resources amounted to 34 per cent and 12 per cent, respectively.

The final data are drawn from a recent Science Policy Research Unit (SPRU) publication, *The Changing Shape of British Science* (1995). The SPRU report notes very interesting trends in UK scientific publication. The report's statistics confirm the now well recognized fact that university-based scientists have long since lost their monopoly supplier position as knowledge workers. The statistics also reveal the tremendous increase in national and international scientific collaboration during the 1980s. Findings in the SPRU report include the following:

- As many as 5000 institutions are now contributing to the scientific literature in the UK.
- Some 60 per cent of scientific papers published in the UK now have non-academic addresses.
- In 1991, 40 per cent of published papers involved collaboration between researchers in different institutions, compared with 28 per cent in 1981.
- International scientific partnerships involving UK researchers increased by 75 per cent in the 1980s.
- The authors predict that, by the year 2000, more than 50 per cent of the UK's scientific papers will each be produced by three or more researchers working in more than two institutions.

These data point to, amongst other things, the crucial role of networking in the new social production of knowledge. As Gambardella (1992), writing of the pharmaceutical industry, has so aptly put it, 'to be part of a network, and to be able to effectively exploit the information that circulates in the network, has become even more valuable than being able to generate new knowledge autonomously' (p. 404).

Normal science is also faced with the challenges from the sociologists of science who have studied the micro processes of scientific conduct (Latour and Woolgar, 1979; Latour, 1987). Woolgar (1994) has convincingly argued that, as the above trends have been emerging and as his own and others' studies of scientific practice have been published, so a more realistic view of the knowledge development process has evolved. With the breakdown of the linear process of science and innovation, which assumed a three-stage process (discover new ideas, transfer ideas, exploit new ideas in new products), so some of the equally simple vocabulary of science, such as the terms 'pure', 'applied', 'strategic' and 'development', are being found wanting. More realist views of scientific development do not assume the complete separation of the producers and consumers of knowledge, do not assume a unidirectional flow of ideas from producers to consumers and are less likely to assume the unchanging character of knowledge during the transfer process.

Although we do not have the empirical data of trends in knowledge production in the social sciences which are available for the natural sciences, we can see a similar questioning process going on in the conduct of social science research. Table 16.2 captures aspects of the debates about the character of knowledge and what it is to know, currently in full sway in the social sciences. Such debates are, of course, highly relevant to the practice of management research. The realist or naturalist view of knowing is increasingly under as much attack as linear views of science and innovation, and yet the realist view remains as deep in the psyche as it is questioned in the brain. But the bastion of scientific knowledge as objective truth continues to be under pressure from the combined assaults of the postmodernists, relativists, contructivists and mediativists.

Table 16.2   Alternative views of knowing

REALIST	Reality is independent of our conceptions of it
PRAGMATIST	Science works; no further justification is required
POSTMODERNIST	There can be no overarching reasons, no one best way of looking at things; truth is undecidable and unobtainable
RELATIVIST	Reality is merely a posit of particular conceptual schemes
CONSTRUCTIVIST	There is no reality beyond the constructs we imply when we talk of reality
MEDIATIVIST	Social circumstances intervene by mediating between nature and accounts of nature, but do not eliminate the effect of nature

Contemporary analysts of social science knowledge tend to emphasize its tentative, partial, theoretical, linguistic and constructed nature (Astley, 1985; Blackler *et al.*, 1993a). There is also a clearer recognition in the natural and social sciences that knowledge derives not just from individual thought but from collective processes of networking, negotiation, interpersonal communication and influence (Dodgson, 1993; Faulkner and Senker, 1995). What we have all treated for years as implicitly given, that informal flows of information are essential to underpin expert practice, is now being explicitly researched and acknowledged. More contentiously, there is also the view that knowledge workers are rarely just in the business of communicating evidence, facts, empirical generalizations or even theories. More often than not, they may also be observed to be communicating inferences from bodies of evidence rather than the evidence itself (Blackler *et al.*, 1993b).

This middle part of the chapter has covered a broad canvas. Drawing on the science policy and sociology of science literatures, an argument has been constructed (and some evidence displayed) to support the Ziman (1994) and Gibbons *et al.* (1994) thesis of major transformation in the social production of knowledge. But what of our own field of inquiry – the study of organizations and management? Is our practice to be challenged by the same environmental pressures, and is our concept of what knowledge is, and what it is to know, likely to be under similar pressure for change?

Research Through Partnership in Management Research: 1985 and 1995

There is no tradition of systematic empirical research on the conduct of management research in the UK or elsewhere. Whitley's papers (1984a, 1984b, 1988) usefully focused our attention on the character and limitations of management research, but they did not stimulate a host of projects researching the researchers. The recent Economic and Social Research Council (ESRC) Commission on Management Research through its consultation process, own debates and published report (ESRC, 1994) managed to reveal many of the contextual pressures on management scholars in the UK and also the perceived value and quality of some management research. A key theme of the 1994 ESRC report was the need for management researchers to build partnerships between themselves and user communities as a stepping stone to meeting the double challenge of scholarly quality and relevance.

Partnerships may, of course, be difficult to form and even more complex to sustain and make work. And as Wensley (1995) has recently reminded us, relevance is itself a complex notion that implies a network and structure of individuals and organizations to make judgements. The practical expression of relevance in the conduct of management research is therefore likely to be highly problematic.

In the absence of any broadly based empirical research on trends in the practice of management research, this chapter will draw on two case studies from the author's research experience. These case studies are separated by a time gap of 10 years, 1985 to 1995. The cases are not presented here as representational or typical of management research in the UK in the mid-1980s and mid-1990s. However, they each represent dimensions of change in management research and thus may well be indicative of trends which are taking shape across the management research community.

The cases have four common features: they have as their major fundor the ESRC; they have the same principal investigator; they are team-based empirical projects and both projects were strongly thematically driven. The big theme in the 1985 project was the link between the capacities of firms to manage change and their long-term performance. The 1995 project has as its general theme innovations in management. The particular focus of study is the diffusion of the Network form of organization and the performance consequences of adopting the N-Form (Pettigrew *et al.*, 1995).[2]

The key research questions in the 1985 project were (1) why do firms operating in broadly similar industry, country and product markets record different performances and (2) what has been the contribution of the way they manage strategic change to their performance? Figure 16.2 captures the key actors involved in this 1985 project. Unusual for its time, the focal research team involved a group of researchers at Warwick Business School's Centre for Corporate Strategy and Change (all with organization behaviour backgrounds) and a team of consultants from Coopers & Lybrand. The methodology used was the comparative longitudinal case method (Pettigrew, 1990), with the comparisons confined to eight UK case organizations. The major results of the research were published in Pettigrew and Whipp (1991).

The key research questions in the 1995 project are:

1   What are the key features of the N-Form that distinguish it from other organizational forms?
2   How far has the N-Form diffused in the wider population of firms, and to what extent is it associated with certain strategies, sectors, size ranges and regions?
3   What are the performance consequences of adopting the N-Form and how sustained are these over time?
4   How is the transition from traditional forms to the N-Form best managed, and what problems should managers anticipate in managing the processes of change?

Figure 16.3 outlines the much more complex character of the 1995 mode of partnership research. A key feature of the 1995 study is that

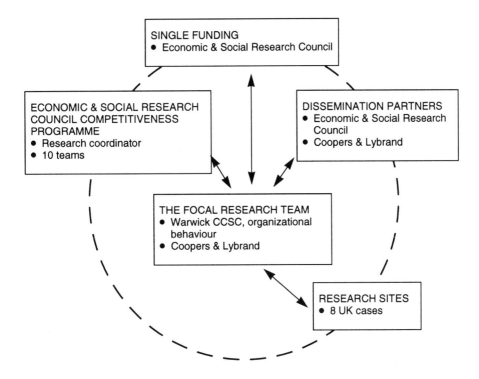

Figure 16.2 Competitiveness and change (research through partnership in 1985)

it involves an international network studying an international network. The focal research team now includes a more interdisciplinary group of Warwick-based scholars aided by a Europe-based rather than a UK-based Coopers & Lybrand team. The methodology involves three large surveys, one each in the UK, Continental Western Europe and Japan, and comparative case studies from the same three geographical locations. The Japanese survey and case studies will be carried out by research partners at Hitotsubashi University and the Continental Western European case studies will be completed by partners at various European universities. Finally, the 1995 project involves co-funding between the ESRC, Coopers & Lybrand and the Centre for Corporate Strategy and Change's consortium of sponsors.

Thus the major changes from the 1985 to the 1995 partnership mode of research are:

- from a unidisciplinary to an interdisciplinary team,
- from single to joint research funding,
- from UK comparisons to UK–international comparisons,
- from a single method to a multi-method research strategy,

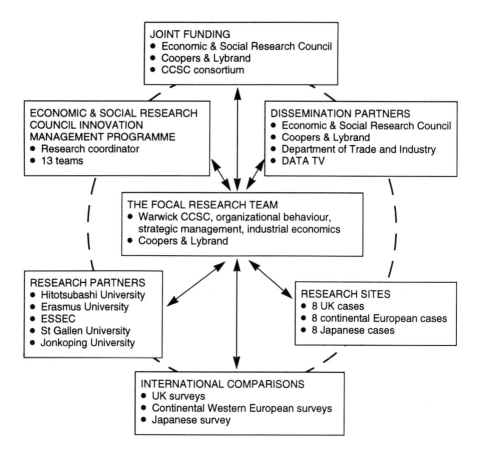

**Figure 16.3   The new internal network organization: process and
performance (research through partnership in 1995)**

- from a unidimensional to a multidimensional dissemination
  strategy, and
- from a limited to an extensive research partnership set.

As we all appreciate, it is not possible to extrapolate an empirical
trend from a single comparative longitudinal case. The 1995 project
is probably not representative of UK management research in the
late 1990s, but it may yet be indicative of a style of research which
will be more commonplace in the early part of the twenty-first century. What is clear from the 1985 to 1995 comparison is that the
direction of change mirrors very closely the Ziman (1994) and Gibbons *et al.* (1994) thesis about the changing character of knowledge
production. In the final part of this chapter, we move on to consider
some of the challenges for management research if, indeed, we are to

move in the direction of greater theme-driven research, with more interdisciplinary involvement, more co-partnerships, more international comparisons and more openness to the double hurdle of scholarly quality and relevance.

The Double Hurdles for Management Research

The Gibbons *et al.* (1994) thesis of a developing Mode 2 knowledge production process alongside the more traditional discipline-driven Mode 1 features a cluster of attributes variously recognizable in different areas of science. The five core features of Mode 2 – research problems framed in the context of application, transdiscipline-driven, diffusion occurring in the process of production, heterogeneous teams of researchers with mixed skill and experience, and a more socially and politically accountable knowledge process and output – are identifiable within existing research practice in management. However, these broad components of practice need to be unpacked and customized to the peculiarities of each area of inquiry. For this writer, the challenges for management research are best captured in a series of concurrent double hurdles which together raise a wide spectrum of cognitive, social and political demands on our skills and knowledge as researchers. The following list draws together some of these challenges:

- mobilizing intellectual themes embedded in social science knowledge and policy and practice;
- big themes, small teams and networks;
- scholarly quality and relevance;
- combining knowledge production and use;
- researchers and users as co-producers;
- internal development of the field alongside engagement with co-beneficiaries and co-producers;
- relevant research has to transcend current beliefs and knowledge whilst engaging with those beliefs;
- balancing involvement and distance;
- management studies has to develop its own autonomous body of knowledge, while drawing on and contributing to social science disciplines;
- seen to supplement not supplant disciplinary knowledge production.

A central tenet of the approach here recommended is that management research should be theme-driven rather than theory or technique-driven. This is not to argue, of course, that management research can make real progress without adequate techniques of data collection or analysis. Neither is it conceivable that knowledge development will flourish in the absence of accessible theoretical languages and insights. The question is the balance and reciprocal relation between themes, theories and techniques. The view taken here is that the themes should drive the process of knowledge production. The themes are the initial problem framer, the necessary condition which exposes the problem, opens up the possibility for interdisciplinary engagement and draws in partners, co-fundors and co-producers from the worlds of policy and practice. With the necessary conditions in place, the sufficient conditions (which include the techniques and theories) can be drawn into play. The mobilizing intellectual themes are thus meant to be liberating of ideas and interactions across disciplinary boundaries and between knowledge producers and consumers in different contexts. The themes also represent new opportunities for disciplines perhaps tired of the customary problems of their academic tribe and territory (Becher, 1989).

Crucially, the themes have to meet the double hurdle of embeddedness in the social sciences and the worlds of policy and practice. The study of change adequately meets this hurdle. All the social sciences have deep conceptual and empirical literatures on change at various levels of analysis. In the 1980s and 1990s, the management of change became one of the major policy challenges in the UK private and public sectors. There may be other themes where this double hurdle is less clearly met. It is doubtful whether research driven by total quality management would adequately meet the test of social science embeddedness. Setting the tone of a theme is very much a question also of symbolism. Whose language is chosen and what messages are given off by the choice of language? Thus a management research programme driven by the theme of corporate governance could well be captured by the particular policy agenda of the day. However, an equivalent programme driven by the linguistic base of the study of managerial elites might provide more open channels into the theoretical and empirical literatures in various social science disciplines, while at the same time engaging with wider policy agendas (Pettigrew, 1992).

The route to scholarly quality and relevance is likely to need the bridgehead of an appropriately defined and resourced mobilizing intellectual theme. The notions of quality and relevance are both problematic and contestable. As such, this hurdle is unlikely to be tidied up in a simple set of definitioned statements. One can see the extremes easily enough: the archetypal 1970s social scientist celebrating the uselessness of their work, or the management researcher caught up in the language and virtues of the latest management fad or fashion. Meeting the double hurdle of scholarly quality and relevance can only be worked out case by case, context by context, project by project. None of this can be contemplated without will and skill from teams of knowledge producers who are reflective enough about their own practice to experiment, learn, unlearn and then try again.

Explicit in the new social production of knowledge is an enhanced openness and capacity for interdisciplinary team working. Some might argue, what is new in this? What seems common to nearly all the scholars who have made a sustained impact from a UK base on organization and management theory is that they have operated over varying lengths of time, and sometimes in different institutions, with an interdisciplinary research team. The obvious case examples to quote are the Aston Group, the Tavistock socio-technical systems group, the Bradford group and, more recently, the Warwick Centre for Corporate Strategy and Change. Such organized research efforts have a number of advantages over the more traditional solo scholar or transient project mode of conducting research. First, they can allow a team of scholars from a number of disciplines to coalesce around a major intellectual theme and develop the theme through several cycles of project work. This cumulative development of work over a five to ten year period is still rare in the social sciences and is one reason why knowledge development in the social sciences appears more like a complex mosaic than a series of deeply lined, cumulative patterns of knowledge development.

Research units may also be capable of bucking the natural conservatism of university teaching departments where patterns of association and the organized curriculum can lock scholars into a rather inner-directed cycle of problem definition. Becher's (1989) excellent account of academic tribes and territories is replete with examples of the way in which the cultures of disciplines shape patterns of intellectual enquiry.

Research centres which survive and flourish beyond the first generation of projects and product champions will have had to stabilize their finances and create a market for their field of intellectual enquiry. It is unlikely that this will occur unless the research group has delivered quality intellectual products to its early sponsors and unless it has built a diverse network of supporters, sponsors, co-beneficiaries and co-producers of knowledge. Drawing on studies of natural scientists, Faulkner and Senker (1995) have recently established the crucial role of informal interaction and barter as significant channels for transferring tacit knowledge between organizations in the innovation process. Dodgson's (1993) work, again with natural scientists, clearly shows that the quality and utility of such scientific networks is dependent, not just on interpersonal trust between different groups of scientists, often in different institutions, but also the quality of trust between the institutions the individuals may represent.

Combining knowledge production and use and organizing projects where researchers and users are co-producers will demand cognitive and social skills of a high order from the management research community. Why are scholars increasingly willing to take on what are clearly more demanding knowledge production processes? Clearly the incentive structure for research in the UK emanating from the White Paper, *Realising Our Potential* (1993) and the Foresight exercise, *Progress Through Partnership* (1995), are important drivers. But if individual scientists are asked why they appear to be collaborating more, other incentives also appear to be important. Diana Hicks, one of the authors of the 1995 SPRU report, *The Changing Shape of British Science*, has indicated (in a personal communication) a range of facilitators and incentives for increased scientific collaboration. Increased travel and the ease of electronic communication are important. Apparently, scientists find international collaboration 'more fun' and it produces 'better results'. As resources are being concentrated more, so there is also a desire to barter, to exchange data sets or offer reciprocal access to instrumentalities. There is also a learning curve effect. As scientists attempt more international collaborative work, so they encounter new intellectual and social challenges. They learn how to deal with these challenges, discover they now have additional skills and knowledge which gives them a competitive advantage, and then wish to further utilize their new competencies.

It is clear that these elements of the new social production of knowledge create a further set of dilemmas and double hurdles. While looking out for opportunities for co-production and co-dissemination, we as management scholars still have to be attentive to the internal development of our own field. Here, of course, the Pfeffer and Van Maanen debate about paradigm development is significant. However, it is doubtful whether the opening up process explicit in the drive for greater user contact and international collaboration will lead, as Pfeffer would prefer, to greater paradigm unity. The greater complexity of the knowledge development process is much more likely to mean that paradigm unity is both unobtainable and undesirable.

In the day-to-day conduct of our work in this new social production of knowledge, there will be the constant pressure to balance involvement and distance with user interests. This is far too complex an issue to be discussed here, and in any case can only be sensibly dealt with in the highly particular negotiations which occur situation by situation, project by project. However, it is clear from our own experience that partnership with users does not need to entail cooptation by users. We are capable of transcending current beliefs and assumptions and not just reproducing them in the way we formulate research problems. There is a role for iconoclasm and criticism in management research, as anyone who has read Pettigrew (1973) and (1985) will appreciate. To work on relevant research is not simply to address problems of current interest to power figures framed in their terms.

There is a revolution going on in the social production of knowledge in the natural and social sciences. We, as management scholars, need to take part in that revolution; indeed, we are especially well equipped to do so because of the fluidity of our interdisciplinary field. To do so is not a strategy for mere image improvement, but will direct us to more fundamental opportunities to alter the substance of our scholarly routines and keep our field intellectually and socially alive.

Notes

1   This chapter was first presented as the Distinguished Scholar Address to the Organization and Management Theory Division of the US Academy of Management, Vancouver, 7 August 1995.
2   The nature of the N-Form organization is discussed in more detail in Chapter 9.

References

Astley, G. (1985), 'Administrative science as socially constructed truth', *Administrative Science Quarterly*, **30**, 497–513.
Becher, T. (1989), *Academic Tribes and Territories: Intellectual Enquiry and the Cultures of Disciplines*, Stony Stratford: SRME and Open University Press.
Blackler, F., Reed, M. and Whitaker, A. (1993a), 'Editorial introduction: knowledge workers and contemporary organizations', *Journal of Management Studies*, **30**, 851–62.
Blackler, F., Reed, M. and Whitaker, A. (1993b), 'Epilogue: an agenda for research', *Journal of Management Studies*, **30**, 1017–20.
Cannella, A.A. and Paetzold, R.L. (1994), 'Pfeffer's barriers to the advance of organizational science: a rejoinder', *Academy of Management Review*, **19**, 331–41.
Cohen, W., Florida, R. and Goe, W.R. (1993), *University Industry Research Centers in the United States: Final Report to the Ford Foundation*, Pittsburgh: Carnegie Mellon University.
Dodgson, M. (1993), 'Learning, trust and technological collaboration', *Human Relations*, **46**, 77–94.
Economic and Social Research Council (1994), *Building Partnerships: Enhancing the Quality of Management Research*, Swindon: ESRC.
Faulkner, W. and Senker, J. (1995), *Knowledge Frontiers*, Oxford: Clarendon Press.
Gambardella, A. (1992), 'Competitive advantage from in-house scientific research: the US pharmaceutical industry in the 1980s', *Research Policy*, **21**, 391–407.
Gibbons, M., Limoges, C., Notwotny, H., Schwartzman, S., Scott, P. and Trow, M. (1994), *The New Production of Knowledge*, London: Sage.

Hassard, J. (1993), *Sociology and Organization Theory: Positivism, Paradigms and Postmodernity*, Cambridge: Cambridge University Press.

HMSO (1993), *Realising Our Potential: A Strategy for Science, Engineering and Technology*, Cmnd. 2259, London: HMSO.

Jackson, N. and Carter, P. (1991), 'In defence of paradigm incommensurability', *Organization Studies*, **12**, 109–27.

Latour, B. (1987), *Science in Action*, Cambridge, Mass.: Harvard University Press.

Latour, B. and Woolgar, S. (1979), *Laboratory Life*, Beverly Hills, CA: Sage.

Office of Science and Technology (1995), *Progress Through Partnership: Report of the Technology Foresight Steering Group*, London: HMSO.

Pettigrew, A.M. (1973), *The Politics of Organizational Decision Making*, London: Tavistock.

Pettigrew, A.M. (1985), *The Awakening Giant: Continuity and Change in ICI*, Oxford: Blackwell.

Pettigrew, A.M. (1990), 'Longitudinal field research on change: theory and practice', *Organization Science*, **3**, 267–92.

Pettigrew, A.M. (1992), 'On studying managerial elites', *Strategic Management Journal*, **13**, Winter Special Issue, 163–82.

Pettigrew, A.M. and Whipp, R. (1991), *Managing Change for Competitive Success*, Oxford: Blackwell.

Pettigrew, A.M., Whittington, R. and Conyon, M. (1995), 'The New Internal Network Organization: Process and Performance', successful research grant application to the Economic and Social Research Council.

Pfeffer, J. (1993), 'Barriers to the advance of organizational science: paradigm development as a dependent variable', *Academy of Management Review*, **18**, 599–620.

Pugh, D.S. (1996), 'A taste for innovation', in A.G. Bedeian (ed.), *Management Laureates*, Vol. 4, Greenwich, Conn.: JAI Press, pp. 235–76.

Science Policy Research Unit (1995), *The Changing Shape of British Science*, Brighton, Sussex: Falmer.

Tsoukas, H. (1994), 'Refining common sense: types of knowledge in management studies', *Journal of Management Studies*, **31**, 761–80.

Van Maanen, J. (1995), 'Style in theory', *Organization Science*, **6**, 2–12.

Webster, A. (1994), 'International evaluation of academic–industry relations: contexts and analysis', *Science and Public Policy*, **21**, 72–8.

Webster, A. and Etzkowitz, H. (1991), *Academic Industry Relations: The Second Academic Revolution?*, SPSG Concept Paper 12, London: Science Policy Support Group.

Wensley, R. (1995), 'Dissent and assent in management thought', unpublished paper, Warwick Business School, September.

Whitley, R. (1984a), 'The scientific status of management research as a practically oriented social science', *Journal of Management Studies*, **21**, 369–90.

Whitley, R. (1984b), 'The fragmented state of management studies: reasons and consequences', *Journal of Management Studies*, **21**, 331–48.

Whitley, R. (1988), 'The management sciences and managerial skills', *Organization Studies*, **9**, 47–68.

Willmott, H. (1993), 'Breaking the paradigm mentality', *Organization Studies*, **14**, 681–719.

Woolgar, S. (1994), 'Rethinking the Dissemination of Science and Technology', CRICT Discussion Paper 44, May.

Ziman, J. (1994), *Prometheus Bound: Science in a Dynamic Steady State*, Cambridge: Cambridge University Press.

17 The Time Dimension in Organizational Research

FRANK HELLER, *The Tavistock Institute*

Introduction

The seminal Aston Studies initiated by Derek Pugh and his colleagues in the 1960s have had considerable impact on the behaviour and organizational science literature. Inevitably, people have appreciated them for different reasons. For me, one important aspect of this work is its systemic theoretical framework developed from the orientation of a psychologist building bridges towards other disciplines (Heller, 1976). Such a psychological orientation was shown most clearly in the methodological approach of the Aston Studies and the choice of statistical methods. Perhaps the most important bridge was its connectedness with sociology and later with administrative and management science (Pugh *et al.*, 1963).

Why is this important? First of all, the social sciences still operate in a very narrow and compartmentalized constituency following the tramlines laid out by the historic development of university departments and, while this helps to develop the intellectual credentials of a discipline, it does little to test its validity on the wider campus of a complex world. This is not a denigration of disciplines, since it is obvious that they have to be developed and show their strength before a cross-disciplinary approach can be expected to yield results. A discipline grows and develops to a state of isolated maturity beyond which it is difficult to achieve further growth without venturing outside the self-imposed boundaries of a given field. I believe that applied psychology reached this stage several decades ago, for instance in the study of leadership, decision making and other facets of organizational life. Moving across disciplinary boundaries requires ingenuity, confidence and perseverance. Kurt Lewin was an early transgressor of boundaries (Lewin, 1936) and he inspired Eric Trist and Fred Emery to venture further into the undercharted territories of technological and organizational life (Trist *et al.*, 1963; Emery, 1982; Emery and Trist, 1973). Another great bridge builder using psychology and economics to explore the limits of rationality in organizations was Herbert Simon (Simon, 1982).

The Aston Studies were from the beginning based on an interdisciplinary group of scholars, bringing together psychology, sociology and anthropology in a conceptual scheme of organizational analysis (Pugh *et al.*, 1963). Rather than continuing the tradition of studying organizational processes, they set out to discover basic structural characteristics and the context in which they occur. Structure and context tend to be fairly stable over time and their cross-sectional design yielded very significant results, explaining often up to 50 per cent of the variance between the variables under investigation. Another reason for the considerable success of their programme of research was their use of a carefully validated interview schedule rather than the more popular and less reliable distributed questionnaire. However, when later they came to look at the interaction between structure, context and individual roles and group behaviour, the statistical relationships were very much weaker (Pugh and Payne, 1977). Such results are not unusual and it is likely that the greater variability of individual and group behaviour, compared with structural dimensions, is a part of the explanation.

In research dealing with structure as well as processes of individual and group behaviour, a strong case can be made out for a longitudinal research design. Even when variances are relatively low, if they are found to be stable over time, the explanatory power is enhanced. If, however, significant differences are found over time, then this has to be considered within an appropriate process-oriented theoretical framework.

In the subsequent discussion I will describe four distinct approaches to longitudinal design and relevant methodological considerations. This is followed by a brief description of two pieces of organizational research – Industrial Democracy in Europe (IDE) and Decisions in Organizations (DIO) – which used different longitudinal methods with some success.

The Case for Longitudinality

In a 1973 symposium on leadership, Ed Fleishman identified the urgent need for longitudinal studies and for a time dimension in research design (Fleishman and Hunt, 1973, pp. 183–4). The logical case for longitudinal research is very strong. Everybody and everything has a history and a future, except at the point of death. So even in selection testing one could make out a case for differentiating results achieved on a Monday morning – maybe after a hectic Sunday – from a Friday afternoon, which may combine signs of fatigue with euphoria anticipating the pleasures of the coming weekend.

The case becomes stronger when we deal with characteristics which clearly vary over time, so the assessment of a manager who has just moved into a job may be substantially different from the same person's attitudes and behaviour after six months, and two years later. A representative and valid leadership profile probably requires a time dimension, particularly if we want to match leader characteristics to success or failure. There is no shortage of examples from the last 10 years or so to show that people who were considered eminently successful suddenly failed. Only a longitudinal study would make it possible to discover the antecedents to success or failure.

The need for longitudinality becomes irresistible when one investigates the activities employees undertake in a working day or in the process of decision making or participation. If we carry out cross-sectional studies on events which occur over time, we make assumptions about representativeness which may not be justifiable. For instance, most research on participation and decision making is carried out cross-sectionally although we know that issues involved in participation take days, weeks or months from beginning to end. The assumption we make is either that the time chosen to solicit an answer to our question is representative of the universe of events we attempt to cover or that the respondent is capable of calculating his/her own average or mode for a representative sample of events. A moment's reflection will suggest that these are risky assumptions to make and we might then fall back on the hope that differences over time do not have any theoretically justifiable pattern or are randomly distributed.

Variations of Longitudinal Design

Having made out the theoretical case and the policy relevance of a longitudinal research design for certain topics of investigation in organizational psychology, I want briefly to discuss a few issues of methodology. In general, a longitudinal approach is more costly than cross-sectional design, but different longitudinal designs incur different costs and probably also yield commensurately different benefits. I will describe four different ways of achieving time-sensitive data collection. In each case the data can be collected through interviews, questionnaires, observation or analysis of available documents.

1   A *two-stage before-and-after longitudinal* design is the most widely used. It is particularly appropriate if the research itself introduces a new factor or wishes to monitor the effect of a given change event. It is also the least costly. The IDE study described below uses this design.

2   *Segmental longitudinal* design consists of more than two cross-sectional stages and is therefore an extension of method (1) above. It covers longer periods and is more suitable for establishing trends.

3   *Processual studies* are designed to create continuity over time. They can take many forms, from participant observation, via case studies, to diachronic research which resembles segmental longitudinal research in method (2) above, but finds some way to establish a degree of continuity between visits and observations. A researcher's visit may occur while a process is going on but, to get continuity, it is possible to link up with past events through what we call retrospective tracing (using interviews or available documents and so on) and from then on carry out process analysis followed later by further retrospective tracing, and so on. Standardized questionnaires can only play a limited role in extensive longitudinal field studies because people soon get tired of filling in forms. We have found a method called Group Feedback Analysis useful in establishing reliable data over time (Brown and Heller, 1981; Heller and Brown, 1995). The method systematically feeds back interview and other material to the people who provided it or are involved in the activity under discussion. This group (or individuals) are asked to verify the data and help interpret them in the light of their experience. The DIO study to be described below uses this method. Processual studies can clearly use a considerable variety of methods. This is a point in their favour.

4   Finally, there is what I call a *simulated longitudinal study*. It uses the conventional cross-sectional design but asks people to focus on specific time periods and describe what happens in each (see, for instance, Fröhlich *et al.*, 1991, pp. 65–71).

Industrial Democracy in Europe (IDE) Research

This project was jointly designed and executed by 16 social scientists from 12 mainly European countries covering a number of disciplines including economics, philosophy, sociology, industrial relations and psychology. It adopted an open systems framework starting with formal, mainly legal, structural variables which are assumed to have an impact on individual and group behaviour and ultimately on individual and group outcomes moderated by a variety of contextual variables. (IDE, 1981a).

The research design was derived from prevailing policy preoccupations relating to organizational democracy, leadership, conflict, organizational climate and individual satisfaction. An important preoccupation in individual countries as well as in the European Commission was to discover the necessary antecedents for successful participative or influence-sharing behaviour at various organizational levels. Was it useful or even necessary to support changes in behaviour at company level, by legal or other formal schemas? More specifically, is influence sharing at various organizational levels dependent on or facilitated by formal structures like the German codetermination scheme?

The research design was complex and I will only describe in outline the basic theoretical model and the main variables (see Figure 17.1). Box 1 was based on a detailed assessment by each of the 12-country teams of four specified context conditions. This descriptive account is contained in a separate book and was consulted in the final assessment of the results (IDE, 1981b). Box 2 contains formal legally prescribed participative measures (such as German codetermination) which were the main dependent measures and varied

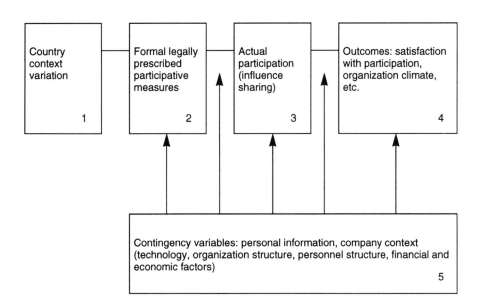

Figure 17.1   The IDE I theoretical model

substantially in the 12 countries. Box 3 describes a measure of actual participation, that is to say, influence and power sharing at all organizational levels. Box 4 describes five outcomes, including satisfaction with participation, satisfaction in general and organizational climate. Finally, box 5 used two types of contingencies which were hypothesized to intervene or moderate the assumed chain of causal relationships. They included several variables derived from the Aston Studies and were based on interviews with managers (IDE, 1981a, ch. 4).

Ten years later, the same international research group carried out a replication study in the same organizations in the same countries.[1] The objective was to test the validity of the previous research conclusions, at the same time extending the design to include some of the most likely variables that had become critical in the intervening 10 years. There are, of course, many methodological and practical problems in carrying out such a large-scale replication study and these are freely acknowledged. The most difficult objective was to see whether a longitudinal link between two cross-sectional studies (we have called this method 'two-stage longitudinal') might give us some insight into possible causal relationships over time (IDE, 1993).

To attempt such an assessment, we had to select a group of contingencies which could be hypothesized to strengthen or weaken the major relationship we had found in the previous study and assess the impact of selected economic and technical changes over the intervening period – in particular the rate of unemployment, which had gone up very substantially.

The theoretical model for the IDE II study is shown in Figure 17.2. The macro variables in box 1 contain the descriptive data on the major political, economic and industrial relations factors which characterize the 1977–87 period. Boxes 2 and 3 are the same as in IDE I but now include comparisons over the 10 years. Outcomes were not considered to be central for the replication study. Box 4 measures a number of contingencies and, in particular, the rate of unemployment and changes in unemployment over the 10-year period.

The replication design allowed us to describe and evaluate the data of the two studies from a cross-sectional as well as longitudinal perspective. It became clear that the longitudinal analysis was more policy-relevant than the conclusions from the cross-sectional material alone. The major conclusion of the replication study is that the relationship between macro variables of formal and legal structure and micro dimensions of influence sharing at the lowest organizational level remains valid. However, in the replication study, the macro variable (formal, legal, participative structure) was less predictive than the indices of unemployment. The 1977–87 period was very turbulent; it included the oil crisis, the subsequent economic

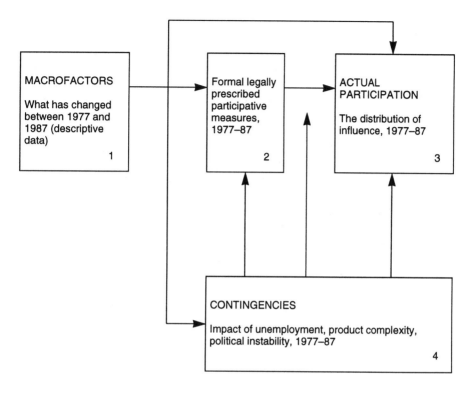

Figure 17.2   The IDE II theoretical model

recession, greatly increased competition and changes in technological sophistication. Our data show that, over the 10-year period, labour
lost ground in organizations, particularly where it had previously
been strong. It seems that, under the umbrella of an economic recession and high unemployment, companies deliberately reduced the
influence of labour where it had previously been strong. Using the
1977 data, it was also possible to conclude that management policy
to reduce the influence of employees by reducing the strength of the
unions was based more on an emotional than a factual interpretation
of employee influence in the decision-making process. We had asked
all employees how much influence they would like to have compared with the influence they currently had and the difference was
very moderate (see also similar evidence from Wall and Lischeron,
1977).

More generally, it was reassuring that, in the two studies separated
by 10 turbulent years, the overall pattern of relationships remained
substantially stable.

Decisions in Organizations (DIO) Research

The two-stage before and after longitudinal IDE research described above was followed up by a subgroup of the original group of researchers in three countries using what we have called a processual longitudinal study. The research lasted five years, four of them on field work. A similar open system theoretical framework was adopted and many of the variables, particularly those measuring the distribution of influence (the influence–power continuum) remained the same. As before, we assessed influence at all organizational levels and in this case in relation to a set of 217 specific tactical and strategic decision issues. Our structural variable was not the country's formal legal provision, but the nearest equivalent at the organizational level, namely formal, usually written, policy on organizational democracy (the structure and function of works councils in particular). This variable was called 'status power'. Since the study covered only seven organizations, the in-depth design over the four years could include a number of additional variables such as three important outcome variables: skill utilization, the efficiency of the decision process and achievement of the decision.

The research methodology was based on interviews, participant observation, access to written records, a detailed interview schedule and frequent use of group feedback analysis (GFA) as a way of validating our interview schedule assessment and exploring the meaning of our data with employees at all levels (Heller, 1969; Brown and Heller 1981; Heller and Brown, 1995). A feature of the processual design was to obtain quantitative as well as ethnographic material relating to the same decision process (Heller *et al.*, 1988).

Our method of following the sample of decisions over time is illustrated in Figure 17.3. Although we visited each company frequently, there was always the possibility that something important had happened between visits. To catch up we used 'retrospective tracing' through interviews and documentation. While we were in the company we observed, talked to various people engaged in the decision and took part in meetings, particularly of the joint consultative procedure (works councils) and safety committees, as well as budget forecasting meetings. This is called 'process registration'. In asking questions to cover the data for the interview schedule it was frequently suggested that we should check with some other people who could tell us more about the issue with which we were concerned. This is called 'snowballing' and covered a variety of levels and functions.

During the pilot investigation we decided to divide the decision process into distinct phases and for the purposes of this chapter we will confine ourselves to a brief description of the phase model used

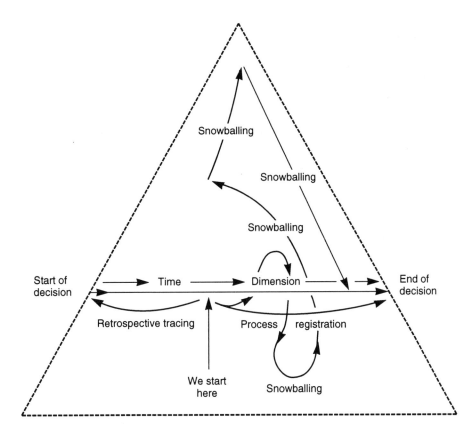

Note: The dotted triangle is used to draw attention to the analysis at different levels of the organization; the diagram illustrates the need to operate in two dimensions: organizational level and time.

Source: Heller *et al.* (1988).

Figure 17.3   The decision process through retrospective tracing, process registration and snowballing

in this research and some of the results achieved. Using the 217 medium- and long-term tactical and strategic decisions as our unit of analysis, we traced each decision over its life cycle of four phases:

1   *start-up*, which contains recognition of issue and definition of goals;
2   *development*, which contains search for responses, investigation of alternatives and creation of possible solutions;

3   *finalization*, which contains evaluation of alternatives, a choice
    among them and ratification of decision; and
4   *implementation* of decision, which contains implementation and
    modification of the decision made in the previous phases.[2]

The degree of participation measured by the influence–power continuum (IPC) had six alternatives: (1) no or minimal information, (2)
information only, (3) opportunity to give advice, (4) advice taken into
consideration, (5) joint decision making and (6) complete control.
These six degrees of influence sharing in the decision process were
scored separately for each of the four phases of our sample of decisions. Previous research on the distribution of power in organizations
had led us to hypothesize that perhaps substantial differences might
result from custom and practice, motivation and variability in competence. The results fully supported these expectations. The
distribution of influence and power over the four phases was significantly different for all levels of organization and in relation to most
decisions. Furthermore, there were significant and consistent differences in the amount of time taken up in each phase. The finalization
phase was nearly always the shortest and the implementation phase
the longest.

A typical distribution of the IPC over the four phases is shown in
Figure 17.4. The lowest level of employee has no real influence over
new product decisions; the difference in scores between phases reflects the amount of information received. Only in the finalization
phase are workers fully informed on new product decisions. When it
comes to consultative procedures, there are substantial differences
over the four phases, rising from very little influence in start-up and
development to considerable influence during finalization and somewhat less in implementation. Managers, of course, have considerably
more influence in all phases. The difference between the four phases
is smaller than for workers but nevertheless statistically significant.
Moreover, the pattern of distribution is reversed between these two
types of decisions.

This distribution is not unexpected, but it does suggest that a
description of the amount of influence a shopfloor worker or manager has cannot usefully be described by a single word or figure. A
number of consequences follow from such a conclusion at the level
of theory as well as of practice.

First of all, it calls into question many of the policy recommendations from the existing literature on participation. In particular, it would
seem necessary to adjust the models used for training managers in
using participative styles of leadership in certain contingencies (for
instance, Vroom and Yetton, 1973). In leadership training, phase should
be considered a contingency. For instance we find that the amount of

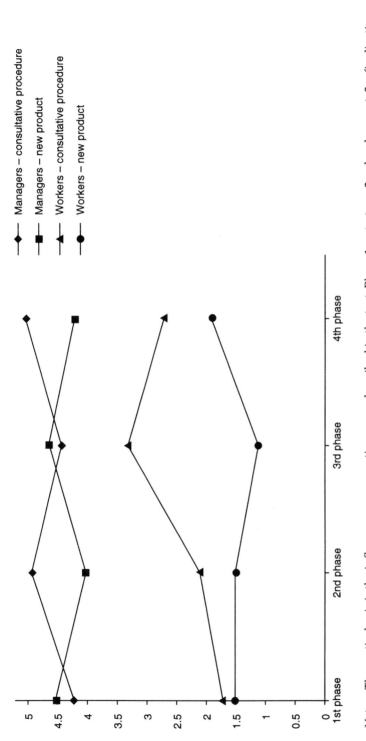

— ◆ — Managers – consultative procedure

— ■ — Managers – new product

— ◀ — Workers – consultative procedure

— ● — Workers – new product

Note: The vertical axis is the influence–power continuum as described in the text. Phase 1 = start-up; 2 = development; 3 = finalization; 4 = implementation.

Source: Heller *et al.* (1988).

Figure 17.4 Differences in influence sharing between workers and managers on two long-term decisions

participation varies significantly between the phases of the decision cycle (see Figure 17.4) and these variations seem to make sense in relation to the experience of the employees engaged in the process. This result of the longitudinal analysis should be used in leadership training and replace the more usual exhortation to use the same method irrespective of the differential conditions characterizing the four phases.

At the theoretical level, it is possible to discern several distinct patterns; we have described six.

1   Dominance without responsibility describes a pattern of partici-pation in which a group has the highest score of involvement in the first phase of decision-making activity and a relatively low score of involvement in the other three phases. The rationale behind this pattern is that the control established through the first stage is not legitimized in the third stage, or elsewhere. This means that another group takes responsibility for the decision.
2   Dominance with responsibility describes a situation where a group has the highest score of involvement in the first and third stage of decision-making activity, and a relatively low score in the second and fourth stages.
3   Overcommitment is the pattern of a group that has a high score of involvement in all four stages of decision-making activity.
4   Controlled participation is created in circumstances where a group is highly involved in the second and third phases, but relatively little involved in the other two phases. In this case the activity of some group or groups is controlled by whoever dominates the first and third phases.
5   Dependent participation appears in cases where a group partici-pates only in the implementation phase and has no great influence on the previous phases of decision-making activity.
6   Zero participation applies to situations where one or more groups have very low involvement scores in all four phases of decision making. This pattern sometimes applies to workers and to rep-resentative bodies.

In the seven organizations of the DIO study we found examples of each of these patterns. We believe that this type of analysis could be helpful for policy making as well as for training to the extent that it imposes an obligation to explain and possibly justify a certain distri-bution of influence. It would be particularly useful if the analysis were to lead to an attempt to match influence sharing with the distri-bution of experience and skill in the organization, thus pinpointing the need for further training.

Another important phase variation applies to 'skill utilization', described in the interview schedule as a rating of the extent to which capacities and experiences of competent people and groups involved in a given process have been utilized. It is a difficult variable to assess accurately and we therefore specified that these assessments must always be checked through group feedback analysis. We considered skill utilization to be a somewhat neglected variable in organizational analysis and in particular in its relation with influence sharing. This was borne out by our findings, which showed very clearly that, in each of the four phases, skill utilization depended on two antecedent conditions: one was the amount of influence sharing practised by management and the other was what we called 'status power', that is to say the amount of formal, usually written, influence assigned to participative bodies like works councils, safety committees and so on.[3] Our ethnographic data from one of the companies provided a number of useful illustrations. In budget forecasting, for instance, the frequent inaccuracies of this procedure could usually be traced back to a lack of consultation with those levels who had the relevant information, for instance the salesperson who knew why customers were not interested in buying the product at certain times of the year. The sequence of events was clear: a lack of participation led to underutilization of the sales staff's experience and this in turn resulted in grossly inaccurate budget forecasts. Looking at this procedure over the four phases, we saw that the lack of consultation was particularly important during the search process of phase 2 and to some extent in finalization during phase 3. It was unimportant in phases 1 and 4. However, in the implementation phase there was a noticeable increase in dissatisfaction for both the sales staff and management since the finance officer held them responsible for not achieving their forecasts and therefore attributed the inappropriate investments in capital equipment to their failure. The other causal factor was status power, which affected the accuracy of the budget decisions because these decisions were not part of the agenda of existing consultative committees; they had their own separate and ad hoc procedure.

There were two ways of improving the situation and both were discussed in our feedback sessions. One was to persuade the senior marketing staff to consult their salesmen regularly, particularly at certain times of the budget forecasting process, the other was to include budget forecasting in the formal joint consultative procedure, particularly in phases 2 and 3. The managing director thought that changing what we called 'status power' was preferable, since he had little confidence in affecting the somewhat autocratic management style of the marketing manager; moreover, he thought that it was easier to confine the sales staffs input during the development and finalization phases within a formal committee procedure. To save embarrassment for the marketing manager, one could, he

thought, start off by bringing the sales staff only into the pre-finaliz-
ation phase. These findings illustrate the policy relevance of the phase
model. We know from previous research and other investigations
that management frequently resists participation on the grounds that
it invades their prerogative. It is likely that this argument has less
force if it can be shown that consultation taps into relevant experiences and skills and therefore improves the quality of decisions and,
furthermore, can be confined to certain phases of the decision cycle.

The utility of a longitudinal design is of course accepted by people
who use the case study method which usually eschews quantification. Even so, our experience with DIO would suggest that a clearly
defined phase structure would produce useful additional descriptive
results. Furthermore, there are issues, particularly in comparative
cross-national research, were some quantification is advantageous
and there is really no reason, except cost, why substantial ethnographic material should not be collected at the same time to extend
the data and deepen our insight into causality and the complexity of
organizational life.

We have seen that there are a number of results that provide links
between the two projects described in this paper. One is the finding
that a formal organization structure at company level (called 'status
power' in DIO) has a very similar effect of increasing the influence of
lower levels to the effect that legal structures at national level had in
the IDE research. The longitudinal dimension adds a refinement by
suggesting that the relationship between structure and behaviour is
more significant and has more useful outcomes in some phases of the
decision cycle than in others.

The Argument

Modern organizations are complex entities and benefit from being
studied from a multidisciplinary perspective and an appropriate variety of methods. It is interesting to see that similar considerations
apply in the physical sciences and that there, too, a multidisciplinary
approach is often resisted. Hawkes (1995) tells us that 'traditional
methods of supporting science do not usually favour interdisciplinary research'. Sir William Mitchell, chairman of the Science and
Engineering Research Council in the 1980s, recalls that, when applications for research grants for projects involving both chemistry and
physics arrived, they would be sent separately to both the chemistry
and physics committees. Each would do their own scoring and then
the Council would take an average. This, he argued, completely
neglected the possibility of cross-fertilization between the two disciplines. Following these experiences, Sir William Mitchell managed to

build up an interdisciplinary research centre in the face of very strong opposition from subject specialists.

Starting with the interdisciplinary and well known Aston Studies on organization structure and context, we have described two other pieces of research (IDE and DIO) which used Aston-like variables of structure and added individual and group dimensions in an attempt to assess the impact of structure on behaviour. Since some of the behaviour variables were processual, it was thought appropriate to use a longitudinal method. Four longitudinal methods were described and two different ones were used in the IDE and DIO projects.

The desirability of tailoring methods to the nature of the research task is widely accepted but not easily practised because of the attitude of funding bodies and the need to limit costs. In some countries, particularly in the United States, the need for frequent publications also mitigates against processual studies like DIO; this pressure is now experienced in many European countries. In these circumstances it becomes important to demonstrate the value added by longitudinality in terms of its relevance for policy and practice as well as theory.[4]

Notes

1   There were some changes in personnel and two additional countries.
2   Mintzberg *et al.* (1976), using students doing a master's degree, had previously used a three-phase model which excluded implementation. In the event, we found this final phase was particularly important.
3   LISREL was the statistical method used for most of the longitudinal analysis. In addition, we collected extensive ethnographic material (see Heller *et al.*, 1988, ch. VI).
4   In this context it may be useful to compare the studies described here with a continuing stream of mechanistic cross-sectional studies on participative decision making that concentrate on psychological variables (see, for instance, Sagie and Koslowsky, 1966).

References

Brown, A.J. and Heller, F.A. (1981), 'Usefulness of group feedback analysis as a research method: its application to a questionnaire study', *Human Relations*, **34**, pp. 141–56.
Emery, F.E. (1982), 'New perspectives on the world of work: sociotechnical foundations for a new social order?', *Human Relations*, **35**, 1095–1122.
Emery, F.E. and Trist, E.L. (1973), *Towards a Social Ecology*. London: Plenum Press.
Fleishman, E. and Hunt, J. (1973), *Current Developments in the Study of Leadership*, Carbondale, Ill.: Southern Illinois University Press.
Fröhlich, Dieter, Gill, Colin and Krieger, Hubert (1991), 'Roads to participation in the European Community: Increasing prospects of employee representatives in

technological change', European Foundation for the Improvement of Living and Working Conditions, Loughlinstown House, Shankill, Dublin.

Hawkes, N. (1995), 'Making the right connections', *The Times*, 29 November 1995, p. 39.

Heller, F.A. (1969), 'Group feedback analysis: a method of field research', *Psychological Bulletin*, **72**, 108–17; reprinted 1973 in D. Graves (ed.), *Management Research: A Cross-Cultural Perspective*, London: Elsevier Scientific Publishing Co., pp. 49–69.

Heller, F.A. (1976), 'Towards a practical psychology of work', *Journal of Occupational Psychology*, **49**, 45–54.

Heller, F. and Brown, A. (1995), 'Group feed-back analysis applied to longitudinal monitoring of the decision making process', *Human Relations*, **48**.

Heller, F.A., Drenth, P.J.D., Koopman, P. and Veljko, R. (1988), *Decisions in Organizations: A Longitudinal Study of Routine, Tactical and Strategic Decisions*, London/ Beverly Hills: Sage.

IDE (Industrial Democracy in Europe) (1981a), *European Industrial Relations*, Oxford: Oxford University Press.

IDE (Industrial Democracy in Europe) (1981b), *Industrial Relations in Europe*, Oxford: Oxford University Press.

IDE (Industrial Democracy in Europe) (1993), *Industrial Democracy in Europe Revisited*, Oxford: Oxford University Press.

Lewin, Kurt (1936), *Principles of Topological Psychology*, New York: McGraw-Hill.

Mintzberg, H., Raisingham, D. and Theoret, A. (1976) 'The structure of "unstructured" decision processes', *Administrative Science Quarterly*, **21**, 246–75.

Pugh, D.S. and Payne, R. (eds) (1977), *Organization Behaviour in its Context. The Aston Programme III*, Aldershot: Dartmouth.

Pugh, D.S., Hickson, D.J., Hinings, C.R., Macdonald, K.M., Turner, C. and Lupton, T. (1963), 'A conceptual scheme for organizational analysis', *Administrative Science Quarterly*, **8**, 289–315.

Sagie, A. and Koslowsky (1996), 'Decision type, organizational control and acceptance of change: an integrative approach to participative decision making', *Applied Psychology*, **45**, 85–92.

Simon, H.A. (1982), 'Rational decision-making in business organization', in H. Simon (ed.), *Models of Bounded Rationality*, Vol. 2, Cambridge, Mass.: MIT Press, pp. 474–94.

Trist, E.L., Higgin, G.W., Murray, H. and Pollock, A.B. (1963), *Organizational Choice*, London: Tavistock.

Vroom, V. and Yetton, P. (1973), *Leadership and decision-making*, Pittsburg: University of Pittsburgh Press.

Wall, T.D. and Lischeron, J.A. (1977), *Worker Participation: A Critique of the Literature and Some Fresh Evidence*, London: McGraw-Hill.

18 Distrust in Dependence: the Ancient Challenge of Superior–Subordinate Relations

VIOLINA P. RINDOVA, *New York University* and **WILLIAM H. STARBUCK**, *New York University*

Foreword

In 1993, Derek Pugh asked William Starbuck to edit readings on premodern management thought, explaining that this meant writings from before 1880. He agreed to attempt this, not as an expert in premodern thought, but to learn about it. A few weeks of reflection brought him to wondering about very ancient management practices – long before Niccolò Machiavelli or Robert Owen – having seen descriptions of ancient practices only in Claude George's *The History of Management Thought* (1968) which was so concise that it mainly aroused curiosity.

Starbuck asked the students in a doctoral seminar to investigate ancient management practices. Each student was to dig out evidence about actual management practices in one society. To keep the students from sliding too easily into well-known works and to push them towards serious library research, they were told to limit their search to times before the year 0CE.

Violina Rindova, co-author of this chapter, looked at ancient China. Other students studied Greece, India and Rome. Starbuck investigated Egypt and Mesopotamia. This chapter reports some findings about China, Egypt and Mesopotamia, the regions with the oldest surviving records.

How Atrahasis Survived The Flood

Among the oldest records that offer practical advice for a manager are Mesopotamian stone tablets engraved with a story of a flood.[1] Scholars say the story of Noah, written around 1000 BCE, was a Judaic adaptation of this Mesopotamian story. Although the oldest substantial copy was composed around 1635 BCE, fragments of tablets suggest that the story probably goes back to at least 3000 BCE in Mesopotamia.[2]

In Mesopotamia, the man who built a boat was named Atrahasis, Ziusudra or Utnapishtim. He lived in a city named Shuruppak (now called Fara) on the Euphrates river. Atrahasis had to contend with quite a few gods, the most powerful of whom, Enlil, led the others in deciding to teach humanity a lesson by drowning everyone in Shuruppak. They chose Shuruppak because it was the 'most fortunate of cities, favoured by the gods'. Although the gods agreed to keep the forthcoming flood secret, two of them broke this pact. Shamash, god of justice and truth, told Atrahasis that an evening shower would foretell the flood. Enki or Ea, god of wisdom who delighted in cunning tricks, saved Atrahasis's life by urging him to build a boat.

Atrahasis's boat was to be so massive that a single family could not build it, and Atrahasis himself had no ship-building experience. How could he induce others to help him build a massive boat? Who would believe a man who claimed that the gods intended to drown everyone? If they did believe him, would they not demand passage in his boat? Atrahasis asked the god Enki how to handle this problem: 'I hear what you say, and I will do it in praise of you. But I will need to explain my actions. What should I tell others? What should I tell the city, the people and their leaders?' Enki advised Atrahasis to deceive them. He should explain that he had to leave Shuruppak because it is dedicated to Enlil, and Atrahasis's own god, Enki, is quarrelling with Enlil: 'Since Shuruppak is the city of Enlil, you can no longer live in the city and you can no longer gaze on the land, which Enlil rules. You must find another place to live and another god to protect you. You have therefore decided to leave Shuruppak and to seek another home. Tell them your patron will be Enki, the god who rules the deep waters, so you will dwell upon the deep waters with Enki.'

Enki told Atrahasis to tell the truth, but to do so using metaphors that hearers would misunderstand. Atrahasis should say, 'As for Shuruppak, he [Enlil, but the ambiguous antecedent allows hearers to substitute Enki] will make abundance rain down on the fortunate city: there will be a flood of bounty. The city will teem with heaven's profusion. The people will see birds and fishes unheard-of in song or story. When the new day dawns, he will pour down loaves of fresh bread and showers of wheat. He will bring a surfeit of everything, yes, more than enough. These are the things to tell the people and their leaders.' However, for Sumerians, bread was a metaphor for darkness and wheat a metaphor for misfortune. Thus Atrahasis's promise had a metaphorical meaning that promised doom: 'When the new day dawns, he will pour down renewed darkness and showers of misfortune.' Thus the god Enki advised Atrahasis, in his supervisory role, to elicit work by deceiving the workers.

Atrahasis also rewarded his doomed helpers generously: 'As for the people who came to help with the work, each day was like a New Year's festival. I slaughtered bullocks for their feasting; every day I slaughtered sheep. To drink, I gave the workers ale and beer, oil and wine aplenty, as if they came from a flowing river.' When he and his family were aboard the boat, and with the storm rising, Atrahasis made his last payment: 'To Puzur-Amuru, the shipbuilder who, outside, caulked up the hatch with pitch, I gave my house with all its contents.'

Thus what may be the oldest surviving advice about management practices concerns leaders' deceptions of followers. Tension-filled, distrustful relations between leaders and followers pervade the ancient texts. This chapter reviews these common issues and people's responses to them. The issues encompass (1) how much leaders and followers should trust each other and speak forthrightly to each other, (2) how leaders manipulate followers and followers manipulate leaders, (3) how much followers respect leaders and leaders respect followers, (4) whether status differences are just, and (5) when leaders act appropriately.

The chapter draws on documents from regions with the oldest surviving documents – Mesopotamia, Egypt and China. Although similar issues doubtless arose in many regions, only these offer records from before 1000 BCE. We do not compare these regions, because records are fragmentary and biased. To justify comparisons, one would need comparable information from all three regions, but invasions and political upheavals created waves of mass destruction that erased disapproved documents. There is no reason to believe this historical editing operated similarly in these regions.

Mesopotamia

Through waves of migration and invasion, Mesopotamia was home to several cultures and several languages. Invasions often involved wholesale destruction of written records, yet quite a lot of writing survives, giving some of the most reliable evidence about ancient practices because people chiselled cuneiform into rock or baked it into clay. Elsewhere, where words were recorded on papyrus, skins or paper, decaying documents had to be copied. Works were copied only if aristocrats approved of and valued them. Copying introduced errors, and some scribes modernized works they were reproducing. Thus Mesopotamian documents offer better insights into attitudes of ordinary people, unfiltered by the editing of their rulers.

The records include contracts, bills of sale, grants by rulers, inventory records and letters to and from rulers. These discuss all sorts of administrative details, from assignments of shepherds, through astronomical observations, to police investigations. However, scholars have found little writing about Mesopotamian management techniques, organization design or strategy.

How Ordinary People Viewed Leaders

The more interesting records to survive include proverbs and sayings used by ordinary people. These sayings date back to at least 2000–1000 BCE and they may be much older. They reveal the ambivalence with which followers regard their leaders.[3] Some assert the necessity of leadership: 'Workers without a supervisor are a canal without someone to regulate it. Workers without a supervisor are a field without a farmer. People without a ruler are sheep without a shepherd.' Others characterize leadership as requiring special talents or embodying special powers: 'A driver of oxen should not try to be a supervisor. To improve government, Shamash [the god of justice and truth] will speak to a ruler even if the ruler is an ignoramus.' Some sayings distinguish between rulers and administrators: 'Acknowledge a lord, acknowledge a ruler, but respect an administrator. Giving is the act of a ruler; doing a favour the act of an administrator.' And still other sayings speak cynically of rulers' doubtful value: 'There are people who support spouses; there are people who support children. Rulers are people who do not even support themselves.'

Protests Against a Ruler's Actions

In a society where rulers could inflict harsh punishment for disobedience or disrespect, protest could be dangerous. A protester had to find a way to tell a ruler that he had erred and yet avoid personal responsibility for this judgement.

One document dating back to 1000–700 BCE seems to protest transgressions by an unnamed ruler against residents of three cities, Sippar, Nippur and Babylon.[4] Instead of accusing a named ruler directly of having taken or threatening to take certain actions, the document offers predictions about what would happen if an unnamed ruler should take certain actions. The actions described, however, are so specific that the author was probably speaking of specific acts by a specific ruler. For example,

> If a ruler denies due process to a citizen of Sippar but grants it to a foreigner, Shamash, judge of heaven and earth, will impose an alien form of due process on the state and neither nobles nor judges will have respect for due process.
> If citizens of Nippur come to the ruler for justice, and the ruler accepts the customary remuneration but denies them due process, Enlil, lord of the world, will bring a foreign enemy to decimate the ruler's army and the army's commanders and officers will prowl the streets like vagabonds.
> If a ruler imposes fines on citizens of Babylon that the ruler usurps as the ruler's own property, or if the ruler hears a plea from Babylonians but dismisses it as trivial, Marduk, lord of heaven and earth, will place the ruler's enemies over the ruler and give the ruler's possessions and property to these foes.

In the original language, the writing style imitated one that Mesopotamians used when describing omens of future events. Thus the document portrays the ruler's transgressions as omens foretelling dire consequences, mainly consequences for the ruler himself but also for the society. The dire consequences are carried out by the populace, gods or foreign invaders (who may have been seen as instruments of the gods). To find this description persuasive, a ruler would have to have believed that Sippar, Nippur and Babylon had strong support from gods. In turn, the document had to emphasize high-minded issues that gods would support: 'If a ruler does not listen to the nobles, the ruler's lifetime will be cut short. If a ruler listens to a scoundrel, the state's morality will change. If a ruler attempts clever deception, the great gods together will harass the ruler endlessly for the sake of justice.'

Egypt

Several surviving Egyptian documents are Instructions that were intended to transmit experience from one generation to another. Typically, an Instruction represented itself as having been written by a father for his sons, but they actually had much wider readership as they served as texts in schools. It appears that Egyptians drew weak distinctions between work and other aspects of life. Their Instructions mix advice on many topics, and none focuses exclusively on management. However, the Instruction of Ptahhotep may be the oldest surviving text on organizational behaviour.[5]

Ptahhotep was mayor of the capital and vizier to King Isesi around 2380–2340 BCE. The vizier was Egypt's highest appointed official, second only to the king. The Instruction states that it is offering advice to Ptahhotep's son. However, scholars debate whether Ptahhotep himself composed the Instruction because the oldest surviving copy has the writing style of works created about 200 years after Ptahhotep died. Works from Ptahhotep's day were shorter and more terse, and they used more archaic language. Surviving copies may be 'expanded and revised editions', or the work's attribution to Ptahhotep may have been a literary device to add the significance of great age. Since Egyptian schools were still using Ptahhotep's Instruction as a text around 1500 BCE, it may have been studied for 900 years.

Ptahhotep's Instruction covers such diverse topics as 'do not let your concubine starve', 'beware of greed', 'do not steal from your neighbours' and reasons why children should listen to their fathers, yet it mainly teaches how to survive and succeed in the Egyptian social system. Its advice sometimes seems more insightful and pragmatic than advice in modern textbooks!

Being a Superior

The Instruction recognizes that rulers need the support of the populace and that superiors need the support of their subordinates. It advises superiors to act virtuously, modestly and with awareness of human needs. It advocates correct behaviour in terms of how people will react, not in terms of demands made by gods. There is no sign that gods intervene in human affairs in order to ensure social justice.

> 4. If you run into opposition from subordinates who are not your equal, show temperance in proportion to your opponents' weakness. If you leave such opponents alone they may rebut themselves. Do not challenge them to make yourself feel better or to vent your feelings. Contemptible is one who bullies uninformed subordinates. When other people will follow your advice, you will subdue your opponents through the judgement of others.
> 14. When among the people, attract supporters by earning their trust. Trustworthy persons speak in ways that do not distort what they think. Their conduct makes them superiors and owners of property. …
> 17. If you are a superior, listen kindly when people make petitions to you. Do not interrupt petitioners until they have unburdened themselves and said what they came to say. Those who think they have suffered wrongs want to vent their feelings more than they want to win their cases. If you interrupt a petition, people will think you rejected it. You cannot grant every plea, but a good hearing soothes the heart.

25. If you hold an important position, earn respect through knowledge and through gentleness of speech. Do not issue commands unless they fit the business at hand. A superior who chafes gets into trouble. Do not act haughty lest you be humiliated. Do not keep silence, but be careful not to offend. When you run into someone who is fuming, avert your face, control yourself, and the flames of anger will sweep past and be gone. ...

30. If you become important having been lowly, or gain wealth having been poor, do not boast of your attainments and do not rely on your wealth. These came to you as gifts from the gods. Otherwise, you might look unworthy in comparison with others who have had similar success.

Being a Subordinate

Ptahhotep's Instruction assumes a sharply hierarchical society and it implies that changes in social status and wealth lie outside the control of normal people, being determined instead by fate, gods or the king. Because superiors exercised great power over their subordinates, and could even inflict death, subordinates had to behave carefully. The Instruction reminds subordinates of their dependency and urges them to behave discreetly and loyally.

7. If you depend on an important person for largess, accept what your superior offers you. Focus on your responsibilities and do not covet a superior's; to annoy a superior tempts fate. Do not offer advice to a superior until asked for it, for you might displease the superior; but answer when a superior asks your advice, for your superior will then welcome it. When superiors are distributing rewards, they can do as they wish. Superiors reward those they favour, and it is fate that determines these decisions. Thus the gods guide your welfare, and only a fool would complain about it.

15. State your business candidly. When your superior asks you to speak, say plainly what you know and do not know. A subordinate who reports fully and impartially will not find it hard to report and will not be asked, 'How do you know such things?' What if a superior does challenge a subordinate's report? The subordinate should remain silent after saying merely, 'I have told all I know.'

26. Do not oppose the actions of important superiors; do not vex the hearts of the burdened. Opposition will rouse their ill-will, whereas support draws their love. Your superiors are your providers, along with the gods, and what they desire should take place. Pacify superiors when they storm in anger. Just as opposition engenders ill-will, support nurtures love.

27. Tell an important superior what is useful; help your superior to win acceptance by other people. This will also benefit you, because your livelihood depends on your superior's success, which clothes your back, and your superior's help protects you. When your superior

receives a promotion, your own desire for rank progresses towards fulfilment, as your superior gives you a helping hand. Thus love will grow stronger among those who love you; it is goodwill that wants to listen.

31. Bow to the one who is over you, your superior who represents the King. In this way, you will preserve your household and earn your pay. Pitiful is one who opposes a superior, for you live only as long as your superior is indulgent. Showing respect does you no harm.

Keeping a Cool Head

Around 1500 BCE, Egyptians began to refer to their king as Pharaoh, and their schools replaced Ptahhotep's Instruction with a similar one composed by Amenemope. Amenemope was Pharaoh's superintendent of cereals, and he addressed his Instruction to his son, explaining that someone who followed its advice would be worthy to serve as an aide to Pharaoh.[6]

Amenemope strongly advocated rational behaviour. He emphasized the desirability of being 'cool-headed' rather than 'hot-headed'. The former seems to denote a composite of considerate, slow to anger, temperate, socially concerned, thoughtful of others and honest, whereas the latter appears to mean a composite of impetuous, quick to anger, rude, selfish, dishonest and treacherous. Amenemope expected gods to punish hot-headed behaviour.

3. Do not quarrel with hot-headed people, or provoke them with words. Act cautiously when dealing with an adversary, and bend to an attacker. Sleep on a response before speaking, for turmoil spreads like fire in hay. Control yourself around hot-headed people, when they appear. If you leave them alone, the gods will answer them.

9. Do not associate with the hot-headed people or consult them. Control your tongue when answering your superiors, and be careful not to malign them. Beware that they may try to entrap you, so be not too free in your replies. Before replying to superiors, discuss the replies with people of your own station, and take care not to speak thoughtlessly. ...

12. Do not covet the property of a superior – do not fill your mouth extravagantly with too much food. If a superior assigns you to manage property, respect the superior's interest, and yours will prosper too. Do not deal with the dishonest people, or associate with disloyal coworkers. If you are sent to transport grain, account for it correctly. People caught in dishonest transactions will never be employed again.

24. Do not listen to the words of your superior indoors and then repeat them outside. To have a clear conscience, do not air your opinions outside the office. A person's conscience is the gods' pointer to right and wrong, so heed it. An aide to an official should be nameless.

The Advantages and Disadvantages of Kingship

Whereas Ptahhotep framed proper actions by superiors in terms of how people would react, another Instruction from before 2000 BCE placed more emphasis on expectations set by gods. Composed around 2150–2050 BCE, this Instruction conveys advice from an unnamed king to his son, Merikare.[7]

Kings saw their worlds quite differently from their subordinates. Merikare's father saw himself as having gods' support: 'The ruler of [our kingdom] is wise. The ruler cannot act stupidly: The ruler receives advice from an entourage; the ruler is wise from birth; and the gods have chosen the ruler over millions of people.' At the same time, he admitted that he needed support from the gods, nobles and populace. He placed emphasis on remaining in control, a complex task that requires balance between contrary needs. He indicated this balance by shifting back and forth between harshness and kindness, idealism and pragmatism, and eliciting support from different constituents.

> Dissatisfied loudmouths make trouble. Suppress them, kill them, erase their names, destroy their kinsfolk, suppress the memory of them and their supporters who love them. Hot-headed rebels incite the citizens and divide the younger people into factions. If you find citizens adhering to them and their movements have grown beyond your control, accuse them publicly and suppress them. ... Bend the multitude to your will and cool its hot heads. Be lenient when you intercede. ... Justify your acts ethically so that people will say that you punish in proportion to the crime. ... A contented citizenry is a ruler's heaven, whereas the curses of the angry are harmful.
>
> Be skilful in speech, that you may prevail. The tongue is a ruler's sword, and speaking is more powerful than fighting. No one can defeat a clever person through physical means. A wise ruler is a school for the nobles, and those who see the ruler's wisdom do not rebel.
>
> Do not be cruel; kindness is good. Build a lasting monument in the citizens' love for you. Benefit the citizens; improve the nation. Then will the citizens praise the gods for your deeds and pray for your health.
>
> Respect the nobles and keep your citizens safe. Strengthen your borders and your patrols in the disputed land beyond the border. It is an investment in the future, because enemies respect the foresighted whereas they attack the trusting. Do not go after your neighbours' lands; one who covets what others possess is a fool. Let your neighbours come to you because of your excellence as a ruler.
>
> Make your nobles very wealthy so that they may carry out your laws. The rich will not be self-serving, for wealthy people do not crave more. The poor, on the other hand, may not speak truly: those who say 'I wish I had' will be unfair, because they give favourable treatment to those who offer bribes.

Cultivate the young people so that the future citizens will love you. Win supporters among those who are going to replenish your towns. Young people happily follow their hearts for 20 years, but then they become the next generation of citizens and raise children themselves. Recognizing that the present comes from the past, I began enlisting the youth's support at my accession. Elevate the young nobles, and promote the young soldiers. Enrich the rising generation of your subordinates: equip them with knowledge, endow them with lands, and reward them with cattle.

Do not favour the children of nobles over those commoners, but choose your aides because of their skills. To be a strong ruler, you will need to have all skills at your disposal. Guard your frontier and staff your fortresses, for troops are useful to their commander.

Yet another Instruction shows the disadvantages of kingship. Although this Instruction describes itself as advice from King Amenemhet (Ammenemes) I to his son King Sesostris I, it was Sesostris who composed it. The Instruction says that, after rebellious nobles murdered Amenemhet in 1965 BCE, Sesostris composed the Instruction 'as an accurate account' of Amenemhet's testimony 'as a god'.[8]

The Instruction restates the mistrust pervading superior–subordinate relationships, the threats arising from political agendas and shifting loyalties. It asserts that proper behaviour and good deeds do not protect a ruler from rebellion by close associates. Self-servingly, Sesostris said nothing about the rebels' motives.

Be on your guard against all subordinates, because you cannot be sure who is plotting against you. Do not be alone with them. Trust no brothers; recognize no friends, make no intimates. Such trust does you no good. Keep your thoughts to yourself, even when you are relaxing. No King has allies when trouble comes.

I gave to the poor. I raised the lowly. I helped the poor and the rich alike. Yet those who ate my food became my opponents. Those I embraced plotted against me. Those who wore my fine linen looked on me as a has-been. Those who put on my perfume undermined me. … They conspired against me without being heard and attacked me without being seen, even though I had adherents throughout the land. They fought me without regard for my good deeds in the past. Good fortune eludes one who overlooks those whom he should watch.

Protests in a Bureaucracy: 'Everything is Going Well, and in Addition…'

The Egyptian bureaucracy had few levels, and even slaves could seek hearings from senior officials in their cities or regions. Civic and regional administrators throughout Egypt sent reports directly to the vizier. These reports show that the bureaucracy was plagued by rampant theft, inefficiency, waste and interpersonal dislike. Thus the reality of Egyptian bureaucracy seems to have violated the high-minded values preached by Ptahhotep and Amenemope. There follow two examples of these reports.[9] Such letters followed a formula in which the reporter first states that all is well, and then adds, almost as an afterthought, that things are not entirely perfect. The first example was written between 1279 and 1212 BCE.

Chief of Police Mininuy communicates to his lord, the Mayor of the Capital and Vizier Khay.
Life, prosperity and health!
This is a letter to inform my lord.
The important locality of Pharaoh that is under my lord's authority is in excellent order, and the guardposts around it are in good shape. We have received the yearly wages, which are in excellent condition, comprising firewood, vegetables, fish and new pottery. I call upon all the gods to keep Pharaoh healthy and to keep my good lord in favour with Pharaoh every day.
In addition, I have been my lord's servant for many years. I ran ahead of Pharaoh's horses, held the reins for him and harnessed them for him. I made various reports to him and he praised me in front of the Council of Thirty. He never found fault in me.
I served as a police officer in Western Thebes, guarding the guardposts of this important locality of Pharaoh. Then I was promoted to a Chief of Police, as a reward for my flawless conduct.
Please note, however, that Chief of Police Nakhtsobeki has been ruining the important locality of Pharaoh in which I work. I am telling my lord of his failings. He has been bullying my police officers in conducting investigations. 'You are an old man and I am young,' he says to me. 'Just keep the locality in order for me. You are a has-been,' he says. He confiscated my fields in the countryside; he took away two fields planted with vegetables, the produce of which belonged to my lord as the Vizier's share. He gave these fields to Chief of Police Monturekh and to the high priest of Montu. He also appropriated grain I had stored in the countryside.
This is a letter to inform my lord.

The second example was written between 1182 and 1151 BCE.

To the fan-bearer on Pharaoh's right, the Mayor of the Capital and Vizier To:
Scribe Neferhotep communicates to his lord.
Life, prosperity and health!
This is a letter to inform my lord.
I call upon many gods to keep Pharaoh healthy and to let him celebrate many jubilees as the ruler of every land, while you continue in his favour every day.
We are working on the nobles' tombs, which my lord commanded us to build. We are working properly and superbly and producing excel-

lent results. Let not my lord worry about the tombs, as we are labour-
ing intensely and not slackening.

In addition, we are exceedingly impoverished. Our supplies – from
the treasury, from the granary and from the storehouse – are all gone.
A load of stone is not light! Indeed, six measures of grain were taken
away and returned to us as six measures of dirt.

Please, my lord, provide us with means to stay alive. We are starving,
and we cannot continue to live if we receive nothing.

China

As in Mesopotamia and Egypt, mass destruction, editing and neglect
erased a great majority of the ancient texts in China. Documents
dating back to 90 BCE blame some of this loss on Confucius, who died
in 478 BCE. According to this legend, Confucius went through the
king's library in the state of Chow, preserved by rewriting documents he regarded as important and discarded the remainder.
However, sources detailing Confucius's life indicate that he never
visited Chow.

Much better documented is a mass destruction in 212 BCE. King
Ch'eng, founding ruler of the Ch'in dynasty, wanted to replace the
old feudal system with a new order, so he tried to erase traditions
that had supported the old ways. He burned nearly all books and
murdered nearly all literate people. Ironically, King Ch'eng ruled for
just three more years after the burning, and his dynasty lasted for
only eight years after his death. Also many documents survived this
destruction, as works were memorized by scholars, hidden in walls
of houses and buried in graves of kings.

Even more losses have occurred since 200 BCE. Of 677 works in the
imperial library of 0 CE, only 152 still exist. If destruction of old texts
was often based on ideological criteria, so was their preservation.
Many scholars rewrote texts and, with them, history. Some scholars
seem to have attributed to their predecessors texts that they themselves wrote.

Most surviving Chinese documents concern kings, presumably because it was kings who maintained libraries and supported scribes.
The documents describe two fundamentally different approaches to
rule: example setting and instrumental control.

Attracting Subordinates by Setting a Good Example

Before 230 BCE, China was not one nation but many feudal states,
with smaller states depending on and subordinate to larger ones.
These political structures aligned with clans, which are quite large

extended families. Typically, one clan controlled each state, although some clans controlled no states. Also cities often operated as independent political units.

One consequence was that larger states sought to acquire smaller affiliates. Of course, warfare was a method of doing so: wars between states and revolts within them created an ever-changing political system. Another method, more talked about in ancient texts, was for a ruler to display virtuous behaviour. For example, the following is some advice that Prime Minister Kaou-yaou gave to King Yu around 2200 BCE.[10]

> Kaou-yaou said, 'If rulers sincerely try to behave virtuously, they will receive intelligent advice and harmonious support.'
> Yu said, 'That sounds right, but explain yourself further.'
> Kaou-yaou replied, 'If rulers attend carefully to their personal improvement, with concern for the long-term, they will be able to show unselfish benevolence and to draw perceptive distinctions among the people in their service. Then all intelligent people will exert themselves to serve the rulers; and through what is near, the rulers will be able to influence what is distant.' Yu acknowledged the wisdom of these admirable words: 'How true!'
> Kaou-yaou counselled, 'Success as a ruler arises from knowing people and keeping people satisfied.'
> Yu sighed, 'Alas, even King Yao found it difficult to attain both of these goals. When rulers know people, the rulers are wise and can assign people to positions that they fit. When rulers keep people satisfied, the rulers are kind and the people cherish them in their hearts. If rulers are both wise and kind, what reason would they have to worry about rebels? what reason to replace bad subordinates? what reason to fear people who have charming words, insinuating styles, and great cunning?'

Some 400 years later, around 1768 to 1765 BCE, T'ang the Successful led a revolution that made him a king. E Yin served as T'ang's prime minister and close advisor. T'ang ruled only 12 years, then two of his sons ruled for a total of seven years. E Yin, who remained extremely powerful, then designated the next king to be T'ang's eldest grandson, T'ae-këa. As the following excerpts show, E Yin thought T'ae-këa needed a lot of guidance.[11]

Around 1750 to 1746 BCE, E Yin offered a sacrifice to the former king [T'ang] and presented the heir to the throne respectfully to his ancestor. ...

> E Yin said, 'Of old, earlier rulers cultivated their virtue earnestly, and so Heaven inflicted no calamities. The spirits of the hills and rivers were all tranquil; and the birds and beasts, the fishes and tortoises, all enjoyed happy environments. But one king failed to follow his ances-

tors' example, with the result that Heaven sent down calamities, employing the services of King T'ang [to overthrow this evil king]. ... Our king T'ang brilliantly displayed his distinguished ability. When, for oppression, he substituted his high-minded gentleness, the millions of the people gave him their hearts.

'Now your Majesty is entering into the estate left by his virtue. Everything depends on how you begin your reign. To generate love, you must love your relations. To generate respect, you must respect your elders. These feelings arise in the clan and state and they consummate in the realm.

'The former king [T'ang] based his actions on careful attention to the bonds that hold people together. He listened to protests and did not seek to suppress them. He recognized the wisdom of bygone people. When occupying the highest position, he displayed intelligence; when occupying a subordinate position, he displayed loyalty. He allowed others to show their good qualities and did not expect them to have every talent. In governing his own behaviour, he was never satisfied.

'It was through these qualities that he came to rule myriad regions. How painstaking was he in these things! He went to great lengths to seek out wise people, whom he expected to be helpful to his descendants and heirs. He defined punishments for wayward officials. ...'

The king would not reflect on these words, or listen to them. On seeing this, E Yin said, 'To develop broad and clear views, the former king meditated in the early morning. He also sought on every side for people of ability and virtue to instruct him and guide his future. Do not frustrate his charge to me and bring on yourself your own overthrow. Be careful to strive for the virtue of self-restraint, and value long-term results. Be like an archer, who looks to see where the arrow is pointing, whether the arrow is aimed properly, and then lets go. Set serious goals for yourself, and follow the ways of your ancestor. If you do so, I will be delighted and be able to show that I have discharged my trust.'

The king was not yet able to change his course. E Yin said to himself, 'This is real unrighteousness, and it is becoming through practice a second nature. I cannot bear to be near such a disobedient fellow. I will build a place in the palace at T'ung, where he can reside quietly near the remains of the former king. This will be a lesson that will keep him from going astray for the rest of his life.' The king went accordingly to the palace at T'ung, and dwelt during the period of mourning.

In the end [having been confined for three years] the king became sincerely virtuous.

Behaving as a Noble Should

One of the most learned people of his time, Confucius had many students during his lifetime and many thousands more afterwards. Sayings by Confucius and his main students were collected in a book titled *The Analects*. The book's origin is murky, as the oldest copies date only to around 2 BCE whereas Confucius lived around 500 BCE. *The Analects* was probably compiled long after Confucius's death by his students and their students, and words that it attributes to Confucius probably reflect his students' esteem for him and their own ideas about what he would have said.

Nearly all biographical statements about Confucius were also written long after he died and they include assertions that contradict better established facts, including claims about his having held exalted positions. Reliable sources indicate that Confucius held minor positions in the state of Lu, including inventory clerk for livestock, and that he earned his living partly by tutoring sons of nobles. Most of Confucius's students aspired to becoming senior officials, and some did so. Confucius himself probably attained his highest rank as Lu's police commissioner around 501 BCE. In that role, he participated in a failed effort to demolish strongholds of three powerful clans. The duke of Lu seems to have held Confucius responsible for this failure because, shortly afterwards, Confucius left Lu unexpectedly, and his stated reasons seem trivial. Over a period of 13 years, Confucius and three students visited the states of Wei, Sung, Ch'en, Ts'ai and Wei again. However, they left Wei quickly after Confucius gave its duke an untactful response; they travelled through Sung in disguise to avoid harm; and they lived in extreme poverty in Ch'en. In 484 BCE, they returned to Lu, where the duke appointed Confucius an official of the lowest rank.

Confucius greatly respected and learned from experiences of ancient rulers and their advisors. His sayings echo ancient teachings about attracting followers by ruling well and leading by setting good examples, although he added his own emphases and sentiments. He extended prescriptions that had been formulated for rulers to all nobles. His teachings focus on nobility, his dominant and never-ending theme being that nobles should behave properly, should follow 'The Way'. We use the phrase 'behave as a noble should' to denote this complex idea. Although Confucius saw The Way as a guide to life in general, not to supervisor–subordinate relations as such, some of his sayings speak to these relations. Indeed, *The Analects* affords the main surviving source about the advice that may have been given to government officials other than rulers.

We offer exemplary passages from *The Analects* on three topics: proper behaviour for nobles, leadership and superior–subordinate relations.[12]

How a noble should behave
2: 3. Confucius said, 'If you guide people with commands and use punishment to keep them in line, they will avoid serving you and

those who do serve you will have no self-respect. If you guide people through proper behaviour and regulate them by behaving as a noble should, they will serve you voluntarily and retain their self-respect.'

13: 13. Confucius said, 'People who are able to manage themselves properly should find no difficulty in filling any administrative position. But if people cannot manage themselves properly, how can they hope to manage others properly?'

17: 6. Tzu-chang asked Confucius about noble behaviour. Confucius said, 'A leader who would practise five principles could induce noble behaviour everywhere.' Tzu-chang asked, 'What are these five principles?' Confucius said, 'Respect, tolerance, truth, diligence and kindness. People respect one who is respectful; the multitude give support to one who is tolerant; people trust one who speaks truthfully; success comes to one who is diligent; people willingly serve one who is kind.'

Leading

13: 6. Confucius said, 'If a leader behaves as a noble should, all goes well even though the leader gives no orders. But if a leader does not behave as a noble should, people will not even obey when the leader gives orders.'

20: 2. Tzu-chang asked Confucius, 'What must one do to be fit to govern the land?' Confucius said, 'A leader should pay attention to five lovely things and avoid four ugly things.' Tzu-chang asked, 'What are these five lovely things?' Confucius said, 'An effective leader can show generosity without falling into extravagance, can assign people work without arousing resentment, can achieve ambitions without acting selfishly, can feel pride without being arrogant, and can inspire awe without displaying ferocity.'

Tzu-chang asked, 'What do you mean by "show generosity without falling into extravagance"?' Confucius said, 'If a leader gives to people only those advantages that are really advantageous to them, is the leader not showing generosity without falling into extravagance? If a leader assigns to people only those tasks that they can perform well, is the official not assigning work without arousing resentment? If a leader aspires to proper behaviour, who can say that the official is selfish? An effective leader, whether dealing with many people or few, with the insignificant or the great, never presumes to slight people. Is not this indeed feeling pride without being arrogant? A properly behaved official wears clothes and hats so elegantly and maintains such a dignified demeanour that people are in awe as soon as they see the official from afar. Is not this inspiring awe without displaying ferocity?'

Tzu-chang asked, 'What are the four ugly things?' Confucius said, 'To put people to death without first having tried to reform them, that is savagery. To demand results without first having given due warning, that is tyranny. To enforce an early deadline having been tardy in ordering work, that is tormenting. And similarly, to be grudging about letting a person have something that one knows they should have, that is acting like a petty functionary.'

Superiors and subordinates

3: 18. Confucius said, 'Were anyone to obey all the established procedures when serving a superior, the subordinate would be thought servile.'

3: 19. Duke Ting asked, 'How should a superior use subordinates and how should subordinates serve their superior?' Confucius replied, 'In employing subordinates, a superior should adhere strictly to established procedures. Subordinates should devote themselves sincerely to their superior's service.'

10: 2. At court, when conversing with junior ministers, Confucius was affable; when conversing with senior ministers, he was respectful and courteous. When the ruler was present, his attitude was constant alertness and solemn readiness.

14: 23. Tzu-lu asked him how to serve a superior. Confucius said, 'Don't oppose covertly. Resist overtly.'

Controlling Subordinates Through Laws, Competition, Rewards and Punishments

Around 350 BCE, the small state of Ch'in began to grow larger and more powerful. At that time, Ch'in's prime minister was Shang Yang, a believer in total control of the populace. Shang Yang's ideas about supervision diverged strikingly from the ancient advice given to kings.[13] For example:

> If a ruler employs virtuous officials, the people will place primary importance on their social relations; but if a ruler employs wicked officials, the people will place primary importance on the statutes. The virtuous respond to others and seek agreement; the wicked spy upon others and argue with them. When the virtuous monitor others' behaviour, they overlook crimes; when the wicked monitor others' behaviour, they punish crimes. In the former case, the people are stronger than the law; in the latter case, the law is stronger than the people. When the people are the stronger, there is lawlessness; when the law is the stronger, the state will be strong. Thus, it is said: 'Governing through good people leads to lawlessness and weakness; governing through wicked people leads to order and strength.'

Shang Yang urged rulers to support laws with rewards, punishments and ideologies.

Historians credit Shang Yang with initiating the totalitarian rule that enabled Ch'in to dominate the entire civilized world (as ancient Chinese viewed the world). Shang Yang himself believed that he had found a formula for total domination and, by 221 BCE, his state had conquered or otherwise seized every state in feudal China. King Ch'eng, who ruled from 246 BCE until 210 BCE, called himself First August Emperor of the Ch'in.

One influence on the First August Emperor was Han Fei Tzu, who admired the works of Shang Yang. The only noble among the renowned Chinese philosophers, Han Fei belonged to the ruling clan in the small and unwealthy state of Han. He was unhappy about his state's ·condition, but felt he could not present his ideas in person because he stuttered so badly. Therefore he frequently sent letters of advice to his king. When the king ignored his letters, Han Fei wrote a book. The king also ignored his book. Although his own king ignored Han Fei's writings, one important ruler did appreciate them – King Ch'eng of Ch'in. When Ch'in attacked Han, the king of Han dispatched Han Fei as a goodwill envoy to Ch'in. However, the suspicious King Ch'eng committed Han Fei to prison, where he committed suicide.

Han Fei wanted to give rulers practical advice about how to strengthen their control and how to remain in power. His ideas differed from traditional ones. He certainly did not intend that his advice should apply to subordinate officials as well as rulers. He never addressed advice to officials, and he told rulers to behave very unlike their subordinates. He saw his contribution as expediting adaptation to changing social values and changing economic conditions: 'People of antiquity strove to be known as moral and virtuous. Those of the middle ages struggled to be known as wise and resourceful. People of today fight for the reputation of being vigorous and powerful …' 'People of old made light of goods, not because they were benevolent, but because goods were abundant. People of today quarrel and pillage, not because they are brutish, but because goods are scarce.'

One of Han Fei's themes was pervasive conflict between superiors and subordinates. He advised rulers to distrust subordinates, to conceal their thoughts and intentions, and to inspire fear in their subordinates.[14]

> It is said: 'A ruler must not reveal desires; for if a ruler reveals desires, the officials put on facades that please the ruler. A ruler must not reveal personal views, because if a ruler does so, the officials show false faces.' Similarly, it is said: 'If a ruler does away with likes and dislikes, the officials show their true feelings. If a ruler shuns wile and cunning, the officials watch their steps. …'
> Rulers stand in danger of being undercut in five ways:
> officials can block their rulers' plans,
> officials can control the wealth and resources of the state,
> officials can issue any orders they please,
> officials can take the credit for doing good deeds, and
> officials can build up cliques.
> If officials can block rulers, the rulers lose the control. If officials can control the wealth and resources, rulers cannot dispense bounty to

others. If officials can issue any orders they please, the rulers lose authority. If officials can take credit for good deeds, the rulers lose the claim to providing benefits. If officials can build up cliques of their own, the rulers lose supporters. Rulers alone should exercise these powers; the powers should never pass into the hands of officials. ...

To control scheming subordinates, rulers should apply rewards and punishments:

Astute rulers control their officials by means of two handles alone. The two handles are punishment and reward. What do I mean by punishment and reward? To inflict mutilation and death on people is to punish; to bestow honour and favour is to reward.

Officials fear punishments and hope for rewards. Hence, if rulers wield the handles of punishment and reward, officials will fear the rulers' sternness and hope to receive the rulers' generosity. However, the evil officials of this age are different. They would take the handle of punishment from their rulers so they can inflict punishments on people they hate, and they would take the handle of reward from their rulers so they can bestow rewards on people they like. If rulers do not reserve to themselves the power to dispense rewards and punishments and instead allow officials to hand these out, then the people fear the officials while holding the rulers in contempt, and they attend to the officials and turn away from the rulers. This is the calamity that results when rulers yield control of punishments and rewards. ...

Yet another contributor to Ch'in's rise was Li Ssu, who became its prime minister some time between 219 BCE and 213 BCE and who was as ruthless as his emperor. On Li Ssu's advice, the First August Emperor abolished the feudal nobility, replaced the feudal states with administrative districts, burned almost all books, standardized weights and measures and writing, built better roads, relocated masses of people and began building the Great Wall.

Li Ssu had no use for rewards and his approach to punishment made Han Fei's seem gentle. Whereas Han Fei said, 'astute rulers never use wise officials or virtuous people for selfish purposes', Li Ssu told his emperor to use his power for personal enjoyment:[15]

Astute rulers should be able to fulfil their duties and use the technique of punishment. Under threat of punishment, officials have to exert their abilities in utmost devotion to their rulers. When rulers define their statuses relative to officials unmistakably, and they make clear the duties of subordinates to superiors, then no one in their empires, whether worthy or unworthy, will dare do otherwise than exert their strength and fulfil their duties in devotion to their rulers. Thus rulers can control their empires single-handedly and cannot be controlled by anyone. As a result, rulers can enjoy themselves to the utmost. How can talented and astute rulers afford not to pay attention to this point? ...

When rulers use punishment effectively, they have no corrupt officials. When rulers have no corrupt officials, their empires are peaceful. When their empires are peaceful, the rulers are venerated and exalted. When rulers are venerated and exalted, they are using punishment without fail. When rulers use punishment without fail, they obtain what they seek. When they obtain what they seek, their states are wealthy. When their states are wealthy, the rulers enjoy abundant pleasures. Therefore, when rulers apply the skill of punishment, they get everything they desire. The officials and the people are so busy trying to correct their faults that they have no time to devise trouble.

Struggling with Inconsistencies

Even the most ancient documents show awareness of difficult relations between superiors and subordinates. Superiors distrust their subordinates and subordinates distrust their superiors, yet each has to depend on the other. One result has been ambivalence. Mesopotamians, for instance, viewed leadership as essential to effective work and leadership skills as distinctive to particular people, but they also joked that rulers are unable to support themselves. The Egyptian Instruction of Merikare oscillates between harshness and kindness, between idealism and pragmatism. Chinese writer Han Fei advised rulers not to trust their subordinates and yet to rely on them to solve problems.

Managers who rise to high positions need to recognize that their subordinates are almost certain to complain and make jokes about their actions and decisions. Fault finding and ridicule are pervasive responses to control by someone else. It is clear that subordinates do not always appreciate their superiors' contributions to organizations and societies. Even when subordinates do acknowledge their superiors' contributions, they also see deficiencies.

Quite a few writers sought to lessen abrasions between superiors and subordinates. They urged superiors to restrain their exercise of power, to focus on behaving properly themselves, to be just and considerate, and to cultivate support of the populace over the long run. They urged subordinates to accept subordination, to demonstrate respect, to act honestly and forthrightly, and to pursue their superiors' best interests rather than their own. On the other hand, other writers advised superiors to be wary of their subordinates, to deal harshly with dissenters and rebels, to pit subordinates against one another, and to manipulate subordinates by means of rewards and punishments. Tales of violent insurrection show that subordinates did not always accept control from above. Although it may have been King Ch'eng's harsh methods that enabled him to unite China, his empire survived him for only four years.

Superiors' control of armed force enabled them to seize property, to alter people's statuses and even to inflict death, so their subjects had reason to fear them and to avoid actions that might arouse their displeasure. Mesopotamians enlisted gods to help them protest a ruler's actions. Egyptian schoolboys were taught to be submissive, circumspect and wary. Although low-level personnel could appeal directly to Egypt's vizier, they did so in a stylized fashion that portrayed their complaints as afterthoughts. Confucius urged subordinates to devote themselves to their superiors. One ancient Chinese legend explains that a powerful prime minister confined his young king in an isolated palace for three years, until 'the king became sincerely virtuous' and followed the prime minister's advice.

Superiors' powers generally increased with their hierarchical positions, but so did the political pressures with which they had to contend. Almost all the documents written by rulers talk about the need for political support from the populace at large and especially from nobles. Many documents also say that rulers need the support of gods. For instance, Prime Minister Kaou-yaou told his king: 'Heaven hears and sees as our people hear and see. Heaven discerningly judges our actions and displays its terrors, as our people discerningly judge our actions and can awe us: such strong connections there are between Heaven and earth! How careful ought to be the rulers of the earth!'

Since differing political interests may make contrary claims, remaining in control required an ability to make the inconsistent less so. The Egyptians and Chinese used schooling to inculcate shared values and acceptance of existing social hierarchies. Such schooling focused on the sons of nobles. However, the Chinese records do contain examples of superiors seeking out unusually able commoners and promoting them to high positions. Indeed, one of the oldest Chinese stories tells how King Yao sought out 'one of the lowly and insignificant who deserves to rise higher' and ultimately made this man his successor.

The roles of superiors and subordinates are complex ones. It is often unclear what actions one should take, what words one should say, what emotions one should feel. All strategies for control entail advantages and disadvantages, as do all strategies for subordination. Clearly, ancient people saw these trade-offs and recognized their complexity. A good example is Confucius's attempt to state the essence of successful leadership. He told leaders to try to see issues from their subordinates' viewpoints and to beware of traps created by power:

13: 15. Duke Ting asked, 'Is there a single phrase that summarizes what makes a ruler succeed?' Confucius replied, 'No single phrase could ever do that. But there is a phrase that comes near to it. It is the saying: "It is hard to be a ruler and not easy to be a subject either." If a ruler really understands the difficulties of rule, would not this understanding be almost enough to produce success?'

Duke Ting asked, 'Is there a single phrase that summarizes what makes a ruler fail?' Confucius replied, 'No single phrase could ever do that. But there is a phrase that comes near to it. It is the saying: "The greatest pleasure in being a ruler is that one can say whatever one chooses and no one dares to disagree." If what a ruler says is good, it is of course all right that the ruler should be obeyed. But if what a ruler says is bad, would not obedience be almost to enough to produce failure?'

Notes

1   Our rendition of Atrahasis's story is based on translations by Ferry (1992), Foster (1993), Gardner and Maier (1984), Heidel (1970), Kovacs (1985), Lambert and Millard (1969), Leonard (1934) and Tigay (1982).) Because translations of ancient works differ, the quotations in this chapter are the authors' own interpretations compiled from several translations. These interpretations rely more strongly on translations with better scholarly documentation, and they use terminology of the late twentieth century.

2   Analysts may produce quite different estimates of the dates of ancient documents. Thus most dates are approximate and some are very inexact. 253 BCE might mean 'between 265 and 240 BCE ' or 'between 300 and 200 BCE'.

3   These interpretations of sayings integrate translations by Foster (1993), Gordon (1968) and Lambert (1960).

4   This interpretation of the protest relies on translations by Foster (1993) and Lambert (1960).

5   These excerpts from Ptahhotep's Instruction are based on translations by Erman and Blackman (1927), Faulkner *et al.* (1972), Foster (1992) and Lichtheim (1973). The numbers preceding paragraphs indicate their positions in the Instruction.

6   These excerpts from the Instruction of Amenemope are based on translations made by Faulkner *et al.* (1972) and Griffith (1926). The numbers preceding paragraphs indicate their positions in the Instruction.

7   These excerpts from the Instruction of Merikare are based on translations made by Erman and Blackman (1927), Faulkner *et al.* (1972), Foster (1992) and Lichtheim (1973).

8   These excerpts from the Instruction of Amenemhet derive from translations made by Breasted (1962), Erman and Blackman (1927), Faulkner *et al.* (1972), Foster (1992) and Lichtheim (1973).

9   These letters interpret translations by Wente (1990).

10   This version of Kaou-yaou's advice interprets a translation by Legge (1865).

11   This interpretation of E Yin's advice builds upon translations by Legge (1865) and Wu (1928).

12   These interpretations of *The Analects* integrate translations by Chan (1963), Lau (1979), Pound (1951) and Waley (1938). The numbers preceding paragraphs designate their positions in *The Analects*.

13 This rendition of Shang Yang's writings is based on Duyvendak's (1928) translation.
14 This version of Han Fei's writings is based on translations by Liao (1959), Peerenboom (1993) and Watson (1963).
15 This interpretation of Li Ssu's writings is based on a translation by de Bary *et al.* (1960).

References

Breasted, J.H. (1962), *Ancient Records of Egypt*. New York: Russell & Russell.
Chan, W.-T. (1963), *Source Book in Chinese Philosophy*, Princeton, NJ: Princeton University Press.
de Bary, W.T., Chan, W.-T. and Watson, B. (1960), *Sources of Chinese Tradition*. New York: Columbia University Press.
Duyvendak, J.J.L. (1928), *The Book of the Lord Shang*, London: Arthur Probsthain.
Erman, A. and Blackman, A.M. (1927), *The Literature of the Ancient Egyptians*, New York: E.P. Dutton.
Faulkner, R.O., Wente, E.F., Jr. and Simpson, W.K. (1972), *The Literature of Ancient Egypt*, New Haven, Conn.: Yale University Press.
Ferry, D. (1992), *Gilgamesh: A New Rendering in English Verse*, New York: Farrar, Straus and Giroux.
Foster, B.R. (1993), *Before the Muses: An Anthology of Akkadian Literature*, Bethesda, MD: CDL Press.
Foster, J.L. (1992), *Echoes of Egyptian Voices*, Norman, OK: University of Oklahoma Press.
Gardner, J. and Maier, J. (1984), *Gilgamesh*, New York: Knopf.
George, C.S. Jr. (1968), *The History of Management Thought*, Englewood Cliffs, NJ: Prentice-Hall.
Gordon, E.I. (1968), *Sumerian Proverbs: Glimpses of Everyday Life in Ancient Mesopotamia*, New York: Greenwood Press.
Griffith, F.L. (1926), *Journal of Egyptian Archaeology*, **12**, 191–231.
Heidel, A. (1970), *The Gilgamesh Epic and Old Testament Parallels*, 2nd edn, Chicago: University of Chicago Press.
Kovacs, M.G. (1985), *The Epic of Gilgamesh*, Stanford, CA: Stanford University Press.
Lambert, W.G. (1960), *Babylonian Wisdom Literature*, Oxford: Oxford University Press.
Lambert, W.G. and Millard, A.R. (1969), *Atrahasis: The Babylonian Story of the Flood*, Oxford: Clarendon Press.
Lau, D.C. (1979), *Confucius: The Analects*, Harmondsworth: Penguin.
Legge, J. (1865), *The Chinese Classics*, Oxford: Oxford University Press.
Leonard, W.E. (1934), *Gilgamesh: Epic of Old Babylonia*, New York: Viking Press.
Liao, W.K. (1959), *The Complete Works of Han Fei Tzu*, London: Arthur Probsthain.
Lichtheim, M. (1973), *Ancient Egyptian Literature: A Book of Readings*, Berkeley: University of California Press.
Peerenboom, P. (1993), *Law and Morality in Ancient China: The Silk Manuscripts of Huang-Lao*, Albany, NY: State University of New York Press.
Pound, E. (1951), *Confucius*, New York: New Directions.
Tigay, J.H. (1982), *The Evolution of the Gilgamesh Epic*, Philadelphia: University of Pennsylvania Press.
Waley, A. (1938), *The Analects of Confucius*, London: George Allen & Unwin.
Watson, B. (1963), *Basic Writings of Mo Tzu, Hsün Tzu, and Han Fei Tzu*, New York: Columbia University Press.
Wente, E.F. (1990), *Letters from Ancient Egypt*, Atlanta: Schools Press.

Wu, K.-C. (1928), *Ancient Chinese Political Theories*, Shanghai: The Commercial Press.

19 From a Universalist to a Polycentric Approach in Organizational Research

TIMOTHY CLARK, *King's College, University of London* and **DAGMAR EBSTER-GROSZ**, and **GEOFF MALLORY**, *Open University Business School*

Introduction

Derek Pugh's last academic appointment before he retired in September 1995 was as Professor of International Management at the Open University Business School. During this time he established and was actively involved in conducting two cross-national research projects, the International Organization Observatory (IOO) and the Anglo-German comparative management study. With this in mind, this chapter has two purposes. The first is to suggest that Derek's career has been characterized by a methodological journey which began by conducting universalist studies (that is, the idea that concepts, theories and models are appropriate and relevant regardless of industry sector or national culture) but which ended with a more polycentric approach to organizational analysis (that is, studies which seek to understand a phenomenon from multiple cultural perspectives). The second and related aim is to suggest that the methodological approach adopted in Derek's more recent work represents a more fruitful approach to comparing organizations across nations.

The focus of this chapter is particularly relevant to current trends in management and OB research. In the last decade there has been an upsurge of interest in cross-national organizational comparative research. As Andrew Pettigrew writes in Chapter 16 of this book, the

337

design of research projects and the composition of research teams are increasingly becoming international. A number of factors are responsible for this trend. First, making cross-national comparisons appears to be a fundamental impulse within mankind. As Lammers and Hickson (1979a, p. 3) note, it is therefore 'not only a sport of scholars; it is also regularly indulged in by the ordinary citizen'. For example, as tourists we make comparisons between the country we are visiting and our home country when we buy currency, order a meal in a restaurant, stay in a hotel, buy a stamp, post a letter and so on. Many of these comparisons are organizational in nature, in that we might note the preponderance of fast-food chains in particular countries, differences in staffing arrangements on the railway system, levels of service in hotels and restaurants and so on. As more of us take our holidays abroad, so an increasing number of people are engaging in 'comparative study' (that is, detecting similarities and/or dissimilarities between nations).

Second, management research becomes more international as management itself becomes increasingly international. Within the last decade there have been many far-reaching changes in the environment of most organizations, whether they be in the private or public sector, not for profit organizations (NFPs), or non-governmental organizations (NGOs). These developments include the maturation of the European Union and the creation of the single European market, the implementation of the North American Free Trade Agreement, the collapse of the former Eastern bloc and the gradual opening up of these markets. In addition, developments in communications technology have brought people close together and the notion of a 'global village' a step further. One consequence of this is that many more people within organizations, and not just the most senior managers, are having to work with people from other nations, with the consequence that they are having to make sense of attitudes and actions which appear strange and unusual within their own cultural frame of reference. Previously, these concerns were limited mainly to expatriate managers and those people who worked for NGOs such as the United Nations, UNICEF, NATO and the International Labour Office in international centres such as New York, Geneva or Brussels. Indeed, much early comparative management research work was directed towards the problems and concerns of those managers who were on secondment or posted to foreign countries.

A related trend has been the increasing importance of international firms to international trade. Dicken (1992) argues that transnational corporations (TNCs) are the most important force in the modern world economy. For example, it is estimated that between one-fifth and one-quarter of total world production in the world's market economies is performed by transnationals, dominated by a core group of 600 such firms. Among these, just 74 firms account for half of all sales, or 10 per cent of total world production.

Finally, management research is occurring within a climate, particularly in the UK and Europe, in which funding bodies are tending to support cross-national research at the expense of intranational research. As national funds supporting research become smaller and competition for these funds increases, researchers are increasingly turning to supranational bodies such as the European Union for funding. Projects funded by such organizations must usually involve partners from more than one country.

To achieve the aims set out above, the chapter is divided into two parts. The first section considers the methodological underpinnings of the organizational studies with which Derek has been involved over the past 30 years. Four projects are considered: the Aston Studies, the cross-national replications of the Aston Studies, the International Organization Observatory and the Anglo-German comparative management study. The second part of the chapter outlines a systemic approach to cross-national comparison. Such an approach emerged from the two projects that Derek directed while at the Open University Business School.

A Methodological Journey

When examining the methodological underpinnings of the organizational studies with which Derek has been involved over the past 30 years, it is possible to discern a shift in approach. This can be portrayed as follows.

1   The initial Aston Studies were essentially a series of single culture studies in that they were originally designed and conducted in Britain on a variety of British organizations by British researchers. Nevertheless, a key objective was to produce instruments and measures which could be used to compare organization structure–context relations in *any* context (that is, regardless of industry or cultural setting). They were therefore universalist in approach.
2   The cross-national extensions of the Aston Studies were also based upon universalist assumptions, in that the original Aston instrument and measures were replicated in a whole host of nations.
3   The International Organization Observatory (IOO) was a cross-national research project based in seven European business schools. This project combined a universalist approach with a polycentric approach.
4   The Anglo-German comparative management study sought to identify how Anglo-German business collaboration could be en-

hanced by focusing on the differences in values and patterns of behaviour in the different national environments. It therefore adopted a polycentric approach.

We now turn to consider each of these projects in a little more detail.

The Aston Studies

Derek Pugh established his long and distinguished academic career as the leading member of the Aston Group (1961–8). The Aston theory which was developed by the group focused on the relationship between measures of organization structure and context. At the time, studying the effects of formal structures was the 'state of the art' in social science, (for example, Chandler, 1962). So the work of the group contributed to the academic demand of its times. The emphasis on the formal aspects of organizations is reflected in the definition of organizational theory put forward by Pugh (1966, p. 235) as 'the study of the structure and functioning of organizations and behaviour of groups and individuals within them'.

The Aston theory provided a rigorous and standardized framework for comparing aspects of organizational structure in different environments. While it has attracted criticism (for example, Aldrich, 1972; Starbuck, 1981; Hage, 1996) its framework was nevertheless used as a 'universal' tool for such research by a number of different researchers around the globe. The Aston theory developed in a climate that supported universalist research and knowledge.

A large majority of studies of organizations of the period took place in Anglo-Saxon countries and adopted the values and methodologies of that culture. Thus most studies, including that of Aston since it was a study of 46 organizations in Birmingham, bore signs of what today may be called Anglo-Saxon parochialism or ethnocentrism. At the time, cross-cultural differences within Europe and the North American countries were not generally accounted for. Talking of a multicultural focus then may well have been understood as a study of the cultures of some remote African tribes. At that time, anthropology was seen to have little relevance to organization studies.

Cross-national Replications of the Aston Studies

The contribution of Aston to the furthering of knowledge on organizations is reflected in the number of replications and adaptations of the methodology by researchers around the globe. Currently the ESRC Data Archive at Essex University holds data from 24 studies which have used the Aston methods and/or instrument. In Chapter

3 of this book, Lex Donaldson identifies 40 such studies (see Table 3.1).

During the 1970s, the Aston Studies gradually became more international as original members of the research team as well as researchers in other countries began to use the Aston measures as a basis for investigating organizational structure in a whole host of countries. These studies have examined organization in countries as diverse as Brazil, Britain, Egypt, Finland, Hong Kong, India, Japan, Jordan and Sweden. All of them replicate the methodology and measures of the Aston Group (see Pugh and Hickson, 1976; Hickson and McMillan, 1981a). Cross-national extensions of the original Aston Studies have been conducted in a diverse range of nations, with the consequence that the relationship between the Aston structure–context measures has been studied in each of the cultural clusters identified by Ronen and Shenkar (1985) which have been elaborated in Hickson and Pugh (1995). Researchers in different countries often set about replicating the Aston Studies on the basis of published material. In some cases, the first time that the Aston Group were aware of a study was when they read the published results. Therefore this group of studies was 'not developed as a single co-ordinated research effort' (Hickson and McMillan, 1981b, p. 187) but rather emerged haphazardly. Nevertheless, they share a common focus in that they are invariably concerned with examining the question first posed by Hickson *et al.* (1974, p. 66): 'Are societal differences overwhelming or are there stable relationships between such contextual factors and structures of work organizations, relationships which hold whatever the society in which the organization is situated?'

Hickson and his colleagues (1974, pp. 63–4) sought to test the universalist 'bold' hypothesis:

Relationships between the structural characteristics of work organizations and variables of organizational context will be stable across societies … This hypothesis implicitly rests on the theory that there are imperatives, or 'causal' relationships, from the resources of 'customers', of employees, of materials and finance, etc., and of operating technology of an organization, to its structure, which take effect whatever the surrounding societal differences.

This means that, 'whether the culture is Asian or European or North American, a large organization with many employees improves efficiency by specialising their activities but also by increasing controlling and co-ordinating specialities' (Hickson *et al.*, 1974, p. 64). From a comparison of 21 American, 25 British and 24 Canadian manufacturing organizations, Hickson *et al.* (1974) claim to find support for their argument. Subsequently, Hickson *et al.* (1979) studied the relationship between the Aston structure–context variables in six countries: America, Britain, Canada, Germany, Japan and Sweden. In this study the contextual variable of autonomy was not included. The results from this study broadly reaffirmed the previous findings, in that consistent relationships were found between structure–context variables across nations. These results can be summarized as follows:

Structure	Context
1. Formalization: positive with	size of organization size of parent organization dependence on parent organization (usually)
2. Specialization: positive with	size of organization size of parent organization
3. Centralization: positive with	dependence but sometimes negative with size of organization

Donaldson (1986) conducted the first meta-analytic review of the cross-national extensions of the Aston Studies. He found that the positive relationship between size and functional specialization does not vary significantly according to global location or organizational type (that is, manufacturing or service). The relationship between size and standardization was similarly unaffected by global location, whereas it does vary across the manufacturing/service distinction. The relationship between size and formalization was unaffected by global location but varied significantly according to organization type. Finally, the negative relationship between size and centralization was not influenced by organizational type but did vary according to global location, although not enough to alter the direction of the relationship. In summary, Donaldson (1986) argues that, 'while the idea of moderator variables is supported ... these are relatively weak in their effects. They make a positive association less positive and a negative association less negative.' His meta-analytic review reveals the effects of moderator variables as being limited. Essentially, he agrees with Lammers and Hickson (1979b, p. 405) that there is a 'modification of strength', not a 'modification of association'. He concludes by suggesting that his study is only a preliminary one, with the consequence that the findings should be 'viewed as tentative and subject to qualification. They are offered only as an initial exploration of the issue' (Donaldson, 1986, p. 91).

Miller (1987) conducted a meta-analytic review of 27 extensions of the Aston studies (nine intranational and 18 international) which supports the main thrust of Donaldson's conclusions. These 27 studies provided a total sample of 1066 organizations from 11 countries. This meta-analytic review has several characteristics in common with the one conducted by Donaldson. First, it focused exclusively on the relationship between size and organization structure, thereby excluding other contextual variables such as size of parent organization, dependence and so on. Second, Miller also examined the effect of two moderator variables on structure–size relationships. The total sample was divided into two subsets reflecting differences in organizational type and country. In the first subset, the studies were classified into those conducted on (1) manufacturing or (2) other types of organization. In the second subset, the studies were classified into those conducted within (1) Anglo-Saxon (Britain, Canada, USA) or (2) other countries. Miller reports that the correlations between organization size and both specialization and formalization were high, positive and significant. As in Donaldson's (1986) study, neither type of organization nor type of country substantially affected these relationships. The relationship between organization size and centralization was not significantly different from zero. Furthermore, neither type of organization nor type of country substantially affected this result.

While the theory suggested that organizational structure–context relationships are likely to be stable across nations and the empirical results gave support to this, the existence of cultural differences was not ignored. It was acknowledged as being part of the environmental contingencies. The awareness of these differences may be seen as a sign of the group's openness to exploring them later.

In terms of the classification outlined at the beginning of this chapter, the initial Aston Studies began as single culture studies, in that they were originally designed and conducted in Britain on a variety of British organizations by British researchers. The cross-cultural extensions pursued an essentially ethnocentric research approach. This occurs when research studies designed and conducted in one culture, by researchers who are members of that culture, are replicated in other cultures. Underpinning ethnocentric studies is a universalist approach, in that instruments and measures developed in one culture are believed to be equally appropriate and applicable in other cultures. As Hickson *et al.* (1979, p. 36) put it: 'Data were collected on standard schedules in structured interviews with chief executives and such other senior managers as were necessary to complete the information. Confirmatory documents etc. were inspected. With this kind of data, no material variations of idiom were required when translating from the original.'

As with all universalist studies, the central aim is replication. The main methodological goal is standardization. As far as is possible, all aspects of the research design and its implementation (with the exception of language) are kept identical across nations. As Hickson and McMillan (1981b, pp. 189–90) write:

> the Aston programme has held to standard data, rather than attempt to define equivalence into different data representing the same concepts. For example, informants in all countries are asked about the same set of specialisms defined in the same way, rather than attempts being made to discover whether the concept of specialization differs in a particular country and to construct a particular measure appropriately.

The aim of the universal standardization described above is at the core of the cross-cultural limitations of the Aston instrument, as a number of the criticisms from both within and outside the group have pointed out (Child, 1981, pp. 312–16; Clark and Mallory, 1992). However, it is debatable whether Hickson and his colleagues could ever account for these variations satisfactorily, since this group of studies have a common origin – the Aston instrument – which was not designed to focus on cultural effects. Maurice (1976, p. 7) has written of 'the implicit perspective of those who support the culture-free thesis and who, in the process of testing for national differences, use concepts and measurements that can only remove all societal or cultural dimensions from organizations and their structures'. In other words, their instrument, like their thesis, is culture-free.

In collecting the same data identically across nations, the Aston cross-national studies set as an ideal the development of 'world measures', that is variables and instruments which would be applicable in all societies since they take account of the full range of variation between societies (Hickson *et al.*, 1979, pp. 27–8). But the extensions have shown that universal world measures of organizational functioning are not obtained by direct translations. Instead, the cultural equivalence of variables needs to be considered. This issue came to the fore in the programme of cross-national research conducted by the network of European business schools which formed the International Organization Observatory group. The IOO study was designed as a study of formal organizations across different cultures. It highlighted the need for a cross-culturally more sensitive approach to defining and operationalizing concepts (such as human resource management) in order to make cross-cultural data comparable.

The International Organization Observatory (IOO)

The IOO is a network of organization researchers based in seven European business schools.[1] The group was inaugurated by Vincenzo Perrone of CRORA at Bocconi University in Milan. Derek established a research team at the Open University Business School in order to conduct the UK part of the research programme. This comprised Derek as project director and two research fellows, Timothy Clark and Geoff Mallory.

The common purpose of this international team is to conduct research which will help in understanding the management implications occasioned by the development of the single European market (SEM). If organizations throughout Europe are to be successful and operate effectively in this new, and rapidly changing, environment they will require a better understanding of, and sensitivity to, the impact of different national settings on the management task. As organizations increasingly develop their international activities in response to the creation of the SEM, they will need to distinguish between those management activities and practices which can be successfully transferred across national boundaries and those which will require modification in view of the divergence between national (that is, cultural and institutional) settings. This can be determined by initially identifying those features of managing organizations which remain constant across national boundaries and those which are divergent and then ascertaining the strength of the forces for convergence or divergence. Initial results from the study are reported in Pugh *et al.* (1995, 1996), Clark and Mallory (1997).

The Italian group had previously collected data from 115 Italian organizations on such characteristics as organization structure, strategy, Human Resource (HR) systems, technology, information technology (IT) investment, R&D activity and so on. The intention was for the other countries to follow suit with a variety of methods and sample sizes but with an identical instrument (except for language) and common sampling frame. Therefore, as with the Aston Studies which preceded it, the IOO began as a universalist project with each national group committed to using the identical instrument in translation. However, during the discussions which took place at the regular meetings of the research team it became apparent that the common language that we use as management teachers and researchers occasionally hides significant differences in meaning. This is important since the way one seeks to operationalize a concept will depend upon the meaning attached to it. This is very apparent when we examine the concept of human resource management (HRM). In a whole host of countries there has been a change in the vocabulary of academics and practitioners with regard to the nature of the employment relationship. Previously popular terms such as 'personnel management', 'personnel administration' and 'industrial relations' have gradually been challenged or replaced by the term 'human resource management', but what does it mean? Although it has been the subject of considerable academic scrutiny, a detailed examination of the Anglo-American literature would show that the precise meaning of the term 'HRM' remains unclear and the subject of considerable controversy (Storey, 1992; Mabey and Salaman, 1995). It has become one of those terms that defy a single all-purpose definition and as a consequence have potentially as many meanings as there are people using them. If the American and British commentators who originated the concept are uncertain as to the meaning of HRM, what does it mean to the Dutch, French or Germans? This is a particularly important question to answer if one is attempting to investigate the incidence and emergence of the concept of HRM in seven countries. What one investigates will depend upon one's conception of HRM and, as a number of writers have suggested, management models and theories developed in one country may not be universally appropriate. These writers suggest that the relevance and validity of a theory are limited by national boundaries (see Azumi, 1974; Hofstede, 1980a, 1993; Laurent, 1983, 1986). For example, Hofstede (1993) argues that 'management scientists, theorists and writers are human too: they grew up in a particular society in a particular period, and their ideas cannot but reflect the constraints of their environment' (p. 82).

In response to this, the research team as an addition did develop a more polycentric approach, rather than seeking to import the conception of HRM contained within the common instrument (which was originally devised and designed by the Italian group) into each country, it sought to determine the extent to which there are 'special understandings' of HRM in different nations. By examining whether HRM is uniquely understood and practised in each nation, the group could then determine whether these differences are centred around a number of common elements which transcend national boundaries, or whether there are divergent understandings of HRM which cannot be integrated into a single truly 'universal' model. In other words, it could determine what was comparable and what was not. In doing this the research team sought to create 'world measures' for measuring the incidence of HRM in different countries by taking account of the full range of variation in meaning across nations. Thus the IOO did not attempt to answer the question 'To what extent are one country's models and notions of HRM present in other nations?' for this is a universalist research approach. Rather, in recognizing that concepts and theories may differ between nations, it sought to examine what people in different nations understand as HRM. This is a polycentric research approach (Clark, 1996).

This research approach contrasts with a universalist one. Those researchers who adopt the latter approach tend to develop their instrument within a single national/cultural context. Since the main methodological goal of this type of research study is standardization, the instrument is subsequently replicated (with the exception of language) in different countries. No account is taken of local variations in meaning and understandings since ideas, concepts, theories and so on are believed to transcend national boundaries. In contrast, the IOO adopted the following approach, which is similar to that first suggested by Berry (1969, p. 125).

1   Descriptions of a concept from within each participating nation are generated.
2   Similarities and differences are noted.
3   Shared categories are then used to build up new, more complete, categories which are valid and appropriate in each nation. These become a derived etic or 'world measure'.
4   The derived etic is then used as the basis for developing measurements and instruments.

In adopting such an approach, the IOO moved from a universalist approach to a polycentric approach and in so doing sought to locate not only organizations but also the concepts and measurements used by researchers within their national settings.

The Anglo-German comparative Management Study

The Anglo-German comparative study was a parallel development of the IOO in collaboration with the German members of the network. The aim of the study was to analyse the major British and German business strengths and to identify how Anglo-German business collaboration can be developed effectively. It was designed as a co-operative venture between the Open University Business School and the Lehrstuhl für Betriebswirtchaftslehre der Universität des Saarlandes. Derek directed the British study, with Dagmar Ebster-Grosz as the research fellow. In Germany, the research team comprised Christian Scholz and Marco Schröter. The British and German teams made their data available to each other, but made their analyses independently (Ebster-Grosz and Pugh, 1996; Scholz, 1993; Schröter, 1994).

   It was a different study from the IOO both in topic focus and methodology. It was designed from the beginning by a cross-cultural group of researchers in Britain and Germany, most of whom had a multicultural background. The focus topic of identifying cross-cultural differences in managerial behaviour and improving cross-national business collaboration allowed a much less structured exploratory study of the relevant differences. Such an approach resulted in two innovations in the study of cross-cultural organizational behaviour. The first stems from the fact that a much larger sample across a range of industries was investigated, compared to other interpretative studies. The chief executive or other senior manager of 99 firms in both countries participated in a wide-ranging interview. Thus both the difficulties of generalizing from a small number of data, which characterizes the interviewing approach of the interpretative type of study, and the rigidity of the quantitative, usually questionnaire-based approach were considerably reduced.

The second innovative aspect stems from the fact that interviewees were not asked to talk about themselves, but to focus on their work relationship with their British and German partners. So the statements which the interviewees gave about themselves were given indirectly, and usually in support of statements about parent company differences. This lessens the pressure on the interviewees to give 'organizationally appropriate' statements, which highlight the positive aspects of their work environment, and to play down the negative ones.

This study has shown that the bulk of cross-national differences in organizational functioning lies in differences in the patterns of behaviour of German and British employees. The behavioural differences were found to stem from differences in cultural values. In contrast, cross-national differences in formal organizational structures were found to be small. The study therefore confirms the conclusions of several wide-ranging reviews of the cross-cultural literature that, whilst there is a trend towards a convergence of organizational structures across British and German firms, differences in the patterns of managerial behaviour remain divergent (see Child, 1981; Adler *et al.*, 1986).

A distinctive feature of this study is that it conducted a systemic analysis of the specific environmental factors (such as social, political, economic and legal institutions) and cultural factors which influence managerial decision making and behaviour in firms in each country. This approach therefore developed the suggestions of previous commentators (for example, Porter, 1990; Whitley, 1992) who highlighted the relevance of environmental factors and the national institutional framework to business performance as well as encompassing the influence of national culture (Hofstede, 1980b; Trompenaars, 1993).

For example, in the study, short-term management (UK) versus long-term management (Germany) and the legitimacy of growth through takeovers (UK) versus organic growth (Germany) were found to be important factors influencing managerial thinking and behaviour. Similarly, the British emphasis on managerial flexibility in market

strategy compared with the German emphasis on managerial efficiency in production and sales led to different managerial responses
to the market, and therefore to different competitive strengths and
weaknesses. As a further example, the study confirmed that the differences between British and German education have an important
managerial impact. In Britain education is independent of industry
and management education is detached from technical training. This
leads to an emphasis on financial results. In contrast, in Germany
education is vocational in overall character, and management education is closely linked to technical education. This results in an emphasis
on product quality and manufacturing efficiency. The findings of the
study enabled the development of a general model to distinguish
between the impact of environmental factors and managerial activities on business performance (see Ebster-Grosz and Pugh, 1996).

The Need for a Systemic Approach in Cross-cultural Studies of Organizations

The main purpose of comparing organizations across nations is to
determine the extent to which, and in what ways, organizations are
similar or different (Lammers and Hickson, 1979a). Child (1981, p.
305) has suggested that this basic purpose can be expressed in terms
of three objectives: first, to determine the extent to which organizational features vary across nations; second, to ascertain the features
of the national setting which account for these variations, or for lack
of variation; third, where national differences are discovered, to offer
an explanation for the process by which organizations become in-
fused with national distinctiveness.

Numerous commentators have noted that cross-national organizational studies have generally fallen short of attaining these objectives
(for example, Roberts and Boyacigiller, 1984; Adler *et al.*, 1986;
Redding, 1994). In the main, progress has been limited to achieving
the first objective. Therefore, while the majority of studies which
compare organizations across nations have tended to note the way in
which they are different or similar, they have failed to offer an explanation for these findings (the second objective). One way of
progressing to the second objective might be to adopt a systemic
approach to the study of cross-national organizational differences.
Such an approach emanates from the IOO and Anglo-German comparative management study. By this we mean an approach to
comparing organizations across nations which seeks to examine them
in the context of their national setting. This approach seeks to incorporate features of the national setting more explicitly into the design
of cross-national organizational studies, thereby ensuring that the

relevant national attributes which account for observed differences between organizations are identified. Two features of the national setting are distinguished:

1   national culture – this refers to the shared attitudes, values and understandings in a society which are shaped by common experiences and result in collective mental programmes; and
2   the national institutional context – this refers to the framework in which organizations operate, and consists of the social, economic, political and legal institutions which define the scope of business activity.

In terms of the Anglo-German comparative management study, this approach suggests that organizational behaviour in British and German firms is not seen as only the result of interactions between individuals, organization structures and management styles. It is also affected considerably by the nature of British and German institutional environments and national cultures and the opportunities and constraints that they present.

Furthermore, an adequate basis for comparison needs to incorporate these features of the national setting in order to interpret economic results correctly. Thus elements such as financial ownership and stability, educational systems and product regulatory frameworks are all part of the distinctive national industrial environment which has its effects on the economic activity of each country. In addition, traditional cultural values of the kind analysed by Hofstede (1980b) and Trompenaars (1993) also affect managerial processes and organizational behaviour which, in turn, affect economic performance.

This systemic perspective leads to a contingency approach to organizational differences between nations. For example, neither British nor German institutions and culture can be described as 'right' or 'wrong' for industry as a whole. Each has different strengths and weaknesses which both support and constrain economic activity and organizational behaviour. Advantages and disadvantages for particular types of organizations and industries are contingent on these institutional and cultural environments. Not all industries will flourish in one national setting, nor will all firms wither in another national setting.

In adopting this approach, comparing organizations across nations is not possible without some reference to the cultural and institutional settings: asserting that organizations in country A differ in this or that respect from organizations in country B is inadequate without an examination of the way cultural and/or institutional factors account for the differences found. Hence this approach to comparison is a two-stage process. At the first stage, organizations in different nations are compared and similarities and differences noted. In the second stage, the national cultures and institutional contexts which may account for the observed similarities and differences are compared, and again elements of uniqueness and comparability are noted.

The experience of the IOO suggests that the national setting is not only relevant when seeking to explain organizational differences across nations but is also applicable to understanding how the concepts which are the focus of the study (for example, HRM) vary across nations. In other words, not only may organizations vary across national settings but so also may the way we come to understand them. Thus cross-national researchers need not only to situate the organization within the national context but also the concepts and measurements they use. When beginning a cross-national study, researchers therefore need to determine the extent to which the concepts and measurements they plan to use are relevant in the different national contexts. This necessitates developing a set of 'world measures' in order to account for variations between nations. If researchers use a fixed and limited number of measures then they will be unable to show the range of societal variation in organizations. The more restricted and culturally specific the measurements, the more organizations in different nations will seem the same. The nearer researchers move to 'world measures', the more differences in organizations will be exposed. Furthermore, such measures will make researchers more aware of the peculiarities of organizations within their 'home' nation since they will be viewed through a different set of lenses. As the experience of the IOO shows, developing 'world measures' is a process of moving not only from local to cosmopolitan measures but also from local to cosmopolitan researchers.

In summary, at the present juncture of the development of the field, we feel that an approach to cross-national comparison which seeks to expose both differences and similarities in organizations and then explain these in relation to various features of the national setting is long overdue. The systemic approach which emerged from the IOO and Anglo-German comparative management study may provide a fruitful way forward.

Note

1   The members of the IOO in 1995 were Enzo Perrone and Nando Penarola (CRORA, Bocconi University, Milan), Josep Baruel (ESADE, Barcelona), Gilles van Wijk and Alan Jenkins (ESSEC, Paris), Marielle Heijltjes and Arndt Sorge (University of Limburg, Maastricht), Timothy Clark, Geoff Mallory and Derek Pugh (Open University Business School, Milton Keynes) and Christian Scholz (University of Saarland, Saarbrücken).

References

Adler, N.J., Doktor, R. and Redding, G.S. (1986), 'From the Atlantic to the Pacific century: cross-cultural management reviewed', *Journal of Management*, Yearly Review, **12**, 295–318.

Aldrich, H.E. (1972), 'Technology and organization structure: a reexamination of the findings of the Aston Group', *Administrative Science Quarterly*, **17**, 26–43.

Azumi, K. (1974), 'Japanese society: a sociological review', in A.E. Tiedemann (ed.), *An Introduction to Japanese Civilisation*, New York: Columbia University Press, pp. 515–35.

Berry, J.W. (1969), 'On cross-cultural comparability', *International Journal of Psychology*, **4**, 119–28.

Chandler, A.D. (1962), *Strategy and Structure*, Cambridge, Mass.: MIT Press.

Child, J. (1981), 'Culture, contingency and capitalism in the cross-national study of organizations', in L.L. Cummings and B.M. Staw (eds), *Research in Organization Behaviour*, Vol. 3, Greenwich, Conn.: JAI Press, pp. 303–56.

Clark, T. (ed.) (1996), *European Human Resource Management: An Introduction to Comparative Theory and Practice*. Oxford: Blackwell.

Clark, T. and Mallory, G. (1992), 'Cross-cultural organization research: a methodological minefield', paper presented to the International Organization Development Association 7th Annual World Conference, Coventry.

Clark, T. and Mallory, G. (1997), 'The impact of strategic choice on the internationalization of the firm', in J. Clegg, G. Chryssochoidis and C. Millar (eds), *Internationalization Strategies*, London: Macmillan, pp. 193–206.

Dicken, P. (1992), *Global Shift: The Internationalization of Economic Activity*, London: Paul Chapman.

Donaldson, L. (1986), 'Size and bureaucracy in East and West: a preliminary meta-analysis', in S.R. Clegg, D.C. Dunphy and S.G. Redding (eds), *The Enterprise and Management in East Asia*, University of Hong Kong, Centre for Asian Studies, Occasional Monograph No. 69, pp. 66–91.

Ebster-Grosz, D. and Pugh, D. (1996), *Anglo-German Business Collaboration: Pitfalls and Potentials*, Basingstoke: Macmillan.

Hage, J. (1996), 'Aston Group', in M. Warner (ed.), *International Encyclopaedia of Business and Management*, London: International Thomson Business, pp. 286–92.

Hickson, D.J. and McMillan, C.J. (1981a), *Organization and Nation: The Aston Programme IV*, Aldershot: Gower.

Hickson, D.J. and McMillan, C.J. (1981b), 'Concluding comments on countries, context and culture', in D.J. Hickson and C.J. McMillan (eds), *Organization and Nation: The Aston Programme IV*, Aldershot: Gower, pp. 187–96.

Hickson, D.J., Hinings, C.R., McMillan, C.J. and Schwitter, J.P. (1974), 'The culture-free context of organization structure', *Sociology*, **8**, 59–80.

Hickson, D.J., McMillan, C.J., Azumi, K. and Horvath, D. (1979), 'Grounds for comparative organization theory: Quicksands or hard core?', in C.J. Lammers and D.J. Hickson (eds), *Organizations Alike and Unlike*, London: Routledge, pp. 25–41.

Hofstede, G. (1980a), 'Motivation, leadership and organization: do American theories apply abroad?', *Organization Dynamics*, 42-63; reprinted in D.S. Pugh (1990), *Organization Theory: Selected Readings*, London: Penguin, pp. 473–99.

Hofstede, G. (1980b), *Culture's Consequences: International Differences in Work-related Values*, abridged version, Beverly Hills: Sage.

Hofstede, G. (1993), 'Cultural constraints in management theories', *Academy of Management Executive*, **7**, 81–94.

Lammers, D.J. and Hickson, D.J. (1979a), 'Towards a comparative sociology of organizations', in C.J. Lammers and D.J. Hickson (eds), *Organizations Alike and Unlike*, London: Routledge, pp. 3–20.

Lammers, D.J. and Hickson, D.J. (1979b), 'Are organizations culture-bound?', in C.J. Lammers and D.J. Hickson (eds), *Organizations Alike and Unlike*, London: Routledge, pp. 402–19.

Laurent, A. (1983), 'The cross-cultural diversity of Western conceptions of management', *International Studies of Management and Organization*, 13, 75–96.

Laurent, A. (1986), 'The cross-cultural puzzle of international human resource management', *Human Resource Management*, 25, 91–102.

Mabey, C. and Salaman, G. (1995), *Human Resource Strategies*, Oxford: Blackwell.

Maurice, M. (1976), 'Introduction: theoretical and ideological aspects of the universalistic approach to the study of organizations', *International Studies of Management and Organization*, 6, 3–10.

Miller, G.A. (1987), 'Meta-analysis and the culture-free hypothesis', *Organization Studies*, 8, 309–25.

Porter, M.E. (1990), *The Competitive Advantage of Nations*, London: Macmillan.

Pugh, D.S. (1966), 'Modern organization theory: a psychological and sociological study', *Psychological Bulletin*, 66, 235–51.

Pugh, D.S., Clark, T. and Mallory, G. (1995), 'Struktur und strukturelle Änderungen in europäischen Unternehmen des produzierenden Gewerbes: Eine vergleichende Studie', in C. Scholz and J. Zentes (eds), *Strategisches Euromanagement*, Stuttgart: Schäffer/Poeschel, pp. 227–45.

Pugh, D.S., Clark, T. and Mallory, G. (1996), 'Structure and structural change in European manufacturing organizations', in P.J.D. Drenth, P.L. Koopman and B. Wilpert (eds), *Organization Decision-making Under Different Economic and Political Conditions*, Amsterdam: North Holland, pp. 225–37.

Pugh, D.S. and Hickson, D.J. (1976), *Organization Structure in its Context: The Aston Programme I*, Aldershot: Gower.

Redding, S.G. (1994), 'Comparative management theory: jungle, zoo or fossil bed?', *Organization Studies*, 15, 323–59.

Roberts, K.H. and Boyacigiller, N.A. (1984), 'Cross-national organizational research: the grasp of the blind men', in B.M. Staw and L.L. Cummings (eds), *Research in Organizational Behaviour*, Vol. 6, Greenwich, Conn.: JAI Press, pp. 423–75.

Ronen, S. and Shenkar, O. (1985) 'Clustering nations on attitudinal dimensions: a review and replications', *Academy of Management Review*, 10, 435–54.

Scholz, C. (1993), *Deutsch–Britische Zusammenarbeit: Organisation und Erfolg von Auslandsniederlassungen*. Munich and Mering: Rainer Hampp Verlag.

Schröter, M. (1994), *Effectivität deutsch–britische Zusammenarbeit in Unternehmen*, Göttingen: Cuvillier Verlag.

Starbuck, W.H. (1981), 'A trip to view the elephants and rattlesnakes in the garden of Aston', in A.H. Van de Ven and W.F. Joyce (eds), *Perspectives on Organization Design and Behavior*, New York: Wiley, pp. 167–98.

Storey, J. (1992), *Developments in the Management of Human Resources: An Analytical Review*, Oxford: Blackwell.

Trompenaars, F. (1993), *Riding the Waves of Culture: Understanding Cultural Diversity in Business*, London: Macmillan/St Martin's Press.

Whitley, R. (1992), *European Business Systems: Firms and Markets in their National Contexts*, London: Sage.

Publications of Derek S. Pugh

(1954), 'A note on the Vorhaus Rorschach-configurations of reading disability', *Journal of Projective Techniques*, **18**, 478–80.

With R.M. McKenzie (1957), 'Human aspects of inspection in industry', *Journal of Institution of Production Engineering*, **36**, 378–87.

With C. Gordon and A.R. Emerson (1959), 'The age distribution of an industrial group (Scottish Railwaymen', *Population Studies*, **12**, 223–39.

With C. Gordon and A.R. Emerson (1959), 'Patterns of sickness absence in a railway population', *British Journal of Industrial Medicine*, **16**, 230–43.

With C. Gordon and K. Levy (1959), Sickness absence among railway clerical staff. *British Journal of Industrial Medicine*, **16**, 269–73.

With J.M. Fraser (1959), 'Wastage in a workshop supervision course', *Technology*.

(1960), 'From business game to management exercise', *British Association for Commercial and Industrial Education Journal*, **14**, 140–43.

(1961), 'Effective staff selection procedures', *Journal of the Institute of Office Managers*, **15**, 197–8.

(1962), 'The industrial administration research unit', *Management Thinking*, **1**, 10–14 (I.A. Department, Birmingham College of Technology).

(1962), 'Management Studies without Research?', *Bulletin of the Association of Teachers of Management*, **6**, 15–18.

With D.J. Hickson, C.R. Hinings, K. MacDonald, C. Turner and T. Lupton (1963), 'A conceptual scheme for organizational analysis', *Administrative Science Quarterly*, **8**, 289–315.

With C.R. Hinings (1964), 'Developments in the empirical study of bureaucracy', paper presented to the British Association for the Advancement of Science, Annual Meeting, Southampton.

(1964), 'The structure of industrial enterprise in industrial society – a comment', *Sociological Review Monograph*, **8**, 63–4.

With D.J. Hickson and C.R. Hinings (1964), *Writers on Organizations*, London: Hutchinson.

With D.J. Hickson (1965), 'The facts about "bureaucracy"', *The Manager*. (1962), 'Games and exercises: A comment on terminology' in E.A. Life and D.S. Pugh (eds), *Business Exercises: Some developments*, Association of Teachers of Management, Occasional Paper No. 1, Oxford: Basil Blackwell.

(1965), 'The profession of management', *Association of Teachers of Management Bulletin*, **16**, 2–4.

(1965), 'T-group training from the point of view of organization theory', in G. Whittaker (ed.), *Group Dynamics for Management Education*, Association of Teachers of Management, Occasional Paper No. 2, Oxford: Basil Blackwell.

(1965), 'Aims and methods of modern management education', *Scientific Business*, **3**, 258–66.

With J.N. Fairhead and W.J. Williams (1965), *Exercises in Business Decisions*, London: English Universities Press.

(1966), 'The social science approach to management', *Scientific Business*, **4**, 23–31.

(1966), 'The first European summer school in social psychology: some impressions', *Bulletin of the British Psychological Society*, **19**, 35–7.

(1966), 'Modern organization theory: A psychological and sociological study', *Psychological Bulletin*, **66**, 235–51.

(1966), 'The profession of management', in D. Pugh (ed.), *The Academic Teaching of Management*, Association of Teachers of Management, Occasional Paper No. 4, Oxford: Basil Blackwell.

(1966), 'The teaching of management theory', in D. Pugh (ed.), *The Academic Teaching of Management*, Association of Teachers of Management, Occasional Paper No. 4, Oxford: Basil Blackwell.

(1966), 'Role activation conflict: A study of industrial inspection', *American Sociological Review*, **31**, 836–42.

(1966), 'Organizational problems of inspection', *Journal of Management Studies*, **3**, 256–69.

With C.R. Hinings, D.J. Hickson and C. Turner (1967), 'An approach to the study of bureaucracy', *Sociology*, **1**, 61–72.

With R.L. Payne and J.H.K. Inkson (1967), 'Extending the occupational environment: the measurement of organizations', *Occupational Psychology*, **41**, 33–47.

With R.L. Payne, D.J. Hickson and J.H.K. Inkson (1967), 'Social behaviour in organizations', paper presented at the Annual Conference of the Social Psychological Section of the British Psychological Society, Oxford.

With D.J. Hickson (1968), 'The comparative study of organizations', in D. Pym (ed.), *Industrial society: The Social Sciences in Management*, London: Penguin Books.

With D.J. Hickson (1968), 'A dimensional analysis of bureaucratic structures', in R. Mayntz (ed.), *Burokratische Organization*. Berlin: Kiepenheuer and Witsch (in German).

With D.J. Hickson, C.R. Hinings and C. Turner (1968), 'Dimensions of organization structure', *Administrative Science Quarterly*, **13**, 65–105.

With J.H.K. Inkson and D.J. Hickson (1968), 'Administrative Reduction of Variance in Organizational Behaviour', British Psychological Society Conference Paper; reprinted in Pugh and Payne (1977).

With D.C. Pheysey (1968), 'Some developments in the study of organizations', *Management International Review*, **8**, 97–107.

With P. Levy (1969), 'Scaling and multivariate analysis in the study of organizational variables', *Sociology*, **3**, 193–213.

With D.J. Hickson, C.R. Hinings and C. Turner (1969), 'The context of organization structures', *Administrative Science Quarterly*, **14**, 47–61.

With D.J. Hickson and C.R. Hinings (1969), 'An empirical taxonomy of structures of work organizations', *Administrative Science Quarterly*, **14**, 115–26.

(1969), 'Organizational behaviour: An approach from psychology', *Human Relations*, **22**, 345–54.

With D.J. Hickson and D.C. Pheysey (1969), 'Operations technology and organization structure: An empirical reappraisal', *Administration Science Quarterly*, **14**, 378–97.

With D.C. Pheysey (1969), 'A comparative administration model', in A. Neghandi (ed.), *Comparative Administration Research*, Kent, OH: Kent State University Bureau of Business Administration.

(1969), 'Organization theory', in T. Kempner (ed.), *A Students Guide to Management Studies*, Association of Teachers of Management, Occasional Paper No. 6, Oxford: Basil Blackwell.

(1969), 'Management education in Britain', in E. Blishen (ed.), *Encyclopaedia of Education*, London: Blond.

With D.C. Pheysey and D.J. Hickson (1970), 'Organization: Is technology the key?', *Personnel Management*, February, 21–6.

With J. Child (1970), 'How to measure organization', *Management Today*, February, 127–9.

(1970), 'The organization of the marketing specialisms in their contexts', *British Journal of Marketing*, **4**, 98–105.

With J.H.K. Inkson and D.J. Hickson (1970), 'Organization context and structure: an abbreviated replication', *Administrative Science Quarterly*, **15**, 318–29.

(Editor) (1971), *Organization Theory: Selected Readings*, London: Penguin Books.

With R.L. Payne (1971), 'Organizations as psychological environments', in P. Warr (ed.), *Psychology at Work*, London: Penguin Books.

With D.C. Pheysey and R.L. Payne (1971), 'Influence of structure at organizational and group levels', *Administrative Science Quarterly*, **16**, 61–73.

With D.C. Pheysey and R.L. Payne (1971), 'Organization structure, organizational climate and group structure: an exploratory study of the relationships in two British manufacturing companies', *Occupational Psychology*, **45**, 45–51.

(1971), 'Organizational behaviour in its context', *Social Science Research Council Bulletin*, **12**, 8–9.

With D.J. Hickson and C.R. Hinings (1971), *Writers on Organizations*, 2nd edn, London: Penguin Books.

With W. Egan (1971), 'Selection for the MSc programme at the London Graduate Business School', in K.M. Miller (ed.), *Managers in the Making*, London: Independent Assessment and Research Centre.

With D.J. Hickson (1972), 'Causal inference and the Aston studies', *Administrative Science Quarterly*, **17**, 273–6.

(1972), 'Developments in organization theory', in R. Piret (ed.), *Proceedings of XVIIth International Congress of Applied Psychology*, Brussels: Editest, pp. 833–6.

(1973), 'Measurement of organization structures', *Organizational Dynamics*, **1**, 19–34.

(1973), 'Colonel Urwick and organization', *Omega*, **1**, 347–52.

With R. Mansfield and M. Warner (1975), *Research in Organizational Behaviour: A British Review*, London: Heinemann.

(1975), 'Organizing for people', *New Behaviour*, **22**, May, 205–7.

With D.J. Hickson (1976), *Organizational Structure in its Context: The Aston Programme I*, Aldershot: Gower.

With C.R. Hinings (eds) (1976), *Organizational Structure: Extensions and Replications: The Aston Programme II*, Aldershot: Gower.

With R.L. Payne (1976), 'Organizational structure and climate', in M. Dunnette (ed.), *Handbook of Organizational Psychology*, Chicago: Rand McNally, pp. 1125–73.

(1976), 'The "Aston" approach to the study of organizations', in G. Hofstede and M.S. Kassem (eds), *European Contributions to Organization Theory*, Amsterdam: Van Gorcum, pp. 62–78.

(1976), 'Going longitudinal', in C. Brown, P. Guillet de Monthoux and A. McCullough (eds), *The Access Casebook*, Stockholm: THS, pp. 234–6.

(1976), 'Motive power', *Accountancy Age*, **7**, 6 August.

With L. Donaldson and P. Silver (1976), 'A comparative study of processes of organizational decision-making: A preliminary report', paper given to Conference on Current Studies on Work Organizations, Berlin, October.

With D.J. Hickson and C.R. Hinings (1976), *Writers on Organizations*, 2nd edn, Tokyo: Tuttle-Mori (in Japanese).

With R.L. Payne (eds) (1977), *Organizational Behaviour in its Context: The Aston Programme III*, Aldershot: Gower.

(1977), 'Communication breakdown', *Accountancy Age*, **8**, 14 January.

(1978), 'Understanding and managing organizational change', *London Business School Journal*, **3**, 29–34.

(1979), 'Effective co-ordination in organizations', *Society for Advanced Management Journal*, (Winter), 28–35.

(1981), 'The Aston programme: Retrospect and prospect', in A. Van der Ven and W.F. Joyce (eds), *Perspectives on Organization Design and Behavior*, New York: Wiley, pp. 135–166.

(1981), 'Rejoinder to Starbuck', in A. Van der Ven and W.F. Joyce (eds), *Perspectives on Organization Design and Behavior*, New York: Wiley, pp. 199–203.

(1983), 'Studying organizational structure and process', in G. Morgan (ed.), *Beyond Method: A Study of Social Research Strategies*, Beverley Hills, CA: Sage, pp. 45–56.

With D.J. Hickson and C.R. Hinings (1983), *Writers on Organizations*, 3rd edn, London: Penguin Books.

(Editor) (1984), *Organization Theory: Selected Readings*, 2nd edn, London: Penguin Books.

(1985), Management classics', in P. Braithwaite and B. Taylor (eds), *The Good Book Guide for Business*, London: Penguin Books/New York: Harper & Row.

(1985), 'International perspectives. Unit 16 Open University Course, "Managing in organizations" (T244)', Milton Keynes: The Open University.

With D.J. Hickson and C.R. Hinings (1985), *Writers on Organizations*, American edn, Beverly Hills, CA: Sage.

(1985), 'What is research?', in A. Chapman (ed.), *Management Research and*

Management Practice, Association of Teachers of Management, Focus Paper, 3–6.

With G. Redding (1986), 'The formal and the informal: Japanese and Chinese organization structures', in S. Clegg, D. Dunphy and G. Redding (eds), *The Enterprise and Management in East Asia*, Hong Kong: Hong Kong University Press.

(1986), 'Modern classics in organization theory', *Management and Labour Studies*, **11**, 111–14, Xavier Labour Relations Institute, Jamshedpur India.

With E.M. Phillips (1987), *How to get a Ph.D*, Milton Keynes: Open University Press.

(1987), 'Organizational development. Block 4 Open University Course, "Planning and managing change" (P679)', Milton Keynes: The Open University.

(1988), 'The Aston research programme', in A. Bryman (ed.), *Doing Research in Organizations*, London: Routledge, pp. 123–35.

(1989), 'Systems and organizations', in R.E. Flood (ed.), *Systems Prospects: The Next Ten Years of Systems Research*, London: Plenum Press.

With D.J. Hickson (1989), *Writers on Organizations*, 4th edn, London: Penguin Books/Newbury Park, CA: Sage.

(1989), (Edited and Introduction), *The Production–Inspection Relationship* (R.M. McKenzie), Edinburgh: Scottish Academic Press.

(Editor) (1990), *Organization Theory: Selected Reading*, 3rd edn, London: Penguin Books.

(1990), 'The convergence of international organizational behaviour?', Open University Business School Working Paper No. 2/90; reprinted 1993 in T. Weinshall (ed.), *Culture and Management*, Berlin: de Gruyter.

(1991), 'Foreword', *Organizational Behaviour*, 2nd edn (A Huczynski and D. Buchanan), London: Prentice-Hall.

With D.J. Hickson (1993), *Great Writers on Organizations: The Omnibus Edition*, Aldershot: Dartmouth.

(1993), 'Organizational behaviour', in W. Outhwaite and T.B. Bottomore (eds), *Dictionary of Twentieth Century Social Thought*, Oxford: Basil Blackwell.

With E.M. Phillips (1994), *How to get a Ph.D.*, 2nd edn, Buckingham: Open University Press.

(1995), 'Culture. Block 5 Open University Course. "International enterprise" (B890)', Milton Keynes: The Open University.

With C. Mabey (1995), 'Strategies for managing complex change. Unit 10 Open University Course, "Managing development and change" (B751)', Milton Keynes: The Open University.

With D.J. Hickson (1995), *Management Wordwide: The Impact of Societal Culture on Organizations Around the Globe*, London: Penguin Books.

(1995), 'International management', in N. Nicholson (ed.), *Encyclopedic Dictionary of Organizational Behavior*, Oxford: Basil Blackwell pp. 251–4.

(1995), 'Organizational design and organizational development', in P. Forrest (ed.), *Croner's A-Z guide for HRM Professionals*, London: Croner Publications.

With T. Clark and G. Mallory (1995), 'Struktur und strukturelle Änderungen in europäischen Unternehmen des Produzierenden Gerwerbes: Eine vergleichende Studie', in C. Scholz and J. Zentes (eds), *Strategisches Euromanagement*, Stuttgart: Schäffer-Poeschel Verlag, pp. 227–45.

With T. Clark and G. Mallory (1995), 'Organization structure and structural change in European manufacturing organization', in P.J.D. Drenth, P.L. Koopman and B. Wilpert (eds), *Organizational decision-making under different economic and political conditions*, Amsterdam: North Holland, pp. 225–37.

With D. Ebster-Grosz (1996), *Anglo-German Business Collaboration: Pitfalls and Potentials*, Basingstoke: Macmillan.

With D.J. Hickson (1996), 'Organizational convergence', in M. Warner (ed.), *International Encyclopedia of Business and Management*, London: Routledge.

With D.J. Hickson (1997), *Writers on Organizations*, 5th edn, London: Penguin Books/Newbury Park, CA: Sage.

(1996), 'A taste for innovation', in Bedeian, A.G. (ed.), Management Laureates, Vol. 4, Greenwich, Conn: JAI Press, pp. 235–76.

(Editor) (1997), *Organization Theory: Selected Readings*, 4th edn, London: Penguin Books.

Index

N.B. Page references to figures and tables are in italics.

361